Norton Townshend Horr, Alton A Bemis

A Treatise on the Power to Enact, Passage, Validity and Enforcement

Of Municipal Police Ordinances

Norton Townshend Horr, Alton A Bemis

A Treatise on the Power to Enact, Passage, Validity and Enforcement
Of Municipal Police Ordinances

ISBN/EAN: 9783337206239

Printed in Europe, USA, Canada, Australia, Japan

Cover: Foto ©ninafisch / pixelio.de

More available books at **www.hansebooks.com**

A TREATISE

ON THE

Power to Enact, Passage, Validity and Enforcement

OF

MUNICIPAL POLICE ORDINANCES

WITH

APPENDIX OF FORMS

AND

REFERENCES TO ALL THE DECIDED CASES ON THE SUBJECT
IN THE UNITED STATES, ENGLAND AND CANADA

BY

NORTON T. HORR AND ALTON A. BEMIS
OF THE CLEVELAND BAR

CINCINNATI
ROBERT CLARKE & CO
1887

Entered according to Act of Congress, in the year 1887, by
ROBERT CLARKE & CO.
In the office of the Librarian of Congress, at Washington, D. C.

PREFACE.

The authors have noticed that very many questions arise in the drafting of municipal ordinances as to the precise extent to which certain powers of police regulation may be exercised, and upon which very little authority can be readily found. Except in those cities and towns where the municipal council has the assistance of regularly employed legal advisers, the limits of lawful legislation are apt to be exceeded. Questions of this nature, too, are seldom adjudicated in courts of last resort—seldom, at least, with reference to the importance of the interests which they may affect. When we consider that the greater part of the capital of this country is invested in enterprises which are located within the territorial limits and subject to the local laws of cities, towns and villages, we realize the importance of having a system of local laws which interfere with and burden the ownership of property as little as possible, but which still preserve good order and the public welfare. The first aim of this book is to show, in as concise a manner as is consistent with clearness, the extent to which police regulation may be exercised, under general and special powers, and to formulate rules that will be applicable in determining the validity of police ordinances.

There seems to be a striking lack of uniformity in the practice observed in enforcing ordinances. Numerous questions arise in the local courts, which must, for want of precedent, be decided by the best judgment of the presiding magistrate, and the rules of pleading, procedure and evidence are consequently both deficient and varied. The rules that are applied in higher courts are often poorly adapted to the peculiar practice in lower courts; and even in cases where local courts might be guided or aided by decided cases, the difficulty of finding them partially destroys their usefulness. We hope to prevent, in a measure, the necessity for laborious research by classifying the decided cases which relate to the practice in magistrates' courts, and, if possible, to aid in making that practice uniform.

Our labor will be amply rewarded if it is found to be of some assistance to those who enact ordinances, or to those who are called upon to enforce and construe them.

DEDICATED

TO THE

CLEVELAND LAW LIBRARY ASSOCIATION,

ITS LIBRARY HAVING FURNISHED THE MATERIAL

FOR THIS BOOK.

TABLE OF CONTENTS.

MUNICIPAL POLICE ORDINANCES.

CHAPTER I.
NATURE OF ORDINANCES.

§ 1.	Definition of an ordinance..	1
§ 2.	Ordinances are laws..	1
§ 3.	Necessity of formal passage..	3
§ 4.	Charter prohibition need not be supplemented by an ordinance..	4
§ 5.	Must be passed by the governing body...........................	4
§ 6.	Must regulate corporate affairs..	5
§ 7.	Must not regulate civil liabilities.....................................	6

CHAPTER II.
CORPORATE POWERS.

§ 8.	Scope of corporate powers..	9
§ 8a.	Corporate powers discretionary.......................................	10
§ 9.	They are continuing..	11
§ 10.	They may not be delegated...	11
§ 11.	What may not be delegated...	12
§ 12.	What may be delegated..	13
§ 13.	Discretion in granting licenses.......................................	14
§ 14.	Source of corporate powers..	15
§ 15.	The rule as to source...	16
§ 16.	Limitations on inherent powers......................................	18

CHAPTER III.
CONSTRUCTION OF CORPORATE POWERS.

§ 17.	Powers construed strictly against the corporation..........	20
§ 18.	Limited to the terms of an enumeration.........................	21
§ 19.	Illustrations..	22
§ 20.	Rule of *ejusdem generis* in enumerations......................	22
§ 21.	Concurrent powers...	23
§ 22.	The greater power includes the less................................	24
§ 23.	Retroactive ordinances...	24
§ 24.	Conditions precedent...	24

HAPTER IV.

Construction of Common Phrases.

§ 25.	Common phrases in grants of power	27
§ 26.	Corporate purposes	28
§ 27.	General welfare	29
§ 28.	Peace and good government	29
§ 29.	Other general expressions	30
§ 30.	To regulate.	31
§ 31.	To suppress and restrain	33
§ 32.	Miscellaneous expressions	34
§ 33.	General rules of construction	34

CHAPTER V.

Passage of Ordinances.

Part I.—Council proceedings.

§ 34.	Necessity of formal enactment	36
§ 35.	Statutory directions are mandatory	36
§ 36.	Council *de facto* can not act	37
§ 37.	Meetings of the council	38
§ 38.	Adjourned and special meetings	39
§ 39.	Joint action of bi-cameral council	40
§ 40.	Quorum in joint session	41
§ 41.	What constitutes a quorum	41
§ 42.	Holdings under statutory provisions	41
§ 43.	Majority of quorum sufficient	42
§ 44.	When the mayor may vote	43
§ 45.	Other charter provisions	43
§ 46.	When a vote may be reconsidered	44
§ 47.	Readings	45
§ 48.	Signature of the clerk of the council	46
§ 49.	Signature of the mayor	46
§ 50.	The mayor's approval	47
§ 51.	How signified	47
§ 52.	Publication	48
§ 53.	Construction of provisions regulating the time of publication	50
§ 54.	The newspaper in which publication may be made	51
§ 55.	Form of the notice published	52
§ 56.	Record of the ordinance	52
§ 57.	What the record must contain	54
§ 58.	Record of votes	54
§ 59.	Informalities subsequently cured	56
§ 60.	Repeal	56
§ 60a.	Must be by the council	56

TABLE OF CONTENTS.

§ 61.	Form of the repealing act	57
§ 62.	Repeal by the legislature by implication	57
§ 63.	Implied repeal by passage of inconsistent ordinance	58
§ 64.	Amendments	59
§ 65.	Summary	59
§ 66.	Saving clause in subsequent ordinance	59
§ 67.	Effect of a repeal on vested rights	60

Part II.—The ordinance itself.

§ 68.	Form of the ordinance	61
§ 69.	Constituent parts	61
§ 70.	Ordinances like resolutions in form	61
§ 71.	The title	62
§ 72.	The introduction	63
§ 73.	Ordinances need not recite authority	63
§ 74.	Scope of the ordinance	64
§ 75.	Reference to existing ordinances	65
§ 76.	Time of going into effect	65
§ 77.	Penalty	65
§ 78.	Definiteness of expression	66
§ 79.	Definiteness as to the penalty	67
§ 80.	License ordinances	67
§ 81.	Ordinances against nuisances	67
§ 82.	Council can not bind its successors	67

CHAPTER VI.
RULES OF VALIDITY.

§ 83.	Introduction	70
§ 84.	United States laws	70
§ 85.	Regulation of commerce	73
§ 86.	United States mails	75
§ 87.	United States license laws	75
§ 88.	Must be consistent with the laws of the state	75
§ 89.	Main conflict as to minor offenses	76
§ 90.	The punishment may be greater	78
§ 91.	Prosecutions under either law no bar to proceedings under the other	78
§ 92.	Alabama	79
§ 93.	Colorado	79
§ 94.	Connecticut	79
§ 95.	Dakota	79
§ 96.	Florida	80
§ 97.	Georgia	80
§ 98.	Illinois	80
§ 99.	Indiana	81

§ 100.	Iowa	82
§ 101.	Kansas	82
§ 102.	Kentucky	82
§ 103.	Louisiana	82
§ 104.	Maryland	83
§ 105.	Massachusetts	83
§ 106.	Michigan	83
§ 107.	Minnesota	83
§ 108.	Missouri	84
§ 109.	Nebraska	84
§ 110.	North Carolina	84
§ 111.	New Jersey	85
§ 112.	New York	85
§ 113.	Ohio	85
§ 114.	Oregon	85
§ 115.	Rhode Island	85
§ 116.	South Carolina	86
§ 117.	Tennessee	86
§ 118.	Texas	86
§ 119.	Utah	86
§ 120.	United States holdings	87
§ 121.	Conflict with state license laws	87
§ 122.	Policy of state legislation must be sustained	90
§ 223.	What is the law of the land	90
§ 124.	Power derived from foreign sovereignties	91
§ 125.	Must be consistent with corporate charter	91
§ 126.	Other requisites of validity	92
§ 127.	Reasonableness	92
§ 128.	When discretion of council final	92
§ 129.	When not final	93
§ 130.	Examples of reasonable ordinances	93
§ 131.	Examples of unreasonable ordinances	97
§ 132.	Restraint of trade	100
§ 133.	What is not a restraint of trade	102
§ 134.	What is not a restraint of trade	102
§ 135.	Discrimination	103
§ 136.	Examples of discrimination	105
§ 137.	Discrimination as to non-residents	106
§ 138.	Once void, always void	107
§ 139.	Partial invalidity	108

CHAPTER VII.

Remedies.

§ 140.	Introduction	110
§ 141.	Territorial limits	111
§ 142.	Extra-territorial effect	112

§ 143.	Ordinances affect what persons	113
§ 144.	When parts of the corporate limits exempt	115
§ 145.	Jurisdiction over railroad property	117
§ 146.	Jurisdiction over streets	118
§ 147.	Penalties	118
§ 148.	The kind of penalty that may be adopted	120
§ 149.	Penalties are not licenses	120
§ 150.	Fines	121
§ 151.	Amount of the fine	121
§ 152.	Cumulative fines	122
§ 153.	Repetition of the offense more heavily punished	123
§ 154.	Costs of the prosecution	124
§ 155.	Imprisonment in default of payment	124
§ 156.	The power strictly construed	125
§ 157.	Such imprisonment does not satisfy the fine	127
§ 158.	Imprisonment as a penalty	127
§ 159.	Forfeiture	128
§ 160.	Illustrations	128
§ 161.	Strays	130
§ 162.	Notice to the owner	131
§ 163.	Judicial determination	132
§ 164.	Forfeiture of real estate	132

CHAPTER VIII.

Procedure—Pleading—Evidence.

§ 165.	Introduction	134
§ 166.	The tribunal	135
§ 167.	Citizenship does not disqualify the magistrate	137
§ 168.	Form of the action	138
§ 169.	Nature of the action	139
§ 170.	Holdings of the different states	141
§ 170a.	General conclusion	145
§ 171.	Joinder of causes of action	145
§ 172.	The complaint	145
§ 172a.	The title of the case	146
§ 173.	The offense must be distinctly alleged	147
§ 174.	Reference made to the ordinance violated	149
§ 175.	Exceptions need not be negatived	152
§ 176.	The conclusion of the complaint	152
§ 177.	Signature to the complaint	153
§ 178.	Arrest before trial	153
§ 179.	What the warrant should contain	154
§ 180.	Arrests made without a warrant	155
§ 181.	Trial by jury	156
§ 182.	Arraignment and plea	157
§ 183.	Evidence	157

§ 184.	Judicial notice	157
§ 185.	How ordinances are proved	159
§ 186.	Record of council proceedings as evidence	161
§ 187.	Proof of publication	162
§ 188.	Presumption that ordinances are reasonable	164
§ 189.	Reasonableness a question of law	169
§ 190.	Proof of time and place of committing the offense	170
§ 191.	Proof that act does not fall within exceptions	170
§ 192.	Testimony of the defendant	170
§ 193.	Construction of ordinances	171
§ 194.	Construction of ordinances	172
§ 195.	Examples of application of rules of construction	173
§ 196.	Defenses to prosecutions	176
§ 197.	Effect of repeal of an ordinance	177
§ 198.	Former conviction	177
§ 199.	Other defenses	178
§ 200.	Doctrine of estoppel applied to defenses	178
§ 201.	Estoppel of the corporation	179
§ 202.	Form of the judgment	180
§ 203.	The order of commitment to jail	182

CHAPTER IX.
PROCEEDINGS IN REVIEW.

§ 204.	*Certiorari*	184
§ 205.	*Habeas corpus*	185
§ 206.	Injunction	185
§ 207.	Appeal	187
§ 208.	Error	188
§ 209.	The record	188

CHAPTER X.
RESOLUTIONS.

§ 210.	Nature and use of resolutions	193
§ 210a.	What may be done by resolution	194

CHAPTER XI.
ORDINANCES CLASSIFIED ACCORDING TO THEIR SUBJECT-MATTER.

§ 211.	Nature of police powers	198
§ 212.	Their general purpose	198
§ 213.	Their general purpose	199
§ 214.	Necessity and scope of health regulation	202
§ 215.	Boards of health	203
§ 216.	Regulation of articles of food	204
§ 217.	Markets	204
§ 218.	Other regulations of the food supply	207

§ 219.	Slaughter houses	208
§ 220.	Other health regulations; cemeteries; offal; dead animals; diseases; miscellaneous health provisions	209
§ 221.	Fire	212
§ 222.	Fire limits	212
§ 223.	Extent of the power	213
§ 224.	Streets	216
§ 225.	Care of the streets	218
§ 226.	Grading	218
§ 227.	Paving	219
§ 228.	Sidewalks	221
§ 229.	Protection of streets	222
§ 230.	Obstructions	224
§ 231.	Examples of lawful obstructions	224
§ 232.	Inclosures	225
§ 233.	Public buildings	226
§ 234.	Other buildings	226
§ 235.	Snow	228
§ 236.	Moving buildings	229
§ 237.	Miscellaneous obstructions	229
§ 238.	Steam railroads	231
§ 239.	Police regulation of steam railroads	232
§ 240.	Street railways	234
§ 241.	Regulations	234
§ 242.	Sewerage system	236
§ 243.	Water supply	237
§ 244.	Gas pipes	238
§ 244a.	Telegraph poles	239
§ 245.	Restrictions on ordinary use of the streets	240
§ 246.	Vehicles	240
§ 247.	Routes and stands	241
§ 248.	Construction of vehicle regulations	242
§ 249.	Strays	243
§ 250.	Nuisances	245
§ 251.	Definition of nuisances	245
§ 252.	Must be an actual nuisance	246
§ 253.	Judicial determination	247
§ 254.	What are nuisances	248
§ 255.	What are not nuisances *per se*	249
§ 256.	Nature of license power	249
§ 257.	Nature of licenses	251
§ 258.	Must not amount to a tax	251
§ 259.	What amount may be charged	252
§ 260.	Examples	254
§ 261.	The license	255
§ 262.	The ordinance authorizing licenses	255

§ 263.	Discretion in officers	256
§ 264.	The penalty	258
§ 265.	Effect of a license	259
§ 266.	Conditions	259
§ 267.	Revocability	260
§ 268.	Grading and discrimination	261
§ 269.	Miscellany	263
§ 270.	Business privileges	263
§ 271.	Transient dealers	264
§ 272.	Peddling	265
§ 273.	Amusements	266
§ 274.	Dogs	267
§ 275.	Liquor licenses	267
§ 276.	Ordinance provisions	268
§ 277.	Other regulations on sale of liquors	269
§ 278.	Definition	270
§ 279.	Evidence in liquor cases	271
§ 280.	Uniformity in licenses	272
§ 281.	Taxation	273
§ 282.	Local assessments	273
§ 283.	Other taxes	274
§ 284.	Mode of exercise of taxing power	275
§ 285.	Amount of tax	276
§ 286.	Constitutional restrictions	276
§ 287.	Discrimination	276
§ 288.	Sunday ordinances	278
§ 289.	Appropriations for police purposes	280
§ 290.	To aid the administration of justice	280
§ 291.	To employ attorneys	281
§ 292.	Wharves	282
§ 293.	Conclusion	285

APPENDIX OF FORMS 287

TABLE OF CASES.

[THE REFERENCES ARE TO SECTIONS.]

A.

Abendroth v. Greenwich, 15.
Academy v. Erie, 62.
Adams v. Albany, 97, 121, 130.
Adgar v. Mayor, 143.
Ah Kow v. Nunan, 84, 193.
Ah Litt, Ex parte, 144.
Ahrens v. Fiedler, 51.
Ah Toy, Ex parte, 121.
Alberger v. Mayor, 188.
Albia v. O'Harra, 187.
Alexander v. Bethlehem, 178.
—— v. Council, 169, 221.
Allen v. Jones, 242.
—— v. Rogers, 75.
—— v. Taunton, 223.
Allerton v. Chicago, 19, 241, 248, 260.
Alton v. Hartford Ins. Co., 188, 284.
—— v. Kirsch, 172a, 207.
—— v. Mulledy, 12, 210a.
Alpers v. Brown, 220.
Amboy v. Sleeper, 98.
Ambrose v. State, 99.
Americus v. Eldridge, 242.
Ames v. Carlton, 7.
Amesbury v. Ins. Co., 139.
Amity City v. Clementz, 147.
Anderson v. Commissioners, 16.
—— v. Gas Co., 11, 244.
Andrews v. Ins. Co., 15.
Anon., 44.
Appleton v. Hopkins, 264.
Argenti v. San Francisco, 200.
Arkell v. St. Thomas, 278.
Arnold v. Holdbrook, 7.
Arnoult v. New Orleans, 8.
Aronheimer v. Stokley, 206.
Ash v. People, 258, 259.
Asheville v. Means, 283.
Ashton v. Ellsworth, 4, 16.
Asylum v. Troy, 224.
Athens v. Long, 268, 287.
—— v. Railroad Co., 195.
Atkinson v. Transportation Co., 131.
Atty. Gen. v. Campbell, 223.
Atty. Gen. v. Heisohn, 237.
Auburn v. Eldridge, 174.
Aull v. Lexington, 220.
Austin v. Murray, 30, 220.

B.

Babcock v. Buffalo, 252.
Baker v. Boston, 188, 214.
—— v. Cincinnati, 259, 260, 273, 280.
—— v. Cushman, 46.
—— v. Normal, 139, 229.
—— v. Paris, 276.
—— v. Scofield, 185.
Baldwin v. Green, 108.
—— v. Murphy, 98, 180.
—— v. Oswego, 24.
—— v. Smith, 67, 253, 265, 267.
Baldwin Co. v. Retailers, 121.
Ball v. Fagg, 186.
Baltimore v. Brannan, 8a.
—— v. Clunet, 188.
—— v. Howard, 12.
—— v. Hughes, 193.
—— v. Johnson, 52.
—— v. Marriott, 8a.
—— v. Pennington, 8a.
—— v. Radecke, 131.
—— v. Scharf, 10.
Bancroft v. Cambridge, 212.
Bank v. Navigation Co., 15, 124.
—— v. Chillicothe, 15, 17.
Banking Co. v. Jersey City, 206.
Barbier v. Connolly, 130.
Barclay, In re, 263.
Barker v. Commonwealth, 237.
—— v. Smith, 63.
Barling v. West, 131, 133.
Barnert v. Paterson, 41, 43.
Barnett v. Newark, 35, 52.
Barr v. Auburn, 58, 185.
Barter v. Commonwealth, 148, 166, 168.
Barthet v. New Orleans, 219.
Barton v. Pittsburgh, 47, 71, 186.

(xv)

TABLE OF CASES.

Baton Rouge v. Crèmonini, 135, 209.
Bauer v. Avondale, 276.
Baumgard v. Mayor, 163.
Baumgartner v. Hasty, 75, 130, 222, 253.
Baxter's Petition, 115.
Bayer v. Hoboken, 54.
Bearden v. Madison, 1, 130, 239.
Beasley v. Beckley, 181, 184, 204.
Beaty v. Gilmore, 234.
Beck v. Hanscom, 40.
Bedell, Ex parte, 52, 56, 157.
Beecher v. People, 166.
Beckman's Case, 39.
Begein v. Anderson, 142.
Bell v. Manvers, 122.
—— v. Quebec, 85.
Benefield v. Hines, 121.
Bennett v. Birmingham, 143, 287.
—— v. People, 121.
Benninger, Ex parte, 260.
Bergen v. Clarkson, 160.
Bergman v. Cleveland, 277.
—— v. Railway Co., 71.
Beronjohn v. Mobile, 131.
Beer Co. v. Mass., 212.
Berry v. People, 98.
Bessoinies v. Indianapolis, 15, 220.
Betbalto v. Conly, 187, 209.
Bickerstaff, In re, 12, 263, 266.
Bills v. Belknap, 229.
Birdsall v. Clarke, 10.
Bishop v. Railroad Co., 195.
Blake v. Walker, 15.
Blanchard v. Bissell, 35, 49, 210a.
Blankley v. Winstanley, 17.
Bliss v. Kraus, 213.
—— v. Ball, 229.
Block v. Jacksonville, 185, 275.
Bloom v. Xenia, 35, 47.
Bloomfield v. Trimble, 28, 100.
Bloomington v. Wahl, 132, 217.
—— v. Strehle, 279.
Board v. Heister, 15, 219, 245.
Board of Excise v. Barrie, 267.
Boehm v. Baltimore, 215, 220.
Bogart v. Indianapolis, 131, 220.
—— v. New Albany, 99.
Bohle v. Stannard, 73.
Bolto v. New Orleans, 160.
Bolton v. Cleveland, 24, 188.
Bonsall v. Lebanon, 164, 235.
Boom v. Utica, 253.
Booth v. Carthage, 63.
—— v. State, 223.
Borough v. Shortz, 242.
Boston v. Richardson, 240.
—— v. Schaffer, 260, 261, 262, 273
—— v. Shaw, 242.
Bosworth v. Hearne, 132.

Bott v. Pratt, 1.
Bowers v. Coulston, 223, 234.
Bowling Green v. Carson, 130, 265.
Bowman v. St. John, 77.
Boyd v. State, 267.
Braddy v. Milledgeville, 213.
Brady v. Gas Co., 222.
—— v. Ins. Co., 213, 223.
Branham v. San Jose, 15.
Brannahan v. Hotel Co., 247.
Branson v. Philadelphia, 265.
Breaux's Bridge v. Dupuis, 50, 68.
Brenham v. Bicker, 132.
Breninger v. Belvidere, 16, 29.
Brewster v. Davenport, 11, 58, 188.
—— v. Hartley, 35.
Brieswick v. Brunswick, 155.
Bright v. McCullough, 287.
—— v. Toronto, 130, 160, 287.
Brodie, In re, 263.
Broeck v. Welch, 137.
Bronson v. Oberlin, 30.
Brooklyn v. Breslin, 10, 13, 134, 229.
Brooklyn v. Cleves, 134, 171, 264.
—— v. Nodine, 246.
—— v. Toynbee, 112.
Brookville v. Gagle, 168, 170.
Brophy v. Perth Amboy, 170.
Brown v. Denver, 84.
—— v. Duplessis, 238, 240.
—— v. Hunn, 223.
—— v. Nugent, 195.
Brownville v. Cook, 28, 109, 170.
Brush v. Carbondale, 188.
Bryan v. Bates, 180.
—— v. Page, 3, 210.
Buell v. State, 84.
Buffalo, In re, 58.
—— v. Mulchady, 145.
—— v. Webster, 196, 217, 277.
Bull v. Quincy, 3, 80, 269, 279.
Bullock v. Gromble, 159.
Burch v. Savannah, 287.
Burckholter v. McConnellsville, 6.
Burgeois, Ex parte, 108.
Burlington v. Baumgardner, 30.
—— v. Dennison, 12, 50, 210.
—— v. Estlow, 63.
—— v. Ins. Co., 210a, 258, 262, 268.
—— v. Kellar, 17, 100, 121, 158.
—— v. Lawrence, 22, 31, 256, 273.
Burmeister v. Howard, 1, 196.
Burmeister, In re, 224.
Burnett, Ex parte, 15, 163, 275.
Burnham v. Chicago, 227.
Burr v. Atlanta, 271, 287.
Burrill v. Boston, 290.
Butler v. Passaic, 210.
Butler's Appeal, 270.

Byars v. Mt. Vernon, 207, 279.
Byers v. Trustees, 275.

C.

Cabot v. Rome, 26.
Cady v. Barnesville, 84.
Cæsar v. Cartwright, 210.
Caine v. Syracuse, 8a.
Cairo v. Bross, 18, 66.
Caldwell v. Alton, 15, 217, 245.
Camden v. Bloch, 203, 204, 207, 209
Camden v. Mulford, 125, 204.
Campbell v. Kingston, 292.
Canal Co. v. St Louis, 292.
Canfield v. Smith, 24.
Cannon v. New Orleans, 292.
Canthorn v State, 178.
Canton v. Nist, 122, 288.
Cantril v. Sainer, 71, 139.
Cape Girardeau v. Riley, 72.
Carlisle v. Baker, 234.
Carlton St., In re, 58.
Carmel v. Wabash, 31.
Carr v. St. Louis, 125.
Carroll v. Tuscaloosa, 284.
—— v Wall. 44.
Carson v Bloomington, 203.
Carter v. Dow, 213, 274.
—— v. Dubuque, 15.
—— v State, 270.
Cartersville v. Lanham, 249.
Carthage v. Buchner, 81, 277.
Casby v. Railroad Co., 238.
Case v Hall, 173.
—— v Mobile, 174, 184.
Cass, Ex parte, 292
Cassinello, Ex parte, 213, 254.
Cedar Rapids v. Holcomb, 220.
Centerville v. Lanham, 143, 213.
—— v. Miller, 31.
Central v. Sears 210a.
Chafin v. Waukesha Co., 170.
Chamberlain v. Evansville, 62.
Chambers v. Trust Co., 7.
Chariton v. Barber, 31.
—— v. Holliday, 200.
Charles v. Hoboken, 10.
Charleston v. Ahrens, 26.
—— v. Benjamin, 288.
—— v. Chur, 174, 186.
—— v. Church, 26, 67, 130.
—— v. Elford, 144
—— v. Goldsmith, 12.
—— v. Kleinback, 181.
—— v. Oliver, 150, 168, 256.
—— v. Reed, 15, 199, 222.
Chastain v. Calhoun, 121.
Chebanse v. McPherson, 213.

Cherokee v. Fox, 177, 272.
Chess v. Birmingham, 287.
Chicago v. Bartee, 131, 272.
—— v. Crosby, 228.
—— v Evans, 6.
—— v. Gosseter, 195.
—— v. Hobson, 195.
—— v. McGinn 130.
—— v. O'Brien, 235.
—— v. Packing Co., 142.
—— v. Quinby, 152.
—— v. Railroad Co., 195.
—— v. Rumpff, 131, 132, 135, 193, 263.
Chicago Packing Co. v. Chicago, 256.
Childress v. Nashville, 213.
Chilvers v. People, 85, 257, 264.
Chin Yan, Ex parte, 130, 188, 202.
Christie v. Malden, 15.
Christopher v. Portage, 228.
Church v. Baltimore, 73, 188.
—— v. New York, 1, 220.
Church, In re, 280.
Cincinnati v. Bickett, 47, 54.
—— v. Bryson, 259, 268.
—— v. Buckingham, 218, 249, 264.
—— v. Gwynne, 170.
—— v. Penny, 242.
—— v. Rice, 288.
—— v. White, 226.
City v. Ahrens, 275.
—— v. Church, 275.
—— v. Duncan, 209.
—— v. Erie Railroad Co., 130, 241.
—— v. Hughes, 209.
—— v. Lenze, 223.
—— v. Railroad Co., 238.
—— v. Telegraph Co., 244a.
City Council v. Church, 60a.
City of Kansas v. Collins, 271.
City of London's Case, 158.
Claiborne v. Brooks, 128.
Clark v. Davenport, 17.
—— v. Elizabeth, 201.
—— v. Fry, 231.
—— v. Le Creu, 132.
—— v. Lewis, 159.
—— v. New Brunswick, 283.
—— v. South Bend, 18, 223.
Clarke's Case, 158.
Clason v. Milwaukee, 130, 189.
Clevenger v. Rushville, 174.
Clinton v. Phillipi, 131.
Clintonville v. Keeting, 277.
Coates v. Dubuque, 114, 188.
—— v. New York, 73, 174, 220.
Coffin v. Nantucket, 12.
Cohens v. Virginia, 87.
Coldwater v. Tucker, 142.
Cole v. Hall, 257, 265.
Coleman v. Railroad Co., 241.

Collins v. Hatch, 15, 16, 17, 19, 131, 249, 254.
Collins v. Louisville, 285.
Collinsville v. Scanland, 195.
Colson v. State, 271.
Columbia v. Harrison, 152, 166.
Columbus v. Cutcamp, 267.
—— v. Flournoy, 284.
—— v. Jacques, 217, 233, 237.
—— v. Street Ry. Co., 241.
Commissioners v. Chissom, 170.
—— v. Detroit, 8.
—— v. Duckett, 8a.
—— v. Gas Co., 131.
—— v. Hudson, 243.
—— v. Mighils, 17.
—— v. Nell, 144.
—— v. Powe, 195.
—— v. Silvers, 210a.
Commonwealth v. Bean, 130, 173.
—— v. Blaisdell, 234.
—— v. Boston, 244a.
—— v. Brennan, 267.
—— v. Brooks, 21, 76, 130.
—— v. Byrne, 264.
—— v. Chase, 185.
—— v. Curtis, 173.
—— v. Davis, 52, 57, 130, 237.
—— v. Dow, 139, 193, 249, 275.
—— v. Duane, 247.
—— v. Elliott, 130.
—— v. Fahey, 73.
—— v. Farnum, 272.
—— v. Gage, 130, 247.
—— v. Gay, 176.
—— v. Goodnow, 105.
—— v. Harris, 234.
—— v. Hartford, 242.
—— v. Jones, 272.
—— v. King, 237.
—— v. Kirby, 267.
—— v. Markham, 213.
—— v. Mathews, 53, 130, 247.
—— v. Passmore, 231.
—— v. Patch, 130, 188, 213.
—— v. Reimer, 234.
—— v. Rice, 218.
—— v. Robertson, 130.
—— v. Rowe, 173.
—— v. Roy, 78.
—— v. Rush, 237.
—— v. Steffee, 130, 213.
—— v. Stodder, 15, 130, 187, 247, 259.
—— v. Stokley, 263.
—— v. Turner, 27, 105, 131, 213, 275.
—— v. Vorhis, 16.
—— v. Wentworth, 234.
—— v. Wilkins, 131, 152.
—— v. Worcester, 130, 167, 160, 176, 189.
Conboy v. Iowa City, 49, 52, 56, 184.

Cook v. Burlington, 243.
—— v. Johnston, 6.
—— v. Pennsylvania, 272.
Cook Co. v. McCrea, 15.
Cooper v. Alden, 124.
—— v. People, 170.
—— v. Savannah, 122.
Corbett v. Duncan, 204.
Cornwall v. West Nissoni, 290.
Cornwallis v. Carlisle, 15, 17, 28, 29.
Corrigan v. Gage, 139, 189.
Corry v. Gaynor, 16.
Corson v. Maryland, 137.
Cory v. Somerset, 69.
Cotter v. Doty, 159, 249.
Coulterville v. Gillen, 121, 207.
Council v. Ahrens, 130.
—— v. Pepper, 143, 167.
—— v. Sceba, 174.
—— v. Van Roven, 279.
Council of Montgomery, Ex parte, 155.
County of Amador v. Kennedy, 135.
County of San Louis Obispo v. Hendricks, 38.
Couteulx v. Buffalo, 15.
Covington v. Boyle, 41.
—— v. Dressman, 200.
—— v. Ludlow, 186.
—— v. Nelson, 24.
Cox v. St. Louis, 184.
Coyne, In re, 262.
Craig v. Bennett, 202.
Cranston v. Augusta, 204, 274.
Crashaw v. Roxbury, 290.
Creighton v. Manson, 34, 52.
—— v. Scott, 227.
Croll v. Village, 63.
Cronin v. People, 73, 134.
Cross v. Morristown, 210, 229.
Crotty v. People, 262.
Crowell v. Hopkinton, 290.
Crowley v. Railroad Co., 145, 239.
Cullen v. Carthage, 292.
Cullinan v. New Orleans, 122.
Cummings v. Fitch, 125.
—— v. Railroad Co., 248.
—— v. Savannah, 84, 85, 160.
Cushing v. Adams, 237.
—— v. Boston, 234.
Cutcomp v. Utt, 47.
Cutliff v. Albany, 268, 287.
Cutter v. Russellville, 58.

D.

Daggett v. State, 223.
Dane v. Mobile, 195.
Daniel v. Richmond, 137.
D'Antignac v. Augusta, 164.
Danville v. Shelton, 15, 17, 35.

TABLE OF CASES.

Darling v. St. Paul, 11, 80, 262.
Darst v. Illinois, 163.
Daublin v. New Orleans, 234.
Davenport v. Bird, 170.
—— v. Kelly, 11, 134, 217.
—— v. Kleinschmidt, 132.
Davies v. Morgan, 162.
Davis v. Clifton, 252.
—— v. Clinton, 243.
—— v. Macon, 268, 287.
—— v. Mayor, 30, 241.
—— v. New York, 15.
—— v. Read, 10.
—— v. State, 121.
—— v. Winslow, 231.
Daws v. Hightstown, 8, 213.
Day v. Clinton, 66, 192.
—— v. Green, 11, 236.
—— v. Jersey City, 34.
Dean v. Borchenius, 227.
—— v. Madison, 15.
DeBere v. Girard, 135.
Decorah v. Bullis, 5.
—— v. Dunstan, 13, 63, 263.
—— v. Gillis, 199.
Deel v. Pittsburgh, 166.
Delaney, Ex parte, 28, 188.
Delphi v. Evans, 3, 9, 58, 210, 226.
Dempsey v. Burlington, 74.
Denniston v. Clark, 226.
Denver v. Mullen, 252.
Des Moines v. Gilchrist, 35.
—— v. Hall, 243.
—— v. Railroad Co., 67.
Desmond v. Jefferson, 223.
Detroit v. Blakeby, 8.
Dietz v. Central, 93, 121, 167, 170, 202.
Dimes v. Petty, 7.
Dinwiddie v. Rushville, 5, 36.
Distilling Co. v. Chicago, 258, 260, 264.
Dist. Columbia v. Waggaman, 188.
Dodge v. Council Bluffs, 206.
Domestic Tel. Co. v. Newark, 244a.
Donnaher v. State, 239.
Donnelly v. Clarke Tp., 268.
Donovan v. Vicksburgh, 163, 249.
Douglass v. Commonwealth, 223.
—— v. Placerville, 15.
—— v. Virginia City, 15.
Douglass, Ex parte, 119.
Douglass, In re, 24.
Douglassville v. Johns, 188.
Drake v. Railroad Co., 210.
Dubois v. Augusta, 180, 220.
Dubuque v. Benson, 243.
—— v. Lieber, 284.
—— v. Maloney, 243.
—— v. Stout, 292.
Ducat v. Chicago, 258, 260, 264.
Duckwall v. New Albany, 30, 248.
Dunbar v. San Francisco, 16.

Dunham v. Hyde Park, 226.
—— v. Rochester, 131, 133, 188.
Durkin, In re, 54.
Dutton v. Hanover, 24.
Dutton v. Aurora, 15.
Dwyer v. Brenham, 56, 184.
Dyer v. Chase, 228.

E.

Eager, In re, 227.
East Hartford v. Hartford Co., 8.
Eastman v. Chicago, 195.
East St. Louis v. Gas Co., 244.
—— v. Trustees, 257, 265.
—— v. Wehrung, 268.
Eddleston v. Barnes, 198.
Edenton v. Capeheart, 143.
Egan v. Chicago, 210a.
Eldora v. Burlingame, 5, 8, 139, 187.
Elizabethtown v. Lefler, 35, 185.
—— v. Woodruff, 209.
Elk Point v. Vaughn, 95, 184, 188, 189.
Ellerman v. McMains, 85.
Elmendorf v. Ewen, 58.
Elwood v. Bullock, 263.
Emporia v. Volmer, 170.
Erie v. Reed's Exec., 114, 188.
Erwin v. Township, 43.
Esling's Appeal, 71.
Eufaula v. McNab, 17.
Evansville v. Martin, 292.
Everett v. Council Bluffs, 229, 252, 255.
Ewbanks v. Ashley, 35, 56, 168, 187, 202, 255.
Express Co. v. Mobile, 130.
—— v. St. Joseph, 287.
Eyerman v. Blaksley, 147.

F.

Faribault v. Wilson, 149, 174, 187, 213.
Farnsworth v. Pawtucket, 16.
Farrel v. London, 172a.
Fant v. People, 98.
Farwell v. Chicago, 248.
—— v. Smith, 175.
Fecheimer v. Louisville, 187.
Fennell v. Bay City, 106.
—— v. Guelph, 283.
Ferguson v. Selma, 15.
Ferrenbach v. Turner, 220.
Ferry Co. v. Davis, 132, 263.
—— v. St. Louis, 257, 268, 270.
Fertilizing Co. v. Hyde Park, 16.
Fielding v. Commissioners, 228.
Fink v. Milwaukee, 170.

Fire Dep't. v. Helfenstein, 280.
First Municipality v. Blineau, 135.
—— v. Cutting, 70, 85, 150, 193, 210.
Fisher v. Graham, 24.
—— v. Harrisburg, 130, 188.
Fiske, Ex parte, 53, 223.
Fitch v. Pinchard, 136.
Flanagan v. Plainfield, 173, 202, 283.
Flora v. Lee, 185, 191, 209.
Florence, Ex parte, 15.
Floyd v. Eutontin, 169, 170.
Fort Smith v. Ayers, 30, 258, 259.
—— v. Dodson, 161.
Foster v. Brown, 100, 121.
—— v. Kenosha, 283.
—— v. Roads, 143.
Fowl v. Alexandria, 256.
Fowler, In re, 242.
Fox v. Winona, 234.
Frank, Ex parte, 134, 136, 283.
Franklin v. Westfall, 22, 31, 62.
Frazee's Case, 131, 245.
Freeport v. Marks, 188.
French v. Quincy, 289.
Fretnell v. Troy, 134.
Friday v. Floyd, 159.
Fuller v. State, 121.
Furman v. Huntsville, 170, 209.
Furman St., In re, 9.

G.

Gabel v. Houston, 1, 2, 130, 188, 288.
Gahagan v. Railroad Co., 239.
Gale v. Kalamazoo, 135, 217, 234.
—— v. South Berwick, 290.
Galerno v. Rochester, 54.
Gall v. Cincinnati, 32, 226.
Garden City v. Abbott, 143.
Gardner v. People, 98.
Garland v. Towne, 234.
Garrett v. James, 63, 74.
—— v. Messenger, 264.
Garrison v. Chicago, 225, 243.
Gartside v. E. St. Louis, 6, 134, 206, 229, 248, 287.
Garver, In re, 227.
Garvin v. Wells, 184.
Gas Co.'s Appeal, 132.
Gas Co. v. Des Moines, 1, 6, 9, 188, 244.
—— v. San Francisco, 210a.
—— v. Toberman, 58.
Gaslight Co. v. Dunn, 11.
—— v. Gas Co., 244.
—— v. Middleton, 225, 244.
—— v. Saginaw, 126.
Gass v. Greenville, 143.
Gates v. Milwaukee, 253.
Geneva, The, 292.
Genoa v. Van Alstine, 201.

Gibson v. Kauffield, 272.
Gilcrist v. Schmiddling, 162, 249.
Gilham v. Wells, 265.
Gillmore v. Lewis, 290.
Gilman v. Wells, 201.
Gilmore v. Holt, 143.
Glasby v. Morris, 242.
Glasgow v. Rowse, 286, 287.
—— v. St. Louis, 224.
Glenn v. Baltimore, 183.
Goddard, In re, 170, 235.
—— v. Jacksonville, 275.
——, Petitioner, 130.
Goldsmith v. New Orleans, 268.
Goldstraw v. Duckworth, 234.
Goldthwaite v. Montgomery, 174, 207.
Goodrich v. Brown, 184.
Gormley v. Day, 67.
Gorsuth v. Butterfield, 279.
Goshen v. Crary, 7.
—— v. Croxton, 170.
—— v. Kern, 174.
Gosling v. Velvey, 43.
Gosselink v. Campbell, 143, 161.
Goszler v. Georgetown, 9.
Graffty v. Rushville, 137, 245.
Graham v. Carondelet, 51.
Grand v. Guelph, 268.
Grand Rapids v. Hughes, 19, 147, 232.
Graves v. Bloomington, 220.
—— v. Shattuck, 231, 236.
Gray v. Brooklyn, 21.
Greely v. Jacksonville, 63.
—— v. Passaic, 170a, 173.
Green v. Canal Co., 145, 239.
—— v. Cape May, 210, 210a, 223.
—— v. Indianapolis, 174, 187.
—— v. Lake, 223.
—— v. Savannah, 213, 254, 277.
Green Bay v. Brauns, 58.
Greencastle v. Martin, 249.
Greenfield v. Mook, 151, 169.
Greensboro v. Mullins, 121.
Greensborough v. Shields, 174.
Greensburgh v. Corwin, 170.
Greenwood v. State, 117.
Gregory v. Bridgeport, 12.
—— v. City of N. Y., 251.
——, Ex parte, 188, 246.
Greystock, In re, 156, 263.
Grierson v. County, 188.
Griffin v. Powell, 248.
Grills v. Jonesboro, 121.
Grimmell v. Des Moines, 210.
Gridley v. Bloomington, 130, 235.
Griswold v. Bay City, 226.
Groove v. Fort Wayne, 255.
Grover v. Huckins, 147, 148.
Guillotte v. New Orleans, 160, 215.
Gunnarsohn v. Sterling, 22, 275.

Gurner v. Chicago, 227.
Guy v. Baltimore, 137.

H.

Hadley v. Mayor, 86.
Hagaman, In re, 292.
Hale v. Houghton, 26.
Hall, In re, 62.
—— v. Minturn, 132.
—— v. Nixon, 150, 223.
Haller v. Sheridan, 213.
Hamilton v. Carthage, 151.
—— v. State, 118.
Hammett v. Philadelphia, 227.
Hanger v. Des Moines, 290.
Hannibal v. Railroad Co., 224.
—— v. Winchell, 224, 272.
Hansom, Ex parte, 287.
Harbaugh v. Monmouth, 139, 191, 207, 275.
Hardenbrook v. Ligionier, 150, 174.
Hardy v. Waltham, 223.
Harker v. Mayor, 174, 184.
Harmon v. Chicago, 85, 254.
Harrington v. Corning, 24.
Harris v. Hamilton, 78.
—— v. Livingston, 188, 220.
Harrison v. Baltimore, 188, 220.
—— v. London, 132.
—— v. Vicksburg, 270.
Hart v. Albany, 148.
—— v. Burnett, 124.
Hartford v. Talcott, 7.
Harvey v. Boyd, 209.
—— v. Sloan, 143.
Haskell v. Bartlett, 54.
Hatcher v. Columbus, 284.
Havanna v. Vanluningham, 213, 248.
Hawk v. Marion Co., 290.
Hawkins v. Huron, 72.
Hayden v. Noyes, 137.
Hayes v. Appleton, 131, 133.
—— v. Vincennes, 78.
Hays v. Jones. 24.
Haywood v. Mayor, 84, 89.
Heath v. Railroad Co., 195.
Heeney v. Sprague, 7
Heilbron, Ex parte, 130, 218, 219.
Heine v. Commissioners, 283.
Heise v. Columbus, 30, 116, 152, 159, 160.
Heisembrittle v. Charleston, 26, 130, 275.
Heiskell v. Baltimore, 41.
Heland v. Lowell, 1.
Hellen v. Noe, 162, 249, 254.
Henback v. State, 121.
Henderson v. Covington, 15.
Hendersonville v. McMinn, 174.

Henke v. McCord, 159.
Hennessy v. Connolly, 181.
Herford v. Omaha, 15.
Hershoff v. Beverly, 71, 168, 172a, 179, 190, 264.
Hesketh v. Braddock, 132, 167.
Herzo v. San Francisco, 15, 35, 123.
Hexamer v. Webb, 234.
Hickey v. Railroad Co. 11, 24.
Highland v. Galveston, 164.
Highley v. Bunce, 17, 52.
Hill v. Atlanta, 121.
—— v. Dalton, 173, 181.
—— v. Thompson, 84.
Himmelman v. Hoadley, 226.
—— v. Satterlee, 228.
Hinckley v. Belleville, 22.
Hine v. New Haven, 223.
Hines v. Lockport, 227.
Hitchcock v. Gulveston, 11, 24.
Hites v. Dayton, 217.
Ho Ah Kow v. Neenan, 15.
Hoblyn v. Rex, 125.
Hoboken v. Gear, 52, 53.
—— v. State 238.
Hodges v. Nashville, 283.
Hoffman v. St. Louis, 9, 226.
Holberg v. Macon, 287.
Holland v. San Francisco, 59, 188, 193.
Hollwedell, Ex parte, 150, 170.
Hooksett v. Amoskeag Co., 147, 229.
Hopkins v. Swansea, 1.
Horn v. People, 6, 7, 10, 292.
Horner v. Rowley, 45.
Horst v. Moses, 225.
Hospital v. Stickney, 260.
House v. State, 256.
Hovey v. Mayo, 226.
Howard v. Robbins, 252.
—— v. Savannah, 23, 155.
Hubbard v. Patterson, 215.
Hudson v. Geary, 288.
—— v. Thorne, 206.
Huffsmith v. People, 89, 93.
Hughes v. People, 93.
Humboldt v. McCoy, 74.
Huntington v. Cheesbro, 31, 173.
—— v. Pease, 173, 174.
Huntsville v. Phelps, 151.
Hurber v. Baugh, 160.
Hurl, Ex parte, 268.
Hutchinson v. Pratt, 56.
Hyde Park v. Borden, 78.
Hydes v. Joyes, 10, 11, 138.

I.

Ill. Cent. R. R. Co. v. Galena, 195.
Independence v. Moore, 213.
—— v. Trouvalle, 185.

Indianapolis v. Blythe, 99.
—— v. Fairchild, 99.
—— v. Gas Co. 1, 18, 224.
—— v. Imberry, 210a.
—— v. Miller, 232.
—— v. Mansur, 24.
Information v. Oliver, 172a, 174, 184, 279.
Ingham v. Railroad Co., 238.
Insurance Co. v. Augusta, 284, 287.
—— v. O'Connor, 131.
Intendant v. Chandler, 204.
Inwood v. State, 181.
Irvine v. Wood, 234.
Israel v. Jacksonville, 168.

J.

Jacks v. State, 273.
Jackson v. Bowman, 256.
—— v. Boyd, 171.
—— v. People, 204.
Jackson Co. v. Brush, 10.
Jackson Co. Ry. Co. v. Inter-State Ry. Co., 132.
Jacksonville v. Block, 168.
—— v. Holland, 209.
—— v. McConnell, 15.
Janesville v. Railroad Co., 27, 174.
Jarman v. Patterson, 249.
Jefferson v. Courtmire, 108.
Jelly v. Dilly, 181.
Jenks v. Williams, 7.
Jenkins v. Cheyenne, 170.
—— v. Thomasville, 97.
Jersey City v. State, 60.
Johnson v. Americus, 180.
—— v. City, 257.
—— v. Philadelphia, 15, 193, 248, 259, 260.
Johnson v. Simonton, 149, 218.
Johnston v. Crow, 132.
—— v. Louisville, 15.
Jones v. Ins. Co., 1, 28.
—— v. McAlpine, 61.
—— v. Richmond, 213.
Jonesborough v. McRee, 15, 167.
Joyce v. E. St. Louis, 248.
Judson v. Reardon, 180.

K.

Kaliski v. Grady, 268.
Kanouse v. Lexington, 156, 209.
Kansas City v. Clark, 197.
—— v. Corrigan, 241.
—— v. Muhlbach, 279.
—— v. White, 60.

Karst v. Railway Co., 9, 226.
Karwisch v. Atlanta, 288.
Kavanaugh v. Brooklyn, 8.
Keasy v. Louisville, 15, 188.
Keeler v. Milledge, 170, 173, 174, 209.
Keely v. Atlanta, 287.
Kellogg v. Corrico, 54.
Kelly v. Dwyer, 268.
—— v. Toronto, 217.
Kelsey v. King, 243.
Kempner v. Commonwealth, 210a.
Kendall v. Camden, 86.
Kennedy v. Phelps, 251.
—— v. Sowden, 143.
Kensington v. Glenat, 171.
Keokuk v. Dressell, 22, 158, 202.
—— v. Packet Co., 292.
—— v. Scroggs, 15, 19, 21.
Keokuk, etc., Co. v. Quincy, 194.
Kepner v. Commonwealth, 50.
Kerr v. Hitt, 54.
Ketchum v. Buffalo, 15, 217, 233.
Kettering v. Jacksonville, 139, 187, 279.
Kiburg, Ex parte, 108, 170, 181.
Kiley v. Forsee, 73.
Kimball v. Marshall, 38, 40.
—— v. People, 98.
Kinder v. Gillespie, 249.
King v. Bellringer, 17.
—— v. Carlisle, 237.
—— v. Cross, 237.
—— v. Davenport, 130, 212, 223.
—— v. Jacksonville, 202, 284.
—— v. Williams, 40.
Kinghorn v. Kingston, 185.
Kinmundy v. Mahan, 10, 158.
Kip v. Patterson, 131, 170, 174, 189, 218.
Kirby v. Market, 235.
Kirk v. Nowill, 159.
Kirkham v. Russell, 15, 17, 129, 189, 237.
Kitson v. Ann Arbor, 258.
Knaust, In re, 71.
Kneedler v. Norristown, 159, 222.
Knief v. People, 52.
Knight v. Kansas City, 49.
—— v. Railroad Co., 186.
Kniper v. Louisville, 17, 270.
Knobloch v. Railway Co., 130, 134, 239.
Knox City v. Thompson, 29.
Knoxville v. Bird, 135, 188, 223.
—— v. King, 143, 196.
—— v. Sanford, 248.
—— v. Vicars, 160.
Korah v. Ottawa, 147, 229.
Kyle v. Malin, 17.

L.

Labrie v. Manchester, 220.
Lackland v. Railroad Co., 241.
Lafayette v. Cox, 17.
Lake v. Aberdeen, 3, 34, 251.
Lake View v. Letz, 138, 220, 251.
Lamarque v. New Orleans, 216.
Lancaster v. Richardson, 147, 229.
Lanfear v. Mayor, 163.
Lanier v. Mayor, 287.
Larney v. Cleveland, 170, 203.
Lauenstein v. Fond du Lac, 10.
Launder v. Chicago, 189, 200, 213, 266.
Launtz v. People, 44.
Lautz v. Hightstown, 267.
Law v. People, 55, 71.
Lawrence v. Killam, 227.
Lawrenceburg v. Wuest, 275.
Leach v. Cargill, 15.
Leathers v. Aiken, 85, 292.
Leavenworth v. Booth, 258, 259, 280.
—— v. Norton, 15.
—— v. Rankin, 15.
Lee Tong, In re, 122.
Leland v. Commissioners, 148.
Lenz v. Sherrott, 63.
Leonard v. Canton, 15, 17, 256, 275.
Lesterjelle v. Mayor, 179.
Levy v. State, 99.
Lewis v. Toronto, 226.
Lewiston v. Proctor, 170.
Lexington v. Curtis, 182.
—— v. Headley, 186.
Lindsley v. Chicago, 117, 185.
Lineman, In re, 220.
Linneus v. Dusky, 108.
Linton v. Carter, 8.
Lippman v. South Bend, 173.
Little Rock v. Barton, 213.
Live Stock Asso. v. Cresent City, 132.
Livingston v. Albany, 122.
—— v. Pippin, 15, 26, 218.
—— v. Trustees, 257, 280.
Loeb v. Duncan, 204.
Logan v. Pyne, 16, 17, 132, 263.
—— v. Tyler, 56.
Logansport v. Crockett, 58, 59.
Logue v. Gillick, 186.
London v. Godman, 132.
—— v. Vanacre, 147.
Long v. Brookston, 202.
—— v. Tax District, 213.
Longbridge v. Huntington, 53.
Lord v. Oconto, 11.
Los Angeles v. Railroad Co., 270.
—— v. Waldron, 188, 210.
Louis v. Cafferata, 288.
Louisburg v. Harris, 151.
Louisiana v. Lathrop, 280.

Louisville v. McKean, 121, 262.
—— v. Osborne, 243.
—— v. Roupe, 137.
—— v. Webster, 223.
—— v. Weible, 132.
Low v. Commissioners, 84.
—— v. Evans, 158.
—— v. Marysville, 8.
Lowell v. Simpson, 231.
Loze v. Mayor, 68.
Lucas v. San Francisco, 59.
Lynch v. People, 175, 195, 209, 288.
Lynchburg v. Railway Co., 241, 258.

M.

Mabry v. Bullock, 272.
Macon v. Bank, 287.
—— v. Patty, 10, 223.
Macy v. Indianapolis, 9, 226.
Madden v. Smeltz, 47, 205.
Madison v. Hatcher, 99.
Maguire, In re, 84.
Main v. McCarty, 180.
Mairs v. Real Estate Asso., 7.
Mankato v. Fowler, 258.
Manufacturing Co. v. Schell City, 70, 210.
March v. Commonwealth, 102, 207, 209.
Marietta v. Fearing, 196.
Marion v. Chandler, 277.
Markham v. Atlanta, 9.
—— v. Mayor, 226.
Markle v. Akron, 1, 170, 277.
Marmet v. State, 268.
Marshaltown v. Blum, 137.
Martel v. E. St. Louis, 267.
Martin, In re, 131.
—— v. People, 256, 275.
Martindale v. Palmer, 49.
Martinsville v. Frieze, 174.
Mason v. Shawneetown, 1, 147, 148.
Mather v. Ottowa, 15.
Mathews v. Alexandria, 11.
—— v. Kelsey, 231.
Matter of Zborowski, 24.
Mauch Chunk v. McGee, 71.
Maxwell v. Jonesboro, 265, 276.
Mayberry v. Franklin, 164.
Mayo v. James, 121.
Mayor v. Allaire, 92, 198, 213.
—— v. Arnold, 179.
—— v. Beasley, 80, 130.
—— v. Hudson, 213.
—— v. Hussey, 97.
—— v. Hyatt, 112.
—— v. Lumpkin, 67.
—— v. Mayberry, 335.
—— v. Nell, 172a, 182, 190.

Mayor v. New York, 52, 58, 197.
—— v. Nichols, 112.
—— v. Railroad Co., 241, 249, 285.
—— v. Rood, 218.
—— v. Rumsey, 15, 223.
—— v. Second Ave. R.R.Co., 241, 248.
—— v. Thorne, 131.
—— v. Wards, 202.
—— v. Williams, 28, 213.
—— v. Winfield, 131.
Mayor Baltimore v. Little Sisters of the Poor, 52.
Mayor New York v. Heft, 7.
Mays v. Cincinnati, 250, 283.
McAlister v. Clark, 195, 254.
McArthur v. Saginaw, 188.
McCaffrey v. Smith, 247.
McCain v. State, 224.
McCarthy v. Boston, 229.
McConvill v. Jersey City, 30, 78, 79, 151.
McCormack v. Patchin, 9, 226, 227.
McCormick v. Bay City, 58.
McCoy v. Briant, 35.
—— v. Railroad Co., 239.
McCracken v. San Francisco, 42, 59.
McCullen v. Charleston, 15.
McDermond v. Kennedy, 29.
McDermott v. Board, 1.
—— v. Miller, 45, 50.
McGear v. Woodruff, 175.
McGraw v. Whitson, 47.
McIntire v. Pembroke, 215.
McKee v. McKee, 162.
McKibbin v. Fort Smith, 213, 223.
McKnight v. Toronto, 255.
McLaughlin v. Stephens, 120.
McLeod v. Kincasdine, 156.
McLin v. Newburn, 29.
McNair v. Ex parte, 143.
McNamara v. Estes, 227.
McPherson v. Chebanse, 288.
McRea v. Americus, 97, 198.
Meech v. Buffalo, 15.
Megowan v. Commonwealth, 288.
Melick v. Washington, 77.
Memphis v. Adams, 291.
—— v. Battaille, 143.
—— v. O'Connor, 173.
—— v. Waterworks, 26.
—— v. Winfield, 213.
Merkee v. Rochester, 156, 178.
Merriam v. Moody, 15.
—— v. New Orleans, 193, 273.
Merz v. Railroad Co., 213, 239.
Meyer v. Bridgetown, 174, 275.
Meyers v. Railroad Co., 141.
Miles v. McDermott, 292.
Milhau v. Sharp, 241, 242, 243, 244.
Miller v. Burch, 252.
—— v. O'Reilly, 170.

Miller v. State, 213.
Milliken v. Weatherford, 84, 131.
Mills v. Gleason, 15.
Milne v. Davidson, 1.
Milwaukee v. Gross, 219.
Minden v. Silverstein, 199, 277.
Minneapolis Gas Co. v. Minneapolis, 12.
Minturn v. Larue, 15, 121.
Mitchell v. Rockland, 220.
—— v. Wiles, 125.
Mixer v. Supervisors, 169.
Moberly v. Wright, 148.
Mobile v. Jones, 170, 192.
—— v. Moog, 16, 292.
—— v. Rouse, 92.
—— v. Yuille, 130, 132, 147, 151, 259.
Monroe v. Gerspach, 253.
—— v. Hoffman, 22, 223.
—— v. Meuer, 169.
Montgomery v. Belser, 204.
—— v. Foster, 203.
—— v. Plank Road Co., 15.
Mooney v. Kennett, 184.
Moore, Ex parte, 156.
—— v. Mayor, 35, 52.
—— v. People, 120.
Moran v. Lindell, 75, 228.
—— v. New Orleans, 85.
Morano v. Mayor, 217.
Morehouse v. Norwalk, 188.
Morey v. Brown, 274.
Morgan v. Cincinnati, 220.
—— v. Nolte, 209.
—— v. Quackenbosh, 36.
Morley v. Carpenter, 227.
Morrill v. State, 272, 280.
Morrison v. Hinkson, 248.
Morton v. Princeton, 195.
Moses v. Railroad Co., 238
Moss v. Oakland, 55, 209.
Mott v. New York, 24.
Moundsville v. Fountain, 181.
Mount, Ex parte, 256.
Mowery v. Salisbury, 274.
Mt. Carmel v. Wabash, 8, 256.
Mt. Keokuk v. Dressell, 31.
Mt. Pleasant v. Beckwith, 15.
—— v. Breeze, 31.
—— v. Vansice, 138.
Mühlenbrinck v. Commissioners, 283.
Municipality v. Dunn, 227.
—— v. Kirk, 231.
—— v. Pease, 188.
Munn v. Illinois, 248.
Murphy v. Jacksonville, 96.
—— v. Montgomery, 292.
—— v. Pance, 284.
—— v. Pearce, 224.
Muscatine v. Packet Co., 292.

TABLE OF CASES. XXV

Musgrave v. Church, 255.
Meyers v. Railroad Co., 239.

N.

Nagle v. Augusta, 229.
Napman v. People, 131, 173, 185.
Nashville v. Althrop, 135, 137, 287.
—— v. Toney, 210.
Nasmith, In re, 130, 160.
Naylor v. Galesburg, 197.
Nealis v. Haywood, 78.
Neilly, In re, 260.
—— v. Owen Sound, 130.
Nelson v. La Porte, 225, 244.
Nevada v. Hutchins, 251.
Newark v. Murphy, 180.
New Hampton v. Conroy 19, 159.
New Haven v. Sargent, 15, 226.
—— v. Water Co., 243.
New London v. Brainard, 15.
New Orleans v. Anderson, 193.
—— v. Blanc, 213.
—— v. Brooks, 38.
—— v. Boudro, 209.
—— v. Clark, 225, 244.
—— v. Costello, 213.
—— v. Dubarry, 268, 287.
—— v. Ins. Co., 15.
—— v. Kaufman, 268, 287.
—— v. Miller, 103.
—— v. Phillipi, 18, 89.
—— v. Savings Bank, 121, 287.
—— v. Wilmot, 144.
Newton v. Aurora, 187.
—— v. Belger, 223.
New York v. Buffalo, 290.
—— v. Hyatt, 62.
—— v. Nichols, 121.
—— v. Ordroneaux, 152.
—— v. Ryan, 124.
Nichols v. Nashville, 17.
Nier v. Railway Co., 127.
Nightingale, Petitioner, 130, 218.
Nolin v. Franklin, 254.
Northern Liberties v. O'Neill, 209.
Norton v. Kearnon, 148.
Noyes v. Ward, 195.

O.

Oakland v. Carpenter, 10, 15, 37.
O'Connor v. Pittsburgh, 226.
Ogdensburgh v. Lyon, 81, 142.
O'Leary v. Sloo, 227, 228.
Olin v. Meyers, 58.
Olinda v. Lothrop, 284.
O'Maley v. Freeport, 28.
O'Mally v. McGinn, 49.

Opelousa v. Andrus, 49.
Ordinary v. Retailers, 256
Osborne v. Mobile, 271.
Oskaloosa v. Tullis, 19.
Oskosh v. Schwarz, 170, 174.
Oswego v. Collins, 248.
Ottawa v. Carey, 15.
Ottoman Cahvey Co. v. Philadelphia, 195.
Ottumwa v. Schaub, 185, 267.
Ouachita v. Monroe, 15.
Ould v. Richmond, 268.

P.

Pacific v. Siefert, 193.
Pacific Junction v. Dyer, 137
Packet Co. v. Catlettsburg, 85, 292.
—— v. Keokuk, 85, 292.
—— v. St. Louis, 85.
Palmer v. Hicks, 142.
—— v. Way, 213.
Palmyra v. Morton, 196, 213.
Parr v. Greenbush, 56.
Parsons v. Trustees, 186.
Paterson v. Barnet, 70, 210.
Paton v. People, 265.
Patton v. Stephens, 290.
Paul v. Detroit, 224.
Paxson v. Sweet, 28, 235.
Peay v. Little Rock, 273.
Peck v. Austin, 7.
Pedrick v. Bailey, 130, 149, 234.
Pekin v. Smelzel, 98, 275.
Pendergast v. Peru, 185, 202, 279.
Penn. Co. v. Frana, 193.
—— v. James, 130, 145.
Penn. Ry. Co. v. Jersey City, 139.
People v. Batchelor, 38.
—— v. Benson, 244.
—— v. Bird, 36.
—— v. Board of Health, 253.
—— v. Brooklyn, 227.
—— v. Brown, 119, 213.
—— v. Buchanan, 185.
—— v. Carpenter, 234.
—— v. Cooper, 9.
—— v. Council, 164.
—— v. Cox, 170a.
—— v. Crotty, 3, 210a, 269.
—— v. Cunningham, 231, 237.
—— v. Detroit, 170.
—— v. Dorr, 13.
—— v. Flagg, 225.
—— v. Johnson, 170.
—— v. Justices, 173, 174.
—— v. Leavitt, 204.
—— v. Lee, 72.
—— v. Marx, 130.
—— v. Mayor, 174, 184.

—— v. McClintock, 223.
—— v. Miller, 178, 188, 213.
—— v. Mitchell, 16.
—— v. Moore, 280.
—— v. Morris, 8.
—— v. Mulholland, 130, 218, 260.
—— v. Murray, 72, 186.
—— v. New York, 263.
—— v. Potter, 184.
—— v. Railroad Co., 67, 202.
—— v. Rochester, 46.
—— v. Russell, 260, 272.
—— v. Sacramento, 154.
—— v. San Francisco, 55.
—— v. Schroeder, 50.
—— v. Starne, 57.
—— v. Stevens, 112.
—— v. Sturtevant, 6.
—— v. Thurber, 85, 292.
—— v. Wharf Co., 292.
—— v. Whitney's Point, 170a.
Peoria v. Calhoun, 188, 189.
Pequignot v. Detroit, 228.
Perchee v. Ellis, 130.
Perry v. Railroad Co., 146, 237.
Pesterfield v. Mayor, 131.
Peters v. London, 151.
Petersburg v. Metzger, 15, 98.
Peterson v. New York, 15, 217.
Pettis v. Johnson, 34, 334.
Philadelphia v. Arrott, 195.
—— v. Board, 234.
—— v. Hughes, 195.
—— v. Roney, 209.
Phillips v. Allen, 159, 160.
Phillips, In re, 227.
Pierce v. Bartrum, 134, 143, 219.
Pieri v. Mayor, 131.
Pimental v. San Francisco, 42, 59.
Piqua v. Zimmerlin, 30, 139, 218.
Plaquemine v. Roth, 18, 19.
—— v. Ruff, 155.
Platteville v. Bell, 276.
Player v. Vere, 133.
Plum v. Canal Co., 226.
Plymouth v. Pettijohn, 143.
Poe v. Machine Works, 204.
Poillon v. Brooklyn, 15.
Polland v. Connelly, 77.
Polinsky v. People, 112, 130, 218.
Pomeroy v. Lapens, 174.
Pool v. Boston, 290.
Porter v. Waring, 184.
Port Huron v. McCall, 17.
Powell v. People, 209.
—— v. St. Joseph, 227.
Powers v. Decatur, 168, 268.
Poyer v. Des Plaines, 206, 255.
Prell v. McDonald, 172, 179, 185.
Prescott v. Battersby, 8a.
—— v. Duquesne, 202.

President v. Holland, 170.
Preston v. Manvers, 48.
Providence v. Railroad Co., 68.
Provision Co. v. Chicago, 248.
Pugh v. Little Rock, 185.
Purdue v. Ellis, 260.
Pye v. Peterson, 222, 252.

Q.

Queen v. Davis, 237.
—— v. Gilbert, 155, 156.
—— v. Justices, 54, 167.
—— v. Milledge, 167.
Quigley v. Aurora, 170.
Quincy v. Ballance, 170.
—— v. Bull, 67, 139, 195, 242, 243.
—— v. Railroad Co., 210.
Quinn v. Heisel, 180.
—— v. Paterson, 146, 224.
Quinette v. St. Louis, 193.
Quong Woo, In re, 11.

R.

Railroad v. Belleville, 240.
—— v. Bloomington, 239.
—— v. Brooklyn, 189, 241.
—— v. Brown, 238.
—— v. Buffalo, 239.
—— v. Burlington, 67.
—— v. Cape May, 67.
—— v. Chenoa, 147, 151, 239.
—— v. Deacon, 79.
—— v. Decatur, 239.
—— v. East Orange, 130.
—— v. Ellerman, 292.
—— v. Engle, 185.
—— v. Ervine, 7.
—— v. Evansville, 24.
—— v. Galena, 239.
—— v. Garside, 238.
—— v. Godfrey, 174.
—— v. Haggerty, 239.
—— v. Jersey City, 139, 239.
—— v. Joliet, 195.
—— v. Klauber, 174.
—— v. Lake View, 241.
—— v. Louisville, 147.
—— v. Long Branch, 224.
—— v. Mt. Pleasant, 227.
—— v. Newark, 238.
—— v. New Orleans, 8.
—— v. Odum, 56.
—— v. People, 261, 239.
—— v. Petersborough, 10.
—— v. Philadelphia, 248.
—— v. Quincy, 8.
—— v. Railroad Co., 238, 240.

TABLE OF CASES. xxvii

Railroad v. Richmond, 135, 241.
—— v. Shields, 238.
—— v. Shires, 185.
—— v. Smith, 240.
—— v. Spearman, 228.
—— v. Springfield, 188.
—— v. St. Louis, 292.
—— v. Transit Co., 240.
Railway Co. v. Baltimore, 12.
—— v. Cambridge, 235.
—— v. Covington, 238.
—— v. Furibault, 224.
—— v. Hoboken, 213, 256, 258.
—— v. Jacksonville, 131, 226, 239.
—— v. Jonesville, 241.
—— v. Lake View, 252.
—— v. Louisville, 238, 241, 242, 265.
—— v. Philadelphia, 213, 241, 248, 250.
—— v. Railway Co., 67.
Raker v. Muquon, 187.
Raleigh v. Dougherty, 116, 220.
Randall v. Van Vechten, 225.
Randolph, In re, 85.
Rau v. Little Rock, 139.
Ravenna v. Penn. Co., 239.
Redden v. Covington, 199.
Reed, Ex parte, 203.
Regina v. Coulter, 271.
—— v. Cuthbert, 271.
—— v. Howard, 223.
—— v. Johnston, 203, 223.
—— v. Osler, 143.
—— v. Pipe, 137, 191.
—— v. Stafford, 267.
Reich v. State, 97.
Reinboth v. Pittsburgh, 15.
Rendering Co. v. Behr, 220.
Rensselaer v. Leopold, 188.
Respublica v. Duquet, 147.
Rex v. Ashwell, 60a.
—— v. Cutbush, 125.
—— v. Harrison, 73.
—— v. Jones, 237.
—— v. Moore, 237.
—— v. Ward, 232.
Reynolds v. Cincinnati, 188.
—— v. Schweinefus, 24.
Rice v. Kansas, 101.
Rich v. Chicago, 58.
Richardson v. Heydenfeldt, 10.
Ridgway v. West. 4, 160.
Robbins v. New Brunswick, 228.
—— v. People, 98.
—— v. Shelby Co., 137.
Roberson v. Lambertville, 173, 175.
Roberts v. Easton, 16.
—— v. Ogle, 137, 249, 254.
Robertson v. Groves, 15, 17.
—— v. Railroad Co., 239.
Robinson v. Franklin, 121.

Rochester v. Close, 133.
—— v. Collins, 29, 32.
—— v. Pettinger, 218.
—— v. Upman, 134, 174, 278.
Rogers v. Jones, 112, 139.
Rome v. Cabot, 15, 218.
Rosebaugh v. Saffin, 152, 162, 249.
Ross v. York, 288.
Rost v. Mayor, 163.
Rothschild v. Darien, 97.
Rudolph, In re, 271.
Ruggles v. Nantucket, 12.
Rulson v. Post, 131.
Runyon v. Bordine, 234.
Russellville v. White, 30.
Ryan v. Jacob, 160.

S.

Sacramento v. Crocker, 268, 270.
—— v. Stage Co., 270.
Safe Co. v. Mayor, 206.
Saginaw Gas Co. v. Saginaw, 132.
Salem v. Maynes, 223.
Salt Lake City v. Wagner, 135, 141.
Sanders v. Butler, 256.
—— v. Elberton, 277.
San Francisco v. Canavan, 8.
—— v. Hazen, 42.
Santa Barbara v. Sherman, 170.
Sargent v. Railway Co., 127, 188.
Satterlee v. San Francisco, 42.
Sauk v. Philadelphia, 46.
Saunders v. Lawrence, 39.
—— v. Russell, 270.
Savannah v. Charleston, 121.
—— v. Feely, 270.
—— v. Hines, 287.
—— v. Wilson, 233.
Saxton v. Beach, 84.
—— v. St. Joseph, 34.
Scammon v. Chicago, 234.
Schenly v. Commonwealth, 59, 227.
Schmidt, Ex parte, 270.
Schneider, In re, 30, 265.
Schott v. People, 185, 188.
Schroder v. Charleston, 116.
Schultz v. Cambridge, 193, 194.
Schuster v. State, 31.
Schwab v. Madison, 206.
Schwartz v. Oshkosh, 52, 57, 64.
Schweitzer v. Liberty, 52.
Schwuchow v. Chicago, 30, 150, 213, 265, 267, 275, 277.
Scott v. Shreveport, 15.
Sears v. Commissioners, 85, 271.
Seebald v. People, 98.
Selectmen v. Murray, 131.
Selma v. Stewart. 203, 209.
Sewell v. St. Paul, 283.

Shaffer v. Mumma, 104.
Shallcross v. Jeffersonville, 30.
Shaw v. Kennedy. 162, 163.
—— v. Pope, 13.
—— v. Poynter, 175.
Sheehan v. Gleason, 11.
Sheffield v. O'Day, 155, 157.
Shelby v. Randles, 274.
Shelton v. Mobile, 139, 264.
Shepherd v. Hees, 144, 249.
Shillito v. Thompson, 254.
Shrader, Ex parte, 254.
Shreveport v. Levy, 131, 136, 288.
—— v. Roos, 78, 147.
Siebenhauer, Ex parte, 121, 135.
Siloam Springs v. Thompson, 89.
Simpson v. Savage, 121.
Sisto Li Protti, Ex parte, 268.
Slatten v. Railroad Co., 238.
Slattery, Ex parte, 28.
Slaughter v. Commonwealth, 280.
Slaughter House Laws, 130.
Slessman v. Crozier, 159, 161.
Smith v. Adrian, 184, 279.
—— v. Buffalo, 35.
—— v. Elizabeth, 209.
—— v. Emporia, 32, 71.
—— v. Gas Co., 244.
—— v. Knoxville, 125, 276.
—— v. Madison, 15, 17, 31, 195, 256.
—— v. Mayor, 130.
—— v. Morse, 10, 15.
—— v. Newburn, 15, 217.
—— v. Rome, 226.
—— v. Sacramento, 291.
—— v. Toronto, 193.
—— v. Washington, 226.
Smith, Ex parte, 188.
Smith, In re, 24, 52.
Snell v. Belleville, 143, 217.
Snyder v. North Lawrence, 20, 194.
Society v. Diers, 273.
Solomon v. Hughes, 58, 186, 207.
Soon Hing v. Crowley, 130.
Southport v. Ogden, 94.
Sower v. Philadelphia, 70, 210a.
Spangler v. Jacoby, 58.
Sparks v. Stokes, 173, 278.
Spaulding v. Lowell, 19, 217.
Specht v. Commonwealth, 288.
Spengler v. Trowbridge, 292.
Spitler v. Young, 143, 199.
Staates v. Washington, 38, 47, 153, 160, 166, 276.
Starr v. Burlington, 1.
State v. Addington, 130.
—— v. Albright, 6.
—— v. Ames, 288.
—— v. Atkinson, 232.
—— v. Atlanta, 15.

State v. Atlantic City, 227.
—— v. Barbour, 46.
—— v. Bayonne, 210a.
—— v. Bean, 213, 283.
—— v. Beattie, 30.
—— v. Bell, 11, 35.
—— v. Bergman, 114.
—— v. Bennett, 265.
—— v. Bill, 204.
—— v. Binder, 108.
—— v. Blauvelt, 204.
—— v. Blaser, 137.
—— v. Brittain, 110.
—— a. Brückhauser, 28, 107.
—— v. Cainan, 139, 151.
—— v. Caldwell, 103.
—— v. Cantieny, 71, 148, 154, 156, 180.
—— v. Canton, 213.
—— v. Carr, 51.
—— v. Chapman, 43, 46.
—— v. Chase, 103.
—— v. Cincinnati Gas Co., 132, 244.
—— v. Clarke, 108, 111, 139, 188.
—— v. Coke Co., 240.
—— v. Columbia, 208.
—— v. Cowan, 108.
—— v. Crenshaw, 151.
—— v. Crummey, 107.
—— v. Douglass, 111.
—— v. Edens, 174.
—— v. Elizabeth, 226, 227.
—— v. Farr, 41, 43.
—— v. Fay, 19.
—— v. Ferguson, 20.
—— v. Fisher, 132.
—— v. Foley, 130, 237.
—— v. Freeman, 27, 130.
—— v. Gening, 279.
—— v. Gisch, 217.
—— v. Gordon, 100.
—— v. Grafmuller, 172a.
—— v. Green, 43.
—— v. Green Co., 16.
—— v. Hardy, 53.
—— v. Hauser, 10.
—— v. Herdt, 154, 155.
—— v. Herod, 141, 157, 265.
—— v. Hoboken, 30, 52, 139, 256.
—— v. Hudson, 74.
—— v. Ironton Gas Co., 188.
—— v. Jersey City, 6, 11, 47, 49, 130, 145, 204, 210a, 227, 230, 239, 242, 251, 252.
State v. Johnson, 23.
—— v. Kantler, 10, 37, 64, 70.
—— v. Keith, 110.
—— v. King, 172a, 185.
—— v. Kirkley, 193.
—— v. Langston, 110.
—— v. Lathrop, 287.

TABLE OF CASES.   xxix

State v. Laverack, 237.
—— v. Lee, 107.
—— v. Ludwig, 107.
—— v. Lufferty, 180.
—— v. McDonough, 28.
—— v. McNish, 195.
—— v. Merritt, 174.
—— v. Mills, 111.
—— v. Mobile, 15, 217, 224, 233, 237.
—— v. Morristown, 15, 224.
—— v. Mott, 188, 252, 255.
—— v. Newark, 35, 47.
—— v. New Brunswick, 12, 146, 224.
—— v. New York, 15.
—— v. Oleson, 107.
—— v. Patamia, 284.
—— v. Patterson, 6, 11, 40, 200.
—— v. Plunkett, 111.
—— v Pollard, 115.
—— v. Railroad Co., 193, 237, 238, 241.
State v. Richards, 174.
—— v. Shelby 117.
—— v. Sims, 28.
—— v. Sly, 114.
—— v. Smith, 17, 270, 283.
—— v. Stearns, 170.
—— v. Swift, 15.
—— v. Taylor, 231.
—— v. Trenton, 11, 12, 240.
—— v Tryon, 1.
—— v. Union, 57.
—— v. Vail, 58.
—— v. Welch, 130, 198, 276, 288.
—— v. West Orange, 226.
—— v Williams, 1, 28, 116.
—— v. Woodward, 232, 237.
—— v Young, 101.
—— v. Zeigler, 77, 151, 168.
State Center v. Barenstein, 11, 21, 130, 167, 188, 263.
St. Charles v. Nolle, 137, 143.
—— v. O'Mailey, 185, 202.
Steckert v. East Saginaw, 58, 228.
Stetson v. Faxon, 237.
—— v. Kempton, 290.
Stevens v. Commonwealth, 173.
Stevenson v. Bay City, 49, 56.
Stewart v. Clinton, 186.
—— v. Commonwealth, 223.
St. John v. New York, 188, 217, 231.
St. Louis v. Bank, 264.
—— v. Bentz, 108, 130, 213.
—— v. Böffinger, 2, 85, 188.
—— v. Buckner, 11.
—— v. Cafferata, 108, 130, 213.
—— v Clemens, 10, 11.
—— v Fitch, 131.
—— v. Fitz, 84, 173.
—— v. Foster, 1, 58, 186.

St. Louis v. Frein, 173.
—— v. Green, 71, 130, 264, 285, 286, 287.
St. Louis v. Herthel, 195.
—— v. Jackson, 217.
—— v. Kase, 125.
—— v. Knox, 130, 173, 182, 188.
—— v. Laughlin, 20, 264, 270.
—— v. Life Asso., 264.
—— v. Oeters, 11.
—— v. Railway Co., 139.
—— v. Siegrist, 277.
—— v. Spiegel, 268.
—— v. Stern, 254.
—— v. Sternberg, 264, 279, 287.
—— v. Tiefel, 71.
—— v. Trust Co., 283.
—— v. Transportation Co., 287.
—— v. Vert, 27, 170.
—— v. Weber, 125, 130, 189, 217.
—— v. Wehrung, 11.
—— v. Withaus, 38.
—— v. Woodruff, 248.
Ry. Co. v. St. Louis, 130, 134, 241.
St. Martinsville v. Mary Lewis, 144, 202.
Stokes v. New York, 134, 209.
—— v. Prescott, 272.
Stondinger v. Newark, 342.
St. Paul v. Colter, 130, 188.
—— v. Laidler, 133.
—— v. Smith, 130, 145, 219.
—— v. Traeger, 20, 131, 245.
—— v. Troyer, 277.
Strabl, Ex parte, 15.
Strauss v. Pontiac, 4, 16, 142, 275, 277.
Strike v. Collins, 124, 217.
Striker v. Kelly, 58.
Stroud v. Philadelphia, 242.
St. Rochs Sud v. Dion, 137.
Stryker v. New York, 142.
Stuhr v. Hoboken, 52.
Sugar Co. v. Jersey City, 224.
Sumner v. Philadelphia, 220.
Sumpter v. Deschampes, 21.
Supervisors v. People, 57.
Sutton v. McConnell, 170.
Swarth v. People, 13, 121, 261.
Sweet v. Wabash, 30, 189, 286.
Sykes v. Columbus, 15.

T.

Taintor v. Morristown, 229.
Tallant v. Burlington, 24.
Tappan v. Young, 10.
Taylor v. Americus, 190, 204, 209.
—— v. Carondolet, 1.
—— v. Palmer, 53.
—— v. Pine Bluffs, 206, 218.

Taylor v. Railway Co., 235.
Taylor, Ex parte, 271.
Taxing District v. Emerson, 273.
Taxtor v. Railroad Co., 239.
Teft v. Size, 187.
Telegraph Co. v. Chicago, 244a.
—— v. Richmond, 268.
Telephone Co. v. Oshkosh, 18.
Temple v. Sumner, 272.
Terre Haute v. Lake, 34, 61.
—— v. Twiner, 255.
Terry v. Haldinand, 263.
Thomas v. Ashland, 169.
—— v. Hot Springs, 20.
—— v. Mt. Vernon, 30, 167, 275.
Thompson v. Boonville, 10.
—— v. Schermerhorn, 10, 11.
Thorpe v. Brumfitt, 237.
Three Rivers v. Mayor, 287.
Tipton v. Norman, 22, 70, 147, 185, 210.
Tisdale v. Minonk, 54, 166, 209.
Toledo v. Edens, 141.
Torbert v. Lynch, 156.
Torrent v. Muskegon, 15, 289.
Touchard v. Touchard, 8.
Towns v. Tallahassee, 160, 188, 267.
Tracy v. People, 58.
Traphagen v. Jersey City, 242.
Trask, Ex parte, 155, 156.
Treadway v. Schnauber, 15.
Trigally v. Memphis, 6.
Triggs v. Lester, 245.
Trimble v. Bucyrus, 213.
Truchelot v. City Council, 138.
Truesdale v. Moultrieville, 173.
—— v. Rochester, 51.
Trustees v. People, 131.
—— v. Roome, 270.
—— v. Schroeder, 203.
Trustees, In re, 12.
Trowbridge v. Newark, 17, 139.
Tuck v. Waldron, 20, 275.
Tucker v. Virginia City, 15.
Tugman v. Chicago, 132.
Tuttle v. State, 223.

U.

Udell v. Brooklyn, 142.
Underwood v. Carney, 234.
—— v Green, 220.
Upington v. Oviatt, 47, 56.
Urquhart v. Ogdensburg, 201.
United States v. Hart, 86.
—— v. Holly, 120.

V.

Van Baalen v. People, 188, 260.

Vance v. Little Rock, 283.
Vanderwater v. New York, 144.
Vandine, Petitioner, 130, 143, 220, 264.
Vandyke v. Cincinnati, 7, 174.
Van Hook v. Selma, 1, 88, 258, 259.
Van Horn v. People, 274.
Van Sant v. Stage Co., 268, 283.
Van Sicklen v. Burlington, 223.
Varden v. Mount, 159, 161, 163, 249.
Vars v. Railway Co., 237.
Vason v. Augusta, 97, 253.
Vicksburg v. Tobin, 85.
Vidal v. Girard, 29.
Vionet v. First Municipality, 213.
Vogel v. Granz, 213.
Vosse v. Memphis, 268.

W.

Waco v. Powell, 249, 254.
Wade v. Newburn, 217.
Wadleigh v. Gilman, 213, 223.
Waite v. Garston, 220.
Waldo v. Wallace, 99.
Waldraven v. Memphis, 60.
Walker v. Evansville, 210a.
—— v. Springfield, 257, 265.
Wallace v. New York, 224.
Walsh v. Railroad Co., 145.
—— v. Union, 195.
Wan Yin, In re, 30, 259.
Ward v. Greenville, 131, 276.
—— v. Little Rock, 252.
Waring v. Mobile, 62.
Warren v. Henly, 227, 228.
—— v. Mayor, 139.
Wartmann v. Philadelphia, 217.
Wasem v. Cincinnati, 55.
Washington v. Frank, 174, 188.
—— v. Hammond, 110.
—— v. Meigs, 84, 274.
—— v. Nashville, 164.
—— v. State, 273, 280.
Waterbury v. Laredo, 15.
—— v. Martin, 67.
Water Commissioners v. Dwight, 71.
Waters v. Leech, 15, 131.
Water Works v. Partlett, 6, 84.
Watson v. Chicago, 74.
—— v. Passaic, 227.
—— v. Turnbull, 188.
Watts v. Scott, 174.
Waupum v. Moore, 206.
Wayne Co. v. Detroit, 106, 169.
Webster v. Harwinton, 15.
—— v. Lansing, 207.
Weeks v. Foreman, 168.
Well v. Ricord, 252, 253.
Weitzel v. Concordia, 170.
Welch v. Hotchkiss, 130, 223, 267.

Welker v. Potter, 35.
Wells v. Atlanta, 15, 26.
Welsh v. Railroad Co., 249.
Welton v. Missouri, 137.
Wendover v. Lexington, 265.
Wertheimer v. Boonville, 209.
West v. Bancroft, 243.
—— v Columbus, 174.
—— v. Greenville, 121.
—— v. Mayor, 206.
Westgate v. Carr, 98.
Wetmore v. Story, 39.
Wetumpka v. Wharf Co., 6.
Wharf Co. v. Portland, 231.
Wheatley v. Covington, 17.
Wheel Co. v. Burnham, 42.
Wheeling v. Black, 184.
White v. Charleston, 12.
—— v. Godfrey, 229.
—— v. Haworth, 162.
—— v. Kent, 127, 180, 188, 237.
—— v. McKeesport, 15.
—— v. Tallman, 159, 160, 249.
Whitehall v. Meux, 171.
Whitfield v. Longest, 249, 254.
Whitlock v. Wilton, 193.
Whitson v. Franklin, 145, 174, 199, 237, 239.
Whitten v. Covington, 11.
Wiggins v Chicago, 166, 169, 202, 267.
Wightman v. State, 113.
Wilcox v. Hemming, 139, 161, 162, 213.
Wilder v. Savannah, 270, 287.
Wiley v. Owens, 260.
Wilkinson v. Charleston, 143.
Willard v. Killingsworth, 17, 185.
Williams v. Augusta, 29, 130, 170.
—— v. Davidson, 1, 17, 84, 131, 213.
—— v. Detroit, 226, 227.
—— v. Warsaw, 99.
—— v. West Point, 82.
Williamson v. Commonwealth, 15.
Williamsport v. Commonwealth, 15.
Willis v. Legris, 163.
Wilmington v. Roby, 143, 272.

Wilson, In re, 8, 10, 30, 204.
Winants v. Bayonne, 11, 19.
Winona v. Burke, 174, 184.
Winooski v. Gokey, 147, 174, 176, 184.
Winpenny v. Philadelphia, 292.
Wistar v. Philadelphia, 227.
Wittler v. Cavender, 24.
Wolf, Ex parte, 38, 63, 276.
Wolfe v. Railroad Co., 237.
Wood v. Brooklyn, 112, 170, 180, 288.
—— v. Mears, 231.
Woodbridge v. Detroit, 235.
Woodruff v. Stewart, 51, 165, 228.
Woodward v. Turnbull, 98.
Worden v. New Bedford, 289.
Workman, In re, 242.
Works v. Lockport, 74.
Worsley v. New Orleans, 35.
Worthington v. Scribner, 213.
Wragg v. Penn. Tp., 98.
Wreford v. People, 131, 219, 252.
Wright v. Atlanta, 284.
—— v. Forrestal, 54, 58.
—— v. Railroad Co., 1, 7, 195.
Wright, In re, 205, 247.
Wyandotte v. Corrigan, 241.
Wythe v. Nashville, 10.

Y.

Yates v. Milwaukee, 218, 292.
Yick Woo v. Hopkins, 136.
Yick Woo, In re, 84, 130, 193.
York v. Forscht, 290.
Young v. St Louis, 73.

Z.

Zanone v. Mound City, 136, 201, 268.
Zborowski, Matter of, 24
Zorger v. Greenbush, 193, 195.
Zottman v. San Francisco, 15.
Zylstra v. Charleston, 15.

MUNICIPAL POLICE ORDINANCES.

CHAPTER I.

NATURE OF ORDINANCES.

§ 1. Definition of an ordinance.
§ 2. Ordinances are laws.
§ 3. Necessity of formal passage.
§ 4. Charter prohibition need not be supplemented by an ordinance.
§ 5. Must be passed by the governing body.
§ 6. Must regulate corporate affairs.
§ 7. Must not regulate civil liabilities.

§ 1. **Definition.**—Municipal ordinances are laws passed by the governing body of a municipal corporation for the regulation of the affairs of the corporation.

The term ordinance is now the usual denomination of such acts, although in England and in some of the states the technically more correct term *by-law* or *bye-law* is in common and approved use. The main feature of such enactments is their local as distinguished from the general applicability of the state laws; hence the word *law*, with the prefix *by* or *bye*, should in strictness be preferred to the word *ordinance*.

§ 2. **Ordinances are laws.**—Ordinances are not merely rules or regulations in the ordinary sense of those terms, but, as the derivation of the word would indicate, they are in the nature of *laws*, being decreed by a body vested with definite legislative authority, coupled with power to enforce obedience to its enactments. That legislative power shall not be delegated is a fundamental principle of our constitutions; and the prohibition is strictly observed in all things that affect the body of the state. But in every thickly-settled locality there is a necessity for more detailed regulation of human affairs than the general legislature could practicably provide, the necessity varying with the physical surroundings, the character of the people, the nature of their employment, and the density of population. As Roberts, C. J., says in a recent case in Texas:[1]

"So far as it relates to the execution of the general laws of the land, there is no more necessity for an incorporation in a city than in the country. Nor does the incorporation exclude within its boundaries the operation of the general laws as applicable to the whole country.

"But when people are placed in close contact in a town or city, the safety of property and persons there, the facility of transacting their business, the preservation of their health, and the comforts and decencies of good society in their midst, require a great many minor, though important, regulations, too minute and varied for general laws and which are peculiar to their condition.

"These regulations are to be made in subordination, and not contrary to the general laws. Still they go far beyond the general laws in prescribing the civil conduct of persons in relation to their personal conduct and property. In order to make these additional regulations binding, the charter must be put in operation by an organization, or by the action of officers under it. An act incorporating a town or city, therefore, is a law of the state, and more than an ordinary law; for it constitutes, when acted on, a sort of organic law, a constitution for a local self-government, within its territorial limits, extending in its scope to the extra regulations required for the good government of the city or town, to be enacted and carried into effect by its municipal officers."

Public policy demands, therefore, and authority sanctions, the delegation of various powers of local legislation to the municipal body. The ordinances enacted in the execution

(1) Williams v. Davidson, 43 Tex. 1.

of these powers have, within the limits of the corporation, the force of laws. They are just as binding as the laws of the state and general government; they are enforced in similar manner and under like rules of construction.[1]

"In the exercise of its regulatory power the government of a city must have as wide a discretion as that possessed by the government of the state, in choosing between different measures for accomplishing the end. When an ordinance is passed under this grant of power, it is in force by the authority of the state, and is to be interpreted and executed as if it had been passed by the general assembly. Such, at least, is its authority when the question under consideration is whether it is inconsistent with the constitution of the United States."[2]

As statutes are tested by the state constitution, so ordinances are tested, not as being of a contractual nature, but, as laws, by the delegated power under which they are enacted. The charter is the local constitution.[3]

§ 3. **Necessity of formal passage.**—Ordinances being in the nature of laws, there is the same necessity for their

(1) Dill. Mun. Corp., § 308; Sedgw. Stat. Law, p. 462; Bish. Stat. Crimes, § 11, a; Cooley Const. Lim, *211; Jones v. Insurance Co., 2 Daly, 307; McDermott v. Board, 5 Abb. Pr. 422; Milne v. Davidson, 5 Martin, 586; State v. Williams, 11 S. C. 288; Gabel v. Houston, 29 Tex. 336; Bearden v. Madison, 73 Ga. 184; Ileland v. Lowell, 3 Allen, 407; State v. Tryon, 39 Conn. 183; Hopkins v. Swansea, 4 M. & W. 621; Burmeister v. Howard, 1 Wash. Ter. 207; Wright v. Railroad Co., 7 Ill. App. 438; Church v. City, 5 Cow. 538; St. Louis v. Bank, 49 Mo. 574; Taylor v. Carondelet, 22 Mo. 105; St. Louis v. Foster, 52 Mo. 513; Mason v. Shawnee, 77 Ill. 533; Bott v. Pratt, 33 Minn. 323; Gas Company v. Des Moines, 44 Ia. 508; s. c., 24 Am. Rep. 756; Starr v. Burlington, 45 Ia. 87; Indianapolis v. Gas Company, 66 Ind. 396. In Markle v. Akron, 14 Ohio, 586, ordinances were held to be mere compacts between the corporators, and not legislation—so held in order to uphold the ordinance in the face of a constitutional provision that "Legislative power shall be vested exclusively in the general assembly." But delegation to local bodies for local purposes is certainly not within that provision, and there was no necessity for such a strained holding.

(2) St. Louis v. Boffinger, 19 Mo. 13.

(3) Gabel v. Houston, 29 Tex. 336.

formal and definite expression. The power given to corporations to legislate is a franchise or privilege, and the extent to which the corporation wishes to exercise it must be defined by the passage of an ordinance. It is not self-executing, but requires an ordinance to put it in force.[1] The existence of the power does not warrant its direct exercise by the ministerial officers of the municipality.[2] Thus power to abate nuisances does not authorize an actual abatement of an existing nuisance, until the erection or maintenance of nuisances has been declared unlawful by ordinance;[3] nor does the power to destroy instruments of gambling authorize a seizure until provided for by ordinance.[4]

§ 4. **Charter prohibition.**—If the municipal charter or creating statute contains an express and definite prohibition of the doing some specified act within the corporate limits, it would not be necessary to enact an ordinance covering the prohibition in order to make it effective, and its non-observance punishable by the local authorities.[5] But the charter prohibition must be accompanied by a prescription of a penalty, and mode of recovery.[6]

§ 5. **Must be passed by governing body.**—The general law usually provides for the election of a body of persons known as the council or assembly, in whom is vested the sole right and duty of regulating the corporate affairs and of exercising its franchises; and no legislative power may be exercised by any other body or agency.[7] The mayor alone could not prescribe an ordinance, neither could any one branch of a compound legislative body enact valid ordinances without the concurrence of the

---

(1) Delphi v. Evans, 36 Ind. 90; Bryan v. Page, 51 Tex. 532; People v. Crotty, 93 Ill. 181; Bull v. Quincy, 9 Ill. App. 27.
- (2) *Idem.*
(3) Lake v. Aberdeen, 57 Miss. 260.
(4) Ridgeway v. West, 60 Ind. 371; 22 Cent. Law Jour. 319.
(5) Ashton v. Ellsworth, 48 Ill. 299; Strauss v. Pontiac, 40 Ill. 301.
(6) Strauss v. Pontiac, *supra*.
(7) Dill. Mun. Corp., § 309.

other branch. In a corporation governed by a council, an ordinance adopted by the whole body of qualified electors would have no validity. Likewise, the electors of the smaller New England towns, in which local legislation is still exercised by the corporators at large, could not, without legislative sanction, delegate their powers to a committee of their number. The body which is recognized or authorized by the law of the state as having the control of the corporate affairs, whether it be the citizens at large, or a council, simple or compound, is the only agency capable of exercising the legislative privileges of the corporation.

The council must be constituted in strict accordance with the law under which it seeks to exercise its powers.[1] So, where a corporation exists under a special charter containing provision for a corporate council to be chosen in a specified manner, and afterward impliedly adopts the benefits of a general law by electing its council in accordance with its provisions, the council so elected will be restricted to the exercise of the powers granted by the general law, because the prior special charter contemplated the exercise of its powers by a council chosen in a different manner.[2]

§ 6. **Must regulate corporate affairs.**—Lastly, the ordinance must regulate corporate affairs. A distinction may be drawn between the mere act of passage and the ordinance itself when passed. In one sense, a council may enact any thing, however absurd or unauthorized; but such an enactment would be a nullity, and injunction would lie to prevent its enforcement.[3] The council would, however, be enjoined from passing a contemplated ordinance, which, if passed, would be wholly void, as in plain excess of its power, whenever surrounding circumstances make the existence alone of such an ordinance a menace to important interests. In order to warrant this remedy the ordinance

(1) Dinwiddie v. Rushville, 37 Ind. 66.
(2) Decorah v. Bullis, 25 Ia. 12. As to the effect of minor irregularities in the constitution of councils, see *post*, §§ 36, 39.
(3) Chicago v. Evans, 24 Ill. 52; Gas Company v. Des Moines, 44 Ia. 405; s. c., 24 Am. Rep. 756.

must be one whose provisions are capable of summary enforcement by the ministerial agents of the corporation, without resorting to any sort of judicial procedure, otherwise the menaced interests would have ample protection in a court of law.[1]

Ordinances, to be valid, must be restricted in their operation to legitimate corporate purposes, those affecting the welfare and security of the community. As will be seen hereafter,[2] this does not mean that an ordinance may not affect persons or property located without the corporate limits, for such an effect might be incidentally unavoidable. Neither does it mean that an ordinance is invalid which is incidentally advantageous or injurious to some individual or class.[3] But the scope and aim of the ordinance must neither be the regulation of extra-territorial affairs, nor of private rights and liabilities. Ordinances are and must be local laws, and absolute equality of burdens can no more be attained by them than by the laws of the state.

Most constitutions provide that all laws shall be of a general or uniform operation throughout the state, but it would obviously be fatal to the purpose of municipal organization to construe such provision to be applicable to ordinances. Ordinances need be general and uniform only throughout the territory over which the legislature intend they shall operate. So, ordinances upon the same subject may be decidedly different in different cities, however like in size or situation.[4]

§ 7. **Must not regulate civil liabilities.**—Due regulation of corporate affairs does not include any interference with civil rights and liabilities. Some courts hold that or-

---

(1) Water-works *v.* Bartlett, 16 Fed. Rep. 52; People *v.* Sturtevant 9 N. Y. 263; State *v.* Patterson, 34 N. J. L. 163; State *v.* Jersey City, 29 N. J. L. 170; State *v.* Albright, 20 N. J. L. 644; Gartside *v.* East St. Louis, 43 Ill. 47.

(2) *Post*, §§ 26, 88–125.

(3) Wetumpka *v.* Wharf Company, 63 Ala. 611; Cook *v.* Johnston, 58 Mich. 437; Horn *v.* People, 26 Mich. 222.

(4) Burckholter *v.* McConnelsville, 20 O. S. 309; Trigally *v.* Memphis, 6 Coldw. 382.

dinances regulating duties that individuals owe to the public may be used as evidence in cases where negligence is charged in the omission to do that which is enjoined by the ordinance; but even in such cases the weight of authority seems to be that the remedy of the individual is in nowise affected by the existence of the ordinance. It has been held that where an act otherwise lawful, such as the storage of oil in considerable quantity within the corporate limits, is prohibited by ordinance, any one specially damaged by an unlawful storage may base his right to recover damages, upon the prohibition of the ordinance.[1]

No kind of civil liability, except to the corporation, can be created by ordinance.[2] Upon an ordinance prescribing a penalty for injuries to shade trees by animals, the owner of the tree injured can not base an action against the owner of the animal that does the injury. His only recourse is to the usual legal remedies.[3] Where an ordinance prohibits the erection of bay-windows so as to obstruct the street, the householder whose view is obstructed by such an unlawful obstruction has no additional remedy by reason of the ordinance.[4] So, the prohibition of a certain trade except under license, does not give a licensee any right of action against the corporation or against a violator of the ordinance for damages resulting from unlicensed competition.[5]

Neither may an ordinance release from civil liability.[6] No one can justify the damaging another's property on the ground that the penalty prescribed by an ordinance for the commission of his injurious act bars all other liabilities.[7]

(1) Wright v. Railroad Co., 7 Ill. App. 439.
(2) Railroad Company v. Ervin, 89 Pa. St. 71; Horn v. People, 26 Mich. 221; Heeney v. Sprague, 11 R. I. 456; Chambers v. Trust Co., 1 Disney (Ohio), 336; Van Dyke v. Cincinnati, 1 Disney, 532; Jenks v. Williams, 115 Mass. 217.
(3) Goshen v. Crary, 58 Ind. 268.
(4) Jenks v. Williams, 115 Mass. 217.
(5) Peck v. Austin, 22 Tex. 261.
(6) Mairs v. Real Estate Association, 89 N. Y. 498; Mayor New York v. Heft, 13 Daly, 301.
(7) Ames v. Carlton, 41 Ill. 261; Dimes v. Petley, L. R. 15 Q. B. 276;

A nuisance can not be so legalized as to supplant ordinary remedies.[1]

The regulation of private property and personal rights and liabilities, and the furtherance of individual interests, must not be made the prime object of an ordinance. Except as incidental to the welfare and good government of the community, they are not included in *corporate affairs*.

Arnold *v.* Holbrook, L. R. 8 Q. B. 96; Hartford *v.* Talcott, 48 Conn. 525.

(1) Chambers *v.* Trust Co., 1 Disney, 336; Van Dyke *v.* Cincinnati, 1 Disney, 532.

CHAPTER II.

CORPORATE POWERS.

§ 8. Scope of corporate powers.
§ 8a. Corporate powers discretionary.
§ 9. They are continuing.
§ 10. They may not be delegated.
§ 11. What may not be delegated.
§ 12. What may be delegated.
§ 13. Discretion in granting licenses.
§ 14. Source of corporate powers.
§ 15. The rule as to source.
§ 16. Limitations on inherent powers.

§ 8. **Scope of corporate powers.**—Under our system of government, the sole legislative power is vested in the state, and municipal corporations must be considered as mere governmental agencies.[1] The organized corporation has some attributes and some powers so distinctly local and disconnected from the interests of the state at large that it often acts in a private capacity. In regard to some matters appertaining to property interests it is simply an agent of the citizens; it may even be a trustee of funds for public charities, and may control a class of affairs in which none but the citizens could be interested; but, so far as the powers that are conferred upon it by the legislature are concerned, the municipality deals, and is treated, as a governmental agency.[2] Its rights and powers which are derived from the state are subject to repeal, diminution, or enlargement, at the will of the legislature, always preserving inviolate such property rights as may have become vested. Its powers are not vested contractual rights, they are simply franchises or privileges.[3] As is said in East

(1) Detroit v. Blakeby, 21 Mich. 84; Low v. Marysville, 5 Cal. 213.
(2) Railroad Co. v. New Orleans, 26 La. An. 478; Touchard v. Touchard, 5 Cal. 306.
(1) Dill. Mun. Corp., §§ 54 and 66 et seq.; Linton v. Carter Company,

Hartford v. Hartford Co., "Towns are liable to have their public powers, rights, and duties modified or abolished at any moment by the legislature. They are allowed to hold privileges or property only for public purposes. Hence, generally, the doings between them and the legislature are in the nature of legislation rather than compact, . . . and to be considered as not violated by subsequent legislative changes."

Corporations are, in short, miniature states, limited in power by their charters. As governmental agencies they must be allowed to exercise all the governmental powers that are pertinent to the purposes of their organization. Their powers are legislative, ministerial, and judicial. Judicial powers have mainly to do with rights of property, and their consideration enters principally into works on taxation and eminent domain. Their exercise is necessary in making provision for public improvements.[1] First, and most important, is the legislative, or the power of making local laws. This branch of municipal power, and the ministerial power necessary to the proper enforcement of the laws when made, constitute the subject-matter before us.

§ 8a. **Corporate power discretionary.**—A question is often raised whether the exercise of the power delegated to municipal corporations is mandatory or only discretionary. It has been held that the corporation becomes charged with some imperative duty to protect those public interests which could be protected by a lawful exercise of its power; for instance, that the corporation would render itself liable in damages to an individual who suffers special injury from a public nuisance, unless it attempts to exercise its power

---

23 Fed. Rep. 535; People v. Morris, 13 Wend. 325; C. B. & Q. Railroad Co. v. Quincy, 12 Ill. App. 184; Mt. Carmel v. Wabash, 50 Ill. 69; Arnoult v. New Orleans, 11 La. An. 54; San Francisco v. Canavan, 42 Cal. 541; Commissioners v. Detroit, 28 Mich. 228; East Hartford v. Hartford Co., 10 How. 511.

(1) In re Wilson, 32 Minn. 144; Dawes v. Hightstown, 45 N. J. L. 501; Kavanagh v. Brooklyn, 38 Barb. 232.

of preventing nuisances.¹ But the true doctrine is, that the exercise of corporate powers rests wholly within the corporate discretion, even though great damage to private interests might result from a refusal.² Legislative powers are given to municipal corporations to be used whenever the council may deem their exercise beneficial to the public good, and the discretion of the council is not to be controlled by others.³

§ 9. **Powers are continuing.**—The powers granted to municipal corporations are continuing; that is, they are not exhausted by one exercise. State legislatures are entirely powerless to restrict the action of subsequent legislatures in regard to any particular subject of legislation; and, analogously, the judgment of one council can not bind its successors. The subjects of municipal control can not always be treated in the same manner at different times and under varying circumstances, and local legislation would prove to be wholly ineffectual if the first exercise of power were held exhaustive. Where property rights are created by ordinance, the further exercise of the same power will be restricted so as to save them; but, with this exception, the council may exercise its powers as often as is deemed necessary.⁴

§ 10. **Power not to be delegated.**—Whenever an agent is clothed with powers the exercise of which involves his personal discretion, they can not be delegated to others without express power so to do. The rule is equally ap-

(1) Commissioners *v.* Duckett, 20 Md. 477; Baltimore *v.* Pennington, 15 Md. 12; Baltimore *v.* Brannan, 14 Md. 227; Baltimore *v.* Marriott, 9 Md. 160.
(2) Cain *v.* Syracuse, 95 N. Y. 88; Prescott *v.* Battersby, 119 Mass. 285.
(3) *Post*, §§ 188, 253.
(4) McCormack *v.* Patchin, 53 Mo. 33; Hoffman *v.* St. Louis, 15 Mo. 651; Karst *v.* Railway Co., 22 Minn. 118; Goszler *v.* Georgetown, 6 Wheat. 593; In re Furman Street, 17 Wend. 649; Delphi *v.* Evans, 36 Ind. 90; Markham *v.* Atlanta, 23 Ga. 402; Macy *v.* Indianapolis, 17 Ind. 267; Gas Company *v.* Des Moines, 44 Ia. 505; People *v.* Cooper, 10 Ill. App. 384.

plicable to public governmental agencies, like municipalities. It is essential that ordinances shall be passed by the properly authorized body, and the council can not delegate its discretion. This statement needs a slight modification, for many classes of powers would be wholly ineffectual were not the officers lawfully intrusted with their execution to have certain powers of choice and discretion. For example, in the exercise of the power to destroy property to prevent the spread of fire, the ministerial agents who are present at the time the emergency arises must of necessity be the sole judges of the advisability of tearing down adjoining buildings. It would be impossible for the council to foresee every emergency, and to prescribe in detail appropriate rules of action. Neither could the council arrange, by ordinance, all the details and steps to be taken in the construction of public improvements. The officers executing or supervising the work must have a degree of discretion. The general proposition is conceded that the exercise of powers of local legislation demands discretion *in the council*, and that such discretion can not be delegated.[1]

The difficulty arises in determining where to draw the line between those matters which must be delegated to others in order to secure efficiency in execution, and those which should be decided by the council alone.

§ 11. **What may not be delegated.**—Among other powers which courts have held can not properly be delegated are the following: to improve the streets;[2] to grade

(1) Tappan *v.* Young, 9 Daly, 357; Thompson *v.* Schermerhorn, 9 Barb. 152; s. c., 6 N. Y. 92; Birdsall *v.* Clark, 73 N. Y. 73; Davis *v* Read, 65 N. Y. 566; Brooklyn *v.* Breslin, 57 N. Y. 591; Railroad *v.* Petersborough, 49 N. H. 281; Baltimore *v.* Scharf, 54 Md. 499; Charles *v.* Hoboken, 28 N. J. L. 202; Macon *v.* Patty, 57 Miss. 378; Whyte *v.* Nashville, 2 Swan, 364; Hydes *v.* Joyes, 4 Bush. 464; State *v.* Hauser, 63 Ind. 155; Smith *v.* Morse, 2 Cal. 524; Oakland *v.* Carpenter, 13 Cal. 540; Horn *v.* People, 26 Mich. 221; Lauenstein *v.* Fond du Lac, 28 Wis. 336; St. Louis *v.* Clemens, 52 Mo. 133; Thomson *v.* Boonville, 61 Mo. 282; In re Wilson, 32 Minn. 144; State *v.* Kantler, 33 Minn. 69; Richardson *v.* Heydenfeldt, 46 Cal. 68; Kinmundy *v.* Mahan, 72 Ill. 462; Jackson County *v.* Brush, 77 Ill. 59; Potter Corp. 374.

(2) Thompson *v.* Schermerhorn, 6 N. Y. 92.

and pave the sidewalks;[1] to ascertain and determine street boundaries;[2] to determine the size of sewers;[3] to establish markets and to choose market sites;[4] to grant to others the privilege of building railways;[5] to permit railroads to use the tracks of other roads previously constructed, or to fix the routes and termini of railroads;[6] to license occupations, or to approve of their existence;[7] to regulate the manner of laying gas mains and pipes;[8] to set a time for a judicial hearing on a claim for damages from a projected improvement;[9] to fix the charge to be made for gas;[10] to regulate the amount of tolls of any kind to be charged for the use of public improvements, such as bridges, turnpikes, and wharves.[11]

§ 12 **What may be delegated.**—It has been held lawful to delegate to the officers of the fire department power to judge of the necessity of pulling down buildings in time of emergency;[12] to delegate to a superintendent of wharves

(1) Hydes v. Joyes, 4 Bush, 464; Hitchcock v. Galveston, 96 U. S. 341 Contra, Brewster v. Davenport, 51 Ia. 427.
(2) State v. Trenton, 36 N. J. 79.
(3) St. Louis v. Clemens, 43 Mo. 395; St. Louis v. Buckner, 44 Mo. 19; Sheehan v. Gleeson, 46 Mo. 577; St. Louis v. Clemens, 52 Mo. 134. Contra, St. Louis v. Oeters, 36 Mo. 456.
(4) Davenport v. Kelly, 7 Ia. 103; State v. Paterson, 34 N. J. 163.
(5) State v. Bell, 34 O. S. 194.
(6) Hickey v. Chicago, etc., Railroad Co., 6 Ill. App. 173.
(7) In re Quong Woo, 13 Fed. Rep. 229; s. c., 7 Sawyer, 526 (consent of vicinage to laundry); St. Louis v. Wehrung, 50 Ill. 29; Winants v. Bayonne, 44 N. J. L. 114 (to license on recommendation of a certain number of neighbors); Darling v. St. Paul, 19 Minn. 389; State v. Fiske, 9 R. I. 94; Day v. Green, 4 Cush. 433; State Center v. Barenstein, 66 Ia. 249. Contra under charter, Whitten v. Covington, 43 Ga. 421.
(8) Anderson v. Gas Company, 12 Daly, 462.
(9) State v. Jersey City, 25 N. J. 309.
(10) Gas Light Co. v. Dunn, 62 Cal. 580.
(11) Lord v. Oconto, 47 Wis. 386; Matthews v. Alexandria, 68 Mo. 115.
(12) White v Charleston, 2 Hill, 571. But see Coffin v. Nantucket, 5 Cush. 269; Ruggles v. Nantucket, 11 Cush. 433.

full power to order and regulate the mooring of vessels;[1] to vest in the overseers of markets full powers of detailed supervision;[2] to appoint committees or agencies to execute and enter into contracts;[3] and in general, to appoint agents to oversee and regulate the details of construction in making public improvements.[4]

§ 13. **Discretion in granting licenses.**—The extent to which discretion may be given to the ministerial officers in the granting of licenses is in dispute. Express power in the charter will warrant such delegation.[5] The authorities differ widely,[6] but the proper conclusion seems to be that as little latitude should be given to the ministerial officer as possible. In exercising a power to license certain occupations, the council should by its ordinance prescribe the exact occupation to be licensed, the amount of the fee to be charged, either uniformly or by reasonable classification, the conditions upon which the license may be issued, and the duration of its validity. And, unless the council desires that all persons may become licensees who choose to comply with the prescribed conditions, it should define the qualifications to be demanded of the applicant. It should leave no duty to the person who issues the license, except to sign the certificate and to see that the applicant has complied with all the conditions and possesses all the qualifications enumerated by the ordinance.[7] The ordinance might, for example, provide that none but persons of reputable character should receive licenses. As to the possession of such a character by the applicant the mayor or

(1) Gregory v. Bridgeport, 41 Conn. 76.
(2) Charleston v. Goldsmith, 2 Spears, 428.
(3) Railway Co. v. Baltimore, 21 Md. 93; Burlington v. Dennison, 42 N. J. L. 165; Alton v. Mulledy, 20 Ill. 76; State v. Trenton, 42 N. J. L. 72. *But see* In re Trustees, 57 How. Pr. 500.
(4) Baltimore v. Howard, 6 H. & J. 383 (street repairs); State v. New Brunswick, 30 N. J. L. 395 (grading).
(5) Brooklyn v. Breslin, 57 N. Y. 591.
(6) Shaw v. Pope, 2 B. & Ad. 465; Swarth v. People, 109 Ill. 621; Decorah v. Dunstan, 38 Ia. 96.
(7) In re Bickerstaff (Cal.), 11 Pac. Rep. 393 (1886).

other officer issuing the license would be the sole judge. It would be a simple question of fact. But, without such a restriction in the ordinance itself, it is very doubtful, indeed, whether the officer could ever refuse a license to a person whom he believed to be wholly unfit to enjoy its privileges.

§ 14. **Source of corporate powers.**—When municipalities first began to come into prominence after the thirteenth century, their privileges were gained from the sovereign by purchase or force, and became at once inalienably vested. At first, specific charters were granted; but as the rule of the sovereign became less arbitrary and powerful, municipalities had no difficulty in usurping many privileges which were never evidenced by formal grant; and, eventually, custom or long usage became their only foundation. Up to a comparatively late day in England, it was frequently necessary to introduce proof of the custom to exercise a certain power in order to recover a penalty ordained in its pursuance. In America, however, the municipality is considered merely as an agency of the sovereign power; and not only are its powers and privileges subject to modification, but its very existence may be terminated at the will of the legislature. No rights are inalienable, and no powers are sustained by force of custom. A few early decisions, rendered before the policy of our municipal system was thoroughly fixed, hold that long usage may sometimes be sufficient proof of a former grant. The municipal corporations of this country have been created within the memory of man, and solely for the regulation of local affairs. In determining their powers we must have recourse to the grant to which they owe their corporate existence, be it charter or general law, and to such subsequent legislation as in any way enlarges or diminishes the original grant. In some cases, corporations have been created without any definite grant of power. Courts consider that there would be no purpose in organizing a community into a corporation, unless it were to possess some powers; hence, recourse is then had to reasonable implication, and the legislative intent is construed to be that the corporation should possess such powers as are essential to its existence and necessary for its good government.

§ 15. The rule.—The powers that may be exercised by municipal corporations are:
1. Those expressly granted.
2. Those necessary to the execution of the express grant.
3. Those absolutely essential to the fulfillment of the purposes of their existence.[1]

A numerous class of cases hold that an express grant of power implies such further powers as are necessary to the perfect exercise of those granted.[2] Some of them hold

(1) Dill. Mun. Corp., § 89; Treadway v. Schnauber, 1 Dak. 227; Couteulx v. Buffalo, 33 N. Y. 333; State v. Mobile, 5 Port. 279; Bank v. Navigation Co., 3 La. An. 294; Christie v. Malden, 23 W. Va. 667; Carter v. Dubuque, 35 Ia. 416; Merriam v. Moody, 25 Ia. 163; Caldwell v. Alton, 33 Ill. 416; Cook County v. McCrea, 73 Ill. 236; Ex parte Mayor of Florence, 78 Ala. 419; Ouachita v. Monroe, 37 La. Ann. 641; Charleston v. Re-d 27 W. Va. 681; State v. Norristown, 33 N. J. L. 57; Herford v. Omaha, 4 Neb. 350; Smith v. Newburn, 70 N. C. 14.

(2) Ex parte Burnett, 30 Ala. 461; Ottawa v. Carey, 108 U. S. 121; Dunbar v. San Francisco, 1 Cal. 356; Smith v. Morse, 2 Cal. 524; Oakland v. Carpentier, 13 Cal. 540; Johnston v. Louisville, 11 Bush, 527; Henderson v. Covington, 14 Bush, 312; Davis v. New York, 1 Duer, 451; State v. New York, 3 Duer, 119; Bank v. Chillicothe, 7 Ohio (pt. 2), 35; Collins v. Hatch, 18 Ohio, 523; Andrews v. Insurance Co., 37 Me. 256; Waterbury v. Laredo, 60 Tex. 519; Kirkham v. Russel, 76 Va. 956; Danville v. Shelton, 76 Va. 325; Robertson v. Groves, 4 Oreg. 210; Cornwallis v. Carlisle, 10 Oreg. 139; Tucker v. Virginia City, 4 Nev. 20; State v. Swift, 11 Nev. 129; Douglass v. Virginia City, 5 Nev. 147; Leavenworth v. Norton, 1 Kan. 432; Leavenworth v. Rankin, 2 Kan. 357; Leonard v. Canton, 35 Miss. 189; Sykes v. Columbus, 55 Miss. 115; Keokuk v. Scroggs, 39 Ia. 447; State v. Atlanta, 72 Ga. 428; Smith v. Madison, 7 Ind. 86; Webster v. Harwinton, 32 Conn. 131; Douglass v. Placerville, 18 Cal. 643; Johnson v. Philadelphia, 60 Pa. St. 445; Bessoinies v. Indianapolis, 71 Ind. 189; Peterson v. New York, 17 N. Y. 449; Meech v. Buffalo, 29 N. Y. 198; Ketchum v. Buffalo, 14 N. Y. 356; Abendroth v. Greenwich, 29 Conn. 263; New Haven v. Sargent, 38 Conn. 50; New London v. Brainard, 22 Conn. 552; Minturn v. Larue, 23 How. 435; Scott v. Shreveport, 20 Fed. Rep. 714; Ho Ah Kow v. Neenan, 5 Sawyer, 552; Petersburg v. Metzger, 21 Ill. 205; Montgomery v. Plank Road Co., 31 Ala. 76; Harris v. Livingston, 28

that the powers expressly granted and those thus incidental are the only powers that may be exercised by the corporation; others merely recognize the existence of these two classes, without expressing an opinion as to whether the corporation may not have still other powers.

A few cases are so strict as to deny to corporations the right to exercise any powers whatever except those expressly granted.[1] The council, or the citizens, surely have no ability to increase their powers by direct enactment, specifically granting additional authority to the council,[2] but the council ought not to be bound down to the strict letter of the law.

Under the system adopted by most of the states of classifying municipal corporations, and granting them powers by classes, it is fairly accurate to say, with the majority of cited cases, that corporate powers are restricted to those expressly granted and those incidental to express powers; but, even then, some powers might be denied whose exercise is indispensable to the purposes of corporate organization. Powers of this class, the third enumerated in the preceding general proposition, ought to be recognized as being inherent in the corporation, needing no express grant as a basis.[3] Such are power to sue, purchase and sell;[4] to grade and pave the streets;[5] to provide a suitable city

Ala. 577; Poillon v. Brooklyn, 101 N. Y. 132; Dean v. Madison, 7 Wis. 688; Mills v. Gleason, 11 Wis. 470; Ex parte Strahl, 16 Ia. 369; Dutton v. Aurora, 114 Ill. 138; Blake v. Walker, 23 S. Car. 517; Mather v. Ottawa, 114 Ill. 659.

(1) Jacksonville v. McConnell, 12 Ill. 138; Waters v. Leech, 3 Ark. 115; McCullen v. Charleston, 1 Bay, 46; Zylstra v. Charleston, 1 Bay, 382; Leach v. Cargill, 60 Mo. 316; New Orleans v. Insurance Co., 25 La. Ann. 390; Zottman v. San Francisco, 20 Cal. 96; Herzo v. San Francisco, 33 Cal. 134; Branham v. San José, 24 Cal. 601.

(2) Torrent v. Muskegon, 47 Mich. 115; Mt. Pleasant v. Beckwith, 100 U. S. 514; Desty on Taxation, § 781.

(3) Bishop Stat. Cr., §§ 18, 19; Commonwealth v. Stodder, 2 Cush. 562; Harris v. Livingston, 28 Ala. 577; and cases cited under note 1, § 15, *supra*.

(4) Jonesborough v. McRee, 2 Yerg. 167.

(5) Keusy v. Louisville, 4 Dana, 154; White v. McKeesport, 101 Pa. St. 394.

hall;[1] to borrow money;[2] to protect the health, peace, and comfort of its citizens;[3] to purchase fire engines;[4] to regulate the use of the streets by droves of cattle;[5] to provide a water supply;[6] and to give bonds for a just debt.[7]

§ 16. **Limitation of inherent powers.**—There are many cases which hold in opposition to the rule enunciated in the preceding section that corporations have no inherent powers.[8] However germane to the general purposes of municipal organization certain inherent powers may be, the right to exercise them should not be upheld for that reason alone. Their exercise must be *absolutely* necessary to the accomplishment of those purposes. The inherent powers claimed should be such as are essential to the welfare of the community. Their exercise should never involve the prescription of a penalty for their non-observance; for, however liberal courts may be to municipal corporations, the imposition of penalties except by the general government in a direct manner is regarded with disfavor.[9] Powers encroaching upon the rights of the public or of individuals must be plainly and literally conferred by the statute or charter.[10] A corporation can not be held to possess any inherent or necessary power, if in the charters of other corporations of the same class that power is made the subject of special mention and grant.[11] A positive power

(1) Torrent v. Muskegon, 47 Mich. 115.
(2) Mills v. Gleason, 11 Wis. 470; Bank v. Chillicothe, 7 Ohio (pt. 2), 35.
(3) Ferguson v. Selma, 43 Ala. 400.
(4) Mayor v. Rumsey, 63 Ala. 352.
(5) Board v. Heister, 37 N. Y. 661.
(6) Rome v. Cabot, 28 Ga. 50; Wells v. Atlanta, 43 Ga. 67; Livingston v. Pippin, 31 Ala. 542.
(7) Reinboth v. Pittsburgh, 41 Pa. St. 278; Williamsport v. Commonwealth, 84 Pa. St. 487.
(8) Mobile v. Moog, 53 Ala. 561; State v. Green Co., 54 Mo. 540; Corry v. Gaynor, 22 O. S. 593; Anderson v. Commissioners, 12 O. S. 635; Roberts v. Easton, 9 O. S. 98; People v. Mitchell, 35 N. Y. 551.
(9) Farnsworth v. Pawtucket, 13 R. I. 82.
(10) Breninger v. Belvidere, 44 N. J. L. 350.
(11) Commonwealth v. Voorhis, 12 B. Mon. 361; Collins v. Hatch, 18 Ohio, 525.

is not conferred by an express charter prohibition of some act or trade.[1] Neither can a power be derived from mere inference.[2] When a certain power, as of police, was granted for a specified length of time, further power does not arise by implication at the expiration of that time.[3]

(1) Strauss *v.* Pontiac, 40 Ill. 301; Ashton *v.* Ellsworth, 48 Ill. 299; *ante,* § 4.
(2) Logan *v.* Pyne, 43 Ia. 524.
(3) Fertilizing Co. *v.* Hyde Park, 70 Ill. 634.

CHAPTER III.

CONSTRUCTION OF CORPORATE POWERS.

§ 17. Powers construed strictly against the corporation.
§ 18. Limited to the terms of an enumeration.
§ 19. Illustrations.
§ 20. Rule of *ejusdem generis* in enumerations.
§ 21. Concurrent powers.
§ 22. The greater power includes the less.
§ 23. Retroactive ordinances.
§ 24. Conditions precedent.

§ 17. **Powers construed strictly against the corporation.**—Corporate powers, being delegated, must be strictly construed and plainly conferred. Whenever a genuine doubt arises as to the right to exercise a certain power, it must be resolved against the corporation and in favor of the general public.[1] Judge Dillon says: "If, upon the whole, there be fair, reasonable, and substantial doubt whether the legislature intended to confer the authority in question, particularly if it relates to a matter extra-municipal or unusual in its nature, and the exercise of which will be attended with taxes, tolls, assessments, or burdens upon the inhabitants, or oppress them, or abridge natural or common rights or divest them of their property, the

(1) Dill. Mun. Corp. §§ 89, 91, and note; Commissioners v. Mighels, 7 O. S. 109; Bank v. Chillicothe, 7 Ohio (pt. 2), 35; Collins v. Hatch, 18 Ohio, 523; Leonard v. Canton, 35 Miss. 189; Robertson v. Groves, 4 Oreg. 210; Cornwallis v. Carlisle, 10 Oreg. 139; Kirkham v. Russel, 76 Va. 956; Danville v. Shelton, 76 Va. 325; Wheatly v. Covington, 11 Bush, 18; Eufaula v. McNab, 67 Ala. 588; Trowbridge v. Newark, 46 N. J. L. 140; Willard v. Killingworth, 8 Conn. 247; Higley v. Bunce, 10 Conn. 435; Lafayette v. Cox, 5 Ind. 38; Kniper v. Louisville, 7 Bush, 599; Burlington v. Kellar, 18 Ia. 59; Logan v. Pyne, 43 Ia. 524; s. c., 22 Am. Rep. 261; Clark v. Davenport, 14 Ia. 495; Nichol v. Nashville, 9 Humph. 252; Sedgw. Const. Law, p. 466, notes; 7 Am. & Eng. Corp. Cas. 670.

doubt should be resolved in favor of the citizen and against the municipality."

The rule is most strictly observed in construing powers that may lead to an infringement of personal or property rights. Where no such infringement is threatened, the tendency of courts is to construe ambiguities in the power so as to effectuate the grant.[1] The application of the rule should not be made to defeat the right to exercise powers which are essential to the good government of the community,[2] and especially not when the power sought to be exercised is such as to concern no one but citizens of the municipality.[3]

Evidence of the construction put upon a doubtful power by the corporation is inadmissible. The intention of the legislature is the sole guide.[4] That intention is to be discovered by a fair construction of the language used, and in no other way. Parol or extrinsic evidence of that intent is inadmissible.

§ 18. **Limited to the terms of an enumeration.**—The charter or statute granting powers to municipal corporations usually enumerates those which may be exercised. It is a general rule that all powers not mentioned in the enumeration, and not incidental to those enumerated, are not intended to be included in the grant. All other powers are impliedly excluded.[5] *Expressio unius est exclusio alterius.* But, "the enumeration of special cases does not, unless the intent be apparent, exclude the implied power

(1) State v. Smith, 31 Ia. 493; Williams v. Davidson, 43 Tex. 1; Kyle v. Malin, 8 Ind. 34.
(2) Smith v. Madison, 7 Ind. 86.
(3) Port Huron v. McCall, 46 Mich. 565.
(4) Otherwise in England, where powers may be acquired by long usage. Blankley v. Winstanley, 3 T. R. 279; King v. Bellringer, 4 T. R. 810.
(5) Cairo v. Bross, 101 Ill. 475; Plaquemines v. Roth, 29 La. Ann. 261; New Orleans v. Phillipi, 9 La. Ann. 44; Telephone Co. v. Oshkosh, 62 Wis. 32.

any further than necessarily results from the nature of the special provisions."[1]

§ 19. **Illustrations.**—Where a power was granted to prohibit the traffic in liquors, and to license and regulate, or prohibit inns and taverns, an ordinance *regulating* the sale of liquors *outside of* inns and taverns was held void.[2]

Power to license specified trades can not be extended to apply to other trades than those mentioned in the enumeration.[3] So, where the corporation is permitted to enforce certain powers by penal prosecutions, the enforcement of other powers in that manner is impliedly prohibited.[4]

When a corporation, originally chartered to exercise general powers, accepts the provisions of a special charter that contains an enumeration of its powers, it may only exercise those that are mentioned in the enumeration.[5] It is held in Massachusetts that an enumeration will not be construed to exclude the exercise of such powers as are necessary to the purposes of corporate existence, for example, to establish markets.[6] Powers are considered to be intentionally omitted when it is the legislative custom to grant them to municipalities.[7]

§ 20. **Ejusdem generis.**—It often occurs in a grant of power that the enumeration of specific rights is followed by some expression of general import. The general expression extends the enumeration only to include things which are of the same kind as those specifically named.[8]

(1) Dill. Mun. Corp., ¿ 316, note; Indianapolis *v.* Gas Company, 66 Ind. 396; Clark *v.* South Bend, 85 Ind. 276; s. c., 44 Am. Rep. 13.
(2) State *v.* Fay, 44 N. J. 474.
(3) Winants *v.* Bayonne, 44 N. J. L. 114; Plaquemines *v.* Roth, 29 La. Ann. 260; New Hampton *v.* Conroy, 56 Ia. 498; Oskaloosa *v.* Tullis, 25 Ia. 440. An apparent exception to the rule in Allerton *v.* Chicago, 6 Fed. Rep. 555.
(4) Grand Rapids *v.* Hughes, 15 Mich. 54.
(5) Keokuk *v.* Scroggs, 39 Ia. 447.
(6) Spaulding *v.* Lowell, 23 Pick. 71.
(7) Collins *v.* Hatch, 18 Ohio, 524.
(8) St. Louis *v.* Laughlin, 49 Mo. 559; Tuck *v.* Waldron, 31 Ark.

Thus a power to license hacks, drays, and other vehicles, would authorize the imposition of a license on all kinds of hacks and drays, but not on vehicles used for other purposes. This implication does not exist if a view of the entire act shows that the legislature intended to extend the enumeration by the general term.[1]

§ 21. **Concurrent powers.**—It also frequently happens that two powers are in a degree concurrent, so that a certain ordinance could be properly enacted in pursuance of either; for example, the power to regulate markets, and the power to regulate streets. Perhaps special formalities in the mode of procedure are attached to the exercise of one power, and not to the other. An ordinance that can be sustained under either is valid if properly passed under either, and need not conform to the formalities of a concurrent power, under which it might equally well have been passed.[2]

But care must be taken not to confound general with special powers in the application of this principle. For instance, an ordinance that might be valid under either of two special powers such as those just mentioned, will be held to have been passed under that power to the formalities of which it has accorded; but if a special power is given to enact ordinances of a certain class, an ordinance of that class must conform to the requirements of that power, and can not be held valid as supported by some other general power, although, did the charter not contain the special power, the ordinance would be valid under the general power.[3] The legislature, by prescribing additional formalities to be observed in the exercise of a certain power, expresses an intention that that power shall not be exercised in any other manner.

462; Thomas *v.* Hot Sgrings, 34 Ark. 553; State *v.* Ferguson, 33 N. H. 426; St. Paul *v.* Traeger, 25 Minn. 248; Snyder *v.* North Lawrence, 8 Kan. 82.

(1) State *v.* Ferguson, 33 N. H. 426.
(2) Commonwealth *v.* Brooks, 109 Mass. 355.
(3) Sumter *v.* Deschamps, 4 S. C. 207 (but see Gray *v.* Brooklyn, 7 Hun, 632); Keokuk *v.* Scroggs, 39 Ia. 447.

§ 22. **The greater includes the less.**—An expression of power must be taken to include the right to exercise any lower degree of that power. The greater includes the less.[1] Thus, a charter authorization to regulate bankers and money changers does not require that the ordinance must be directed against both bankers and money changers.[2] An ordinance that regulates bankers alone would be perfectly valid. Power to prohibit includes power to partially prohibit, to license, regulate, or restrain.[3] Conjunctive words may always be read disjunctively in order to authorize the exercise of any part of the power granted.[4]

§ 23. **Retroactive ordinances.**—Corporations can no more pass *ex post facto* laws than can the legislature. Vested rights can not be interfered with, nor acts made unlawful which were lawful when committed. But unless some vested right is disturbed, or some additional burden imposed, there seems to be no objection to giving an ordinance retroactive effect. Thus, the provisions of an ordinance regulating the mode of deciding contested elections to local offices may be made applicable to contests arising in an election held prior to the passage of the ordinance.[5] It has been held that municipal ordinances may not operate retroactively unless explanatory of a statute, declaratory of the common law, or regulatory of ministerial acts.[6]

§ 24. **Conditions precedent.**—A numerous class of powers is usually vested in municipal corporations, the right to exercise which depends upon the prior fulfillment of some condition. The exercise of the power to undertake many kinds of public improvements affects

---

(1) Tipton v. Norman, 72 Mo. 380; Monroe v. Hoffman, 29 La. Ann. 651.
(2) Hinckley v. Belleville, 43 Ill. 183.
(3) Keokuk v. Dressell, 47 Ia. 597; Burlington v. Lawrence, 42 Ia. 681; Gunnarssohn v. Sterling, 92 Ill. 569; Franklin v. Westfall, 27 Kan. 614.
(4) *Post*, § 195.
(5) State v. Johnson, 17 Ark. 407.
(6) Howard v. Savannah, T. U. P. Charlt. 173.

property rights, and the benefit of the improvement may accrue mainly to those citizens whose property is adjacent to the proposed improvement, and only remotely to the community at large. In such cases it is only just that those who are specially benefited should bear the burden, or the larger part of the burden. But it is also just that those who must bear the burden should have some voice in determining the need for the improvement; hence the customary charter or statute provision that a corporation can only undertake certain improvements upon the petition or approval of the property owners most affected thereby. The right to make improvements which will affect a limited number of persons ought not to be exercised without giving them notice and an opportunity to be heard in opposition. When a certain step to be taken by the adjoining owners is prescribed as a condition precedent to an exercise of the corporate power, the condition must be strictly and faithfully observed, else those who are holden for the cost will not be bound by the corporate action.[1]

If the condition precedent is ignored the ordinance is absolutely void, and the local assessments levied in pursuance of its authority can not be collected.[2] When the condition precedent is the presentation of a petition signed by a certain proportion of the adjoining owners, it is the duty of the council to see that the petition presented has the requisite number of signers, and their determination of that fact can not be attacked collaterally.[3] If the petition should be signed by a majority of the owners *to be benefited*, the condition is sufficiently complied with by a petition signed by *all* the *adjoining* owners, asking that the

---

(1) Mott v. New York, 2 Hilton, 358; Harrington v. Corning, 51 Barb. 396; Canfield v. Smith, 34 Wis. 381; Railroad Co. v. Evansville, 15 Ind. 395; Hickey v. Railroad Co., 6 Ill. App. 173; Tallant v. Burlington, 39 Ia. 543; Hitchcock v. Galveston, 3 Woods, 287. But notice of intention to make a local improvement is unnecessary unless prescribed by the organic law of the corporation. Matter of Zborowski, 68 N. Y. 98.

(2) Wittler v. Cavender, 3 Mo. App. 580; In re Smith, 52 N. Y. 526; In re Douglass, 46 N. Y. 42; Covington v. Nelson, 35 Ind. 532.

(3) Railroad v. Evansville, 15 Ind. 395.

improvement be made and the expense assessed on *their* land.¹ Any material variation is fatal. Still it has been held, though surely not in accordance with the reason and justice of the rule, where a petition is signed by less than the required two-thirds of the lot-owners, that the ordinance enacted will be valid if passed by more than two-thirds of the council.² Property owners can withdraw their signatures at any time before final action on the petition.³

The rule of strict observance is equally applicable where the condition precedent consists in the recommendation of some board, or the declaration by the council of the necessity for the improvement.⁴ But the written recommendation of the board of improvements is not rendered worthless by immaterial irregularities, such as the omission of the clerk of the board to sign the same, even though the statute says that the recommendation shall be signed by him.⁵

The necessity of close adherence to the formalities prescribed by statute is more fully treated in Chapter V, *post*.

(1) Baldwin *v.* Oswego, 2 Keyes, 132.
(2) Indianapolis *v.* Mansur, 15 Ind. 112.
(3) Dutton *v.* Hanover, 42 O. S. 215; Hays *v.* Jones, 27 O. S. 218.
(4) Reynolds *v.* Schweinefus, 18 O. S. 85; Bolton *v.* Cleveland, 35 O. S. 319; Fisher *v.* Graham, 1 Sup. Ct. Rep. (Ohio) 113.
(5) Fisher *v.* Graham, *supra*, note 4.

CHAPTER IV.

CONSTRUCTION OF COMMON PHRASES.

§ 25. Common phrases in grants of powers.
§ 26. Corporate purposes.
§ 27. General welfare.
§ 28. Peace and good government.
§ 29. Other general expressions.
§ 30. To regulate.
§ 31. To suppress and restrain.
§ 32. Miscellaneous expressions.
§ 33. General rules of construction.

§ 25. **Common phrases.**—It is the policy of modern legislation to enumerate in considerable detail the power which it shall be lawful for municipal corporations to exercise, at least to group them into classes according to their subject-matter. Each group or class contains a definition of the subject to which it applies and specifies the degree of power that may be exercised. The definition of the subject-matter must be construed according to the general rules of statutory construction and with regard to the special circumstances of each case. The grant of power is generally expressed by certain words and phrases which are more or less common to all charters and empowering statutes. Such expressions as "*to regulate,*" "*to control,*" "*to govern,*" "*to suppress,*" "*to restrain,*" and "*to establish,*" are most frequent, and their exact scope has often been the subject of judicial determination.

Whenever corporate powers are not granted in such detail, expressions of much broader import are used, and the municipality is given power to enact all ordinances essential to its "*corporate purposes,*" to the preservation of "*peace and good order,*" to "*good government,*" to the "*general welfare of the community,*" and the like. The scope of such general expressions is much more difficult to define, and the rules by which courts are governed in their interpretation are numerous and indefinite. As a general rule all such expressions are construed strictly against the right to exercise a disputed or doubtful power, unless the essential purposes of municipal organization would thereby be defeated.

§ 26. Corporate purposes.—Municipal organization is resorted to for the better administration and execution of the police powers of the state; and, hence, where no more definite grant of power is made than for "*corporate purposes*" generally, the grant must include all things usually classed under *police* powers, together with such as are absolutely essential to the proper organization and conduct of the local government. The expression "corporate purposes" is practically equivalent to the definition of police powers, and includes the regulation of all subjects which affect the peace and good order of the community, and the health, welfare, and comfort of its inhabitants. So long as only objects of a police nature are sought to be attained, the judgment of the corporate authorities is generally a safe guide.[1]

The main corporate purposes are the preservation of good order and health; the protection of life and property against such special dangers as arise from peculiar physical characteristics of the locality, or from the nature of the industries prosecuted in it; the control of all public ways, places, and streets; the improvement of streets, walks, canals, and rivers within the corporate limits; the provision of hospitals, markets, pounds, jails, and suitable buildings for the accommodation of the local government; the construction of public wharves and bridges; the prevention of fire and flood; the abatement of public nuisances; the provision of adequate supplies of water, gas, and sewerage facilities;[2] the erection and regulation of public cem-

(1) Potter Corp. 376.
(2) Cabot v. Rome, 28 Ga. 50; Wells v. Atlanta, 43 Ga. 67; Livingston v. Pippin, 31 Ala. 542; Hale v. Houghton, 8 Mich. 458; Memphis v Water-works Co., 5 Heisk. 495.

eteries;[1] and the regulation of all trades, occupations, and businesses, that might by improper exercise injure the health and morals of the inhabitants.[2]

§ 27. **General welfare.**—Care must be taken not to confound the term "*general welfare*" as used by many courts with other terms of narrower scope. General welfare is merely synonymous with corporate purposes. Such expressions as "peace and good order" and "peace and good government" are much more restricted. Many things are essential to the public welfare which belong neither to the preservation of peace and order nor to the exercise of good government. The general welfare clause does not allow local regulation of acts, such as assaults, riots, libel, slander, and forcible entry, which are within the cognizance of the statutes of the state.[3] Nor does it warrant any kind of local taxation.[4] General welfare extends, among other things, to preventing the obstruction of streets;[5] to regulating the hours of closing places where liquors are sold;[6] and to prohibiting the carrying of concealed weapons.[7]

§ 28. **Peace and good government.**—Under power to pass ordinances "*to preserve the peace and good order or good government*" of the community, any reasonable provision for the health, security, comfort, and protection of the citizens may be adopted.[8] Among other things that have been held lawful under such an expression of power are the prohibition of the use of obscene or profane language in public places;[9] the prohibition of bawdy

---

(1) Charleston *v.* Church, 4 Strobh. L. 306.
(2) Nichol *v.* Nashville, 9 Humph. 252; sale of liquors, Heisembrittle *v.* Charleston, 2 McMullen, 233; Charleston *v.* Ahrens, 4 Strobh. L. 241.
(3) Commonwealth *v.* Turner, 1 Cush. 493.
(4) Dill. Mun. Corp., § 764.
(5) Janesville *v.* Railroad Co., 7 Wis. 484.
(6) State *v.* Freeman, 38 N. H. 426.
(7) St. Louis *v.* Vert., 84 Mo. 204.
(8) Paxson *v.* Sweet, 13 N. J. L. 196. See page 205.
(9) Ex parte Slattery, 3 Ark. 484; Ex parte Delaney, 43 Cal. 478.

houses;[1] the abatement of nuisances;[2] the requiring sales of coal to be made by established weights and measures and the imposition of a fee of five cents per load for the remuneration of the corporate authorities, upon whom rests the duty of enforcing the ordinance;[3] requiring the owners of buildings to which the public has access to properly guard their elevator shafts;[4] prohibiting the keeping in stock of certain kinds of explosive fireworks;[5] the provision of facilities for the education of youth and for the care of the poor within the limits of the corporation;[6] punishing the public commission of such acts as are otherwise covered by the penal laws of the state;[7] punishing willful trespasses upon and injury to property;[8] provision for the arrest and punishment of persons found publicly intoxicated;[9] the establishment of an adequate police force.[10]

§ 29. **Other general expressions.**—The term "public peace," alone is not synonymous with "public policy." The subjects regulated under it must be such as directly effect the peace, and do not include things merely germane to peace.[11] Thus, it does not authorize the prohibition of billiard saloons.[12] It has even been held that the passage of Sunday ordinances as necessary to the peace of the community is unlawful.[13] A simple power of "police" regulation does not authorize the imposition of a license fee on the use of wagons.[14] Power to preserve "the order,

(1) State v. Williams, 11 S. C. 288.
(2) Paxson v. Sweet, 13 N. J. L. 196.
(3) O'Maley v. Freeport, 96 Pa. St. 24.
(4) Mayor v. Williams, 4 E. D. Smith, 516.
(5) Jones v. Insurance Co., 2 Daly, 307.
(6) State v. McDonough, 8 La. Ann. 171.
(7) State v. Bruckhauser, 26 Minn. 301.
(8) Brownville v. Cook, 4 Neb. 101.
(9) Bloomfield v. Trimble, 54 Ia. 399.
(10) State v. Sims, 16 S. C. 486.
(11) Cornwallis v. Carlile. 10 Oreg. 139.
(12) Breninger v. Belvidere, 44 N. J. L. 350.
(13) Cornwallis v. Carlile, *supra*.
(14) Knox City v. Thompson, 19 Mo. App. 523.

health, and quiet," extends to the erection and maintenance of guard-houses,[1] and to the abatement of nuisances and to the imposition of penalties for their maintenance.[2] Under power to pass ordinances "for the security, welfare, and convenience" of the corporation, an ordinance is valid which regulates the storage and traffic in gunpowder within the city limits.[3] The "promotion of trade, industry, and happiness" includes educational purposes.[4] But local taxation for the aid of railroads is not "for the benefit and advantage" of the municipality in the sense given to those words in grants of local power.[5] Under general powers of any kind the streets may be kept free from obstructions.[6] Under a power to enact ordinances "as at common law," a city may provide for the protection of its streets and lake front by a suitable breakwater.[7]

No absolute rules can be laid down by which the construction of these various general expressions of power is to be governed. Rights will, however, rarely be denied under them, which are essential to the attainment of the purposes of local government, and they will be construed to include all powers which are usually exercised by corporations in furtherance of police regulation, unless restricted in their operation by more definite and detailed grants in other parts of the organic law.

§ 30. "**To regulate.**"—"*To regulate*" is the expression most frequently used to define the degree of power that it shall be lawful to exercise over the subject under local supervision. It means to govern, to control, to subject to governing laws, and, in this connection, the determination and enforcement of the condition and restriction under which certain things may be done, or certain public

(1) McLin v. Newburn, 70 N. Car. 12.
(2) Rochester v. Collins, 12 Barb. 559.
(3) Williams v. Augusta, 4 Ga. 509.
(4) Vidal v. Girard, 2 How. 127.
(5) McDermond v. Kennedy, Brightly, 332.
(6) Janesville v. Railroad Co., 7 Wis. 484.
(7) Miller v. Milwaukee, 14 Wis. 642.

or private rights exercised. The word itself implies that the act controlled is lawful, but that certain restrictions are necessary to preserve the public free from harm. It can never be extended to include prohibition, for the very essence of regulation is the existence of something to be regulated.[1]

It is held that the power of regulating slaughter-houses implies power to fix their location, to direct the manner of their use and to prohibit their continuance whenever necessary to the welfare of the community. The only thing that the power recognizes as unavoidable is their right to exist, but the corporation may say how, when, and where.[2]

Under a power to regulate certain trades or occupations their exercise may be restricted to certain places, and restrictions may be laid on the manner of conducting them.[3] Power to regulate does not imply power to tax.[4] So, an ordinance assessing a certain amount for the privilege of building vaults under the street is not sustained by power to regulate vaults.[5] But this power authorizes ordinances which prescribe the hours of closing places of business whenever the business is of a nature to need safeguards.[6]

The power to regulate includes power to restrain, so long as the restraint imposed is reasonable. The restraint must not so confine the exercise of any occupation as to amount to a prohibition.[7] Nor may the regulation virtually effect the creation of a monopoly. Thus power to regulate the streets does not authorize a grant to a street rail-

---

(1) Heise v. Columbus, 6 Rich. 404; Sweet v. Wabash, 41 Ind. 7; McConvill v. Jersey City, 39 N. J. L. 38; Bronson v. Oberlin, 41 O. S. 476; Austin v. Murray, 16 Pick. 12; Duckwall v. New Albany, 25 Ind. 283; Shallcross v Jeffersonville, 26. Ind. 193.

(2) Cronin v. People, 82 N. Y. 318.

(3) Livery stables, State v. Beattie, 16 Mo. App. 131; liquor traffic, In re Wilson, 32 Minn. 144.

(4) Desty on Taxation, 1380; Mayor v. Beasley, 1 Humph. 232.

(5) State v. Hoboken, 33 N. J. 280.

(6) Schwuchow v. Chicago, 68 Ill. 444.

(7) Piqua v. Zimmerlin, 35 O. S. 507; Thomas v. Mt. Vernon, 9 Ohio, 290.

road company of the exclusive right to lay tracks and to operate its cars in a particular street.[1]

The means adopted to effect the regulation are immaterial so long as they do not violate any constitutional or statutory provision, or result in marked injustice to those who bear the burden of the regulation. Their validity is measured by their effect, and their choice lies within the sole discretion of the council. The occupation or trade may be limited to certain localities whenever its neighborhood is offensive. It may be limited to certain hours of the day whenever its nature is such that it needs supervision, or irresponsible persons can be prevented from its pursuit by the exaction of a license fee.[2] Some courts deny the right to license unless specifically granted.[3]

§ 31. **To suppress and restrain.**—Power "to suppress and restrain" imports more than simple regulation and little less than total prohibition. It may be exercised in any degree and through any reasonable means. Thus, under power to suppress and restrain disorderly houses, an ordinance may declare them to be nuisances and prescribe definite punishment for those who conduct them.[4]

As a general rule restraint may be exercised through a license system.[5] It is noticeable that the courts of Alabama hold the contrary. They do so in adherence to the well-established legislative policy of that state against all

---

(1) Davis v. Mayor, 14 N. Y. 506; *post*, § 132.

(2) In re Wan Yin, 22 Fed. Rep. 701; Russellville v. White, 41 Ark. 485; Fort Smith v. Ayers, 43 Ark. 82.

(3) Burlington v. Baumgartner, 42 Ia. 673; In re Schneider, 11 Oreg. 288.

(4) Centerville v. Miller, 57 Ia. 56; s. c., 57 Ia. 225, limiting Charitan v. Barber, 54 a. 360, where punishment was held illegal; and Mount Pleasant v. Breeze, 11 Ia. 399.

(5) Burlington v. Lawrence, 42 Ia. 681; (bowling alleys) Smith v. Madison, 7 Ind. 86; (hawking and peddling) Huntington v. Cheesbro, 57 Ind. 74; (sale of liquors) Mt. Carmel v. Wabash, 50 Ill. 69; (liquors) Franklin v. Westfall, 27 Kan. 614. *Contra* (liquors), Keokuk v. Dressell, 47 Ia. 597; Schuster v. State, 48 Ala. 202.

measures that facilitate the traffic in liquors, and particularly against any license system. Aside from any consideration of state policy, the power under discussion plainly implies the right to license as a proper mode of restraint.

§ 32. **Miscellaneous expressions.**—Under power to abate and remove nuisances it is unlawful to impose penalties for their erection, or to attempt by ordinance to prevent their creation. The law presumes that every act is lawful and proper and without express authority, citizens can not be hampered by restrictions, until the results of their undertakings are proven to be injurious.[1]

Power "to establish" certain works of public usefulness receives a broad construction. It is held to warrant measures, not only to establish, but also to regulate and alter the public improvement after its establishment. So, under power to establish pounds, penalties may be provided for breaking them open;[2] and a similar power over markets authorizes their removal or abandonment to meet the needs of a growing city.[3]

§ 33. **General rules of construction.**—In construing any of these general terms the ordinary and accepted definition of the words used should be the first guide. And further, the rule that a grant of power includes all degrees of that power is applicable, unless some declared policy of the state indicates that the power is mandatory rather than permissive, in which case it must be exercised to its full extent, if at all. The presumption is that the grant of a power expresses the *limit* of the corporate discretion, and that any exercise of the power falling short of or not exceeding that limit is valid.

(1) Rochester v. Collins, 12 Barb. 559.
(2) Smith v. Emporia, 27 Kan. 528.
(3) Gall v. Cincinnati, 18 O. S. 563.

CHAPTER V.

PASSAGE OF ORDINANCES.

PART I.

COUNCIL PROCEEDINGS.

§ 34. Necessity of formal enactment.
§ 35. Statutory directions are mandatory.
§ 36. Council *de facto* can not act.
§ 37. Meetings of the council.
§ 38. Adjourned and special meetings.
§ 39. Joint action of bi-cameral council.
§ 40. Quorum in joint session.
§ 41. What constitutes a quorum.
§ 42. Holdings under statutory provisions.
§ 43. Majority of quorum sufficient.
§ 44. When the mayor may vote.
§ 45. Other charter provisions.
§ 46. When a vote may be reconsidered.
§ 47. Readings.
§ 48. Signature of clerk of council.
§ 49. Signature of the mayor.
§ 50. The mayor's approval.
§ 51. How signified.
§ 52. Publication.
§ 53. Construction of provisions regulating the time of publication.
§ 54. The newspaper in which publication may be made.
§ 55. Form of the notice published.
§ 56. Record of the ordinance.
§ 57. What record must contain.
§ 58. Record of votes.
§ 59. Informalities subsequently cured.
§ 60. Repeal.
§ 60a. Must be by the council.
§ 61. Form of the repealing act.
§ 62. Repeal by the legislature by implication.
§ 63. Implied repeal by passage of inconsistent ordinance.
§ 64. Amendments.
§ 65. Summary.
§ 66. Saving clause in subsequent ordinance.
§ 67. Effect of a repeal on vested rights.

PART II.

§ 68. Form of ordinances.
§ 69. Constituent parts.
§ 70. Ordinances like resolutions in form.
§ 71. The title.
§ 72. The introduction.
§ 73. Ordinance need not recite authority.
§ 74. Scope of the ordinance.
§ 75. Reference to existing ordinances.
§ 76. Time of going into effect.
§ 77. Penalty.
§ 78. Definiteness of expression.
§ 79. Definiteness as to the penalty.
§ 80. License ordinances.
§ 81. Ordinances against nuisances.
§ 82. Council can not bind its successors.

§ 34. **Necessity of a formal enactment.**—The powers granted to municipal corporations are not self-executing. They require formal exercise by a legislative enactment of the municipal council, or governing body, before the ministerial officers can proceed to enforce them.[1] Municipal corporations can not act at all except through the bodies in which the law vests their legislative functions.[2] And the legislative department can only act through the medium of a formal expression of its will, whether in the form of an ordinance, resolution, or mandate.[3] This rule applies to police and contractual powers alike.[4]

§ 35. **Statutory directions are mandatory.**—"It is the policy of our jurisprudence to require of municipal corporations a strict observance of their powers, and that in the exercise of these powers they should observe the forms the law has directed. All tribunals of special and limited jurisdiction must show the authority under which they

---

(1) *Ante*, § 3; Lake v. Aberdeen, 57 Miss. 260.
(2) Saxton v. St. Joseph, 60 Mo. 153; Saxton v. Beach, 50 Mo. 488.
(3) Day v. Jersey City, 19 N. J. Eq. 412; Creighton v. Manson, 27 Cal. 613.
(4) Terre Haute v. Lake, 43 Ind. 480; Pettis v. Johnson, 56 Ind. 139, 151.

act, and act in the manner pointed out."[1] Statutory directions as to the mode of procedure to be followed in the enactment of ordinances are mandatory and must be strictly observed. They are conditions precedent and if omitted the ordinance is *ab initio* void.[2] The statutory mode becomes the measure of the power, and all enactments must be passed in strict subordination to the conditions and directions prescribed.[3] The compliance must be *literal*, and not merely substantial.[4] When a power is granted to be exercised in a particular manner, or through specified means, there is an implied prohibition upon the exercise in a different manner, or by different means,[5] and the corporation can not so legislate as to alter the mode of the exercise of that power, or to change the persons who may exercise it.[6]

Conditions precedent to the passage of ordinances are such as relate to the mode of procedure in the common council, or to any thing that it would be necessary to record in their journal. The journal should show compliance with each statutory direction.[7] It might be that some of the prescribed formalities seem wholly useless, or that omission to observe them could not possibly prejudice the rights of any one; but the obligation to follow them would be just as imperative. All exercise of discrimination is precluded between expressions of the legislative will.

§ 36. **Council de facto can not act.**—It is equally important as a condition precedent to the enactment of

(1) Wright, J., in Bloom v. Xenia, 32 O. S. 461, 466.
(2) State v. Bell, 34 O. S. 194; Bloom v. Xenia, *supra*; Welker v. Potter, 18 O. S. 85; Blanchard v. Bissell, 11 O. S. 101; Herzo v. San Francisco, 33 Cal. 134; State v. Newark, 25 N. J. 399; Elizabethtown v. Lester, 23 Ill. 90; Ewbanks v. Ashley, 36 Ill. 177; Barnett v. Newark, 28 Ill. 62; Danville v. Shelton, 76 Va. 325.
(3) McCoy v. Briant, 53 Cal. 250; Smith v. Buffalo, 1 Sheldon, 493.
(4) State v. Newark, 25 N. J. 399.
(5) Des Moines v. Gilchrist, 67 Iowa, 211.
(6) Brewster v. Hartley, 37 Cal. 15.
(7) Moore v. Mayor, 73 N. Y. 238.

police ordinances that the corporate council should have been lawfully created. Acquiescence on the part of those affected by contractual ordinances until rights have vested may estop them from afterward claiming that the council was improperly constituted; but the principle is not applicable to ordinances of a police or penal nature. In order to enact valid police ordinances the members of the council, or at least those who voted in favor of its passage, must have been duly elected and qualified, although it is apprehended that an ordinance passed by more than the requisite number of votes would not be void if one of those who voted for it should prove to have been disqualified to act. Where the council is the judge of the election and qualification of its own members, its decision when once invoked is determinate.[1] Every provision of the statute regulating the election of councilmen is material, and must be fulfilled; thus, if the official inspector of elections fails to file a certificate of the election, as the law requires, those elected can not enact ordinances.[2]

§ 37. **Meetings of the council.**—The times of holding council meetings is usually fixed by statute, but, if not, it may be regulated by the council itself in any manner that will charge its members with due notice. At the first meeting of a newly elected council a majority present can effect an organization, and then proceed to the transaction of any business, regardless of the fact that some are absent, or even that the absentees have not yet qualified as members. The full power given to the council may be exercised at its first meeting.[3]

When the charter or statute declares that stated meetings shall be held, but makes no provision for fixing the time, the council may exercise its own discretion, and in

---

(1) Kendell *v.* Camden, 47 N. J. 64; Hadley *v.* Mayor, 33 N. Y. 603; Morgan *v.* Quackenbosh, 22 Barb. 78. *Contra*, quo warranto still lies, People *v.* Bird, 20 Ill. App. 568.
(2) Dinwindie *v.* Rushville, 37 Ind. 66.
(3) Oakland *v.* Carpentier, 13 Cal. 540.

any manner it chooses. If the times have been once fixed by a formal resolution, approved by the mayor and published, the council is not precluded thereby from changing the dates of meetings, but may do so by simple motion.[1]

§ 38. **Adjourned and special meetings.**—There is considerable conflict of authority as to the validity of acts performed at adjourned and special meetings. Technically, the term meeting, used in the corporate charter or organic law, does not include *adjourned* meetings.[2] A distinction seems to have been made between special and adjourned meetings. If the statute or charter provides for the transaction of specified business at a stated meeting, it is doubtful whether those present at that meeting can appoint a *special* meeting for the transaction of that business at a later day;[3] but all difficulty may be avoided by simply *adjourning* the stated or regular meeting. Members of the council are supposed to attend each regular meeting, and they are charged with notice of all the business there transacted. They are thus charged with notice of the time and place of the adjournment of that meeting, if one is had, and of the unfinished business to be taken up at the adjourned meeting.[4] If members are absent from a regular meeting, at which an election was postponed to another day, they can not attack the validity of the election when held, on the ground that they were not notified.[5] And the adjournment could be voted by a minority of the council in the absence of a quorum.

If it is true that councilmen are charged with notice of all that is done at regular meetings, they have notice of any adjourned meeting, and it seems that adjourned meetings should stand on an equal footing with the regular meetings. It is certain that unfinished business may be completed,

(1) State *v.* Kantler, 33 Minn. 69.
(2) Staates *v.* Washington, 44 N. J. 605.
(3) People *v.* Batchelor, 22 N. Y. 128.
(4) People *v.* Batchelor, 22 N. Y. 128.
(5) Kimball *v.* Marshall, 44 N. H. 465.

and the reasonable rule is that any business may be transacted that could have been brought up at the preceding regular meeting.[1]

When special or adjourned meetings are held by virtue of statutory authority, an ordinance is void that is enacted at a special meeting held after the repeal of the empowering statute.[2] A statutory provision is mandatory which directs that no business shall be transacted at a special meeting called by the mayor, except such as is mentioned in his proclamation.[3]

§ 39. **Joint action of bi-cameral council.**—In municipalites that have adopted the bi-cameral system of local government, ordinances must be duly passed by both branches of the council before they attain validity. The *council* consists of both parts. Enactments must receive the sanction of the two branches that hold office at the same time. An ordinance that passed one branch just before the expiration of its term of office, or of the term of office of a part of its members, can not be taken up by the other branch, newly elected, and passed as unfinished business. It can not be said to have been passed by the council.[4]

In order to have valid joint action there must be a meeting of the minds of the two branches, and there can be none such between two bodies which have had no contemporaneous existence. In a case where concurrent action of both branches was necessary to elect a city solicitor, the lower house elected A., and sent a report of their vote to the upper house. The latter refused to concur and adjourned. At their next meeting the upper house in its turn elected A., and reported to the lower house. The official notices of the refusal to concur and of

---

(1) New Orleans *v.* Brooks, 36 La. Ann. 641; Ex parte Wolf, 14 Neb. 24.

(2) County of San Louis Obispo *v.* Hendricks, 11 Pac. Rep. 682.

(3) St. Louis *v.* Withans, 16 Mo. App. 247; Allen *v.* Rogers, 20 Mo. App. 290.

(4) Wetmore *v.* Story, 22 Barb. 414; Beekman's Case, 11 Abb. Pr. 164; s. c., 19 How. Pr. 518.

the subsequent election reached the lower house at the same time, which then in its turn refused to concur in A.'s election, but elected B., which last election received the ratification of the upper house. B. was adjudged elected, A not having received the *concurrent* vote of both houses.[1]

§ 40. **Quorum in joint session.**—Where the two branches of the council meet in joint session, they do not merely vote together as two separate bodies, but constitute *one* assembly, and a quorum for the transaction of business is obtained, if a majority of the total number of members in both houses are present.[2] It is, however, held in New Jersey, in the absence of any statutory regulation, that a majority of *each* body must be present.[3]

§ 41. **What constitutes a quorum.**—Any power vested in the corporate council may be lawfully exercised by a majority of its members, unless otherwise prescribed by law.[4] The state may make any other provision that it sees fit, but if it is silent the common-law rule prevails. The council has no power to declare that more than a majority shall be necessary.[5]

§ 42. **Holdings under statutory provisions.**—Where the statute provided in terms that a majority of those *elected* to the council should constitute a quorum, and eight members were elected, of whom one was an alien and therefore incapable of acting, it was held that five qualified members were still necessary to the quorum, it not being the legislative intent to throw special stress

---

(1) Saunders *v.* Lawrence, 141 Mass. 380.
(2) Beck *v.* Hanscom, 29 N. H. 213; Kimball *v.* Marshall, 44 N. H. 465, 468. And in England, see King *v.* Williams, 2 M. & S. 141.
(3) State v. Patterson, 35 N. J. 190; see page 194.
(4) Covington *v.* Boyle, 6 Bush, 204; Heiskell *v.* Baltimore, 65 Md. 125; s. c., 20 Am. L. Rev. 640; State *v.* Farr, 47 N. J. 208; Barnert *v.* Paterson, 48 N. J. 395.
(5) Heiskell *v.* Baltimore, *supra*, note 4.

on the word *elected*.¹ The same construction was put upon the same statute where one of the eight members elect resigned, and an ordinance was declared void that had been passed by a vote of four to three.² The intent is always that the measure shall receive the requisite majority or proportion of the total number that constitute the council when filled.

If the statute provides that no councilman shall vote who is personally, that is, pecuniarily, interested in the proposed measure, the vote thus disqualified must not be counted. In a council of nine members, requiring two-thirds to pass a certain ordinance, the votes of six, one being thus disqualified, are not sufficient.³ No vote can be thrown out for this reason, except in pursuance of express provision of the statute.

§ 43. **Majority of quorum sufficient.**—When a quorum is obtained the body may then proceed to the transaction of business, and unless contrary to the express provision of the organic law of the corporation, an ordinance is properly passed for which a majority of the quorum have voted.⁴ This is strictly in conformity to the rule observed in political elections, a majority of those voting deciding the issue.⁵

Those who are present and who help to make up the quorum are expected to vote on every question, and their presence alone is enough to make the vote decisive and binding, whether they actually vote or not. The objects of legislation can not be defeated by the refusal of any one to vote, when present. If eighteen are present and nine vote, all in the affirmative, the measure is carried, the

---

(1) Saterlee v. San Francisco, 23 Cal. 314.

(2) San Francisco v. Hazen, 5 Cal. 169; McCracken v. San Francisco, 16 Cal. 591; Pimental v. San Francisco, 21 Cal. 351, 362.

(3) Wheel Company v. Burnham, 60 Iowa, 493.

(4) State v. Farr, 47 N. J. 208; State v. Chapman, 44 Conn. 1; Barnert v. Paterson, 48 N. J. 395.

(5) Erwin v. Township, 21 U. C. C. P. 330.

refusal of the other nine to vote being construed as a vote in the affirmative so far as any construction is necessary.¹

As was said by Sheldon, J., in Launtz v. People, 113 Ill. 137, quoting from Wilcock on Corporations: "After an election has been properly proposed, whoever has a majority of those who vote, the assembly being sufficient, is elected, although a majority of the entire assembly altogether abstain from voting, because their presence suffices to constitute the elective body; and if they neglect to vote it is their own fault, and shall not invalidate the act of the others, but be construed an assent to the determination of the majority of those who do vote; and such an election is valid, though the majority of those whose presence is necessary to the assembly protest against any election at that time, or even the election of the individual who has the majority of the votes."

§ 44. **When the mayor may vote.**—Although it was the rule of the common law that the mayor has no casting vote except as given by charter or founded on custom,² it is usual now to allow the mayor, like the presiding officer of any other legislative body, to vote in case of an equal division of the council. Recent decisions are very favorable to the exercise of the right. Thus, where the charter gave the mayor a right to vote in case of tie, and of the eight councilmen present four voted and four refused to vote, the mayor considered the refusal as a negative vote, and voted with the other four, as the court said, lawfully.³ If the mayor has the power to "appoint by and with the consent of the council," and the council divides evenly upon a motion to approve an appointment, the mayor may decide in favor of his nomination by casting his vote.⁴

§ 45. **Other charter provisions.**—Provisions authorizing the suspension of the rules for any purpose must be

(1) State v. Green, 37 O. S. 227; Gosling v. Veley, 4 H. L. Cas. 679; Angell & Ames Corp., § 127; Grant on Corporations, 71.

(2) Anon. Lofft, 315.

(3) Launtz v. People, 113 Ill. 137.

(4) Carroll v. Wall, 35 Kan. 36.

strictly observed. So, where the council is made to consist of seven members, including the mayor and recorder, or clerk, and four of the trustees, the mayor and the recorder are present, the rules can not be suspended by vote of the four trustees alone, the charter or regulation requiring a three-fourths vote.[1] In another case the charter provided that six should constitute the council and that the concurrent vote of four should be necessary to elect an officer. The number of councilmen was afterward increased by law to eight, but it was held that four could still elect.[2]

§ 46. **When a vote may be reconsidered.**—As a rule a municipal council may reconsider any action taken at the same meeting, though the votes of a specified number are usually required, or sometimes, a suspension of the rules. If a two-thirds vote is necessary to suspend the rules, and the vote taken upon the pending measure after a motion to reconsider has prevailed shows that two-thirds of those present voted in its favor, it may be presumed that the motion to reconsider was also carried by the requisite proportion.[3] If a condition to the action of the council has been fulfilled, and the measure defeated, a subsequent reconsideration, and passage of the measure would not be invalid; the condition precedent is considered sufficiently observed.[4]

The right to reconsider is doubtful when the rights of others have become vested by virtue of the action of the council. If a power of appointment has been once exercised, and the council is not vested with a right of removal without cause, the appointment can not lawfully be reconsidered and defeated.[5] When the council has attempted to pass an ordinance over the mayor's veto and failed, its power is exhausted, and the motion to pass the ordinance over the veto can not be reconsidered.[6]

(1) Horner *v.* Rowley, 51 Ia. 620.
(2) McDermott *v.* Miller, 45 N. J. 251.
(3) Sank *v.* Philadelphia, 8 Phila. 117.
(4) People *v.* Rochester, 5 Lans (N. Y.) 11.
(5) State *v.* Barbour, 53 Conn. 76. *Contra*: **Baker** *v.* **Cushman**, 127 Mass. 105; State *v.* Chapman, 44 Conn. 601.
(6) Sank *v.* Philadelphia, 8 Phila. 117.

§ 47. **Readings.**—The usual statutory direction is that every ordinance shall be read at three different meetings before its final enactment. The direction is necessary as a safeguard against too hasty legislation, and its observance mandatory. If neglected, the ordinance is *ab initio* void.[1] But it is not necessary that the readings should be at regular meetings; they may be at adjourned meetings not held on the same day.[2] On the ground that the letter of the statute was complied with, it has just been held in Ohio that an ordinance is valid which was passed at an adjourned meeting under a suspension of the rules, although at the foregoing regular meeting a motion to suspend the rules as to the same ordinance was defeated.[3]

Ordinances should represent the will of the local legislative body, and can not for that reason be proposed by one council and enacted by their successors. Each council must finish its own business, otherwise any action in which separate and distinct councils have had a voice is not the expression of the same legislative will. If, after an ordinance has passed two readings, an election is held and a part of the council superseded by new members, the newly constituted body can not take up the same ordinance, read it the third time and pass it.[4]

Likewise, the requisite readings must all be of the same ordinance. Any change or alteration of substance made between readings destroys the effect of the first or previous reading. An immaterial change in the title during the passage of an ordinance would not affect its validity.[5] And this difficulty can not be avoided by formally reconsidering the previous reading after making an alteration, for the

(1) Weill *v.* Kenfield, 54 Cal. 111. *Contra*: Barton *v.* Pittsburgh, 4 Brewster, 373.
(2) Cutcomp *v.* Utt. 60 Ia. 156.
(3) Madden *v.* Smeltz, 2 O. Circ. Ct. 168.
(4) The only direct decision is, however, contrary to the text. McGraw *v.* Whitson, 69 Ia. 348; s. c., 34 Alb. Law Jour. 59.
(5) State *v.* Newark, 30 N. J. 303; State *v.* Jersey City, 34 N. J. 429; Staates *v.* Washington, 44 N. J. 605.

provision that the readings must be on different days would then be violated.¹

The provision of a state constitution that all acts " of a general or permanent nature" must be read on three separate days does not apply to a resolution awarding a contract, nor to a resolution declaratory of the necessity of a certain proposed public improvement.²

Any provision whereby the three readings may be had at the same meeting, as by suspending the rules, must be strictly observed. Thus, where the rules have been suspended, only one ordinance may be passed under that suspension. If two are enacted, the second is void.³

§ 48. **Signature of clerk of council.**—When the signature of the clerk of the council is required to be attached to an ordinance, the act is entirely ministerial and he can not refuse to comply. In case of refusal the presiding officer may appoint a substitute or deputy to act in his place.⁴

§ 49. **Signature of the mayor.**—A broad distinction exists between the simple signature of the mayor and his approval. His signature may be the means adopted to designate his approval when his approval is required; but if his signature alone is necessary the element of approval is absent. Unless his signature is made *essential* to the validity of an ordinance by the express terms of the statute or charter, the requirement is only directory, and the absence of his signature not fatal to the ordinance.⁵ So, where the statute directed the mayor to sign all ordinances, but he omitted to perform his duty with regard to an ordinance which was properly passed and published as though

(1) State v. Newark, 30 N. J. 303.
(2) Cincinnati v. Bickett. 26 O. S. 49; Upington v. Oviatt, 24 O. S. 232.
(3) Bloom v. Xenia, 34 O. S. 461.
(4) Preston v. Manvers, 21 U. C. Q. B. 626.
(5) Stevenson v. Bay City, 26 Mich. 44; Martindale v. Palmer, 52 Ind. 411; Conboy v. Iowa City, 2 Ia. 90; Blanchard v. Bissell, 11 O. S. 96.

it had been signed by him, the ordinance was sustained.[1] In such case the signature of a person presiding in the mayor's absence is effective.[2] If the statute only directs the mayor to sign a certain class of ordinances or resolutions, the provision will receive a liberal construction to excuse any omission.[3]

§ 50. **The mayor's approval.**—The mayor's *approval*, when required, is essential to the validity of an ordinance, and the requirement receives strict construction. There is, however, no common-law rule making his approval necessary. The requirement must be embodied in the statutes or charter governing the municipality.[4] Where the charter requires the sanction of the mayor to all council enactments, an ordinance is inoperative till approved.[5] A provision requiring his approval of "every ordinance or resolution" is imperative, and extends to all acts of the council.[6] Where the charter gives the corporate council power to pass "by-laws, ordinances, resolutions, and regulations," and requires that "by-laws and ordinances" shall be subject to the mayor's approval, the requirement is held to extend to *resolutions* as well as to ordinances.[7] And even resolutions appointing officers whose duties do not affect any of the interests of the public are included.[8]

§ 51. **How signified.**—The mayor's signature alone does not constitute an approval, and especially so if it is merely affixed to the journal of the council meeting.[9] Neither is his signature the only method of expressing his approval. In a case where the statute required his approval and sig-

(1) Opelousas *v.* Andrus, 37 La. Ann. 699; Knight *v.* Kansas City, 70 Mo. 231.
(2) O'Mally *v.* M'Ginn, 53 Wis. 353.
(3) State *v.* Jersey City, 30 N. J. L. 148.
(4) Burlington *v.* Dennison, 42 N. J. 165.
(5) Breaux's Bridge *v.* Dupuis, 30 La. Ann. 1105.
(6) People *v.* Schroeder, 76 N. Y. 160.
(7) Kepner *v.* Commonwealth, 40 Pa. St. 124.
(8) McDermott *v.* Miller, 45 N. J. 251.
(9) Graham *v.* Carondelet, 33 Mo. 262.

nature, and his approval appeared on the record of the council proceedings in that he appears as voting "yea" to the passage of a "revised code" containing old and new ordinances, and affixed his name to the minutes, the compliance with the statute was held sufficient, as his approval and not his signature was the object sought, and his affirmative vote testifies to his approval.[1]

A *veto* is the positive expression of the mayor's disapproval, and is conclusive unless some method is provided for passing the ordinance over the veto. If such a method is provided, the veto power once exercised is exhausted, and the subsequent passage of the measure by the requisite majority gives it immediate effect.[2] A statute requiring the mayor to return his reasons with the veto is imperative. A veto unaccompanied by reasons is wholly inoperative in such case.[3] If the statute says that the ordinance shall take effect, if not returned by the mayor with his veto, within ten days from its passage, the provision can not be defeated and an expected veto avoided by the adjournment of the legislative body before the ten days have expired. The mayor may have ten days in which to announce his veto, whether the council is in session or not.[4]

§ 52. Publication.—In nearly every state of the Union statutory direction is made for the publication of all ordinances enacted by municipal corporations. If no publication at all, or an imperfect publication, be made of an ordinance requiring assessments upon property, and involving the contractual relations of the city, the better opinion seems to be that the assessment is unlawful, but that any contract entered into by virtue of its provisions will bind the corporation.[5] The object of publishing *police* ordinances is to give notice to all who must obey them, and since this class of ordinances restrict the personal rights

(1) Woodruff v. Stewart, 63 Ala. 208.
(2) Ahrens v. Fiedler, 43 N. J. 401.
(3) Truesdale v. Rochester, 33 Hun, 574.
(4) State v. Carr, 67 Mo. 38.
(5) Moore v. Mayor, 73 N. Y. 238; Creighton v. Manson, 27 Cal. 616.

of the citizens, it is the policy of the law to insist upon strict compliance to the publication required. There seems to be some authority for the doctrine that the requirement of publication is only directory and not a condition precedent to the validity of the ordinance. In such case the ordinance goes into effect from the moment of its passage.[1] Though this may be true with regard to property ordinances, it does not apply to police ordinances. If statutory provision has been made for publication, its object, that of giving notice, is deemed essential, and without it the legislative intent has not been fulfilled. If the legislative act expressly provides that failure to publish shall not affect the validity of the ordinance, the ordinance is in force from the date of its passage.[2] But in the absence of such limitation the publication in the manner and form prescribed is essential to the validity of the ordinance.[3] A good illustration of the distinction between police and other ordinances is found in the case of Stuhr v. Hoboken, 47 N. J. L. 148. A statute prohibited any change in the salaries of municipal officers during their terms of office, and another section required all ordinances to be published twenty days before going into effect. An ordinance was enacted altering the salary of one of the officers. Before the twenty days had expired, but after the passage of the ordinance, the office became vacant and was filled by an election. The new incumbent was held to be entitled to the salary provided by the new ordinance. Within the intent of the statute the change had been effected as soon as the ordinance had passed the council. But, in the

---

(1) Commonwealth v. Davis, 140 Mass. 485; In re Smith, 65 Barb. Barb. 283; Mayor v. New York, 25 Wend. 693. If a revision of all the ordinances contains a prior existing ordinance unchanged, the revision as to that part needs no publication. Ex parte Bedell, 20 Mo. App. 125.

(2) Schweizer v. Liberty, 82 Mo. 309.

(3) Kneif v. People, 6 Hun, 238; State v. Hoboken, 38 N. J. 110; Baltimore v. Johnson, 62 Md. 225; Higley v. Bunce, 10 Conn. 435; Conboy v. Iowa City, 2 Ia. 90; Barnett v. Newark, 28 Ill. 62; Hoboken v. Gear, 27 N. J. 265.

passage of *police* ordinances, the element of notice is made essential, and until notice is given in the manner prescribed the ordinances do not go into effect. Where publication is required, the fact that power is given to the corporation to prescribe the mode does not presume any discretion in the corporate authorities to avoid the necessity of publishing the ordinance by omitting to designate how it shall be done. Some kind of publication must be made by order or direction of the corporate authorities.[1]

§ 53. **Construction of provisions regulating the time of publication.**—If the publication is directed to be made for a certain length of time, as is usually the case, the first day of the period is the day of the first publication. If in a newspaper, and the newspaper is dated later than actually issued, the day of its issuing and delivery to the public is the first day of the period. If the period is so many days, Sundays and holidays are not excluded from the count.[2] The ordinance does not go into effect until after the expiration of the full period. If twenty days' publication is necessary, an offense committed on the twentieth day is not punishable.

Publication must usually be made for a certain number of consecutive weeks. The term week is used as equivalent to seven days, and three weeks means twenty-one days.[3] The publication may be made in a weekly newspaper or once a week in a daily paper.[4] If one week's publication is required a single insertion in a weekly paper suffices, and the ordinance is in operation on the eighth day from the date of its actual issue.[5]

(1) Higley v. Bunce, 10 Conn. 435; Schwartz v. Oshkosh, 55 Wis. 490; Baltimore v. Little Sisters, 56 Md. 400.

(2) Taylor v. Palmer, 31 Cal. 240; Ex parte Fiske, 13 Pac. Rep. 310 (Cal. 1887),

(3) Longbridge v. Huntington, 56 Ind. 253.

(4) Hoboken v. Gear, 27 N. J. 265.

(5) State v. Hardy, 7 Neb. 37; Commonwealth v. Matthews, 122 Mass. 60; Hoboken v. Gear, 27 N. J. 265.

§ 54. **The newspaper in which publication may be made.**—If no method of publication is prescribed, the publication need not be in a newspaper, but the old system of posting copies and notices in public places may be used. A posting in five or six places would be sufficient.[1] But publication is generally directed to be made in a newspaper of general circulation within the corporation. If the paper must simply be of general circulation, it need not be a local paper. A paper issued in a neighboring city, but circulating generally in the corporation, would suffice.[2] Publication in a newspaper published and issued in the corporation, but having no local circulation, would be defective.[3] Where the publication is directed to be made in an *adjoining* municipality, in the absence of any local paper, a leading paper in a large city not far distant which circulates in the community, may be resorted to in preference to the local paper of a village lying nearer, in point of fact, than the city.[4] A newspaper which is edited and issued in a city is in a legal sense *printed and published* in the city, though the type and press-work are done out of the city.[5]

If the duty of the council to designate the particular newspaper has been neglected, the clerk may make a lawful publication in any paper in the city.[6] And after the publication is begun a designation of a different paper by the council would take effect only as to subsequent ordinances.

The council is not obliged to select a publication devoted entirely to news, but its contents may be of a legal, commercial, scientific, or political nature. The word *newspaper* is a generic term for periodical, unbound publications of all kinds, and its contents need not be current

(1) Queen *v.* Justices, 4 Q. B. D. 522; s. c., 29 Moak Eng. Rep. 61.
(2) Tisdale *v.* Minonk, 46 Ill. 9.
(3) Haskill *v.* Bartlett, 34 Cal. 281.
(4) Gallerno *v.* Rochester, 46 U. C. Q. B. 279.
(5) Bayer *v.* Hoboken, 44 N. J. 131.
(6) In re Durkin, 10 Hun, 269. A paper once designated is de facto the official paper, and publications made therein are valid, though the appointment was irregular. Wright *v.* Forrestal, 65 Wis. 341.

news.¹ It is, however, implied that the paper must be one printed in the English language. A publication in a German newspaper alone would be void.²

§ 55. **Form of the notice published.**—In the absence of any express direction as to the form of the advertisement, any thing will be sufficient which gives the body of the ordinance its title and the signatures required by law. It is not necessary to state that the publication is made in compliance with the statute requiring it, neither need the power authorizing the ordinance be recited.³ The ordinance may be published as a part of the proceedings of the council session at which it was passed.⁴ It may be published, too, in more ways than are necessary without laying grounds for an injunction at the instance of a taxpayer.⁵ Errors in printing, or slight variation from the text of the ordinance, are not fatal so long as the intent and purport of no material provision are concealed.⁶

§ 56. **Record of the ordinance.**—Municipal councils should keep a journal of all their proceedings, and record in it every thing that transpires, and especially every thing connected with the passage of ordinances. This is essential because the record is the best, if not the only means of proving that certain ordinances have been lawfully enacted. Compliance with those formalities in the passage of ordinances which do not go to the validity of the council's action, and which, as matters of mere detail, are considered only directory, may perhaps be shown by evidence outside of the record, but compliance with mandatory provisions, and with formalities that are considered as conditions precedent to the validity of the ordinance, can

(1) Kellogg v. Corrico, 47 Mo. 157; Kerr v. Hitt, 75 Ill. 51.
(2) Cincinnati v. Bickett, 26 O. S. 49.
(3) People v. San Francisco, 27 Cal. 655. See also Moss v. Oakland, 88 Ill. 109.
(4) Law v. People, 87 Ill. 389.
(5) Wasem v. Cincinnati, 2 Sup. Ct. Rep. 84 (Ohio).
(6) Law v. People, 87 Ill. 389; Moss v. Oakland, 88 Ill. 109.

only be shown by the record. In order to avoid any question the record should omit nothing at all. The extent to which extrinsic testimony is admitted is considered in the treatment of rules of evidence, *post*, § 186. The object of a record is apparent, but it is not very important that it should be made in any particular manner, so long as testimony can be procured, if the record is not self-explanatory in that respect, to identify the writing as the record of the proceedings of the council. If the statute directs the recording of all ordinances "in a separate book," the provision is merely directory and the ordinance is valid, though recorded only in the council journal.[1] It is not necessary for the clerk or other official intrusted with making up the record to do the manual labor himself. It need only be done under his general supervision and direction.[2] Irregularities in the performance of purely ministerial duties are not fatal to the ordinance, if the substantial formalities of passage have been observed. So, the alteration, by interlineation in the record book, of an ordinance that had been properly passed, would have no effect.[3] And if the statute directs the mayor to sign the record book at the end of the record of the proceedings of each session of the council, his omission is merely a neglect of a ministerial duty and is not fatal to the validity of the proceedings.[4] There is always implied power to have the ordinances printed.[5]

The record, as has been said, should be a true account of all the proceedings, or, if a separate book is kept in which formal enactments are copied, it should not only contain the ordinances, but also every regulation, rule, or resolution of however temporary a character.[6] Still, a contract entered into by the corporation in pursuance of a

(1) Upington *v.* Oviatt, 24 O. S. 232.
(2) Hutchinson *v.* Pratt, 11 Vt. 402.
(3) Railroad Co. *v.* Odum, 53 Tex. 343.
(4) Stevenson *v.* Bay City, 26 Mich. 44; Conboy *v.* Iowa City, 2 Ia. 90.
(5) Dwyer *v.* Brenham, 65 Tex. 526.
(6) Logan *v.* Tyler, 1 Pittsburgh Rep. 244.

resolution would not be voidable for failure to record the resolution.[1]

§ 57. **What the record must contain.**—The record or journal must show compliance with all the formalities which are considered mandatory. These may be summarized as :[2]

(a) The body of the ordinance, its title, and the date, or dates, of its consideration.

(b) The requisite number of readings on different days, or, if on the same day, a suspension of the rules for the consideration of the ordinance in question.

(c) The vote, or action, on the final motion to adopt the ordinance.

(d) The approval of the mayor and the signatures of the officers, mayor or clerk, or both, when required. If vetoed, the vote of the council on passage of the ordinance over the veto.

(e) The publication, specifying date and newspaper, or places of posting notices, generally required to be evidenced by the certificate of the publisher, or of the clerk of the council.

(f) Any other requirements specially provided by statute, charter, or council rules.

§ 58. **Record of votes.**—Where any of the steps necessary to the construction of a public improvement must be passed by a certain vote of the council, the record must enumerate those who voted affirmatively and negatively in order that no doubt may arise as to the compliance with the requirement. The presence or participation of any member can not be left to presumption.[3]

---

(1) Parr v. Greenbush, 72 N. Y. 463.

(2) Schwarz v. Oshkosh, 55 Wis. 490; State v. Union, 32 N. J. 343. *Contra as to readings :* People v. Starne, 35 Ill. 121 ; Supervisors v. People, 25 Ill. 181. Special rule in Boston, Commonwealth v. Davis, 140 Mass. 485.

(3) Steckert v. East Saginaw, 22 Mich. 104; In re Carlton Street, 16 Hun, 497; In re Buffalo, 78 N. Y. 362; Delphi v. Evans, 36 Ind. 90;

In regard to ordinances that define and prescribe penalties for offenses, the same rule prevails. The calling the vote is a condition precedent to the validity of the ordinance passed. If the ayes and nays are required, the record must show that they were taken.[1] But unless the statute expressly requires the vote as called to be recorded, it will suffice that the record shows indirectly a compliance with the condition. Thus, if a three-fourths vote is necessary to suspend the rules, and the record of a session shows that six of the seven members being present, the rules requiring three readings were suspended and the ordinance adopted by a vote of *all those present*, the conclusion is inevitable that the motion to dispense with the second and third readings was carried by a three-fourths vote of the council.[2] There seems, likewise, to be no necessity of spreading the ayes and nays on the record, whenever the record shows that a measure was adopted *unanimously*.[3] Compliance with the requirement may be shown indirectly, unless the statute or charter expressly directs that the ayes and nays shall be *recorded* as well as taken, in which case the statute is mandatory and the ordinance void if the record is defective.[4] No record of the vote taken on a motion to adjourn need be kept.[5] If several resolutions are passed together, there need be no separate record of the vote for each ordinance.[6]

Spangler *v.* Jacoby, 14 Ill. 297; Rich *v.* Chicago, 59 Ill. 286. *Contra:* Striker *v.* Kelly, 7 Hill, 9 (dissenting opinion, mandatory); St. Louis *v.* Foster, 52 Mo. 513; Mayor *v.* New York, 25 Wend. 693.

(1) Tracy *v.* People, 6 Col. 151.

(2) State *v.* Vail, 53 Ia. 550. The rule in Iowa is, however, more lenient than in any other state in which the courts have considered the question. Brewster *v.* Davenport, 51 Ia. 427; Eldora *v.* Burlingame. 62 Ia. 32; and see McCormick *v.* Bay City, 23 Mich. 457.

(3) Elmendorf *v.* Ewen, 2 N. Y. Leg. Obs. 85; Solomon *v.* Hughes, 24 Kan. 211; Barr *v.* Auburn, 89 Ill. 361.

(4) Steckert *v.* East Saginaw, 22 Mich. 104; McCormick *v.* Bay City, 23 Mich. 457; Gas Company *v.* Toberman, 61 Cal. 199; Cutler *v.* Russellville, 40 Ark. 105; Logansport *v.* Crockett, 64 Ind. 319; Olin *v.* Meyers, 55 Ia. 209.

(5) Green Bay *v.* Brauns, 50 Wis. 204.

(6) Wright *v.* Forrestal, 65 Wis. 341.

§ 59. **Informalities subsequently cured.**—Any informality in the passage of an ordinance is incurable by subsequent supplementary action, except the last in order of procedure. If the record has been omitted, and no time limit is imposed by statute, it may be supplied and the ordinance validated.[1] But this could only be done by the council which had voted on the ordinance, not by its successor. All other defects in the passage of police or punitive ordinances are fatal so far as subsequent action is concerned.[2]

§ 60. **Repeal.** Power to enact ordinances is legislative, and, as we have already seen, continuing. The power is not exhausted by once being exercised, but the municipality may change its laws to accord with its growing and varying needs, and it may provide suitable remedies for each new mischief. This implies the right to repeal existing ordinances, and either to omit to supplant them or to enact others of a different character in their places. Power to enact implies power to repeal.[3] The right to reconsider its enactments is inherent in the municipal council as a legislative body.[4] This applies to ordinances establishing municipal offices as well as to remedial ordinances; power to erect an office gives power to abolish it, saving the rights of the immediate incumbent.[5]

§ 60a. **Must be by the council.**—No *express* repeal may be made except by the same body that enacted the ordinance—that is, by the council.[6] The legislature can not, by express intendment, repeal ordinances, though a repeal

---

(1) Schenley *v.* Commonwealth, 36 Pa. St. 29. *Nunc pro tunc* entry of ayes and nays may be made. Logansport *v.* Crockett, 64 Ind. 319.

(2) McCracken *v.* San Francisco, 16 Cal. 591; Pimental *v.* San Francisco, 21 Cal. 362. The rule is different as to property ordinances. Lucas *v.* San Francisco, 7 Cal. 413; Holland *v.* San Francisco, 7 Cal. 361; Cory *v.* Somerset, 44 N. J. 445.

(3) Kansas City *v.* White, 69 Mo. 26.

(4) Jersey City *v.* State, 30 N. J. 529.

(5) Waldraven *v.* Memphis, 4 Coldw. 431.

(6) Rex *v.* Ashwell, 12 East, 22.

may be effected by the passage of a general law that is inconsistent with the ordinance. The legislature can not be restricted in the freedom of its action by any exercise of the powers previously delegated by it to municipal corporations. Neither can the mayor or a single branch of a compound council effect a repeal. Only the power that enacts can expressly repeal.[1]

§ 61. **Form of the repealing act.**—Express repeals can only be effected by an act of equal grade with that by which the ordinance was originally put into operation. No part or feature of an existing ordinance can be changed by a mere resolution of the council, even though signed by the mayor and recorded. A new ordinance must be passed.[2] So, contracts that were made by vote of the council can only be rescinded in similar manner.[3]

§ 62. **Repeal by the legislature by implication.**—Though the state legislature is powerless to effect the repeal of municipal ordinances directly, there are various ways in which it may be done impliedly. If the legislature amends the grant of power to the municipality, the ordinances, or parts of ordinances, that were valid under the old power, but inconsistent with the new power, are repealed by implication. The effect amounts to a repeal, for to that extent the ordinance can not be enforced. But if the ordinance contains several provisions and the alteration in the power affects a part only of those provisions and does not disturb the validity of the mode of punishment adopted, the ordinance is only repealed *pro tanto*. The balance remains in effect.[4] A change in the state statute does not repeal the ordinance unless conflicting with it.[5] The alteration must go to the substance and not

(1) City Council *v.* Church, 4 Strobh. 306.
(2) Jones *v.* McAlpine, 64 Ala. 511.
(3) Terre Haute *v.* Lake, 43 Ind. 480.
(4) Chamberlain *v.* Evansville, 77 Ind. 542; Franklin *v.* Westfall, 27 Kan. 614.
(5) In re Mollie Hall, 10 Neb. 537.

merely to the form of the general law. Thus, the change of a village to a city leaves the ordinances of the village operative as ordinances of the city.[1] So, if the new statute confers upon the municipality the same rights and powers in a different form or under a new name, together with additional powers, the ordinances enacted before the change are not interfered with.[2] It is not the policy of the law to consider municipal powers repealed by implication.[3]

§ 63. **Implied repeal by passage of inconsistent ordinance.**—The rules governing the repeal of statutes by implication are equally applicable to questions arising under municipal ordinances. The enactment of an ordinance containing provisions directly repugnant to those embodied in the previously existing ordinance on the same subject repeals the former ordinance by implication.[4] For example, an ordinance prohibiting persons from allowing animals to run at large, would be repealed by a subsequent ordinance, containing the same prohibition " as may from time to time be designated by resolution."[5] But repeals by implication are not favored, and will only be sustained when the terms of the subsequent ordinance are so directly inconsistent with those of the prior ordinance that they can not be reconciled. Otherwise both exist concurrently, until one is expressly repealed.[6] The repeal operates to the extent of the direct conflict.[7] As a general rule a subsequent ordinance which covers the entire field occupied by the prior ordinance will be considered to repeal the prior ordinance by implication. Effect will be given

(1) Academy v. Erie, 31 Pa. St. 515.
(2) Waring v. Mobile, 24 Ala. 701.
(3) New York v. Hyatt, 3 E. D. S. 156.
(4) Ex parte Wolf, 14 Neb. 24.
(5) Lenz v. Sherrott, 26 Mich. 139.
(6) Croll v. Village, 40 O. S. 340; Barker v. Smith, 10 S. Car. 226; Providence v. Railroad Co., 12 R. I. 473. An ordinance relating to a *special locality* is not repealed by a subsequent *general ordinance.* Garret v. James 65 Md. 250.
(7) Greely v. Jacksonville, 17 Flor. 174.

to an evident intent on the part of the council to revise the whole system of regulation of some subject of municipal control, but the intent must be plain.[1]

§ 64. **Amendments.**—A repeal by implication can be effected by the enactment of an amendment to an existing ordinance that is inconsistent with it, as well as by the passage of a new and separate ordinance. If an ordinance is expressly repealed by reference to title and date of passage any amendments which have been made fall with the main ordinance.[2] For this reason, and in order to preserve the ordinances in an orderly manner, amendments, except of a very minor character, should be avoided.

§ 65. **Summary.**—Repeals, then, may be effected in four various ways:

(1) By withdrawal by the state of the delegated power under which ordinances are passed.

(2) By the enactment by the state of a statute containing provisions clearly repugnant to those of the ordinances.

(3) By express act of the municipal legislative body.

(4) By implication from a subsequent ordinance, (a) containing provisions plainly repugnant to those of the prior ordinance; (b) covering the entire subject-matter of the prior ordinance, and in a different manner.

§ 66. **Saving clause in subsequent ordinance.**—Whenever it is not intended that the passage of an ordinance shall affect existing ordinances, a saving clause should be inserted. Even such a clause would not, however, apply to any ordinance or resolution that was in excess of the power of the municipality at the time of its enactment, so

---

(1) Burlington v. Estlow, 43 N. J. 13; Decorah v. Dunstan, 38 Ia. 96; Booth v. Carthage, 67 Ill. 103.

(2) Schwartz v. Oshkosh, 55 Wis. 490. A valid amendment of an ordinance will not fall because that *part* of the ordinance which it amends was invalid. Otherwise, if the whole of the amended ordinance was invalid. State v. Kantler, 33 Minn. 69.

as to validate it.¹ Neither will a saving clause have any retroactive effect. After the repeal of a police ordinance, the corporation can not, by a subsequent ordinance, declare that the former repeal shall not affect proceedings for the punishment of offenses against the ordinance. repealed which had already been committed. In order to diminish the effect of a repeal, the reservation must be incorporated in the repealing act.²

The repeal of a repealing ordinance does not revive the original ordinance. It must be enacted anew.³

§ 67. **Effect of a repeal on vested rights.**—No repeal of an existing ordinance can operate to destroy rights of property that have been vested by virtue of its provisions. The most that can lawfully be done is to subject those rights to any degree of police regulation that would be lawful had they arisen independently of the ordinance. No person can claim immunity from proper police regulation of his vested interests because they were based upon the privileges or under the protection of a municipal ordinance.⁴ The right of a municipal officer to the enjoyment of his office, or of his full salary, belongs to a different class of rights. If an elective officer, his salary may be reduced or his office abolished during his incumbency for good cause and upon some kind of judicial determination; but if appointive, at the pleasure of the appointing power.⁵

(1) Cairo v. Bross, 101 Ill. 476.
(2) Day v. Clinton, 6 Ill. App. 476.
(3) *Idem*.
(4) Quincy v. Bull, 106 Ill. 337; Gormley v. Day, 114 Ill. 185; Baldwin v. Smith, 82 Ill. 162; People v. Railroad Co., 18 Ill. App. 125; Railway Co. v. Railway Co., 14 Fed. Rep. 525; Mayor v. Lumpkin, 5 Ga. 447; Railroad Co. v. Burlington, 49 Ia. 144; Des Moines v. Railroad Co., 41 Ia. 569; Railroad Co. v Cape May, 35 N. J. Eq. 419; Charleston v. Church, 4 Strob. 306. *Post*, §§ 257-265, as to rights under municipal licenses.
(5) 4 Am. & Eng. Corp. Cas. 658, note; 6 Am. & Eng. Corp. Cas. 97, note; 4 Am. & Eng. Corp. Cas. 690 and 705. *Contra*, when appointive, Waterbury v. Martin, 46 Conn. 479.

Part II.

§ 68. Form of ordinances.—Too much care can not be exercised in drafting ordinances, especially police ordinances, as the omission of any material part may prove a fatal defect, and because even mere irregularities afford opportunities to question their validity. Of course, the ordinance must be in writing or print, and must be composed in the English language.[1] An ordinance of the city of New Orleans, enacted in 1830 in the French language, when French was the language of the city, the statute being silent as to the proper language to be used, was held valid.[2]

§ 69. Constituent parts.—Where an ordinance is in regular form it contains certain regular parts, viz:

(1) *The title*, generally in form like, "An ordinance to regulate" [*some subject of municipal control*].

(2) *The introduction*, in form, "Be it ordained by the council of the [city] of ———."

(3) *The definition* of the thing regulated, or of the act prohibited, and the command or direction in that regard.

(4) *The designation of the penalty* imposed for an offense against the ordinance.

(5) The direction as to the time when the ordinance shall go into operation.

§ 70. Ordinances like resolutions in form.—If no definite direction is made by the statute governing the form of the ordinance, it may be drawn in the form of a resolution. If then passed with all the formalities of a regular ordinance, it will be in effect an ordinance. The substance of an ordinance must be present, and no steps

---

(1) Breaux's Bridge *v.* Dupuis, 30 La. Ann. 1105.
(2) Loze *v.* Mayor, 2 La. 427.

omitted.[1] A mere temporary or informal *motion* can never amount to an ordinance.[2]

§ 71. The title.—The title is not a substantial part of the ordinance. It serves to direct attention to the nature of the provisions of the ordinance. Not being of the substance of the ordinance, its wording can not be taken into consideration when construing ambiguous provisions in the body of the ordinance. It in no sense controls the ordinance.[3] For the same reason, an ordinance is not affected by any slight irregularities or mistakes in the wording of the title. If the title uses the words "common council" instead of "city council," the error is immaterial.[4] Generally, the statutes, or charter, by which power is given to enact ordinances, provide that the title shall clearly express the nature of the ordinance, or that the ordinance shall cover one subject only, which shall be expressed in its title. Such provisions are intended to prevent fraud and surprise, both on the council and on those who must take notice of and obey the ordinance, and honest legislation should not be embarrassed by observance of the requirement. Any matter congruous to the main object of the ordinance may nevertheless be included.[5] The title need merely express the general subject so as to fairly give notice of the contents of the ordinance.[6] If the title reads, "An ordinance to regulate and prohibit the running at large of animals," a section may lawfully be inserted in the ordinance providing a penalty for breaking

(1) Manufacturing Co. *v.* Schell City, 21 Mo. App. 175; State *v.* Kantler, 33 Minn. 69; Sower *v.* Philadelphia, 35 Pa. St. 236; First Municipality *v.* Cutting, 4 La. Ann. 336; Tipton *v.* Norman, 72 Mo. 380; Paterson *v.* Barnet, 46 N. J. 62.

(2) Manufacturing Co. *v.* Schell City, 21 Mo. App. 175.

(3) Hershoff *v.* Beverly, 45 N. J. 288.

(4) Law *v.* People, 87 Ill. 389.

(5) St. Louis *v.* Green, 70 Mo. 562; s. c., 7 Mo. App. 468; St. Louis *v.* Tiefel, 42 Mo. 578.

(6) Barton *v.* Pittsburgh, 4 Brewst. 373; Esling's Appeal, 89 Pa. St. 205; Mauch Chunk *v.* McGee, 81 Pa. St. 434; Bergman *v.* Railway Co., 88 Mo. 678; State *v.* Cantieny, 34 Minn. 1.

open the public pounds.¹ If the title indicates that the ordinance is *regulatory* in its scope, it may in fact be prohibitory.² It has even been held in New York that a title simply reading, "An act for the relief of the village of C.," is not in violation of the constitutional requirement that the subject-matter shall be designated by the title.³

§ 72. **The introduction.**—Although it is customary and advisable to preface the body of an ordinance with words signifying that it is ordained or enacted by the proper legislative body, such as, "Be it ordained by the common council of A.," this introduction is not essential. The fact that the ordinance was regularly passed and entered on the council journal is considered a sufficient declaration that it is the formal act of the council⁴—a variance in the name of the corporation when used in the introduction is immaterial. An ordinance is valid if it appears on the face to have been enacted and passed by a municipal body having authority to make such an enactment, under the power granted.⁵

§ 73. **Ordinance need not recite authority.**—Where no reference is made in the body of an ordinance to the particular grant of power under which it is sought to be enacted, the ordinance will be valid if it is within any of the powers granted to the municipality. Whereas, if the power is recited in the ordinance and proves inadequate to support it, the ordinance can not be sustained under another power which is adequate. It is, therefore, not only unnecessary, but also unadvisable to incorporate the power into the ordinance, or to refer to it in any way.⁶

Likewise, if the right to pass an ordinance on a given

(1) Smith *v.* Emporia, 27 Kan. 528.
(2) Cantril *v.* Sainer, 59 Ia. 26.
(3) Water Commissioners *v.* Dwight, 101 N. Y. 9; In re Knaust, 101 N. Y. 188.
(4) People *v.* Lee, 112 Ill. 113, see p. 121; People *v.* Murray, 57 Mich. 396; Cape Girardeau *v.* Riley, 52 Mo. 424.
(5) Hawkins *v.* Huron, 2 U. C. C. P. 72.
(6) Church *v.* Baltimore, 6 Gill, 391; Commonwealth *v.* Fahey, 5 Cush. 408.

subject depends upon the existence of a necessity for regulation, or upon some condition precedent, the ordinance, when passed, need neither recite the existence of the necessity nor compliance with the condition precedent.[1] Compliance with conditions precedent appears, or should appear in the records of council proceedings, and the fact that the council has passed an ordinance is conclusive evidence that it considers such action necessary or advantageous.

§ 74. **Scope of the ordinance.**—In the absence of statutory restrictions there is no limit to the ground which an ordinance may be made to cover. A compilation of proposed ordinances might be passed as a single enactment.[2] Where its scope is, however, restricted to "*one subject*," only such things as are of the same nature may be contained in the same ordinance. Thus, all the offenses connected with the sale of intoxicating liquors, or in regard to the public markets, might be covered by one enactment. The ordinance will not be considered too extensive so long as the nature of each and every provision is reasonably indicated by the catch words used in the title. If any provision should be improperly included, the rest of the ordinance would not thereby be affected, unless the pertinent and impertinent provisions are in some way mutually dependent on one another. A constitutional provision that *no bill* shall contain more than two subjects is not applicable to ordinances. The term *bill* is used as the technical designation of the enactments of the state legislature.[3]

Contiguous public improvements, or improvements asked for in the same petition of the property owners, are properly provided for by a single ordinance.[4]

(1) Young v. St. Louis, 47 Mo. 492; Coates v. New York, 7 Cow. 585; Cronin v. People, 82 N. Y. 318; Bohle v. Stannard, 7 Mo. App. 51; Kiley v. Forsee, 57 Mo. 390; Rex v. Harrison, 3 Burr. 1328.
(2) Garrett v. Janes, 4 East. Rep. 609 (Md., 1886).
(3) Humboldt v. McCoy, 23 Kan. 249.
(4) State v. Hudson, 29 N. J. 104; Works v. Lockport, 28 Hun, 9; Watson v. Chicago, 115 Ill. 78; Dempsey v. Burlington, 66 Ia. 687.

§ 75. **Reference to existing ordinances.**—If it becomes necessary in the framing of an ordinance to adopt an existing ordinance *in toto*, or to incorporate some provision of an existing ordinance, it may be done by referring to the prior ordinance or section of an ordinance, without incorporating it bodily into the new enactment. Any language is sufficient that clearly indicates the ordinance referred to, either by its title and date of passage or by its date of passage alone, when only one ordinance was passed on the same day. Reference may then be had in an ordinance to any extrinsic matter of public record, to the general statutes of the state, to the corporate charter, to the system of rules and regulations adopted by a municipal board, or to the regulations adopted by the council itself for its own government.[1]

§ 76. **Time of going into effect.**—If no statutory direction is made as to the time when an ordinance shall go into operation, it will be in force from the date of its passage; that is, the expiration of the prescribed period for publication. This would be true even though the statute provides that ordinances shall take effect from the time indicated by the council, and the council fails to fix a time.[2] Although seldom necessary, it is nevertheless better to always indicate in the ordinance itself when it shall operate. By so doing all room for doubt is avoided.

§ 77. **Penalty.**—An ordinance is entirely inoperative that contains no penalty clause. After the act has been declared a misdemeanor, some provision must be made, in the same enactment, conferring jurisdiction on the municipal court and decreeing a definite penalty.[3] The magis-

(1) Moran *v.* Lindell, 52 Mo. 229; Baumgartner *v.* Hasty, 100 Ind. 575.
(2) Commonwealth *v.* Brooks, 109 Mass. 355.
(3) Bowman *v.* St. John, 43 Ill. 337.

trate has no power to fix the penalty. He can only follow the express provision of the ordinance.¹

§ 78. **Definiteness of expression.**—The terms of ordinances will not be construed so strictly as to defeat their purposes if definite enough to be understood within a reasonable certainty. Thus, if it is necessary to define certain territorial limits within which an ordinance shall operate, and the description is slightly inaccurate but clear enough to show the legislative intention, that intention will be followed.² An ordinance is sufficient which follows the words of an express power; for instance, under a power to license the sale of "small ware," an ordinance forbidding the sale of "small ware" on the streets, and not defining what constitutes "small ware" is definite enough.³ But the term of the power, or the expression used in the ordinance, must, as in the case just cited, be one that has a recognized and definite meaning. An ordinance against keeping a bawdy house in an "indecent" manner is definite, as it would be impracticable to state what is indecency in the conduct of such houses.⁴ And it is sufficiently definite to say that no one shall drive on the streets faster than at an "ordinary trot."⁵ But an ordinance that merely prohibits driving at an "immoderate" speed, is indefinite. The determination of what constitutes immoderate speed should not be left to the court, as the idea of no two men would harmonize on that point.⁶ So it is too indefinite to prohibit the driving "any drove or droves of horned cattle, except milch cows, through any of the public streets." The number of animals constituting a drove should be specified.⁷

(1) Melick v. Washington, 47 N. J. 254; State v. Zeigler, 3 Vroom, 262.
(2) Poland v. Connelly, 16 O. S. 64; Hays v. Vincennes, 82 Ind. 178; Hyde Park v. Borden, 94 Ill. 27.
(3) Harris v. Hamilton, 44 U. C. Q. B. 641.
(4) Shreveport v. Roos, 35 La. Ann. 1010.
(5) Nealis v. Hayward, 48 Ind. 19.
(6) Commonwealth v. Roy, 140 Mass. 432.
(7) McConvil v. Jersey City, 39 N. J. 38.

§ 79. **Definiteness as to penalty.**—As will be seen later on, there is some disagreement in the decided cases as to whether the penalty must be named to a certainty, or whether certain maximum limits may be set, within which the court may exercise its discretion. The better rule seems to be that it is definite enough to set limits to the amount of the fine that may lawfully be exacted, or the length of the imprisonment that may be inflicted.[1]

§ 80. **License ordinances.**—An ordinance requiring a license should specify the person to issue it, the amount to be paid, the time and manner of payment, its duration, and such other requirements as it may be deemed necessary to prescribe, for as little discretion as possible should be reposed in the ministerial agent who issues the license.[2]

§ 81. **Ordinances against nuisances.**—Under power to prevent or abate nuisances, the ordinance need not declare the thing or class of things ordained against to be nuisances.[3] The ordinance need not show on its face that its subject-matter is within the terms of the power. Thus, under power to prevent the depositing of filth in water channels, an ordinance prohibiting such deposits in a designated river need not declare that that particular river is a water channel.[4]

§ 82. **Council can not bind its successors.**—An ordinance imposing a license fee of $500 can not lawfully provide that during the time for which any license is granted under that ordinance, no other license shall be granted for the same purpose for a less amount, because a subsequent council, or the same council, might at any time amend,

---

(1) *Post*, §§ 150, 151, McConvil *v.* Jersey City, 39 N. J. 38; Railroad Co. *v.* Deacon, 63 Ill. 91.
(2) Buell *v.* Quincy, 9 Ill. App. 127; Darling *v.* St. Paul, 19 Minn. 388. *Post*, § 263; *ante*, § 13.
(3) Carthage *v.* Buckner, 4 Ill. App. 317.
(4) Ogdensburg *v.* Lyon, 7 Lans. 215.

repeal, or supplant that ordinance and make new provisions. The council can not bind or hamper the free exercise of the powers vested in it by any such device.[1]

(1) Williams *v.* West Point, 68 Ga. 816.

CHAPTER VI.

RULES OF VALIDITY.

§ 83 Introduction.
§ 84. United States laws.
§ 85. Regulation of commerce.
§ 86. United States mails.
§ 87. United States license laws.
§ 88. Consistency with the laws of the state.
§ 89 Main conflict as to minor offenses.
§ 90. The punishment may be greater.
§ 91. Prosecution under either law no bar to proceedings under the other.
§ 92. Alabama.
§ 93. Colorado.
§ 94. Connecticut.
§ 95. Dakota.
§ 96. Florida.
§ 97. Georgia.
§ 98. Illinois.
§ 99. Indiana.
§ 100. Iowa.
§ 101. Kansas.
§ 102. Kentucky.
§ 103. Louisiana.
§ 104. Maryland.
§ 105. Massachusetts.
§ 106. Michigan.
§ 107. Minnesota.
§ 108. Missouri.
§ 109. Nebraska.
§ 110. North Carolina.
§ 111. New Jersey.
§ 112. New York.
§ 113. Ohio.
§ 114. Oregon.
§ 115. Rhode Island.
§ 116. South Carolina.
§ 117. Tennessee.
§ 118. Texas.
§ 119. Utah.

§ 120. United States holdings.
§ 121. Conflict with state license laws.
§ 122. Policy of state legislation must be sustained.
§ 123. What is the law of the land.
§ 124. Power derived from former sovereignties.
§ 125. Must be consistent with corporate charter.
§ 126. Other requisites of validity.
§ 127. Reasonableness.
§ 128. When discretion of council final.
§ 129. When not final.
§ 130. Examples of reasonable ordinances.
§ 131. Examples of unreasonable ordinances.
§ 132. Restraint of trade.
§ 133. What is a restraint of trade.
§ 134. What is not a restraint of trade.
§ 135. Discrimination.
§ 136. Examples of discrimination.
§ 137. Discrimination as to non-residents.
§ 138. Once void, always void.
§ 139. Partial invalidity.

§ 83. **Introduction.**—In earlier days, before the enactment of municipal governments were often attacked, courts were not aided by any very definite rules to be followed in determining the validity or invalidity of ordinances. It was said in a very general way that ordinances or by-laws must be *fide, legii et rationalii*, that they must be lawful and reasonable and enacted in good faith, but beyond this courts were left to their own judgment. Now these general expressions mean but little unless their scope is more accurately defined, and in the light of modern decisions many distinct, well settled rules may be formulated, which courts will follow in considering any point raised to invalidate an ordinance.

§ 84. **United States laws.**—The supreme law of the land, as embodied in the federal constitution and in the statutes of congress, is the ultimate test to which all inferior legislation, whether state or municipal, is subjected, and any ordinance is void that violates its provisions or infringes upon its guaranties.[1] The general law of the land

(1) Haywood v. Mayor, 12 Ga. 404.

§ 84.] RULES OF VALIDITY. 71

is not subject to exclusion or alteration by the exercise of powers of local legislation.¹

The constitutional safeguard that no man shall be deprived of his life, liberty, or property, except by due process of law, is as binding on the exercise of municipal powers as upon state legislation. Although the nature of local regulation is such that more summary remedies and more rapid procedure must be resorted to to make it effective than are lawful or customary in the enforcement of those laws which are operative throughout the whole state, still the constitution must be observed with equal strictness. Local courts acquire no exemptions or privileges by reason of their inferiority. In every proceeding which may result in depriving the individual of his personal liberty, the right of trial by jury can not be denied. It is held, however, that imprisonment, when resorted to merely to enforce the payment of a previously adjudged fine, is not such imprisonment as entitles to a jury trial.² A jury trial can not be demanded when the only direct penalty is a pecuniary fine.³ The judicial determination by the court is considered due process of law. Many restrictions attempted to be placed on personal liberty have been held void as contrary to common right, and beyond the legitimate scope of police regulation. Except in extreme cases the law presumes that the intentions of all men are lawful and it should never base a punishment upon a mere supposition that a person intends to violate the law. Thus "the knowingly associating with persons having the reputation of being thieves and prostitutes" can not be made an offense against the community.⁴ So, an ordinance is void which prohibits females from attending or waiting in a dance-cellar, bar-room, or place where liquors are sold, and from being present in such places in any capacity between six o'clock in the evening and six in the morning, because it precludes a woman from

(1) Williams v. Davidson, 43 Tex. 1. See page 34.
(2) *Post*, §§ 155, 181.
(3) Low v. Commissioners R. M. Charlt. 316.
(4) St. Louis v. Fitz, 53 Mo. 582; nor walking with prostitutes, Cady v. Barnesville, 4 Ohio Law Bull. 101.

a lawful business.¹ Any thing in itself immoral, as visiting such place in licentious costumes, or dancing in a public dance hall where liquors are sold, or perhaps even serving as waiters in saloons, might well be prohibited. But a woman could lawfully act as cashier, musician, door tender, or proprietress of such a place. Discrimination between the sexes is lawful and commendable in such vocations as would bring them into contact under circumstances peculiarly advantageous to immoral practices. It is contrary to common right to ordain a penalty against the renting of houses to lewd women, without regard to the uses to which they are intended to be put, because lewd women have just as much right to occupy habitations as virtuous women, so long as they do not use them for unlawful purposes.² It would be equally unjust, even under the broadest power, to impose a penalty upon any person bearing the reputation of being a prostitute who should be found within the city limits.³

It is contrary to the fourteenth amendment to ordain that the hair of every convict shall be shorn, without exempting from the operation of the ordinance, or at least omitting to enforce it against all whose natural or artificial growth of hair is held sacred by them.⁴

Laws of police may, and often do, disturb personal rights of property by imposing restrictions and conditions upon the right to own certain kinds of property the vicinity or mode of uses of which would be dangerous to health or security, and without providing for compensation. All property rights are subject to such regulation, but the regulation must not amount to total deprivation. For instance, it is lawful, under power, to license the ownership of dogs, but not to absolutely prohibit their being kept.⁵

(1) In re Maguire, 57 Cal. 604.
(2) Milliken *v.* Weatherford, 54 Tex. 388.
(3) Buell *v.* State, 45 Ark. 336.
(4) Ah Kow *v.* Nunan, 5 Sawyer, 552.
(5) Washington *v.* Meigs, 1 McArthur, 53; Hill *v.* Thompson, 48 N.

Distress can not be resorted to to collect fines.[1] Nor may any form of forfeiture of property be exercised, unless after due notice to the offender and allowing him an opportunity to be heard. Ordinances are void which tend to deprive a person of his property, or to create a charge against it, preliminary to, or which may be made the basis of, taking it without a provision affording the owner due notice of the pendency of proceedings.[2]

§ 85. **Regulation of commerce not permitted.**—It frequently becomes a serious question whether ordinances passed to regulate some matter of local importance do not conflict with the provision of the constitution which prohibits the states from regulating inter-state or foreign commerce. Any ordinance which directly aims at regulating commerce is plainly void, but a large class of police measures which are necessary to secure the protection, convenience, and health of cities located on state boundaries, indirectly affect commerce, without for that reason being void, or exceeding the competency of the state government.[3]

It is just that the citizens of a community should be protected against frauds practiced upon them by dealers who represent foreign mercantile houses, and who are in a measure beyond the control of local authority; hence it is lawful to demand the payment of a license fee from non-resident traders who vend foreign products,[4] and to regulate the business done by foreign insurance companies.[5] Nor is the imposition of a tax on all goods of foreign production, sold on commission by any person in the city, levying a duty or impost within the meaning of the con-

Y. Sup. Ct. 481. See Water-works *v.* Bartlett, 8 Sawyer, 555; s. c., 16 Fed. Rep. 615; In re Yick Woo, 68 Cal. 294.

(1) Cumming *v.* Savannah, R. M. Charlt. 26.
(2) Brown *v.* Denver, 7 Col. 305.
(3) St. Louis *v.* Boffinger, 19 Mo. 13.
(4) Sears *v.* Commissioners, 36 Ind. 267, In re Randolph, 6 Sawyer, 295.
(5) People *v.* Thurber, 13 Ill. 554.

stitutional prohibition.¹ Such an ordinance might, however, be held void as unjustly discriminating between foreigners and citizens of the municipality, and the charge, as a tax, would have to be expressly authorized by the state.

Cities located on the seaboard or on navigable waters generally have power to regulate the public wharves, and, as a means of regulation, wharfage dues are frequently imposed upon the vessels that use them. The corporation is under expense to maintain and police its wharves, and it is right that it should be treated in this respect as a private individual, warranted in demanding a reasonable indemnity for the use of its property; hence it is held that the levy of a reasonable wharfage fee on all packages handled over the public wharves does not constitute a regulation of commerce.²

A license fee on a ferry running from the city of Detroit across the Detroit river to the Canadian shore is lawful, and if reasonable in amount, is neither a tax nor a regulation of commerce.³ While an ordinance taxing every person running *tow-boats* from New Orleans to the Gulf of Mexico has been held void.⁴

Power to build an aqueduct and to furnish the city with water does not authorize any obstruction of a navigable river.⁵

In order to protect the health and for the convenience of the citizens, it is lawful to declare the smoke from tugs and vessels using the navigable water adjacent to a city a nuisance, and to prescribe a penalty for failure to abate the same. It is only the effect of the use of the vessels on the

(1) Cumming v. Savannah, R. M. Charlt. 26.
(2) Worsley v. New Orleans, 9 La. 324; First Municipality v. Pease, 2 La. Ann. 538; Ellerman v. McMains, 30 La. Ann. 190; Packet Co. v. Keokuk, 95 U. S. 80; Packet Co. v. St. Louis, 100 U. S. 423; Vicksburg v. Tobin, 100 U. S. 430; Packet Co. v. Catlettsburg, 105 U. S. 559; Leathers v. Aiken, 9 Fed. Rep. 679.
(3) Chilvers v. People, 11 Mich. 43.
(4) Moran v. New Orleans, 112 U. S. 69.
(5) Bell v. Quebec, 2 Quebec, 305.

convenience of the community, and not their relations to commerce that is sought to be regulated.[1]

§ 86. **United States mails.**—An ordinance which limits the speed of all vehicles using the streets, and which applies to carriers of the the government mail, is not void as being against the federal statute punishing willful stoppage of the mails.[2]

§ 87. **United States licenses.**—The fact that a certain trade or business is specially licensed by the United States does not prevent a corporation, under power from the state, from imposing additional restrictions, even to total prohibition. The licensing of lotteries under the federal law does not override the power of the state over lotteries, whether directly exercised or by delegation to municipal corporations.[3]

§ 88. **Must be consistent with the laws of the state.** According to the American theory of municipal existence, the legislation permitted to be exercised by municipal corporations is a mere delegation of the power of the state, and the ordinances enacted by virtue of this delegated authority are as much a part of the general scheme of legislation as are the laws of the state. It is therefore necessary that they should be consistent with the state laws. If the state legislature enacts a law whereby some act is forbidden, which under a prior law was expressly permitted, the courts hold that the subsequent law, as the latest expression of the legislative will, repeals the former law by implication; but municipalities have no power to repeal, directly or indirectly, the laws of the state, and their legislation must accord with the policy of the legislation of the state. If the only measure of authority were the terms

(1) Harman v. Chicago, 110 Ill. 400.
(2) United States v. Hart, Pet. C. C. 390; s. c., 3 Wheeler's Criminal Cases, 304.
(3) Cohens v. Virginia, 6 Wheat. 264.

of the charter, there would often be ordinances plainly within the granted power, but irreconcilable with some state law, or contrary to the settled policy of the state, a result neither lawful nor intended. Some charters, by express language, restrict the ordinances that may be passed to such as are consistent with the laws of the state. Others are silent upon the subject, but the restriction exists, whether expressed or not, and becomes very important in its application.

§ 89. **Main conflict as to minor offenses.**—The class of general legislation with which ordinances are most apt to come in conflict is that which declares certain acts or occupations either absolutely unlawful or lawful under certain restrictions. The police powers conferred upon municipalities cover the same class of acts governed by the state laws, and their execution must be effected in the same manner, by penalties. As a general rule, it is evident that ordinances are void whenever contrary to the laws of the state.[1] The difficulty lies in determining the meaning of the phrase, "contrary to the laws of the state." An ordinance that is expressly authorized by the charter or organic statute is not void because it differs from the state law on the same subject. The express grant of power to the municipality is considered to be an expression of the legislative intent to supersede the state law already existing within the limits of the corporation.[2] Or, it is expressive of an intent to punish the same act by additional penalties when committed within certain territorial limits. But when no additional power of legislation is expressly conferred, it is doubtful whether the municipality may, by its ordinances, inflict additional penalties to those already prescribed by the state, or whether it may legislate at all upon matters covered by the general statutes. A wrongful act is, wherever committed, an injury to the public good, and contrary

(1) Sedgwick on Stat. Law, p. 469; New Orleans v. Phillipi, 9 La. Ann. 44; Siloam Springs v. Thompson, 41 Ark. 461; Haywood v. Mayor, 12 Ga. 404.
(2) Huffsmith v. People, 8 Col. 175.

to the peace and dignity of the state. But the very foundation for the necessity of municipal government is the idea that the needs of certain localities, by reason of density of population, or other circumstances, are more extensive and urgent than those of the general public in the same particulars. The obstruction of the public highways, for example, is wrong, but a certain obstruction on a road little traveled would be of very slight inconvenience to the public as compared with the inconvenience of the same obstruction maintained in one of the thoroughfares of a large city, and the necessity of preventing and removing all obstructions to travel would be a hundred-fold more urgent in the city. It would be a greater obstruction. So, loud and noisy conduct on the streets of a city constitutes a much more aggravated offense than would the same degree of disorderly behavior in a sparsely-populated rural district. The public peace and good order are disturbed in each case, but, in the one case, the necessity for a speedy and effective remedy, and the actual inconvenience and annoyance, is much greater. Some acts would be entirely innocent in one locality and decidedly reprehensible in another. In this sense, then, it may be truly said that the same act may be a wrong to the public at large and an additional wrong to the community where committed. It would be an offense against the dignity of the state, and also an offense against the good order of the municipality. The act is single, its effect double; and for each effect there may properly, and without working injustice to the rights of the offender, be a separate remedy or penalty. The offense is *per se* contrary to the good order of the state, and therefore a certain punishment is prescribed for it wherever committed; but the offense, if committed within the limits of a populous town or city, may work much greater injury to the local peace and good order, and it is proper that the town or city should have its remedy and a separate right to punish for the special and additional wrong done to it. Perhaps on no subject connected with municipal corporations is there greater diversity of authority than upon the extent to which ordinances may lawfully trespass upon the territory covered by the laws of the state. Courts are rightfully jealous of the rights of the person, and are loth to hold that one and the same act may render a person twice liable, unless, in the particular case, considerations of public good are plainly superior to the individual rights; but, on principle, the law of the state is best upheld and subserved by permitting municipal corporations to exercise separate and distinct jurisdiction over offenses of a minor character, for which the offender is already amenable to the state. It is useless to attempt to reconcile the numerous decisions, but a careful consideration of the more recent holdings leads one to the belief that their tendency is to sustain the concurrent jurisdiction of state and municipality under their respective laws, and their varying punishments for the same offense. Especially is this so in the states whose courts have had frequent occasion to consider the question.[1]

§ 90. **The punishment may be greater.**—In those states where this double legislation is allowed, difficult questions of practice arise. It is doubted whether the municipality may prescribe heavier penalties than the state law for the same offense. The safer course is to restrict the amount of the fine, or the length of the imprisonment, to the limit set by the state law; but where the offense is specially obnoxious to the municipality, the state limit is seldom adequate, and, if local regulation is to be allowed at all, it should be made effective and the punishment proportionate to the offense. Here, again, the states are not in harmony.

§ 91. **Prosecution under either no bar to proceedings under the other.**—It is inconsistent with the theory of double penalties to hold that a prosecution under either the statute or ordinance is a bar to proceedings under the other. It seems to be the better opinion that either remedy

---

(1) Bish. Cr. Law, § 897a; Bish. Stat. Cr., §§ 23, 25; Cooley Const. Lim. 199.

may be pursued without barring or affecting the right of recourse to the other.

§ 92. **Alabama.**—In Alabama ordinances may cover the same ground as the state law.[1] It is held that an ordinance punishing assault and battery does not in any way interfere with the punishment prescribed by the law of the state, and may be enforced.[2]

§ 93. **Colorado.**—The Colorado courts hold the same act may be considered as a double offense, against the state and against the municipality,[3] and where the ordinance is authorized, but no limit set to the penalty, the penalty may be made greater than that prescribed by the state law;[4] and an exclusive grant of power to the municipality repeals the state law within the municipal limits as soon as the power has been followed by the enactment of an ordinance.[5]

§ 94. **Connecticut.**—There is one decision in this state which tends to the doctrine that additional local regulation is not permissible. The town of Southport had express charter power to prohibit the taking of oysters in the adjacent waters. The state afterward passed a statute covering the subject, and it was held to abrogate the power given by the charter, and to prevent the enforcement of the ordinance.[6]

§ 95. **Dakota.**—The powers granted to municipalities are superadded to those exercised by the state through its laws, and both the general law and the ordinance are enforceable.[7]

(1) Mobile v. Rouse, 8 Ala. 515.
(2) Mayor v. Allaire, 14 Ala. 400.
(3) Hughes v. People, 8 Col. 536.
(4) Dietz v. Central, 1 Col. 323.
(5) Huffsmith v. People, 8 Col. 175.
(6) Southport v. Ogden, 23 Conn. 128.
(7) Elkpoint v. Vaughn, 1 Dak. 108.

§ 96. **Florida.**—The conservative doctrine seems to prevail in Florida, and it is held that taxes are illegal, if levied to assist in prosecuting offenses under the ordinances which are also offenses under the state law.[1]

§ 97. **Georgia.**—All the earlier cases in this state adhere to the rule that acts can not be punished by both state and city, and that the state law alone may be enforced.[2] But the latest expression from their supreme court leans the other way, but holding that a conviction under either bars proceedings under the other. "The state may deal only with the central element of a transaction which is fringed around with adjuncts that ought to be prohibited by ordinance, as highly mischievous to the quiet of municipal society."[3]

§ 98. **Illinois.**—The courts of Illinois have had numerous occasions to deal with these questions, but their holdings are far from harmonious. The first decision was that authority given to a city to pass ordinances declaring the sale of intoxicating liquors a nuisance does not supplant any of the provisions of the state law *regulating the sale*.[4] This was followed by decisions to the effect that the amount of the fine or the severity of the punishment prescribed by ordinance need not be limited to that imposed by the state law, unless the corporation is restricted in that respect by the express terms of the charter.[5] Then it was held that the remedies were plainly concurrent, unless the municipal power is made exclusive by the grant, and that punishment under either is a bar to the other.[6] But later,

(1) Murphy v. Jacksonville, 18 Flor. 318.
(2) Mayor v. Hussey, 21 Ga. 80; Adams v. Albany, 29 Ga. 56; Rothschild v. Darien, 68 Ga. 503; Jenkins v. Thomasville, 35 Ga. 145; Reich v. State, 53 Ga. 73; Vason v. Augusta, 38 Ga. 542.
(3) McRea v. Americus, 59 Ga. 168.
(4) Gardner v. People, 20 Ill. 430; Kimball v. People, 20 Ill. 349.
(5) Petersburg v. Metzger, 21 Ill. 205; Pekin v. Smelzel, 21 Ill. 464; also, Amboy v. Sleeper, 31 Ill. 499; Baldwin v. Murphy, 82 Ill. 486.
(6) Berry v. People, 36 Ill. 423.

the court refused to consider whether the remedies are concurrent.[1] For a time the court seemed to favor the theory that an express authorization to exact ordinances upon some subject regulated by the statutes supersedes the state law *pro tanto*, and that it can not be enforced within the corporate limits.[2] Although it was declared that that principle is to be applied with extreme caution.[3] When the question next arose, the court reviewed all the decisions, and adopted what may now be considered settled law in that state. It held that the same act may constitute a double offense, each punishable by itself, and that a conviction under either law would be no bar to a conviction under the other, for the accused would not be twice in jeopardy for *one offense*, but only once in jeopardy for each offense.[4] Still, the court soon took occasion to avoid the question, in a case where the ordinance prescribed a smaller fine than the state law. It held that the statute is paramount; that its full punishment must obtain, and that a conviction under the ordinance was no bar, because its penalty was inferior in degree.[5]

§ 99. **Indiana.**—The earlier holdings are against the right to enact ordinances punishing acts that are already misdemeanors against the state.[6] But the later decisions have gone to the other extreme, and are uniform in holding, not only that such ordinances may be passed, but that a conviction under both the law and the ordinances is permissible.[7] As the court says in Waldo *v.* Wallace, 12 Ind. 584: "The powers which are exercised by a city govern-

(1) Fant *v.* People, 45 Ill. 258.
(2) Westgate *v.* Carr, 43 Ill. 450; Woodward *v.* Turnbull, 41 Ill. 1.
(3) Seebold *v.* People, 86 Ill. 33.
(4) Wragg *v.* Penn Township 94 Ill. 11.
(5) Robbins *v.* People, 95 Ill. 175.
(6) Madison *v.* Hatcher, 8 Blackf. 341; Indianapolis *v.* Blythe, 2 Ind. 75.
(7) Bogart *v.* New Albany, 1 Ind. 38; Indianapolis *v.* Fairchild, 1 Ind. 315; Ambrose *v.* State, 6 Ind. 351; Waldo *v.* Wallace, 12 Ind. 582; Levy *v* State, 6 Ind. 281; Williams *v.* Warsaw, 60 Ind. 457.

ment are, it thus appears, superadded to those exercised by the state in the same locality. The people of towns and cities are governed that much more than are the people of the state generally. This is deemed a necessary incident to a dense population."

§ 100. **Iowa.**—Unless *specially* authorized, corporations in Iowa can not punish acts that are made penal by the state law.[1] But when authorized, the two enactments subsist together, and are both enforceable.[2]

§ 101. **Kansas.**—An ordinance passed under express power repeals the state law as to the limits of the corporation, if plainly irreconcilable with it.[3] The jurisdiction over double offenses is considered concurrent, the first court that gains jurisdiction retaining it till final judgment, to the exclusion of the other.[4]

§ 102. **Kentucky.**—The enactment of an ordinance does not supersede the state law on the same subject. Either law may be enforced, but conviction under one bars proceedings under the other.[5]

§ 103. **Louisiana.**—Corporations can not, under general powers, punish acts that are misdemeanors under the statutes.[6] And in case of express power, they are limited to the amount of the fine imposed by the statute.[7] A license by a corporation to do an act which is unlawful under the state law can not be used to defeat a prosecution under the state law, but might be considered by the court in mitigation of the penalty.[8]

(1) Foster v. Brown, 55 Ia. 686; Burlington v. Kellar, 18 Ia. 65.
(2) Bloomfield v. Trimble, 54 Ia. 399.
(3) State v. Young, 17 Kan. 414.
(4) Rice v. Kansas, 3 Kan. 141.
(5) March v. Commonwealth, 12 B. Mon. 25.
(6) New Orleans v. Miller, 7 La. Ann. 651.
(7) State v. Chase, 33 La. An. 287.
(8) State v. Caldwell, 3 La Ann. 435.

§ 104. **Maryland.**—In Maryland it is held that the power exercised under ordinances by the mayor of a corporation is a part of the police power of the state, in contradistinction from the regular judicial power, and its exercise does not extinguish the liability for an offense committed against the peace and dignity of the state.[1]

§ 105. **Massachusetts.**—Municipalities may, within express powers, impose additional regulations upon trades, occupations, and other things regulated by statute and not of a criminal nature. Thus, the statute allows bay-windows to project one foot only from the side of buildings, but by ordinance it may be unlawful to allow them to project at all.[2] An ordinance on a subject covered by a criminal statute is void.[3]

§ 106. **Michigan.**—It seems that in Michigan no ordinance that is directed against an act prohibited by state law can be valid unless expressly authorized;[4] and when authorized the ordinance in no way supersedes the statute.[5]

§ 107. **Minnesota.**—The policy of Minnesota is as far advanced in the doctrine of double control as that of any other state. Ordinances may be enacted against the public commission of any crime or misdemeanor as tending to a breach of the peace.[6] The ordinance does not repeal or supersede the statute,[7] nor the common law.[8] Whatever offends against the ordinance also offends against the statute. The offenses are distinct in their legal character, both as to the jurisdiction offended against and as to the nature and quality of the offense. A conviction of either offense

(1) Shafer v. Mumma, 17 Md. 331.
(2) Commonwealth v. Goodnow, 117 Mass. 114.
(3) Commonwealth v. Turner, 1 Cush. 493.
(4) Fennell v. Bay City, 36 Mich. 186.
(5) Wayne County v. Detroit, 17 Mich. 399.
(6) State v. Bruckhauser, 26 Minn. 301.
(7) State v. Oleson, 26 Minn. 507; State v. Lee, 27 Minn. 445.
(8) State v. Crummey, 17 Minn. 72.

is no bar to the punishment of the other,[1] nor is it a valid objection that the penalty prescribed by the ordinance is either different from or greater than that attached to the offense against the state.[2]

§ 108. **Missouri.**—Indictable offenses can not be further punished by ordinance under general powers of police,[3] nor under any "general welfare" clause.[4] But under power to pass ordinances regulating any special subject of municipal concern any act may be made a double offense, and offenders are subject to prosecution under both laws.[5] The better rule seems to be that a prosecution under either does not act as a bar.[6] If the power given is expressly exclusive, or incompatible to the state law, the latter is thereby *pro tanto* superseded; otherwise the exercise of the municipal power does not interfere with the operation of the state law.[7]

§ 109. **Nebraska.**—The only decision is a general one that ordinances may be directed against acts that are already subject to penalties under state laws.[8]

§ 110. **North Carolina** courts hold that the power to enact ordinances is subordinate to the state law on the same subjects, and that additional burdens imposed by ordinances are unlawful.[9] But *quaere*, as to whether the legislature might not expressly authorize a corporation to enact additional penalties for the same act.[10]

(1) State v. Lee, 27 Minn. 445.
(2) State v. Ludwig, 21 Minn. 202.
(3) Jefferson v. Courtmire, 9 Mo. 683.
(4) Ex parte Bourgeois, 66 Mo. 663.
(5) St. Louis v. Cafferata, 24 Mo. 94; St. Louis v. Bentz, 11 Mo. 61; Ex parte Kiburg, 10 Mo. App. 442; State v. Clarke, 54 Mo. 17; Linneus v. Duskey, 19 Mo. App. 20.
(6) St. Louis v. Cafferata, 24 Mo. 94. *Contra*, State v. Cowan, 29 Mo. 330.
(7) Baldwin v. Green, 10 Mo. 410; State v. Binder, 38 Mo. 451. As to exclusive power of city of Liberty, see State v. Gordon, 60 Mo. 383.
(8) Braunville v. Cook, 4 Neb. 101.
(9) Washington v. Hammond, 76 N. C. 33; State v. Langston, 88 N. C. 692; State v. Brittain, 89 N. C. 574; **State** v. Keith, 94 N. C. 933.
(10) State v. Brittain, 89 N. C. 574.

§ 111. **New Jersey.**—An early case holds that the passage of an ordinance in no way abrogates a similar statute, but doubt was expressed as to whether an offender, who had been punished under the state law, would be liable to a subsequent proceeding under the ordinance.[1] As to property rights, a grant of power to a municipality, inconsistent with some statute, operates to repeal the statute by implication within the corporate limits.[2]

§ 112. **New York.**—The fact that the state law regulates certain things done does not prevent the corporation from making further regulations if covered by its powers.[3] It matters not that the same act is covered by a general statute.[4] The ordinance is not restricted in the amount of the fine, or severity of the punishment, by the limit of the statute.[5] And a conviction under the ordinance is no bar to a subsequent prosecution by the state.[6]

§ 113. **Ohio.**—An ordinance covering the same ground as a state law, and not inconsistent with it, is valid, but a fine under the one is a bar to proceedings under the other.[7]

§ 114. **Oregon** is also among the most advanced states. Its supreme court holds that the same act may constitute two separate offenses, and that a conviction under either ordinance or statute is no bar to prosecution under the other.[8]

§ 115. In **Rhode Island** the statutes expressly prohibit

(1) State v. Plunkett, 18 N. J. L. 5.
(2) State v. Clarke, 25 N. J. L. 54; State v. Douglass, 33 N. J. L. 363; State v. Mills, 34 N. J. L. 180.
(3) Rogers v. Jones, 1 Wend. 261; Mayor v. Hyatt, 3 E. D. S. 167.
(4) Polinsky v. People, 11 Hun, 390; Brooklyn v. Toynbee, 31 Barb. 282.
(5) Wood v. Brooklyn, 14 Barb. 425. *Contra,* Mayor v. Nichols, 4 Hill, 209.
(6) People v. Stevens, 13 Wend. 341.
(7) Wightman v. State, 10 Ohio, 452.
(8) State v. Sly, 4 Oreg. 277; State v. Bergman, 6 Oreg. 341.

the passage of any ordinance directed against acts that are already punishable under the state law.[1]

§ 116. **South Carolina.**—The courts of South Carolina held at first that an ordinance is void that prescribes a penalty for an act already covered by the state law,[2] but that holding was overruled later, and the policy of the state law is now pretty well settled that it is lawful for ordinances to cover the same ground.[3] Among other grounds for adopting that policy is the ingenious argument that because the same act frequently comes within the prohibition of two different statutes, it is equally proper that it should be covered by an ordinance and a statute, ordinances as well as statutes being enacted by legislative authority.[4]

§ 117. **Tennessee,** too, held at first to the strict rule,[5] but it was subsequently declared that offenses are aggravated when committed within the limits of a thickly settled community; that the additional offense to the corporation should be punished, and that ordinances may, therefore, be lawfully enacted against acts punishable by the state. And conviction under either law is no bar.[6]

§ 118. **Texas.**—The theory of double offenses and entirely separate remedies is adopted in Texas by the only decision on the point.[7]

§ 119. The **Utah** court says that it sees no reason why there may not be a statute and an ordinance covering the same act and both enforceable;[8] still, an ordinance against

(1) Baxter's Petition, 12 R. I. 13; State *v.* Pollard, 6 R. I. 290.
(2) Schroder *v.* Charleston, 3 Brev. 533.
(3) Heise *v.* Columbia, 6 Rich. 404.
(4) State *v.* Williams, 11 S. C. 288.
(5) Raleigh *v.* Dougherty, 3 Humph. 11.
(6) Greenwood *v.* State, 6 Baxt. 567; State *v.* Shelby, 16 Lea, 240.
(7) Hamilton *v.* State, 3 Tex. App. 643.
(8) Ex parte Douglass, 1 Utah, 108.

assault and battery was soon thereafter declared void as trespassing upon the state law.[1]

§ 120. United States.—The general doctrine of the federal courts is well expressed by Justice Greer in the following language:

"Every citizen of the United States is also a citizen of a state or territory. He may be said to owe allegiance to two sovereigns, and may be liable to punishment for an infraction of the laws of both. That either or both may, if they see fit, punish such an offender, can not be doubted. Yet it can not be truly averred that the offender has been twice punished for the same offense, but only that *by one act* he has committed *two offenses*, for each of which he is justly punishable. He could not plead the punishment by one in bar to a conviction by the other."[2] And this doctrine is fully adhered to when the apparent conflict is between statutes of a state and municipal ordinances.[3]

It would be much better if the various state tribunals were more harmonious in their views upon this much disputed question, but their tendency and the burden of their authority are certainly in favor of the adoption of the broader rule.

§ 121. **Conflict with state license laws.**—Statutes and ordinances come into further conflict in regard to acts which are permitted by the state law under certain restrictions, and either prohibited by the ordinance, or permitted under additional restrictions to those imposed by the state. The true test to be applied in such cases is based upon the nature of the authority for the passage of the ordinance. When the state law allows a certain traffic to be carried on under a license, a municipality can not impose an additional license under its general welfare or police power, even though the imposition of a local license

(1) People v. Brown, 2 Utah, 462.
(2) Moore v. People, 14 How. 13.
(3) McLaughlin v. Stephens, 2 Cranch C. C. 148; United States v. Holly, 3 Cranch C. C. 656.

would be entirely free from objection, were there no state law on the subject.[1] When the state law is silent the corporation may safely exercise any regulation within the legitimate scope of its power.[2] If the corporation has express power to license, the grant is considered additional to the power of regulation exercised by the state, and the local license is lawful and limited in amount only by the terms of the power.[3] The court of Georgia seems to be alone in considering the state license to vest such property rights in the licensee, that municipal ordinances, though enacted under express power subsequently granted to the corporation, can not be enforced as to those who have procured the state license.[4] A somewhat similar holding was made by the Illinois court, which decided in a late case that a license taken out under an ordinance would exempt the licensee from an additional fee imposed by a subsequent statute.[5] These decisions do not mean, however, that both laws could not be enforced against a person who engages in the traffic after both laws have gone into effect. The ordinance may go farther than the statute when the power is plain. So, under power "to license, regulate, and prohibit peddlers," a corporation may require a license from *all* peddlers, even though a statute of the state exempts those peddlers from any license tax, who vend the products of the state.[6] But, unless the power is plain, an ordinance can not require inspection when the statute allows the sale of a certain commodity without inspection.[7] Such permis-

(1) Grills *v.* Jonesboro, 8 Bax. 247; Robinson *v.* Franklin, 1 Humph. 156; Savannah *v.* Charlton, 36 Ga. 460.
(2) Burlington *v.* Kellar, 18 Ia. 59.
(3) Deitz *v.* Central, 1 Col. 323; Fuller *v.* State, 48 Ala. 291; West *v.* Greenville, 39 Ala. 69; Greensboro *v.* Mullins, 13 Ala. 341; Ex parte Siebenhauer, 14 Nev. 365; Simpson *v.* Savage, 1 Mo. 359; Dill. Mun. Corp., § 86; New Orleans *v.* Savings Bank, 31 La. Ann. 637.
(4) Chastain *v.* Calhoun, 29 Ga. 333; Hill *v.* Atlanta, 54 Ga. 645; Baldwin County *v.* Retailers, 42 Ga. 325.
(5) Swarth *v.* People, 109 Ill. 621.
(6) Ex parte Ah Toy, 57 Cal. 92.
(7) New York *v.* Nichols, 4 Hill, 209.

sion must, however, be express, and can not be implied from the silence of the state law.

The existence or exercise of express power by the municipality does not impair the power of the state over the same subject nor excuse any one from strict compliance with the state law.[1] Permission from the corporation is no defense against the statute.[2] The application of this rule must be restricted to cases where the ordinance and statutory provisions are concurrent in their nature, and not directly inconsistent with each other. Thus, when the statute expressly permits liquor to be sold or drank *anywhere*, an ordinance restricting its consumption to the place where sold would be inconsistent and void.[3] Under express authority the corporation could even prohibit that which the state law permits under restriction.[4] The grant of power to the municipality of a nature inconsistent with the existing state law will, if express, be considered as the latest expression of the legislative mind and supersedes the state law. If the privilege of granting licenses is made *exclusive* in the corporation, no state license need be procured,[5] and this, too, even though the corporation does not see fit to exercise its power.[6] This theory is certainly most consistent with the principle of local regulation, and yet it has been held that the grant of a license by a corporation, under exclusive power to grant or withhold licenses, is not interfered with by the imposition of an additional burden by a state law.[7]

If the state law absolutely prohibits, the corporation may not permit under license.[8]

(1) Henback v. State, 53 Ala. 523; Davis v. State, 2 Stew. & Port. 83 Minturne v. Larue, 23 How. 435; Dill. Mun. Corp., § 86.
(2) Davis v. State, 2 Stew. & Port. 83
(3) Adams v. Albany, 29 Ga. 57.
(4) Mayo v. James, 12 Gratt 17.
(5) Bennett v. People, 30 Ill. 389.
(6) Coulterville v. Gillen, 72 Ill. 599.
(7) Benefield v. Hines, 13 La. Ann. 420; Louisville v. McKean, 18 B. Mon. 10.
(8) Foster v. Brown, 55 Iowa, 686.

§ 122 Policy of state legislation must be sustained.—
In order that municipal ordinances may be perfectly consistent with the law of the state, the construction placed upon the wording of the charter or organic law must accord with the declared policy of the state legislation. When, for example, the qualifications of voters are prescribed by the general law, the municipality can not add to those qualifications by ordinance.[1] If the state constitution declare that only *ad valorem* taxes shall be levied, and power is given to the corporation to tax "all sales of horses made by drovers," a tax of one dollar for each horse sold is void because not *ad valorem*.[2] So, when the state law guarantees freedom of religious opinion to all citizens, it would be unlawful to enact an ordinance requiring shops to be closed on Sunday, without excepting from its operation persons who observe some other day of the week;[3] and an ordinance is void which discriminates in effect against persons of color.[4]

With regard to ordinances of a punitive nature, it must be observed that the corporation is restricted in their passage to any definition of the thing or act ordained against that is found in the statutes. For example, the state law makes gaming an offense and *defines* it. The ordinance must be directed against the act of gaming as thus defined.[5]

§ 123. What constitutes the law of the land.—We have seen that ordinances must accord with the federal constitution and laws and with the legislation of the state in which the municipality is situated. Sometimes an exercise of corporate power is attempted to be supported by decisions of the English courts, on the theory that English common law forms a part of the law of our land

(1) Bell *v.* Manvers, 3 U. C. C. P. 349.
(2) Livingston *v.* Albany, 41 Ga. 22; Cullinan *v.* New Orleans, 28 La. Ann. 102.
(3) Canton *v.* Nist, 9 O. S. 439.
(4) Cooper *v.* Savannah, 4 Ga. 68.
(5) In re Lee Tong, 18 Fed. Rep. 253.

in the absence of any definite expression of policy by our courts or legislatures. Generally speaking, it would only be misleading to give weight to English authorities, because many of the powers exercised by the municipalities of that country rest solely upon prescription, a source not recognized in America.[1] Still in cases where no applicable decision or expression of legislative policy can be found except in England, the English decision would be considered in construing corporate powers unless clearly inapplicable.[2]

§ 124. **Powers derived from former sovereignties.** Some of the older American cities may still have property rights which had their origin under the laws of some foreign power,[3] but they may exercise only such *legislative* powers as are granted by and consonant with the laws of the United States, or its members. New Orleans, for instance, existed as a municipality under the government of France and under that of Spain, but it may now exercise only the powers granted under the code of Louisiana, and its ordinances must conform to the policy of existing American legislation. It contains none of the rights formerly exercised under its French charter, and none that were sanctioned by the Spanish *cabildo*, unless confirmed by its present organic law.[4]

§ 125. **The corporate charter.**—The most obvious restriction upon the passage of ordinances is that they must be consonant with the provisions of the municipal charter or organic law. Both their aim and form must fall within the powers conferred.[5] The charter is the

(1) Herzo v. San Francisco, 33 Cal. 134.
(2) Claiborne County v. Brooks, 111 U. S. 400.
(3) For example, San Francisco, Hart v. Burnett, 15 Cal. 530.
(4) Bank v. Navigation Company, 3 La. Ann. 294. For special holdings as to other cities, see (New York) Mayor v. Ryan, 2 E. D. S. 368; (Detroit) Cooper v. Alden, 1 Harr. Ch. 72.
(5) Camden v. Mulford, 26 N. J. 49; Carr v. St. Louis, 9 Mo. 190; Mitchell v. Wiles, 59 Ind. 364; St. Louis v. Kase, 9 Ill. App. 409; Smith

primary test of the validity of an ordinance. In the application of this test as well as the others just considered it is always better to err in restricting than in extending the scope of corporate powers.

§ 126. **Other requisites of validity.**—The restrictions so far noted are those based upon constitutional and statutory laws of express character, and are of much easier application than those further restrictions which are based on general principles of law, and depend for their expression upon the decisions of courts.

§ 127. **Reasonableness.**—The restriction most frequently appealed to by those desirous of defeating ordinances is that ordinances must be *reasonable*. And of all restrictions this is the least capable of precise formulation and definition. An ordinance to be void for unreasonableness must be *plainly and clearly* unreasonable.[1] There must be evidence of weight that it took inception either in a mistake, or in a spirit of fraud or wantonness on the part of the enacting body.[2]

§ 128. **When the discretion of the council should be final.**—If an express power is given to a corporation to enact ordinances of a certain kind, the legislature thereby trusts to the discretion of the council to determine just how far they shall go within the limits imposed; and there is every presumption that the council are not only actuated by pure motives, but that they are so familiar with the mischief to be remedied, and with the defects of the prior regulations, as to be the best possible judges of the necessity for the enactment of the new law, and of the extent to which it is advisable to exercise the power granted. The

---

v. Knoxville, 3 Head, 245; St. Louis v. Weber, 44 Mo. 547; Cummings v. Fitch, 40 O. S. 56; Rex v. Cutbush, 4 Burr. 2204; Hoblyn v. Rex, 2 Bro. P. C. 329; Dill. Mun. Corp. § 319.

(1) White v. Kent, 11 O. S. 550; Neier v. Railway Co., 12 Mo. App. 25.

(2) Sargent v. Railroad Co., 1 Handy (Ohio), 52.

council, and not the court, is the proper repository of this public trust, and it should be a plain case indeed to justify the latter in interfering with the determination of the council, or of questioning either their motives or the cogency of their reasons for enacting the ordinance. Surely, when an ordinance is, upon its face, plainly within the terms of an express power, the court ought not to interfere on the ground of unreasonableness. It is restricted to consider the constitutionality of the act granting the power.

§ 129. **When not final.**—When the ordinance is passed in order to exercise some power necessary to effectuate an express grant, or under some implied or inherent power which it is the policy of the courts to allow municipalities to exercise, or under a power accompanied by no express direction governing the mode of its exercise,[1] then it is proper for the court, in cases of doubt, to look beyond the face of the ordinance in order to inquire if it is reasonable. And, in fact, as is evidenced by the best considered decisions on the subject, the evidence is looked into in those cases alone. The reasonableness of an ordinance ought never to be questioned when it is enacted in accordance with the terms of an express power.

§ 130. **Examples of reasonable ordinances.**—Decisions as to the reasonableness of ordinances will be particularly considered under the subsequent treatment of the various special subjects of municipal control,[2] but an enumeration here of some leading cases will aid in fixing the general rule. The following ordinances have been held reasonable :

Railroads: That railroad trains shall not be run at a greater rate of speed than six miles per hour within the corporate limits ;[3] regulating the speed of trains and wagons.

(1) Kirkham *v.* Russell, 76 Va. 956; Ex parte Chin Yan, 60 Cal. 83.
(2) *Post,* §§ 211 to 292.
(3) Knobloch *v.* Railway Company, 31 Minn. 402.

within the city;[1] that trains shall not be allowed to stand across a public street longer than two minutes at one time;[2] that railroad companies shall keep flagmen at street crossings during the day, and that they shall protect the street crossings by colored lights at night;[3] that boys and other persons not connected with the management of the railroad, except passengers, and those about to take passage, shall not get on trains or cars within the city limits;[4] that street railway companies shall report quarterly the number of passengers carried;[5] requiring railroads to pave the sides of the streets through which they run.[6]

Vehicles: That hackney carriages shall not stand within thirty feet of any public place of amusement;[7] fixing the rates of fare that may be charged by hackney coachmen;[8] prescribing routes of travel for omnibus lines, and prohibiting their passing over other streets;[9] fining persons who impede the progress of street cars by allowing their vehicles to stand on the tracks;[10] requiring hackmen who stand near railroad depots to obey the orders of the police;[11] imposing a moderate tax on all vehicles that are used on the streets;[12] assigning certain stands for vehicles used for hire.[13]

Markets: That wagons loaded with produce shall not stand in the market-place for over twenty minutes during certain hours;[14] prohibiting those who were not licensed occupants of market stalls from offering fresh meat for

(1) Commonwealth *v.* Worcester, 3 Pick. 461; Pennsylvania Co. *v.* James, 32 *P. F. Smith, 202.
(2) State *v.* Jersey City, 37 N. J. 348.
(3) D. L. & W. R. R. Co. *v.* East Orange, 41 N. J. 127.
(4) Bearden *v.* Madison, 73 Ga. 184.
(5) St. Louis *v.* St. Louis Railway Co., 89 Mo. 44.
(6) City *v.* Erie Passenger R. R. Co., 7 Phila. 321.
(7) Commonwealth *v.* Robertson, 5 Cush. 438.
(8) Commonwealth *v.* Gage, 114 Mass. 328.
(9) Commonwealth *v.* Stodder, 2 Cush. 562.
(10) State *v.* Foley, 31 Ia. 527; s. c., 7 Am. Rep. 166.
(11) St. Paul *v.* Smith, 27 Minn. 364.
(12) St. Louis *v.* Green, 70 Mo. 562.
(13) Commonwealth *v.* Mathews, 122 Mass. 60.
(14) Commonwealth *v.* Brooks, 100 Mass. 355.

sale in less that quarters;[1] fixing market-hours at from dawn to nine o'clock A. M., and prohibiting the sale of fresh beef at other times in quantities less than a quarter.[2]

Sale of commodities: Prescribing that gunpowder shall not be kept in quantities over a certain number of pounds, that it shall be kept in copper canisters, and imposing a fine of from $50 to $500 for each violation of the ordinance;[3] prohibiting the sale of milk without a license from the mayor;[4] requiring a license to sell certain commodities in certain streets;[5] requiring a $200 license fee from each butcher;[6] requiring all imitations of lacteal products to be plainly marked;[7] prescribing any regulations to prevent the adulteration of milk;[8] providing for and regulating the weight and price of bread;[9] and requiring the weight of the loaf to be stamped thereon, the bread to be forfeited if the provision is neglected;[10] restricting the slaughter of animals in certain localities;[11] forbidding sales of goods on Sunday;[12] requiring a license fee from persons engaged in peddling goods from house to house;[13] and from those who stand on the streets to sell papers;[14] that every horse and cattle dealer shall take out a license and furnish a certificate of moral character.[15]

Intoxicating liquors: Levying a tax of $100 on each re-

(1) St. Louis v. Weber, 44 Mo. 547.
(2) Bowling Green v. Carson, 10 Bush (Ky.) 164.
(3) Williams v. Augusta, 4 Ga. 509.
(4) People v. Mulholland, 82 N. Y. 324.
(5) Nightingale, Petitioner, 11 Pick. 168.
(6) St. Paul v. Colter, 12 Minn. 41.
(7) State v. Addington, 77 Mo. 110.
(8) Polinsky v. People, 73 N. Y. 65.
(9) Mayor v. Yuille, 3 Ala. 137.
(10) In re Nasmith, 2 Ont. 192.
(11) Slaughter-House Laws, 16 Wall. 63; Ex parte Heilbron, 20 Cent. L. Jour. 183.
(12) Gabel v. Houston, 29 Tex. 335.
(13) State Center v. Barenstein, 66 Ia. 249.
(14) Commonwealth v. Elliott, 121 Mass. 367.
(15) St. Louis v. Knox, 6 Mo. App. 247.

tailer of spirituous liquors;[1] placing the tax at $500;[2] punishing the sale of liquors in quantities of a quart or more to be drunk on the premises;[3] punishing retail grocers who keep spirituous liquors on their premises;[4] that dram shops shall close at nine o'clock P. M.;[5] closing them from 10:30 P. M. till 5 A. M.;[6] and from midnight till five A. M.;[7] requiring that there shall be no avenue of direct communication between billiard rooms and places where liquors are sold.[8]

Other occupations: Requiring an annual license fee of $500 from express companies whose business extends beyond the state, and $100 on all others;[9] requiring restaurants to close at ten o'clock in the evening;[10] and confectioneries to remain closed on Sunday after nine o'clock in the morning;[11] prohibiting gambling and bawdy houses from being located in certain parts of the city;[12] prohibiting work in laundries at night within certain territorial limits.[13]

Health and security: Prohibiting persons from allowing their cattle to run at large;[14] compelling boats laden with produce apt to become putrid to anchor in the adjoining waterway until inspected and permitted to unload by a city officer;[15] punishing vagrants;[16] preventing the establishment

(1) Mayor v. Beasly, 1 Humph. 426.
(2) Perdue v. Ellis, 18 Ga. 586.
(3) Adams v. Albany, 29 Ga. 56.
(4) Council v. Ahrens, 4 Strob. L. 241; Heisembrittle v. Charleston, 2 McMull. 233.
(5) Smith v. Mayor, 3 Head, 245.
(6) State v. Welch, 36 Conn. 215.
(7) Bright v. Toronto, 12 U. C. C. P. 433.
(8) Neilly v. Owen Sound, 37 U. C. Q. B. 289.
(9) Express Co. v. Mobile, 49 Ala. 404.
(10) State v. Freeman, 38 N. H. 426.
(11) St. Louis v. Cafferata, 24 Mo. 94.
(12) Ex parte Chin Yan, 60 Cal. 78.
(13) Soon Hing v. Crowley, 113 U. S. 703; Barbier v. Connelly, 113 U. S. 27.
(14) Commonwealth v. Patch, 97 Mass. 221; Commonwealth v. Bean, 14 Gray, 52.
(15) Dubois v. Augusta, Dudley (Ga.), 30.
(16) St. Louis v. Bentz, 11 Mo. 61.

of new burial-grounds within the city limits;[1] prohibiting unlicensed persons from removing offal and garbage;[2] imposing a fine of ten dollars upon the owner of any dog that shall bite any one.[3]

Miscellaneous ordinances: Prohibiting the owners of lots abutting on the lake shore from removing sand;[4] prohibiting the erection of awnings over the sidewalks;[5] fixing a price for the privilege of tapping the public sewers;[6] requiring adjoining owners to clear the snow from the sidewalks;[7] prohibiting the erection of wooden buildings within certain territorial limits;[8] requiring a license for building;[9] prohibiting any one from delivering sermons, lectures, or addresses in the public common without first having obtained permission from the council;[10] making it unlawful to keep draw-bridges open more than ten minutes at one time, and fining vessels that neglect to observe the bridge signals;[11] restricting laundries to certain kind of building.[12]

§ 131. **Examples of unreasonable ordinances.**—Among others, the following ordinance regulations have been declared unreasonable, and for that reason void:

Railroads: That a railroad company shall keep a flagman by day and a red light by night at a street crossing which is not particularly dangerous.[13]

(1) Charleston v. Church, 4 Strob. L. 306.
(2) Vandine, Petitioner, 6 Pick. 187; s. c., 17 Am. Dec. 351.
(3) Commonwealth v. Steffee, 7 Bush, 161.
(4) Clasen v. Milwaukee, 30 Wis. 316.
(5) Pedrick v. Bailey, 12 Gray, 161.
(6) Fisher v. Harrisburg, 2 Grant Cas. 291.
(7) Goddard, Petitioner, 16 Pick. 504. *Contra,* Gridley v. Bloomington, 88 Ill. 555.
(8) King v. Davenport, 98 Ill. 305; Baumgartner v. Hasty, 100 Ind. 575.
(9) Welch v. Hotchkiss, 39 Conn. 140.
(10) Commonwealth v. Davis, 140 Mass. 485.
(11) Chicago v. McGinn, 51 Ill. 266.
(12) In re Yick Woo, 68 Cal. 294.
(13) Railway Co. v. Jacksonville, 67 Ill. 38; s. c., 16 Am. Rep. 611.

Vehicles: That porters and hackmen shall not approach within twenty feet of a depot, when their presence is expressly sanctioned by the railroad company.[1]

Markets: Prescribing a penalty for each hour that a wagon is kept within the limits of the public market.[2]

Sale of commodities: That fruit and lemonade shall not be sold at temporary stands without a license;[3] imposing a fee of five cents on each sale of produce;[4] that producers shall pay an annual fee of twenty-five dollars for the privilege of vending their produce on the streets;[5] forbidding the sale of goods on Sunday;[6] imposing a license fee on all hucksters;[7] forbidding sales by auctioneers except to the highest bidder;[8] prohibiting auction sales after sundown.[9]

Intoxicating liquors: That licensed venders of spirits shall not sell between six o'clock P. M. and six o'clock A. M.;[10] requiring druggists, under a heavy penalty for neglect, to furnish a quarterly statement, verified by affidavit, of the kind and quantity of liquors sold;[11] prohibiting sales of liquors in less quantities than twenty-eight gallons.[12]

Other occupations: Permitting one person, to the exclusion of others, to carry on a dangerous business;[13] prohibiting the slaughtering of animals on one's own premises unless in a regular slaughter-house;[14] restricting all slaughtering to a single specified building;[15] prohibiting non-residents from taking fish from a navigable river

(1) Napman v. People, 19 Mich. 352.
(2) Commonwealth v. Wilkins, 121 Mass. 356.
(3) Barling v. West, 29 Wis. 307; s. c., 9 Am. Rep. 576.
(4) Kip v. Patterson, 2 Dutch. 298.
(5) St. Paul v. Traeger, 25 Minn. 248; s. c., 33 Am. Rep. 462.
(6) Shreveport v. Levy, 26 La. Ann. 671; s. c., 21 Am. Rep. 553.
(7) Dunham v. Rochester, 5 Cow. 462.
(8) In re Martin, 27 Ark. 467.
(9) Hayes v. Appleton, 24 Wis 542.
(10) Ward v. Greeneville, 8 Baxter, 228; s. c., 35 Am. Rep. 700.
(11) Clinton v. Phillips, 58 Ill. 102; s. c., 11 Am. Rep. 52.
(12) Commonwealth v. Turner, 1 Cush. 493.
(13) Mayor v. Thorne, 7 Paige, 261.
(14) Wreford v. People, 14 Mich. 41.
(15) Chicago v. Rumpff, 45 Ill. 90.

within the city limits;[1] requiring a license fee for each milk-cart;[2] requiring owners of theaters to pay a police officer for attendance at every performance.[3]

Health and security: Compelling the removal, from the city, of a steam engine that is not *per se* a nuisance;[4] prohibiting a gas company from opening paved streets for the purpose of making new connections;[5] forbidding the use of a certain kind of approved fire-extinguishers at fires;[6] compelling the removal of property not shown to be a nuisance;[7] punishing those whose animals are found running at large in the streets;[8] giving authority to police officers to make arrests without warrants for offenses not committed in their presence;[9] punishing those who associate with persons of bad character;[10] limiting the burial of the dead to one locality, the prohibited territory being unreasonably large;[11] subjecting private burial-grounds to the control of the city sexton;[12] forbidding the renting of buildings to prostitutes, without regard to the use to which they intend to put them;[13] prohibiting the use of steamboats not provided with a spark-arrester "as effectual as the same can be made by any means known or in use."[14]

Miscellaneous ordinances: Requiring the arrest of all free negroes found on the streets after ten o'clock P. M.;[15] levying a tax to build a sidewalk in an uninhabited part of the city, where it would not be connected with other side-

(1) Hayden v. Noyes, 5 Conn. 391.
(2) Chicago v. Bartree, 111 App. (1887).
(3) Waters v. Leech, 3 Ark. 110.
(4) Baltimore v. Radecke, 49 Md. 217; s. c., 33 Am. Rep. 239.
(5) Commissioners v. Gas Company, 12 Pa. St. 318.
(6) Insurance Co. v. O'Connor, 27 La. Ann. 371.
(7) Pieri v. Mayor, 42 Miss. 493.
(8) Collins v. Hatch, 18 Ohio, 522.
(9) Pesterfield v. Mayor, 3 Coldw. 205.
(10) St. Louis v. Fitz, 53 Mo. 582.
(11) Selectmen v. Murray, 16 Pick. 121.
(12) Bogart v. Indianapolis, 13 Ind. 134.
(13) Milliken v. Weatherford, 54 Tex. 189.
(14) Atkinson v. Transportation Co., 60 Wis. 141.
(15) Mayor v. Winfield, 8 Humph. 707.

walks;[1] requiring the expulsion from the public school of any child that shall decline, under its parents' direction, to study some branch of the curriculum;[2] excluding a scholar from promotion in the public schools for inability to pass an examination in a study which his parents do not desire him to pursue;[3] providing that the city sexton, whose fees are paid out of the estates of deceased persons, shall expend $500 on the public burying-grounds, and bury paupers free of charge;[4] granting a franchise to maintain a toll-bridge across a river;[5] requiring consent of mayor to march through the streets in procession with flags, torches, and music.[6]

§ 132. **Restraint of trade.**—At common law, any one might carry on any trade in any place unless some custom forbade.[7] Any restraint of trade is burdensome to the community at large, and especially so to those engaged in the trade or occupation that is restrained. But many trades are of such a nature that they may easily be made injurious or dangerous to health and security, if improperly conducted. Any regulation of trade that has restraint as its object is unlawful, but any degree of restraint is permissible that is actually necessary to secure and maintain health and good order. A simple regulation for police purposes alone is valid.[8] "A law which unnecessarily and oppressively restrains a citizen from engaging in any traffic, or disposing of his property as he may see fit, although passed under the specious pretext of a preservation of the health of the inhabitants, would be void. Such a law would be unreasonable, and would deprive the people of

(1) Corrigan *v.* Gage, 68 Mo. 541.
(2) Rulison *v.* Post, 79 Ind. 567.
(3) Trustees *v.* People, 87 Ill. 305.
(4) Beronjohn *v.* Mobile, 27 Ala. 58.
(5) Williams *v.* Davidson, 43 Tex. 1.
(6) Frazee's Case, Mich. (Oct. 28, 1886), 35 Alb. L. J. C.
(7) Clark *v.* Le Creu, 9 B. & C. 52; Hesketh *v.* Braddock, 3 Burr. 1847; Bosworth *v.* Hearne, 2 Str. 1085; Harrison *v.* London, 1 Burr. 16; London *v.* Godman, 1 Burr. 12.
(8) Mobile *v.* Yuille, 3 Ala. 137.

the rights guaranteed to them by the organic law of the land. But if the regulation or prohibition contains nothing more than the necessary limitation, and is passed in good faith for the purpose of preserving the good health and abating nuisances, it is not liable to objection. No man has an inalienable right to produce disease or trade in that which is noxious."[1]

If the degree of the restraint is reasonable, and its necessity obvious, the ordinance imposing it is valid. But the restraint must not be such as to create a monopoly, or to entirely prevent any trade, the exercise of which is useful to humanity, so long as properly conducted. *Monopolies are obnoxious to the spirit of our laws, and should not, even indirectly, be created.*[2]

It tends to create a monopoly, to designate a single place as a market-house and to prohibit the sale of fresh meats at any other place, at any time, and in any quantity;[3] to grant the exclusive right of maintaining a market-house to one person for a term of years, and to confine the sale of produce to his house.[4]

Privileges that have once been conferred can not subsequently be made exclusive, unless additional authority has in the meantime been granted.[5] A grant of an exclusive privilege of selling water to the city for a term of twenty years, creates a monopoly.[6] Monopolies may be created by delegating police powers to persons or corporations.[7]

Thus, no one person ought to have the exclusive right to run omnibus lines,[8] or to carry on the business of slaughtering.[9]

(1) State v. Fisher, 52 Mo. 174.
(2) Gas Light Co. v. Saginaw, 28 Fed. Rep. 529; Tugman v. Chicago, 78 Ill 405; Railway Co. v. Railway Co., 24 Fed. Rep. 306; State v. Cin. Gas Light, etc., Co., 18 O. S. 262; Live Stock Association v. Crescent City, 1 Abb. U. S. 388; Gas Company's Appeal (Pa.), 4 Atl. Rep. 733.
(3) Bloomington v. Wahl, 46 Ill. 489.
(4) Gale v. Kalamazoo, 23 Mich. 344.
(5) Johnson v. Crow, 87 Pa. St. 184.
(6) Davenport v. Kleinschmidt, 13 Pac. Rep. 249.
(7) Louisville v. Weible (Ky.), 1 S. W. Rep. 605.
(8) Logan v. Pyne, 43 Ia. 524.
(9) Chicago v. Rumpff, 45 Ill. 90.

Still, express power to grant exclusive privileges may be exercised. Thus, a mere power to license gives no right to create a monopoly by confining the license granted to one or a few persons; but, where the corporation has power to *grant or refuse* a license, an exclusive license may be conferred.[1]

Business investments, upon which the prosperity of a community depends, should be hampered by as few restraints as are compatible with the health and security of the people; and whenever any doubt exists as to the urgency of the necessity, or the dangerous character of the occupation, it should be resolved against the validity of the restraint.

§ 133. **What is a restraint of trade.**—The following ordinance regulations have been declared invalid as in restraint of trade: A prohibition of aution sales after sundown;[2] requiring petty grocers to procure licenses;[3] prohibiting the sale of lemonade, nuts, and fruit, at temporary stands;[4] imposing *numerous* conditions upon the right to sell fresh meat outside of the market stalls;[5] limiting the number of carts that should be allowed to be used, and requiring licenses;[6] under power to *regulate* the ringing of bells and the crying of goods and other commodities for sale at auction or otherwise, an ordinance unnecessarily restrains trade which forbids all sales of watches and other jewelry after sunset by public auction.[7]

§ 134. **What is not a restraint of trade.**—It is not a restraint of trade to impose reasonable regulations on the speed of railway trains;[8] or to require *all* persons selling

---

(1) Ferry Co. v. Davis, 48 Iowa, 133. See further, *post*, § 256 *et seq.*
(2) Hayes v. Appleton, 24 Wis 542.
(3) Dunham v. Rochester, 5 Cow. 462.
(4) Barling v. West, 29 Wis. 307.
(5) St. Paul v. Laidler, 2 Minn. 190.
(6) Player v. Vere, Raym. 288.
(7) Rochester v. Close, 35 Hun, 209.
(8) Knobloch v. Railway Co., 31 Minn. 402.

liquors to obtain a license, druggists included;[1] or to prohibit the maintenance of slaughter-houses within certain limits;[2] or to impose a license fee of four dollars a day upon auctions;[3] or to prohibit the sale at retail of fresh meat outside of market-stalls;[4] or to prohibit such sale except under license;[5] or to require a license from persons engaged in carrying coal from places within to places without the city;[6] or to require, under penalty for omission, every hackman and drayman to obtain a license;[7] or to require coal, when sold, to be weighed by the city weigher;[8] or to require street railway companies to make quarterly reports of the number of passengers carried;[9] or to impose licenses, if moderate, on all business, under general power to license trade and occupations.[10]

§ 135. **Discrimination.**—Municipal ordinances are passed by a body that represents the whole community, and for the purpose of regulating matters which affect the general welfare, and their provisions should, so far as practicable, affect each member of the community alike. Ordinances should neither favor nor discriminate against any person or class of persons, or any particular portion of the municipal territory. Their burdens and their benefits should rest equally upon all. Laws of a municipality, like the laws of a state, should be uniform and of a general operation within the corporate limits, and any unnecessary, distinct discrimination between persons, classes, or locations, will invalidate them. Slight inequalities of benefit are unavoidable in proper police regulation. "A slight, incidental damage

(1) Rochester v. Upman, 19 Minn. 108.
(2) Cronin v. People, 82 N. Y. 318; Pierce v. Bartrum, Cowp. 270.
(3) Fretwell v. Troy, 18 Kan. 272.
(4) Davenport v. Kelly, 7 Ia. 103.
(5) Brooklyn v. Cleves, Hill & Den. Sup. 231; Strike v. Collins, 54 L. T. Rep. (N. S.) 152.
(6) Gartside v. East St. Louis, 43 Ill. 47.
(7) Brooklyn v. Breslin, 57 N. Y. 591.
(8) Stokes v. New York, 14 Wend. 87.
(9) St. Louis Railway Co. v. St. Louis, 89 Mo. 44.
(10) Ex parte Frank, 52 Cal. 606.

done to one individual, or even more, could never be held to be an oppression or wrong such as would invalidate an ordinance of a city. It must certainly be one working a general and public, or a permanent and continued wrong to a private individual or class."[1] Penal ordinances must be general in their effect; they must affect all, who are thereby restricted, equally. If directed against single persons or concerns, or against part only of a class, they are contrary to common right and void.[2] The effect of one ordinance that is general in form may in reality be as discriminating as one that is in terms partial. Regard must be had to the reason of ordinances. It is, for example, proper to impose a license tax on all liquor dealers in order to prevent wholly irresponsible persons from engaging in the traffic, and to thereby preserve the public peace; but if the corporation extends over districts which are wholly unsettled and remote from the thickly inhabited parts of the city, it would be manifestly unjust to subject a liquor dealer located in such district to the same degree of restriction as other dealers. Such an ordinance would impose a burden largely out of proportion to the benefits of police protection which it affords.[3] On the other hand, an ordinance that is *prima facie* discriminating, because governing the conduct of a specific railroad, is still valid so long as there are no other railroads to be regulated.[4]

In order that burdens may in fact be equably imposed, it is often necessary to classify the citizens of a municipality for the purposes of police regulation. The same principle is recognized in state legislation by the classification of municipalities according to their size. The classification must, however, be well defined and based on some reason-

---

(1) Knoxville v. Bird, 12 Lea. 121; s. c., 47 Am. Rep. 326; Gale v. Kalamazoo, 23 Mich. 344; s. c., 9 Am. Rep. 80; Chicago v. Rumpff, 45 Ill. 90.

(2) Baton Rouge v. Crémonini, 36 La. Ann. 247; De Bere v. Gerard, 4 La. Ann. 30; First Municipality v. Blineau, 3 La. Ann. 688; Nashville v. Althrop, 5 Coldw. 554.

(3) Salt Lake City v. Wagner, 2 Utah, 400.

(4) Railroad Co. v. Richmond, 96 U. S. 521.

able distinction. If the members of each class are then treated alike the ordinance is unobjectionable.¹ If a regulation of some business is the object of the ordinance, the amount or extent of the business done may be taken as a basis of classification; or, in regard to other subjects, the degreee of ability to work injury to the rights of the community. But no man can object to an ordinance directed against a certain business because he has less business than his competitors, claiming that discrimination should be made in his favor. His opportunities are equal to those of all others, and the right to classify lies solely within the discretion of the local legislators.

§ 136. **Examples of discrimination.**—A tax ordinance directed against dram-shops must include all dram-shops within its operation, either equally or by classes.² Taxes for general revenue must be levied equally on all persons according to the tax basis adopted by the state.³ No distinction can be made between goods in store and goods *in transitu*.⁴ So, an ordinance regulating the observance of the Sabbath can not exclude Jews from its operation, because in the eyes of the law all persons are equal, and a man's religious belief is in no way violated by prohibiting him to engage in certain occupations on a certain day.⁵ Power to regulate the lighting of the streets does not authorize an ordinance granting an exclusive right to light the streets, for every man may lawfully provide street lights in front of his own premises if he does not disturb the public easement.⁶ The same principle goes to prevent a corporation from imposing any discretion in its ministerial agents who are to issue licenses for certain trades or occupations. It is proper for the council to direct them

(1) Ex parte Siebenhauer, 14 Nev. 365; *post*, §§ 268, 287; County of Amador *v.* Kennedy, 11 Pac. Rep. 757.
(2) Zanone *v.* Mound City, 103 Ill. 553.
(3) Fitch *v.* Pinchard, 5 Ill. 69.
(4) Ex parte Frank, 52 Cal. 606.
(5) Shreveport *v.* Levy, 26 La. Ann. 671.
(6) Gas Light Co. *v.* Saginaw, 28 Fed. Rep. 529.

to follow certain general classifications, to refuse licenses to those who are incompetent, irresponsible, or of bad reputation, but discretion vested in the mayor to thus classify applicants might easily be so exercised as to result in unjust discrimination between races, or between persons of exactly the same responsibility and competency.[1]

§ 137. **Discrimination as to non-residents.**—Municipalities are not in any sense close corporations. They are not vested with rights of local legislation, in order that they may arrogate to their own inhabitants additional rights and privileges to those enjoyed by other citizens of the state or nation. Neither may rights be denied to its citizens and still allowed to be exercised by non-residents who may come within the corporate limits. Discrimination *against* residents is equally odious to discrimination in their favor. If an ordinance declares that the tires of wagon-wheels shall be of a certain width according to the weight carried, non-residents who pass through the corporation, or who reside more than two miles from the limits, can not be excluded from its operation.[2] It has been held, however, in Kentucky, that an ordinance may discriminate against citizens of the municipality, however peculiar its provisions.[3] A grant of exceptional immunities to non-residents might, it is true, be of advantage to the municipality by attracting trade, but the furtherance of the material interests of the people is not one of the legitimate objects of corporate organization. Without express legislative authority, municipal corporations are restricted to matters of government and of police regulation.

Under power to regulate fisheries, an ordinance prohibiting all persons not residents of the town from fishing within the corporate limits is void.[4] It is unlawful discrimination to prohibit, except under license, non-residents from running lines of coaches into or within the city,

(1) Yick Woo v. Hopkins, 118 U. S. 356.
(2) Regina v. l'ipe, 1 Ontario, 43.
(3) Louisville v. Roupe, 6 B. Mon. 591.
(4) Hayden v. Noyes, 5 Conn. 391.

without imposing an equal burden on the same occupation when exercised by residents.¹ So, non-resident peddlers and sales-agents can not be restricted to any further extent than residents, neither can additional burdens be imposed on the sale of goods that are not of local manufacture.² And no discrimination in wharfage fees can be lawfully made against citizens of other states than the one in which the municipality is located.³ An ordinance is void for the same reason that prohibits swine belonging to non-residents from running at large in the town when no such restriction is made upon residents.⁴

§ 138. **Once void, always void.**—If the corporate power is exceeded at the date of the enactment of an ordinance, no subsequent grant of additional power could validate the prior ordinance. An ordinance which is void at its inception is always void, and neither the council nor the legislature can lend it validity by subsequent affirmance or legislation.⁵ And even when subsequent legislation is held to validate a void ordinance, the ordinance does not gain any retrospective effect.⁶ An ordinance that has been declared void for inconsistency with the provisions of a state law does not acquire validity through the repeal of the law to which it is obnoxious.⁷

(1) Commonwealth v. Stodder, 2 Cush. 562.
(2) Marshalltown v. Blum, 58 Ia. 184; Welton v. Missouri, 91 U. S. 275; Pacific Junction v. Dyer, 64 Ia. 38; St. Rochs Sud v. Dion, 1 Quebec, 242; Graffty v. Rushville, 107 Ind. 502; Fecheimer v. Louisville (Ky. 1886), 35 Alb. L. J. 155; Nashville v. Althrop, 5 Cold. 554; Daniel v. Richmond, 78 Ky. 542; St. Charles v. Nolle, 51 Mo. 122; Robbins v. Shelby County (U. S. Sup. Ct. 1887), 7 Sup. Ct. Rep. 592; Corson v. Maryland, 7 Sup. Ct. Rep. 655.
(3) Guy v. Baltimore, 100 U. S. 434; Broeck v. Welch, 18 Blatch. 54; s. c., 2 Fed. Rep. 364.
(4) Roberts v. Ogle, 30 Ill. 459.
(5) Hydes v. Joyes, 4 Bush, 464; Mt. Pleasant v. Vansice, 43 Mich. 361. *Contra*, Truchelot v. City Council, Nott & McC. 227.
(6) Lake View v. Letz, 44 Ill. 81.
(7) Mt. Pleasant v. Vansice, 43 Mich. 361.

§ 139. **Partial invalidity.**—Ordinances passed in pursuance of an express power are often so worded as to include some provisions which are not authorized by the power. The unauthorized provisions do not invalidate the whole ordinance if they can be separated from the rest of the ordinance without so mutilating it as to render it inoperative; but whenever the void portion is an essential element of the whole, when the provisions are mutually dependent, then the whole ordinance falls.[1]

"When an ordinance is entire, each part being essential and connected with the rest, the invalidity of one part renders the whole invalid, but when it consists of several distinct and independent parts, as when it prohibits disjunctively two or more acts, the invalidity of one part does not affect the validity of the others."[2]

The fact that an ordinance covers matters which the city has no power to control, is no reason why it should not be enforced as to those which it may control.[3] So, when a double penalty is imposed upon some offense, one of them being unauthorized by the charter does not prevent the enforcement of the other.[4] But, if the penalty is void, the whole ordinance is void.[5] When an ordinance contains several sections, each defining a different offense, the sections are not mutually dependent, and one may be void without affecting the validity of the others.[6] If the prohibition of the ordinance is against enumerated offenses, or if its subject-matter is expressed by an enumeration, in

---

(1) State v. Hoboken, 38 N. J. 110; Trowbridge v. Newark, 46 N. J. 140; Baker v. Normal, 81 Ill. 108; Harbaugh v. Monmouth, 74 Ill. 367; Quincy v. Bull, 106 Ill. 337; Cantril v. Sainer, 59 Ia. 26; Eldora v. Burlingame, 62 Ia. 32; Commonwealth v. Dow, 10 Metc. 382; Warren v. Mayor, 2 Gray, 84; Amesbury v. Insurance Co., 6 Gray, 596; St. Louis v. Railway Co., 14 Mo. App. 221; State v. Clarke, 54 Mo. 17; Rogers v. Jones, 1 Wend. 237; Piqua v. Zimmerlin, 35 O. S. 507; Rau v. Little Rock, 34 Ark. 303; St. Louis v. Railway Co., 89 Mo. 44.

(2) Penna. Railroad Co. v. Jersey City, 47 N. J. 286.

(3) Kettering v. Jacksonville, 50 Ill. 39.

(4) Wilcox v. Hemming, 58 Wis. 144.

(5) State v. Cainan, 94 N. C. 883.

(6) Rogers v. Jones, 1 Wend. 260.

which some things are contained over which the corporation has no power, the enumeration is separable.[1] An ordinance regulating the speed of railroad trains over the public streets is not wholly void because its provisions are unreasonable when applied to one or two suburban streets.[2]

Separability of the void from the valid parts of the ordinance is the only test, and a fair doubt should be so resolved as to effectuate the ordinance.

(1) Shelton v. Mobile, 30 Ala. 540.
(2) Railroad Co. v. Jersey City, 47 N. J. 286.

CHAPTER VII.

REMEDIES.

§ 140. Introduction.
§ 141. Territorial limits.
§ 142. Extraterritorial effect.
§ 143. Ordinances affect what persons.
§ 144. When parts of the corporate limits exempt.
§ 145. Jusisdiction over railroad property.
§ 146. Jurisdiction over streets.
§ 147. Penalties.
§ 148. The kind of penalty that may be adopted.
§ 149. Penalties are not licenses.
§ 150. Fines.
§ 151. Amount of the fine.
§ 152. Cumulative fines.
§ 153. Repetition of an offense more heavily punished.
§ 154. Costs of the prosecution.
§ 155. Imprisonment in default of payment.
§ 156. The power strictly construed.
§ 157. Such imprisonment does not satisfy the fine.
§ 158. Imprisonment as a penalty.
§ 159. Forfeiture.
§ 160. Illustrations.
§ 161. Strays.
§ 162. Notice to the owner.
§ 163. Judicial determination.
§ 164. Forfeiture of real estate.

§ 140. Introduction.—Most municipal ordinances would be entirely ineffective if there were no way of compelling obedience to their provisions. Those which are passed in the exercise of the powers of local police regulation must, like the police laws of the state, be capable of proper enforcement. Ordinances of a quasi-ministerial nature, such as those providing for the improvement of the streets, do not need to contain such positive provisions for their enforcement, because the execution of the contracts entered into by their authority is a matter independent of the local police, and the taxes levied to bear the expense are usually collected and enforced by the ministerial agents of the state or city in some manner prescribed by general law. Their burdens are imposed upon the property affected, whereas police ordinances primarily affect rights of the person, and provision must be made to enforce them against the person, else they are of no avail. The gist of the ordinance is that part which prescribes the penalty, and the necessity of keeping within the limits of authority as to the penalties imposed, and as to the persons subjected to their enforcement, is far greater than that of observing the strict limits of the degree of lawful regulation, or of the extent of the subject-matter incorporated into the ordinance. Penalties are to be construed strictly, without exception, against the body in whose favor they are imposed. The remedy to be adopted in enforcing ordinances must be cautiously selected, and strictly confined to the limits of the existing authority.

§ 141. Territorial limits.—As has been stated, one of the prime essentials of police ordinances is that they shall aim at corporate purposes alone. Unless the special circumstances surrounding the necessity for a certain regulation require it to be of only limited territorial application, police ordinances take effect over the whole territory included within the corporate limits, both at the time of their passage and at all times thereafter. If the limits of the corporation should subsequently be extended, those within the added territory would, *ipse facto*, come within the operation of all the ordinances then in force.[1] Any other rule would not only produce innumerable complications, but it would necessitate the re-enactment of the whole body of local laws, whenever any material addition is made to the territorial extent of the corporation.

Ordinances that do not fall within the operation of the rule are such as limit certain occupations or acts to prescribed portions of the municipal territory; and, to a very limited extent, ordinances general in their form, but which

---

(1) Toledo *v.* Edens, 59 Ia. 352.

would work decided inequalities of burdens if enforced over the entire limits. For example of the latter class, it is lawful to limit the speed of railway trains within a city, but if the city covers considerable tracts of agricultural, or sparsely settled land, it would be useless and oppressive to demand a moderation of speed in such portions of the city equal to that exacted in the heart of the city.[1] It would be equally oppressive to impose the same degree of restriction on occupations carried on in such virtually rural districts as is necessary in the thickly peopled parts of the city.[2] But the circumstances in each case must be such as make the inequality of burden very plain in order to warrant a departure from the general rule.

§.142. **Extraterritorial effect.**—The same reasons that necessitate any kind of local regulation apply to demonstrate that many acts may be injurious to the inhabitants of a town or city when performed without its territorial limits. And the inhabitants are often greatly in need of power to provide for adequate sewerage or water supply by using and regulating the use of property beyond the limits. It would seem eminently proper that some means should be provided by which the corporation in such cases may exercise some degree of control over the immediately adjoining territory. Still, the spirit and the letter of our laws are plain that no power of this kind may be exercised unless it is expressly granted by the state legislature, and that the authority must be clear and undoubted.[3] Municipal corporations may exercise power of police control over adjoining navigable waters, where such control comes in conflict with no provision of the maritime law of the land. But such jurisdiction is limited to police purposes, and must not interfere with or create property rights. Thus

---

(1) Meyers v. Railroad Co., 57 Ia. 555; s. c., 42 Am. Rep. 50.

(2) Salt Lake City v. Wagner, 2 Utah, 400.

(3) Strauss v. Pontiac, 40 Ill. 301; Chicago Packing Co. v. Chicago, 88 Ill. 221; Coldwater v. Tucker, 36 Mich. 474; s. c., 24 Am. Rep. 601. The erection of a cemetery just outside the city limits can not be prevented by a municipality. Begein v. Anderson, 28 Ind. 79.

fishing in adjoining waters could not be prohibited.¹ If a municipal corporation is bounded by navigable water, on the other side of which another municipality is located, each would be allowed to exercise police control to the center of the stream. In one instance, that of New York city, the state legislature, in view of the importance of the interests exposed, has extended the jurisdiction of the city over the navigable rivers surrounding it up to the opposite shore line of those rivers, to the exclusion of the power of the adjoining cities.²

§ 143. **Ordinances affect what persons.**—In order that ordinances shall serve the purposes of their enactment, it is evident that they must bind the actions of every one who is at any time found within the corporate limits, not only regular citizens, but non-residents and even transient visitors. This proposition is as applicable to municipal regulations as to those of a state or nation.³ An early decision in New York deviates from the strict rule, and holds that a stranger could not be prosecuted in a municipal court for trespassing upon the commons in violation of the provision of an ordinance passed under authority to improve the public commons and to prescribe regulations to govern their use.⁴

Whoever comes in person, or allows his property to be in the corporate limits, tacitly consents to submit to all local laws, and his property rights are as much subject to their regulations as he himself. If a non-resident's business interests are located within the corporate limits they

(1) Palmer *v.* Hicks, 6 Johns. 133; Ogdensburg *v.* Lyon, 7 Lans. 215.

(2) Udall *v.* Brooklyn, 19 Johns. 175; Stryker *v.* New York, 19 Johns. 179.

(3) Plymouth *v.* Pettijohn, 4 Dev. Law, 591; Wilmington *v.* Roby, 8 Ired. Law, 250; Gilmore *v.* Holt, 4 Pick. 258; Vandine, Petitioner, 6 Pick. 187; Ex parte McNair, 13 Neb. 195; Gosselink *v.* Campbell, 4 Ia. 296; Pierce *v.* Bartrum, Cowp. 269; Regina *v.* Osler, 32 U. C. Q. B. 324; Cooley Const. Lim, *p. 199; Harvey *v.* Sloan, Smith (Ind.), 136.

(4) Foster *v.* Rhoads, 19 Johns. 191.

enjoy the full benefit and protection of the local laws, and ought not to be exempt from their burdens. If animals belonging to a non-resident stray into a corporation the local authorities may execute the ordinance against strays against them to the same extent as though they were the property of a citizen. The accident of ownership can not alter the degree of the offense.[1] The fact that a business man lives outside of the city does not excuse him from the payment of a tax imposed by the city upon all businesses of the same nature as his.[2] If an ordinance imposes a license tax on all vehicles used for hire on the public streets, the tax must be paid for each vehicle of the kind, by whomsoever owned.[3] So a tax imposed on the owner of all vehicles kept or used for free delivery within the limits of a city can be collected from the proprietors of iron works whose drays are sent into the city to deliver goods.[4]

In these cases, as in all others, regard must be had for the purpose and reason of the law. Its spirit as well as letter must be observed. Non-residents are subject to the local laws, because their interests and rights are protected, and they should therefore help bear their burdens, and also because their interests or occupations are injurious to some corporate right. If the reason for holding a non-resident fails, he ought to go free. Thus, if a tax is imposed on every vehicle using the paved streets, intended reference is had to such as use them *habitually*, and the ordinance would not operate to bind a non-resident who uses the paved streets incidentally in passing through the corporation.[5] Neither would such a provision apply to one who lives at a distance, but who occasionally brings a load into the city

---

(1) Kennedy *v.* Sowden, 1 McMull. 323; Knoxville *v.* King, 7 B. J. Lea, 441; Spitler *v.* Young, 63 Mo. 42; Centerville *v.* Lanham, 67 Ga. 753.

(2) Wilkinson *v.* Charleston, 2 Spears, 623; Edenton *v.* Capeheart, 71 N. C. 156.

(3) Council *v.* Pepper, 1 Rich. L. 364.

(4) Memphis *v.* Battaile, 8 Heisk. 524.

(5) Bennett *v.* Birmingham, 31 Pa. St. 15.

and takes another back. Such use is not habitual.[1] Under power to regulate all hucksters living in the city or within one mile thereof, the ordinance must be drawn so as not to be applicable to any one living more than a mile away.[2] Likewise an ordinance providing for the payment of a tax on "all hay bought or brought within the corporation" applies only to persons who sell hay in the city for *use in the city*. It would not apply to a non-resident who buys hay in the city for use without the city.[3]

A power to restrict "residents" in some manner can not be extended to warrant the same regulation of non-residents.[4] The fact that the word is used in the power implies the exclusion of all other persons, and whenever a serious doubt exists, it must be resolved in favor of a non-resident who has been proceeded against.

§ 144. **When parts of the corporate limits exempt.**— The proposition that all persons within the limits of a corporation are subject to the corporate ordinances must be accepted with some limitation as to the place where the offense is committed. Every act that is prohibited as a police regulation is considered injurious or threatening injury to the public welfare, and distinction must be drawn between various unlawful acts according to the degree of their capability of doing harm. In a municipality the only places that are really public are the streets, squares, commons, and public buildings to which all have access, and there are classes of acts that are not injurious to the public in any sense unless committed in a public place. A person who is seen publicly in a state of intoxication may cause a breach of the peace, and is at any rate a spectacle that works harm upon the standard of public morals and decency, but the public is not affected if a person gets intoxicated in the seclusion of his own house.

(1) St. Charles *v.* Nolle, 51 Mo. 122. Likewise as to carriages, Adgar *v.* Mayor, 2 Spear, 719.
(2) Snell *v.* Belleville, 30 U. C. Q. B. 81.
(3) Gass *v.* Greeneville, 4 Sneed, 62.
(4) Garden City *v.* Abbott, 34 Kan. 283.

The public has no right of access to his house. Likewise, it would be of no import to the public that a man supports a billiard room for the use of his family and invited guests. So long as not every one may have access to and partake in the thing otherwise unlawful, no offense can be committed. If the ordinances directed against such offenses do not expressly restrict their own operation to public places, the courts will, when called upon, supply the deficiency by construction.

Purely private rights can not be regulated by ordinance except when they still threaten the public good. Many occupations that are conducted wholly on one's own premises may have results that are evil. Slaughtering, manufacturing chemicals, tanning, operating noisy or ponderous machinery, are things which thus in fact harm or disturb the health and convenience of the public. The storage of explosives, or of combustibles, or the use of inflammatory material in the construction of buildings, are things that may easily do injury, and by reason of their threatening character may be prohibited. In such cases police regulation may invade and control private premises and the mode of their use, regardless of whether the public has access.

But under power to prevent and suppress opium smoking, only those can be punished who smoke in a place kept for public use for that purpose.[1] And under an ordinance providing that "all hogs shall be kept up," the running of hogs in public places may be prevented, but no additional remedy is thereby created against a person who allows his hogs to escape into an adjoining lot.[2] So, power to regulate wharves does not extend to regulation of wharves that are owned and conducted by private enterprises. The reason of the power is that the public may be compensated for the outlay in providing public wharves, and that the wharves so provided may be protected from improper use. The reason no longer exists when the ownership and con-

(1) Ex parte Ah Litt. (Oregon, 1886)'
(2) Shepherd v. Hees, 12 Johns. 433.

trol is private.[1] The lowering of cotton bales on to an open private space where they are exhibited for sale, and which is open to the public, is dangerous enough to need regulation.[2]

§ 145. **Jurisdiction over railroad property.**—Railroads are often called semi-public institutions, and their property is likewise semi-public. Their tracks, grounds, and depots, when located in a thickly settled community, are unavoidably used more or less by the general public, and their conduct is accompanied by danger even on the company's private grounds. It is, therefore, eminently proper that municipalities should exercise some degree of control over the details of their management. This right is evident in regard to street crossings and other places where the right to use the space is open to the railroad and the public alike. It has been held that the speed of trains can only be regulated over the streets, squares, and public grounds,[3] but the generally accepted view is that such regulation may be exercised over the whole line of the right of way through the corporation,[4] and even over the switch yards of the company.[5] Where an ordinance prohibited the running of any car or engine at a higher rate of speed than ten miles an hour within the city limits, it was held that it was not intended to apply to engines used in the yards and private premises of the railroad company, but the court intimated that an ordinance might have been lawfully passed that would apply to even the private yards.[6]

Under power to regulate hacks, an ordinance may be made to apply to their conduct on the depot grounds of a

(1) Vanderwater *v.* New York, 2 Sandf. 258; Commissioners *v.* Nell, 3 Yeates, 54; New Orleans *v.* Wilmot, 31 La. Ann. 65; St. Martinsville *v.* Mary Lewis, 32 La. Ann. 1293.

(2) Charleston *v.* Elford, 1 McMull. 234.

(3) State *v.* Jersey City, 29 N. J. L. 170.

(4) Pennsylvania Co. *v.* James, 32 P. F. Smith, 194; Whitson *v.* Franklin, 34 Ind. 392.

(5) Crowley *v.* Railroad Co., 65 Iowa, 658.

(6) Green *v.* Canal Co., 38 Hun, 51.

railroad as well as upon the public streets, and that they may be compelled to occupy certain stands under the direction of a public officer.[1] But it has been held in New York that under power to license and regulate vehicles used for public hire, an ordinance prescribing certain stands for hacks would not prevent their occupying other stands on private railroad premises.[2]

§ 146. **Jurisdiction over streets.**—Police regulation is always properly exercised over the streets of a corporation, without regard to the title to the streets. Even private streets may be generally used by the public. Power over streets, the fee in which belongs to the adjoining owners, is limited to police regulation and to such measures as are necessary to insure the serviceability of the roadway. The city could not alter the physical characteristics of a private street publicly used, nor could it authorize a railroad company to run over a street to which the fee remains in the land-owners, unless express authority is granted by the state.[3] But the fact that a turnpike company owns the fee does not prevent the exercise of any grade of police regulation.[4]

§ 147. **Penalties.**—A penalty is a punishment for doing a prohibited act or omitting some imperative duty. It does not include imprisonment, when used with reference to municipal ordinances.[5] Ordinances would be inoperative if no power was vested in the municipality to enforce obedience to them. Provision is usually made by statute or charter for the means that may be adopted to enforce ordinances; but if it is not expressly made, the municipality is not thereby barred from its remedy. Although penal-

---

(1) Walsh v. Railroad Co., 27 Minn. 367; St. Paul v. Smith, 27 Minn. 364.
(2) Buffalo v. Mulchady, 1 Sheldon, 431.
(3) Quinn v. Paterson, 28 N. J. 35; Perry v. Railroad Co., 55 Ala. 425.
(4) State v. New Brunswick, 30 N. J. 395.
(5) Lancaster v. Richardson, 4 Lans. 136.

ties are rightfully looked upon with disfavor, no grant of power would be made if it were not within the legislative intent that the exercise of the power should be made effective by the imposition of adequate penalties. Power to ordain implies, of necessity, power to provide and enforce reasonable penalties.[1] The penalties imposed under implied power must be reasonable, that is, they must not be too severe to accomplish their purpose—that of insuring obedience to the ordinances. Regard must be had for the policy of the state as evidenced in grants to other corporations, or to the same corporation over other subjects of local control.

Power to establish, erect, and keep bridges in repair implies power to provide by ordinance for the punishment of persons who willfully injure the bridges that are erected under the grant.[2] Under power "to open, widen, establish, improve, and keep in repair the streets, avenues, etc.," and to pass ordinances to effectuate that power, fines may lawfully be imposed for obstructing the public streets.[3] Power to prevent nuisances necessitates the imposition of definite penalties for their erection or maintenance.[4] So, a power to prevent, as the council "may judge proper," the erection of wooden buildings authorizes an ordinance prescribing a penalty to be enforced by a prosecution in the municipal courts.[5] Under a general power of police regulation, a city may impose pecuniary penalties for injuries to the public property.[6] And power to levy a license tax implies power to enforce payment by appropriate proceedings.[7] If a municipality has power to suppress bawdy houses, power

---

(1) Tipton v. Norman, 72 Mo. 380; Eyerman v. Blaksley, 78 Mo. 145; Winooski v. Gokey, 49 Vt. 282; Grover v. Huckins, 26 Mich. 476; Mobile v. Yuille, 3 Ala. 137; London v. Vanacre, 12 Mod. 270; Mason v. Shawneetown, 77 Ill. 533; Shreveport v. Roos, 35 La. Ann. 1010; Hooksett v. Amoskeag Co., 44 N. H. 105.

(2) Korah v. Ottawa, 32 Ill. 122.

(3) Railroad Co. v. Chenoa, 43 Ill. 209.

(4) Railroad Co. v. Louisville, 8 Bush, 415.

(5) Respublica v. Duquet, 2 Yeates, 493.

(6) Korah v. Ottawa, 32 Ill. 122.

(7) Amite City v. Clements, 24 La. Ann. 27.

to adopt means to suppress them follows by implication.[1] But if the charter enumerates certain powers that may be enforced by *penal* prosecution, such enumeration excludes the implication of right to impose penalties in other cases.[2]

§ 148. **The kind of penalty that may be adopted.**— Whenever the organic law of the corporation defines the mode of enforcement of ordinances, the definition must be strictly adhered to.[3] Thus, under a power to punish by fine *or* imprisonment, an ordinance is void which imposes a certain fine or a certain imprisonment, *or both*.[4] When the mode of enforcement is specified in the act containing the grant of power, or otherwise, all other modes are precluded.[5] The usual means are to be resorted to if no others are indicated;[6] and within the limits of those usual means the council may exercise its discretion.[7]

§ 149. **Penalties are not licenses.**—The penalties imposed by ordinances, like those imposed by the laws of the state, can in nowise be construed as legalizing the acts subjected to punishment. Penalties are not licenses. The acts punished are thereby made unlawful. Express grant of power, for example, to kill dogs, for the keeping of which no license has been obtained, does not prevent the imposition of a penalty on the owner for violation of the ordinance in refusing or omitting to procure a license. The imposition of a penalty amounts to an authoritative prohibition.[8]

(1) Shreveport *v.* Roos, 35 La. Ann. 1010.
(2) Grand Rapids *v.* Hughes, 15 Mich. 54.
(3) Barter *v.* Commonwealth, 3 Pen. & W. 253; Norton *v.* Kearon, 6 Ir. R. C. L. 126.
(4) Leland *v.* Commissioners, 42 N. J. 375.
(5) Hart *v.* Albany, 7 Wend. 571; Moberly *v.* Wright, 19 Mo. App. 269.
(6) Grover *v.* Huckins, 26 Mich. 478.
(7) Mason *v.* Shawneetown, 77 Ill. 533, State *v.* Cantieny, 34 Minn. 1. (Costs).
(8) Pedrick *v.* Bailey, 12 Gray, 161; Johnson *v.* Simonton, 43 Cal. 242; Faribault *v.* Wilson, 34 Minn. 254.

§ 150. **Fines.**—Fines are not debts in the sense of a constitutional provision which prohibits imprisonment for debt.[1] They are strictly penalties, and are in the nature of liquidated damages, established as such in lieu of the damages which a court of law would be authorized to assess for the injury done to the public by the offense punished.[2]

At common law fines constituted the only lawful mode of punishing breaches of ordinances.[3] And unless express power is given to punish in some other mode, as by imprisonment, the rule still obtains.[4] But it has been held that authority to impose "the ordinary penalties" does not restrict a city to the imposition of fines alone in cases where a license is exacted. Offenses may be punished by revocation of the license.[5]

§ 151. **Amount of the fine.**—Fines, as penalties, must be reasonable in amount; but when the limit is not prescribed, the amount fixed by the council in the exercise of its discretion is presumptively reasonable. If a limit is prescribed by statute, it must be strictly observed, and no penalty for a single offense may exceed the maximum. If fifty dollars is the prescribed maximum and an ordinance authorizes the imposition of any amount between twenty and one hundred dollars, any fine levied under that ordinance will be enforceable if not greater than fifty dollars. It would seem that the mere attempt to authorize an unlawful fine is not fatal to the validity of the ordinance so long as the minimum fine prescribed would be lawful.[6]

When the charter of a city gives it "the same power" to impose fines that had previously been given to other towns, and as to other towns there was no restriction as to

---

(1) Hardenbrook v. Ligonier, 95 Ind. 70; Ex parte Hollwedell, 74 Mo. 395; Charleston v. Oliver, 16 S. C. 47.
(2) First Municipalty v. Cutting, 4 La. Ann. 335.
(3) Hall v. Nixon, 10 L. R. Q. B. 159.
(4) Sedgwick Stat. Law, p. 473.
(5) Schwuchow v. Chicago, 68 Ill. 444.
(6) Greenfield v. Mook, 12 Ill. App. 281.

amount, the amount of the fine that could lawfully be imposed would be limited only to the jurisdiction of the tribunal provided for the trial of violations of the ordinances.[1]

Fines must be not only reasonable, but certain in amount. Neither of these requirements should, however, be construed to mean that the ordinance should name the exact amount. If the offense were of such a nature that the circumstances of its commission could not operate to aggravate it, it would be best to fix upon an invariable amount of the fine; but most offenses do vary materially in degree according to the accompanying circumstances, and the best ends of justice are subserved by recognizing this fact by prescribing certain limits within which the court trying the offender may exercise its discretion. A provision that a certain offense shall be punished by a fine *not over* a certain amount, but fixing no minimum, would impose too much confidence in the discretion of the magistrate, who might adjudge a very nominal fine against an offender and thus virtually make the penalty no punishment at all. An ordinance is both reasonable and definite which fixes a maximum and a minimum limit.[2] In those states where actions brought to enforce penalties under municipal ordinances are considered to be criminal prosecutions, it is held that the ordinance should fix the exact amount of the fine.[3]

§ 152. **Cumulative fines.**—In determining the validity of a judgment imposing a fine, care must be had to discriminate between offenses that are several and distinct and those that are continuing. Distinct offenses of the same nature may, under some codes of procedure, be pros-

---

(1) Hamilton *v.* Carthage, 24 Ill. 22; Railroad Co. *v.* Chenoa, 43 Ill. 209; Zylstra *v.* Charleston, 1 Bay (S. C.), 382; Dill. M. C., § 438.

(2) McConville *v.* Jersey City, 39 N. J. 38; State *v.* Crenshaw, 94 N. C. 877; State *v.* Cainan, 94 N. C. 883.

(3) Louisburg *v.* Harris, 7 Jones (N. C.), 281; State *v.* Zeigler, 32 N. J. 262; Mobile *v.* Yuille, 3 Ala. 137 (overruled in Huntsville *v.* Phelps, 27 Ala. 55); Peters *v.* London, 2 U. C. Q. B. 543.

ecuted in one and the same action; in which case the full limit of the law may be adjudged against the offender for each offense, regardless of the fact that the total fine thus imposed far exceeds the bounds of the jurisdiction of the local court.[1] For instance, one might make any number of unlawful sales of intoxicating liquors on the same day, and each sale would be a distinct offense punishable separately.

Other acts that constitute offenses against ordinances are continuing; that is, they may have numerous consecutive results, each of which may be considered an offense. Thus, if a person erect a nuisance, not only the primary erection but also each day's continuance, is a menace to public rights. A prosecution, however, would needs cover the total offense prior to the date of its institution. In such cases, the limit of the lawful fine for maintaining a nuisance could not be exceeded for the same nuisance, but it is lawful to provide an initial fine for creating the nuisance and an additional fine for each day of its continuance. The fine, as thus computed, must not be made to exceed the limit prescribed for that kind of an offense. It is no ground of objection to such an ordinance that the fine might, under its provisions, be computed to exceed the limit.[2] An ordinance that imposes a fine of five dollars for every barrel of flour sold without having been inspected by a certain officer, is only operative up to the $100 limit fixed by statute as the amount of fine that the municipality may lawfully impose.[3] So, under power to regulate the sale of gunpowder and to punish all offenses against the city by fines not to exceed $250, an ordinance that imposes a fine of $125, on each hundred pounds kept in store, could only be enforced up to the $250 limit.[4]

§ 153. **Repetition of an offense more heavily punished.**—It is proper that a distinction should be drawn be-

(1) Columbia *v.* Harrison, 2 C. C. (S. Car.) 215; Heise *v.* Columbia, 6 Rich. 404.
(2) *Contra*, Commonwealth *v.* Wilkins, 121 Mass. 356.
(3) Chicago *v.* Quimby, 38 Ill. 274.
(4) New York *v.* Ordrenaux, 12 Johns. 122.

tween the first and a subsequent commission of an offense. The repeated act is more of an offense, because the offender's attention has been forcibly attracted to the provisions of the law, and the disregard thus shown for the rights of the public is less pardonable. Special authority is often given by statute to distinguish between a first offense and subsequent offenses by imposing a heavier fine for each repetition of the unlawful act; but, without express authority, such discrimination is still lawful, so long as the higher penalty is within the limit of the amount that the municipality may impose for breaches of its ordinances.[1]

§ 154. **Costs of the prosecution.**—In computing the amount of a fine, the costs of the proceeding are not to be considered as a part of the penalty.[2] Municipal corporations are generally obliged to enforce their own ordinances, and the expense incurred in securing the punishment of offenders should be repaid by those whose digression from the path of duty has caused the expense. Being proceedings to punish the commission of offenses against the community, the community should not only be made good for its outlay, but whatever fines are imposed should be paid into the municipal treasury, and inure to the benefit of the corporation.[3]

§ 155. **Imprisonment in default of payment.**—Fines imposed for violations of ordinances may be collected by levying upon the personal property of the offender and selling it, as upon an execution in a civil proceeding, only when the authority is express. If any remedy exists against his real estate, it can only be enforced in a separate action brought in a state court. In Canada the sole remedy is against personalty,[4] and in the United States neither realty nor personalty can be subjected to the payment of a fine in the absence of special authority.[5]

(1) Staats v. Washington, 45 N. J. L. 318.
(2) State v. Herdt, 40 N. J. L. 264.
(3) People v. Sacramento, 6 Cal. 422.
(4) Queen v. Gilbert, 2 Pug. & Bur. 619; Ex parte Trask, 1 Pug. & Bur. 277.
(5) Howard v. Savannah, T. U. P. Ch. 173.

In order, therefore, that the imposition of fines for offenses against municipalities may be made effective against impecunious offenders, it is usually provided by statute or charter that the offender may be imprisoned for a certain length of time in case default is made in paying the fine and the costs of prosecution. Such imprisonment is not looked upon as a punishment for the offense, but simply as a necessary means of enforcing the pecuniary penalty.[1] Neither does it fall within the meaning of imprisonment as used in the constitution, and does not entitle the offender to the protection of any of the rights or guaranties which are accorded to persons who stand accused of an offense punishable by imprisonment.[2] By paying the fine imposed, an offender can escape this kind of imprisonment. Although this option to pay or be imprisoned is virtually of no value to one whose poverty prevents him from exercising it to escape confinement, and thus, in fact, amounts to a punishment, it is just that class of offenders who escape punishment if no such procedure were lawful.

The charter or general law must, however, expressly authorize this mode of enforcing fines. Thus, power to punish by fines or imprisonment does not include power to imprison for the non-payment of a fine.[3]

Neglect to take out a license required by ordinance is as much a violation of the ordinance as other offenses more positive in their nature, and the payment of the fine provided for such neglect may be enforced by imprisonment whenever a failure to pay a fine imposed for any other offense might be so punished.[4]

§ 156. **The power strictly construed.**—In adjudging the alternative of payment or imprisonment for a certain time unless the fine is paid, the terms of the power to so

(1) Sheffield *v.* O'Day, 7 Ill. App. 339; State *v.* Herdt, 40 N. J. 264.
(2) State *v.* Herdt, 40 N. J. 264; Inwood *v.* State, 42 O. S. 186.
(3) Brieswick *v.* Brunswick, 51 Ga. 639.
(4) Ex parte Council of Montgomery, 64 Ala. 463. See Plaquemine *v.* Ruff, 30 La. Ann. 497.

imprison must be closely followed, and the imprisonment must conform exactly to the wording of the decree. Where a magistrate is empowered to commit offenders, in default of payment, to "the county jail," and "for such time as the council may have directed," a commitment to any other than the *county* jail would be unlawful, and no commitment at all could be sustained if the council had neglected to make the contemplated direction as to the duration of the imprisonment. The power is not perfect until such direction has been made.[1] So, where the statute allows six months' imprisonment, the judgment of the court should *in terms* decree imprisonment for six months, *or until the fine is paid*, a mere general judgment of imprisonment being unlawful in not providing for the possible termination of the necessity for such a penalty.[2] If the charter authorizes such imprisonment for twenty-one days, an ordinance is void which permits or authorizes a commitment for from one to thirty days.[3] If the state law directs that fines shall be collected by levying execution on the goods and chattels of the offender, and also allows imprisonment for failure to pay fines, an attempt to collect a pecuniary penalty by execution must be made before the right to imprison can lawfully be exercised.[4]

The terms of the judgment rendered must be closely observed. Thus, if a statute make it lawful to imprison at hard labor for failure to pay a fine, but the judgment or sentence, as rendered, simply decrees imprisonment until the fine and costs are paid, to subject the offender to imprisonment at hard labor would render the authorities who execute the sentence liable to the offender in an action for false imprisonment.[5] Costs can not be included in the amount for which the offender is imprisoned, without express authority.[6]

(1) Merkee *v.* Rochester, 13 Hun. 137.
(2) Kanouse *v.* Lexington, 12 Ill. App. 318.
(3) McLeod *v.* Kincasdine, 38. U. C. Q. B. 617.
(4) Queen *v.* Gilbert, 2 Pug. & Bur. 619; Ex parte Trask, 1 Pug. & Bur. 277; In re Greystock, 12 U. C. Q. B. 458.
(5) Torbert *v.* Lynch, 67 Ind. 474; Ex parte Moore, 62 Ala. 471.
(6) State *v.* Cantieny, 34 Minn. 1. See *post*, § 203.

§ 157. **Such imprisonment does not satisfy the judgment.**—Consistently with the theory that imprisonment in default of payment is not in itself a punishment, but merely a mode of compelling payment, it is held that such imprisonment is in no sense a satisfaction of the fine imposed, unless some provision is made that the prisoner shall work out the amount of the fine during the imprisonment. It would, therefore, be no bar to an action of *scire facias* on an appeal bond to collect the fine and costs, neither would it prevent subsequent execution to collect the sum due.[1]

An offender can not, however be compelled to labor during his imprisonment in order to satisfy the judgment against him unless by virtue of express statutory provision, and the labor imposed must conform to the letter of the power.[2]

§ 158. **Imprisonment as a penalty.**—Ordinances may prescribe imprisonment as a penalty for their non-observance only when express authority is given. The only remedy at common law was an action in the nature of debt to collect the pecuniary penalties attached to violation. The power to imprison never arises by implication.[3] When this power is conferred, it must, like all other final provisions, be strictly construed. The literal meaning conveyed by the terms of the grant must be followed. It could not authorize an ordinance inflicting imprisonment for failure to pay a license fee, if no power is given the municipality to make such failure a misdemeanor.[4]

Imprisonment as a direct penalty means imprisonment in pursuance of a proper judicial determination of the guilt of an offender, in a prosecution for an offense actually committed. If that is the penalty prescribed by ordinance, no authority is thereby given to imprison a person before

(1) Sheffield *v.* O'Day, 7 Ill. App. 339.
(2) Ex parte Bedell, 20 Mo. App. 125.
(3) Clarke's Case, 5 Coke, 64; City of London's Case, 8 Coke, 127; Burlington *v.* Kellar, 18 Ia. 59; Kinmundy *v.* Mahan, 72 Ill. 462.
(4) Desty Taxation, 770.

a judicial determination of his liability. He can not be imprisoned before trial.[1]

Whenever a limit is set to the duration of the imprisonment that may be inflicted by ordinance, it must never be exceeded. An ordinance, however, that provides a method of determining or computing the length of the term, whereby it would be possible to exceed the constitutional or statutory limit, may be enforced up to that limit. The ordinance would not *ipso facto* be void.[2]

§ 159. **Forfeiture.**—At common law and in England to-day fines alone are lawful as penalties for violation of municipal ordinances, and unless express authority exists to collect them by taking the property of the offender. Collection can only be made by a separate action in the nature of debt. Distress against the goods of the offender and imprisonment are alike unlawful.[3] The rights of private property are equally sacred to the common law of this country. Except under plain authority, forfeitures to secure the payment of fines are unlawful;[4] and when conferred, the power must be exercised in strict conformance to its terms.[5] But if a double penalty of fine and forfeiture is imposed by ordinance, the fine is lawful, although the forfeiture is not. The two penalties are severable, and the fact that one is in excess of the power granted would not affect the validity of the other.[6]

§ 160 **Illustration.**—An ordinance authorizing the arrest and punishment of persons who keep or visit gam-

(1) Low v. Evans, 16 Ind. 486.
(2) Keokuk v. Dressell, 47 Ia. 597.
(3) Kirk v. Nowill, 1 Term Rep. 118.
(4) Heise v. Columbia, 6 Rich. 404; Hart v. Albany, 9 Wend. 571; Cotter v. Doty, 5 Ohio, 394; Rosebaugh v. Saffin, 10 Ohio, 31; White v. Tallman, 26 N. J. L. 67; Phillips v. Allen, 41 Pa. St. 481; Kneedler v. Norristown, 100 Pa. St. 368; Henke v. McCord, 55 Ia. 378; New Hampton v. Conroy, 56 Ia. 498; Varden v. Mount, 78 Ky. 86; Slessman v. Crozier, 80 Ind. 487.
(5) Clark v. Lewis, 35 Ill. 417; Friday v. Floyd, 63 Ill. 50; Bullock v. Gromble, 45 Ill. 218.
(6) Kneedler v. Norristown, 100 Pa. St. 368.

bling houses, does not warrant the seizure and destruction of the instruments of gambling that may be found in such houses.[1] Power to regulate markets authorizes the passage of an ordinance requiring the true capacity of all baskets in which produce is sold to be plainly marked on the baskets, but could not warrant forfeiture of all baskets not so marked.[2]

But where the thing prohibited is of itself dangerous to the health of the community, provision may be made to abate the nuisance on duly compensating the owner for any actual loss. Thus, it is held that bread may be forfeited if the loaves fall below the prescribed standard weight, which is required to be stamped thereon.[3] The ultimate object of such regulation is to keep light loaves out of the market, and this is not accomplished by a simple punishment of the baker or vender.

The occasions just referred to furnish the key to an important distinction between those cases where forfeitures are and where they are not allowable. If the gist of the offense is some personal act that tends to break the peace of the community, the fine imposed can not be made out of the offender's property, but if the offense is based on the erection and maintenance of a structure which menaces public health or security, or on the keeping or production of some article which is such a nuisance, the remedy ceases to be directed purely against the individual, but it is all important that the structure or article should be removed or altered beyond the possibility of doing harm. In the case of light weight loaves of bread, the defect can not be remedied by rebaking the bread, and the only way of keeping such bread from consumers is to withdraw it entirely from the market.

If a person is conducting a trade or business under a license from the town, and commits some offense against the ordinance regulating the manner in which he shall

(1) Ridgeway v. West, 60 Ind. 371.
(2) Phillips v. Allen, 41 Pa. St. 481.
(3) Guillotte v. New Orleans, 12 La. Ann. 482; In re Nasmith, 2 Ontario, 192.

conduct his business, the offense is of a personal nature and may not be punished by forfeiture of his license.[1] The license is property, and so is the right to conduct the business. Without express authority no place of business can be closed for a violation of the ordinance regulating its conduct.[2] Such a procedure would amount to a distress, and is contrary to common right.[3]

In all cases where the remedy of the municipality in order to be effective must be enforced against the property the improper use of which constitutes the offense, considerable expense is incurred by the municipality, and this should in some way be reimbursed by the offender. Under a power to prevent the erection of wooden buildings within defined limits, an unlawful structure may be removed. The materials removed still belong to the person who is building, but the corporation may lawfully have its remedy against them in order to secure compensation for the expenses incurred in their removal. The same is true with regard to any nuisance that the corporation has power to abate.

§ 161. **Strays.**—The most frequent application of the rule against forfeiture is in cases arising under ordinances for the prevention of strays and the running at large of animals.[4] Power to restrain cattle from running at large and to enact such ordinances as are necessary to make the restraint effectual does not authorize a sale of the animals taken up in order to satisfy the penalty imposed upon their owner.[5] The animals may be held and sold to defray the *cost* of abating the nuisance, but not to pay the penalty.

(1) Heise v. Columbia, 6 Rich. 404; Staats v. Washington, 44 N. J. L. 605. *Contra*, Hurber v. Baugh, 43 Ia. 514.

(2) Ryan v. Jacob, 6 W. L. Bull. (Ohio) 139; Bolte v. New Orleans, 10 La. Ann. 321; Bright v. Toronto, 12 U. C. C. P. 433. *Contra*, Towns v. Tallahassee, 11 Fla. 130.

(3) Bergen v. Clarkson, 6 N. J. L. 352; White v. Tallman, 26 N. J. L. 67; Cumming v. Savannah, R. M. Charlt. 26.

(4) Varden v. Mount, 78 Ky. 86.

(5) Sleesman v. Crozier, 80 Ind. 487; Wilcox v. Hemming, 58 Wis. 144.

The ordinance is only indirectly aimed at the owner of the stray animals; he may, in fact, be wholly beyond the corporate jurisdiction. The corporation is put to trouble and expense in taking up the strays and in providing a suitable pound for their retention until claimed by the owner. The animals must be fed and cared for. To meet this expense the animals may be sold, even against the owner's consent, although the owner thereby forfeits his property.[1]

§ 162. **Notice to the owner.**—Every principle of justice demands that no man shall be deprived of his property, even though by his own act or neglect he may have allowed it to be so used or placed as to violate the local laws, without first affording him an opportunity to contest the fact of the violation, and, when the fact is determined, of saving the forfeiture by paying such fines as have been imposed, and by compensating the public for its outlay. Such is the almost uniform holding of the courts, although the Supreme Court of Wisconsin, deeming the necessity of the remedy of paramount importance, holds that an ordinance that authorizes the seizure, impounding, and sale of strays without any prior judicial inquiry, does not work a forfeiture within the constitutional prohibition of forfeitures of property without due process of law and compensation.[2]

Before a sale can be made either actual or constructive notice must be given to the owner. It may be personal or by advertisement.[3] Due notice can not be dispensed with without legislative authority.[4] And the prescribed mode of giving notice must be strictly followed in order to justify the proceeding.[5] So, where an ordinance against allowing

(1) *Contra*, Gosselink v. Campbell, 4 Ia. 296. *Pro*, Fort Smith v. Dodson, 46 Ark. 301.

(2) Wilcox v. Hemming, 58 Wis. 144.

(3) Davies v. Morgan, 1 C. & J. 587; Rosebaugh v. Saffin, 10 Ohio, 31; Hellen v. Noe, 3 Ired. L. 493; Shaw v. Kennedy, N. Car. Term. Rep. 158; Gilchrist v. Schnidling, 12 Kan. 263; McKee v. McKee, 8 B. Mon. 433.

(4) Rosebaugh v. Saffin, 10 Ohio, 31.

(5) Wade on Notice, § 1122.

hogs to run at large gives the owner five days to redeem the strays, and allows a sale to defray expenses after three days' advertisement of the sale, the owner has five full days time *exclusive* of the day on which the animals are seized, and a sale could not be made until three days after the expiration of the five days, or until the ninth day after the day of seizure.

§ 163. **Judicial determination.**—Although the acts of seizure, impounding, and sale are ministerial, to be performed by the police authorities of the corporation, some formal proceding should be had to determine the fact that the animals seized were actually running at large, and in which the owner may have an opportunity of being heard and contesting the justice of the seizure or sale.[2]

If possible, personal service of summons should be made upon the owner of the animals, but if he is not known, or is beyond the jurisdiction of the court, it is sufficient that the procedure be *in re* and that some public notice be given of the time and place of sale.

§ 164. **Forfeiture of real estate.**—Those are really police ordinances which make the construction of sidewalks or fences obligatory upon the owners of property adjacent to the public streets, and which provide that in case of failure to comply with the requirement after due notification, the corporate authorities may proceed to construct the walk or fence, and charge the owner with the cost of construction. The cost is generally assessed upon the land, by authority of law, and if not paid the land may be sold to satisfy it, as for any delinquent taxes due to the state or county, thus indirectly working a forfeiture for disobeying the ordinance. This is considered more as a tax than as a penalty and is looked upon with favor.[3] It

---

(1) White *v.* Haworth, 21 Mo. App. 439.

(2) Varden *v.* Mount, 78 Ky. 86; Baumgard *v.* Mayor, 9 La. 119; Rost *v.* Mayor, 15 La. 129; Lanfear *v.* Mayor, 4 La. 97; Shaw *v.* Kennedy, N. Car. Term Rep. 158; Darst *v.* Illinois, 51 Ill. 286; Willis *v.* Legris, 45 Ill. 289; Donovan *v.* Vicksburg, 29 Miss. 247; Ex parte Burnett, 30 Ala. 461; Dill. Mun. Corp., § 353.

(3) Bonsall *v.* Lebanon, 19 Ohio, 418.

does not result in unequal taxation within the meaning of that term as used in constitutions.[1] The primary burden is upon the person upon whom the duty is imposed by statute or authorized ordinance,[2] but as the improvement is a benefit to the land, it is eventually charged upon the land, and any person who has an interest therein, or who acquires an interest after the construction is completed, is liable to have his interest sold to satisfy the lien.[3] As in other proceedings which result in imposing a burden on persons or property, every step must conform strictly to the mode prescribed by the charter or statute.[4]

(1) Mayberry v. Franklin, 6 Humph. 368; Washington v. Nashville, 1 Swan (Tenn.) 177.
(2) People v. Council, 54 N. Y. 507.
(3) Highland v. Galveston, 54 Tex. 527.
(4) D'Antignac v. Augusta, 31 Ga. 700.

CHAPTER VII

PROCEDURE—PLEADING—EVIDENCE.

§ 165. Introduction.
§ 166. The tribunal.
§ 167. Citizenship does not disqualify the magistrate.
§ 168. Form of the action.
§ 169. Nature of the action.
§ 170. Holdings of the different states.
§ 170a. General conclusion.
§ 171. Joinder of causes of action.
§ 172. The complaint.
§ 172a. The title of the case.
§ 173. The offense must be distinctly alleged.
§ 174. Reference made to the ordinance violated.
§ 175. Exceptions need not be negatived.
§ 176. The conclusion of the complaint.
§ 177. Signature to complaint.
§ 178. Arrest before trial.
§ 179. What the warrant should contain.
§ 180. Arrests made without a warrant.
§ 181. Trial by jury.
§ 182. Arraignment and plea.
§ 183. Evidence.
§ 184. Judicial notice.
§ 185. How ordinances are proved.
§ 186. Record of council proceedings as evidence.
§ 187. Proof of publication.
§ 188. Presumption that ordinances are reasonable.
§ 189. Reasonableness a question of law.
§ 190. Proof of time and place of committing the offense.
§ 191. Proof that act does not fall within exceptions.
§ 192. Testimony of defendant.
§§ 193, 194. Construction of ordinances.
§ 195. Examples of application of rules of construction.
§ 196. Defenses to prosecutions.
§ 197. Effect of repeal of an ordinance.
§ 198. Former conviction.
§ 199. Other defenses.
§ 200. Doctrine of estoppel applied to defenses.
§ 201. Estoppel of the corporation.
§ 202. Form of the judgment.
§ 203. The order of commitment to jail.

§ 165. **Introduction.**—The enforcement of municipal ordinances is intrusted to the local authorities, and must be accomplished through proceedings in a local court. The state laws seldom prescribe detailed rules of practice and procedure in these local courts, and we therefore find a deplorable state of confusion in the methods ordinarily followed. They are based partly upon direct statutory provisions, partly on custom, partly on the by-laws of the corporation itself, but more often on an attempt to imitate the rules laid down for analogous proceedings in the state courts. When we consider that the offenses are of a minor character, that the necessity for a speedy remedy is more urgent, that local courts are seldom organized under complete systems such as underlie the existence of state tribunals, and that the ordinances to be enforced are of a confusing variety and scope, it becomes apparent that the rules observed in higher courts are often wholly impracticable or inapplicable to practice before the municipal courts. Rules must be varied and modified to meet the necessities of each case. Rules of evidence are about the only rules that can well be applied in the local courts without some modification. Because the practice in these courts is usually left to its own development and is seldom regulated by extensive legislation, it is much easier to formulate rules which will be applicable to procedure in all the states, than it is in regard to actions brought in the state courts.

§ 166. **The tribunal.**—In England all actions to enforce ordinances are in the nature of debt or assumpsit to recover the specific fine, and are brought before the ordinary tribunals having jurisdiction to entertain such actions. In America the practice is very diverse, but some special tribunal is usually created for the trial of causes based upon violation of local ordinances. Its jurisdiction is often, for the sake of convenience, extended over petty offenses against the laws of the state. Remedies under ordinances will, however, never be allowed to fail for want of a tribunal, and if no special tribunal is provided, actions to enforce penalties may be brought in the established courts of the state.[1] If a special tribunal is provided by general law such actions are restricted to it. It acquires exclusive jurisdiction unless the general law plainly indicates that such is not the intention of the state legislature. The power to hear and decide actions brought to enforce ordinances involves the liberty and rights of property of the individual. It is derogatory to common right and can only be exercised by such tribunals as have plain, unmistakable authority, and in strict accordance with the terms of the grant. If the charter provides that justices of the peace shall hear proceedings based on the ordinances of the municipality, the municipality can not supplement the charter by giving concurrent jurisdiction to the mayor.[2] The corporation can not erect its own tribunals if none are provided by the law under which it is established, nor can it erect different tribunals from those that are expressly authorized.[3]

When special tribunals are created for the purpose of entertaining actions to enforce municipal ordinances, their jurisdiction is limited strictly to that purpose, and only extends to such proceedings as may be necessary to compel obedience to the local laws. They may control the person of the offender and his property so far as concerns the manner of its use. It may be necessary to determine the title to property incidentally, but such determination is only effective as regards the remedy being pursued. No claim to the property can be based on it. It could not even be used in evidence in an action in a state court involving the title to the same property.[4] Local courts are, in short, limited in their jurisdiction strictly to the purposes of their creation.

Objection to the jurisdiction must be made before submission to the process and judgment of the court. If the person whose rights are in jeopardy fails to question the

(1) Columbia v. Harrison, 2 C. C. (S. Car.) 213.
(2) Staates v. Washington, 45 N. J. L. 318.
(3) Barter v. Commonwealth, 3 Pen. & W. 253; Deel v. Pittsburgh 3 Watts, 363.
(4) Beecher v. People, 38 Mich. 289.

jurisdiction at the first step, he will be estopped from so doing in the appellate court.¹ If suit be begun before one justice, but for some insufficient reason is continued before a different justice, and the defendant allows the trial to proceed without objection, his appearance and silence will be a bar to subsequent objection.²

The jurisdiction of the court is in no sense dependent upon the validity of the ordinance; that is, an objection to the jurisdiction by demurrer or motion will not be sustained by proof of the invalidity of the ordinance sought to be enforced.³

§ 167. **Citizenship does not disqualify the magistrate.** Every citizen of a municipality has an interest in the prompt and vigorous enforcement of its ordinances. This interest may be only such as all public spirited persons have in the peace and good order of the community, or it may be pecuniarily material as in cases where the fines collected inure to the benefit of the local revenue, and thereby slightly reduce the burdens of taxation. No one would think of claiming that the judge of a state court is disqualified from hearing prosecutions brought under the penal laws of the state, by reason of his interest, as a public-minded citizen, in the due enforcement of those laws. Earlier English corporations were not municipal, but were close corporations, composed of those who followed the same trade, and it was held that the local magistrate was disqualified to try violations of their by-laws, if he chanced to be a member of the prosecuting corporation.⁴ Reasoning from the false analogy of such holdings, the claim has often been seriously made that the personal interest of a local justice, mayor, or magistrate is so direct and material as to disqualify him to try actions brought to enforce the penalties imposed by the ordinances of the municipality of which he is a citizen. The authorities are uniformly opposed to the validity of

(1) Tisdale v. Minonk, 46 Ill. 9.
(2) Wiggins v. Chicago, 68 Ill. 372.
(3) Woodruff v. Stewart, 63 Ala. 208.
(4) Hesketh v. Braddock, 3 Burr. 1847.

such an objection. The magistrate's personal interest in the fine is far too remote to defeat his jurisdiction.[1]

§ 168. **Form of the action.**—The common-law remedy for violation of ordinances consisted of a civil action either of *debt* or *on the case in assumpsit*, brought against the offender to recover the amount of the penalty imposed; *debt*, when the penalty was considered as a certain amount of liquidated damages, and *assumpsit*, when the act complained of was merely considered as a violation of a duty owed to the community by the offender.[2] And in this country an action in the nature of debt is still the proper remedy unless, as is generally the case, the charter or general law contains some other provision.[3] When the statute is silent it is proper, though unnecessary, for the corporation to ordain that penalties shall be recovered by action in debt; such an ordinance would simply be a formal recognition of the rule of law.[4] In the majority of the states the general municipal code or the charter provides for a special proceeding to be instituted before some local magistrate. This special proceeding is more or less summary, and is usually divested of many of the formalities and technicalities of actions in higher courts.

Whether the fine or penalty is definitely fixed by ordinance, or is only restricted to certain limits within which the magistrate is to exercise his discretion, the action is always brought to enforce a penalty, the benefit of which inures to the corporation, and unless the law of the state requires the action to be brought in the name of the state

---

(1) Commonwealth v. Worcester, 3 Pick. 462; Thomas v. Mt. Vernon, 9 Ohio, 290; Deitz v. Central, 1 Col. 323; Jonesborough v. McKee, 2 Yerg. 167; Council v. Pepper, 1 Rich. 364; Queen v. Justices, 4 Q. B. Div. 522; s. c., 29 Moak Eng. Rep. 61; Queen v. Milledge, 4 Q. B. Div. 332; s. c., 28 Moak Eng. Rep. 784.

(2) Dill. Mun. Corp., § 409; 1 Roll. Abr. 366, 1. 48; Clift. 901.

(3) Brookville v. Gagle, 73 Ind. 117; Jacksonville v. Block, 36 Ill. 507; Israel v. Jacksonville, 2 Ill. 290; Ewbanks v. Ashley, 36 Ill. 177; Weeks v. Foreman, 16 N. J. L. 237; State v. Zeigler, 32 N. J. 262; Williamson v. Commonwealth, 4 B. Mon. 146.

(4) Barter v. Commonwealth, 3 Pa. 253

the corporation is the proper party plaintiff. If the statute makes any direction it must be closely followed.[1] No other form could be legalized by an ordinance than the one prescribed.[2] If authorized to sue "in the name of the corporation," the name conferred or recognized by the charter or general law must be used, though a slight variation would be considered immaterial.[3]

Where no direction at all is made it is advisable to use such name as may be incidentally used in the charter or statute, or in the absence of such a name, that by which the municipality is generally known, or by which it is accustomed to appear in court. In such case, an action in the name of the council, of the overseers, or of the president and trustees would be unobjectionable.[4]

§ 169. **The nature of the action.**—The rules of procedure and evidence applicable to proceedings to enforce penalties for the violation of ordinances depend largely upon the nature of the action, whether civil or criminal. At common law the only means of enforcing ordinances was an action in debt brought before tribunals of general jurisdiction, and the action was therefore purely civil. Certainly, the erection of special tribunals for such actions, and the prescription of different modes of procedure and practice, does not alter the civil nature of the action so long as a fine only is sought to be enforced. And, as we have seen, the imprisonment that is often inflicted for failure to pay a fine is considered a means of enforcing payment and not as a punishment. Great diversity of opinion exists as to the nature of actions which may result in imprisonment as a part or the whole of the punishment. Fines may be considered as debts or as liquidated damages, but imprisonment is a penalty directed against the person of the offender, one that deprives him of liberty. For the pur-

(1) State v. Zeigler, 32 N. J. 262.
(2) Weeks v. Forman, 16 N. J. 237.
(3) Powers v. Decatur, 54 Ala. 214.
(4) Charleston v. Oliver, 16 S. C. 47; Williamson v. Commonwealth, 4 B. Mon. 146; Hirschoff v. Beverly, 45 N. J. L. 288.

poses of determining rules of procedure, actions of this class are best divided into quasi-criminal and criminal actions. The majority of ordinances are directed against offenses which have no existence except as defined by the ordinance. These offenses are not of the same grade with offenses against the state, and the actions brought to punish them are only *quasi-criminal*.[1] But actions brought to enforce the punishment of imprisonment for acts, which are already crimes or misdemeanors under the laws of the state, are *criminal*, and the same right or rights equally efficient should be secured to the accused in the municipal court that are reserved to him in the state courts.

There is no objection to a double punishment for the same act considered as two distinct offenses, one against the public at large, the other against the peace of the local community, but the local community should not be allowed to provide or follow modes of procedure that might make conviction easier under the ordinance than under the statute. This last class of actions are not very numerous, and still we apprehend that they are more apt to work unlawful infringement of the personal rights of citizens than any other proceeding, and their conduct should be guarded with closer scrutiny than simple civil or quasi-criminal actions. For instance, the constitutional guarantee of trial by jury, whenever a person is tried for an offense punishable by imprisonment, would defeat the jurisdiction of a local magistrate over such cases, unless the law creating his tribunal makes provision for jury trial.[2] But the applicability of the constitutional guarantee to prosecution under ordinances ceases whenever the act complained of is not included among the offenses punishable by the laws of the state.[3]

Much confusion arises from a careless use of the words "crime" and "criminal." A *crime* is technically an act made penal by the laws of the state or general govern-

---

(1) Wiggins v. Chicago, 68 Ill. 373; Floyd v. Eutontin, 14 Ga. 355; Greenfield v. Mook, 12 Ill. App. 281; State v. Lee, 27 Minn. 445.

(2) Thomas v. Ashland, 12 O. S. 124.

(3) Monroe v. Meuer, 35 La. Ann. 1192.

ment, and the proceeding brought to enforce the punishment prescribed by the state law is a *criminal prosecution*. It is preferable not to extend the application of these terms to offenses against ordinances, unless in relation to offenses common to both the state and the municipal law, in which case the rules of procedure in the local court should conform to those in the state court in all their essential features.[1]

The extent to which proceedings brought to punish quasi-criminal offenses must conform to the criminal codes and rules of practice in the state courts is decided very differently in different states.

§ 170. **Holdings of the various states.**—The following digest of decided cases shows the tendency to be toward very much less strict rules of procedure in the enforcement of ordinances :

(*a*) *Alabama.* Such actions are so far criminal as to disqualify the defendant from testifying in his own behalf, as is the rule in regular criminal proceedings.[2] And, in general, stricter rules of procedure are observed than in civil cases.[3]

(*b*) *California.* Such actions are criminal and, unless some contrary provision is made by statute, they should be brought in the name of the people like prosecutions under the penal laws of the state.[4]

(*c*) *Georgia.* The right of trial by jury is not violated by imposing fines for violations of municipal ordinances to be recovered by actions before a tribunal that is not provided with a jury.[5]

(*d*) *Illinois.* Actions for violations of penal ordinances are in the nature of actions on tort, but they are not such

(1) Mixer *v.* Supervisors, 26 Mich. 422; Wayne County *v.* Detroit, 17 Mich. 390; Alexander *v.* Council, 54 Miss. 659

(2) Mobile *v.* Jones, 42 Ala. 630.

(3) Fuhrman *v.* Huntsville, 54 Ala. 263.

(4) Santa Barbara *v.* Sherman, 61 Cal. 57; People *v.* Johnson, 30 Cal. 98.

(5) Williams *v.* Augusta, 4 Ga. 509; Floyd *v.* Eutontin, 14 Ga. 354.

penal actions as require security to be given for costs, under a statutory provision that security for costs must be given by the informer in penal actions.¹

(e) *Indiana.* The remedy under ordinances is a civil action brought to recover the common-law penalties.² It makes no difference that the action is begun by the service of a warrant of arrest.³ And the rules of practice in civil cases must be followed.⁴

(f) *Iowa.* Such actions need not be brought in the name of the state, not being *criminal* prosecutions. The complaint filed is not a *process* within the meaning of the statutory provision that all process in criminal prosecution shall be in the name of the state.⁵

(g) *Kansas.* The municipality can sue in its own name, unless the act complained of is also a penal offense against the laws of the state, in which case the proceeding is a criminal prosecution, which must be governed by the rules of criminal procedure.⁶

(h) *Massachussetts.* Such actions are public prosecutions governed by the penal code of procedure, although unlike actions under the state laws, in that no costs are allowed the accused in case of acquittal.⁷

(i) *Michigan.*—Prosecutions under municipal ordinances are not criminal proceedings within the provisions of the penal code of procedure, but are merely penal actions on the part of the municipality for local purposes.⁸

(1) President v. Holland, 19 Ill. 271; Quincy v. Ballance, 30 Ill. 185; Lewiston v. Proctor, 23 Ill. 533.

(2) Brookville v. Gagle, 73 Ind. 117; Quigley v. Aurora, 50 Ind. 28; Greensburg v. Corwin, 58 Ind. 518.

(3) Goshen v. Croxton, 34 Ind. 239; Commissioners v. Chissom, 7 Ind. 688.

(4) Goshen v. Croxton, 34 Ind. 239; Miller v. O'Reilly, 84 Ind. 168 (as to appeal bonds).

(5) Davenport v. Bird, 34 Ia. 524.

(6) Weitzel v. Concordia, 14 Kan. 446. *Contra,* Emporia v. Volmer, 12 Kan. 622.

(7) Dill Mun. Corp., § 412; In re Goddard, 16 Pick. 504; Commonwealth v. Worcester, 3 Pick. 462.

(8) Cooper v. People, 41 Mich. 403; People v. Detroit, 18 Mich. 445.

(j) In *Minnesota* such actions are called quasi-criminal, and statutory provisions for the regulation of procedure in prosecutions for crimes are not applicable.[1]

(k) *Missouri.* Such proceedings are purely civil, and it is wholly immaterial whether the form of the action be civil or criminal.[2]

(l) In *Nebraska* the statute is practically the same as in Iowa, but contrary to the holding in Iowa actions of this kind are considered criminal.[3]

(m) *New Hampshire* courts hold likewise that prosecutions for offenses against ordinances are criminal in their nature.[4]

(n) *New Jersey.* Proceedings in this state more clearly adhere to the old common-law procedure than in the other states. Actions brought to enforce pecuniary penalties under ordinances are civil, and even if in the form of an information, part of the penalty going to the informer, the action is *qui-tam* and civil.[5]

(o) *New York.* Offenses against ordinances, however punished, are neither crimes nor misdemeanors.[6]

(p) *Ohio.* In this state it is apprehended that such actions would be considered quasi-criminal only. Its supreme court has called attention incidentally to the fact that the common-law civil action in the nature of debt is still lawful, unless expressly superseded, to recover pecuniary penalties;[7] and it has also been said that "many offenses, decidedly immoral and mischievous in their tendencies, are only quasi-criminal and properly fall under the jurisdiction of a justice or mayor.[8] Still, where the complaint failed to allege that an action was for a second offense against an

(1) State *v.* Lee, 27 Minn. 445.
(2) St. Louis *v.* Vert, 84 Mo. 204; Ex parte Hollwedell, 74 Mo. 395; Ex parte Kiburg, 10 Mo. App. 442.
(3) Brownville *v.* Cook, 4 Neb. 102.
(4) State *v.* Stearns, 31 N. H. 106.
(5) Brophy *v.* Perth Amboy, 44 N. J. L. 217; Kip *v.* Patterson, 26 N. J. L. 298; Keeler *v.* Milledge, 24 N. J. L. 142.
(6) Wood *v.* Brooklyn, 14 Barb. 431.
(7) Cincinnati *v.* Gwynne, 10 Ohio, 192.
(8) Markle *v.* Akron, 14 Ohio, 586.

ordinance that imposed heavier fines for each repetition of an offense, the court held that it was a fatal omission, and that the rule of criminal pleading would apply.[1]

(*r*) *Wisconsin.* In no other state has this question received more thorough consideration than in Wisconsin, and the position finally adopted by the courts is the most logical and the one to which other states are tending, if they have not already adopted it. At first it was held that even actions brought to enforce the payment of a fine are criminal prosecutions within the meaning of the state bill of rights, which provides that "in all criminal prosecutions the accused shall be entitled to demand the nature and cause of the accusation against him."[2] Referring to that decision, Judge Dillon expresses his belief that such a broad principle can not be maintained where the act charged "is not a crime at common law or in its essential nature;"[3] and the later decisions in Wisconsin fully maintain him and go even farther. If the offense is a crime under the state law, the action is criminal, but otherwise, at most quasi-criminal.[4] In cases punishable by imprisonment, and probably in all cases whether the offense is also covered by the state law or not, the right of trial by jury may be waived by stipulation between the parties.[5] The action is purely civil, so far as the remedy under the ordinance is concerned, and an offense is not a misdemeanor, if prohibited by the ordinance alone, and not by the state law.[6]

(*s*) *Wyoming.* In order to avoid all question it is provided by the code of Wyoming that actions brought to enforce municipal ordinances are purely civil, to be governed by civil procedure.[7]

(1) Larney *v.* Cleveland, 34 O. S. 599.
(2) Fink *v.* Milwaukee, 17 Wis. 26.
(3) Dill. Mun. Corp., § 412, note.
(4) Oshkosh *v.* Schwarz, 55 Wis. 483; Sutton *v.* McConnell, 46 Wis. 269.
(5) Sutton *v.* McConnell, 46 Wis. 269.
(6) Chafin *v.* Waukesha County, 62 Wis. 463.
(7) Jenkins *v.* Cheyenne, 1 Wy. Ter. 287.

§ 170a. **General conclusion.**—In general it may be said that every rule of procedure provided by statute or ordinance must be strictly followed, and especially so when the action may result in a forfeiture of property, or in imprisonment as a penalty.[1] If no provision at all be made, the procedure should conform as closely as practicable to procedure in similar actions. Thus, if jurisdiction over offenses against ordinances is given to an existing tribunal, the same rules should be observed that are prescribed for procedure in other causes brought before it.[2] So, a justice would have no right to refuse a jury trial if compulsory in other cases brought before him.[3]

§ 171. **Joinder of causes of action.**—If the action be considered as brought to recover a debt, or liquidated damages, as at common law, there could be no objection to joining claims for several penalties in one action.[4] It seems, however, that the offenses must be against the same ordinance, and not against two different ordinances, however closely related by their nature.[5] Even where it is customary to join such causes of action it is optional with the complainant, and several causes of action need not be joined so that the aggregate of the penalties exceeds the limits of the magistrate's jurisdiction.[6] In Iowa special authority is conferred by statute to proceed against several offenses in a single information, and the same provision may be made by ordinance.[7] For further treatment of joinder of claims see *ante*, sec. 152.

§ 172. **The complaint.**—In a proceeding to enforce the penalty for a violation of an ordinance, the first step to be taken is to file with the proper magistrate a complaint or

(1) People *v.* Whitney's Point, 32 Hun, 508.
(2) Greeley *v.* Passaic, 42 N. J. 87.
(3) People *v.* Cox, 76 N. Y. 47.
(4) Brooklyn *v.* Cleves, Hill & Den. Sup. 231.
(5) Kensington *v.* Glenat, 1 Phila. 393.
(6) Whitehall *v.* Meaux, 8 Ill. App. 182.
(7) Jackson *v.* Boyd, 53 Ia. 536.

pleading in the nature of an information. This must be in writing.[1] A sentence would be wholly void unless based upon a formal complaint, even though the accused should appear before the magistrate and acknowledge his guilt. Such a sentence could, however, only be impeached by the offender himself. This preliminary pleading may be called an information, petition, complaint, affidavit, or by any other name, but in order to be sufficient it must contain a clear statement of the offense charged and a reference to the ordinance violated. Great formality is seldom required, and even when the remedy is an action of debt brought before the local court it is not at all necessary to file a common-law declaration.[2] So, when the action is considered criminal, the strict formality of an indictment need not be observed, so long as the principal element, the offense, be definitely described and alleged. In order that the complaint may not be open to any manner of objection, it should, however, contain the name of the tribunal before which it is filed, a formal title, a full and complete allegation of the commission of an offense, a reference to the ordinance prohibiting the act complained of, and a conclusion. The complaint must be signed by the informer, and sworn to before the magistrate or some other officer having power to administer such an oath. It then becomes the duty of the magistrate to institute such further action as will bring the accused before the court in a lawful manner, and as will enable some formal decision to be rendered.

§ 172a. The title.—Every complaint should be entitled for the purpose of identification, if for no other reason, but the total lack of a title will not be fatal to its validity if the complaint concludes "against the form of the ordinance in such case provided by the city of X," or "against the peace and dignity of the city of X," so that it shows on its face that the proceeding is brought on behalf of the city of X.[3] The object of a formal title is to inform the offender

(1) Prell v. McDonald, 7 Kan. 445.
(2) Dietz v. Central, 1 Col. 323.
(3) Information v. Oliver, 21 S. Car. 318.

of what law he is charged with violating. This object is attained with sufficient accuracy if the information is conveyed by the wording of the body of the complaint. The issue is fully formed and apparent without any title.[1] Whenever a title is made necessary by statute, but no particular form is prescribed, any form is sufficient. Slight mistakes are immaterial.[2] They are mere irregularities and not fatal.[3] It was held, however, in an early case in Pennsylvania, that the name of the corporation must be accurately given.[4] If the identity of the corporation is plain in spite of an error, there is no ground for a valid objection to a verdict or sentence.[5] Even though the error consist in entitling the case, as though brought by the state instead of by the corporation, exception must be taken in the court below on the trial of the case or the error will be effectually waived.[6]

§ 173. **The offense must be distinctly alleged.**—It is essential to the validity of a prosecution that the complaint contain allegations of every fact necessary to inform the accused with reasonable certainty of the act for which he is sought to be punished.[7] It is sufficient if he is informed to a reasonable certainty.[8] Neither the strictness of the common-law requirements nor the technical accuracy of indictments need be observed.[9] Still, a complete statement of the offense must be made.[10] The requirement is not satisfisd by a simple allegation that the defendant has violated a certain ordinance. The act of violation must be described

(1) Alton v. Kirsch, 78 Ill. 261.
(2) Hershoff v. Beverly, 45 N. J. 288.
(3) State v. Graffmuller, 26 Minn. 6.
(4) Mayor v. Nell, 3 Yeates, 475.
(5) Farrel v. London, 12 U. C. Q. B. 343.
(6) State v. King, 37 Ia. 462.
(7) Memphis v. O'Connor, 53 Mo. 468.
(8) St. Louis v. Frein, 9 Mo. App. 590.
(9) Keeler v. Milledge, 24 N. J. 145; Memphis v. O'Connor, 53 Mo. 468; Commonwealth v. Rowe, 141 Mass. 79.
(10) People v. Justices, 12 Hun, 65.

and not left to implication.¹ It is best, if not necessary, to plead the acts constituting the alleged offense at least as accurately and definitely as the description of the offense contained in the ordinance.² If the same language is used the complaint will hold good.³ Under an ordinance against the maintenance of nuisances in¹ the shape of obnoxious and injurious trades, it is not enough to allege that the defendant keeps in store a large quantity of hides and tallow which emit a disagreeable odor. The complaint must also allege that the odor is injurious to health or obnoxious to the comfort of the citizen, or other facts which would make it amount to a nuisance.⁴ So, if it is made unlawful to "suffer" hogs to go at large, the complaint must aver that the defendant's hogs were at large *by his sufferance*.⁵ Any *material* deviation from the elements of the offense as defined by the ordinance is fatal. Thus, under an ordinance declaring it an offense for any one to allow his animals to *stop and feed* along the highway, a complaint is defective which avers that the defendant's animals were allowed by him to stop *to* feed. The animals must have not only stopped, but they must also have fed on the highway. If the feeding had not been considered a material element of the offense, it should and would have been omitted from the provision of the ordinance.⁶

There must be a positive allegation that the act was committed. A complaint is bad for uncertainty that simply alleges that the informer has "just cause to suspect and does suspect that B. is guilty of a certain offense.⁷

It is, however, no ground of objection to a complaint that it aver *more* than is necessary to constitute the offense. If any one of several distinct acts that are alleged is suffi-

---

(1) Huntington v. Pease, 56 Ind. 305; Huntington v. Cheesbro, 57 Ind. 74.
(2) Truesdale v. Moultrieville, Rice (S. C.), 158.
(3) St. Louis v. Knox, 74 Mo. 79.
(4) Lippman v. South Bend, 84 Ind. 276.
(5) Case v. Hall, 21 Ill. 632.
(6) Commonwealth v. Bean, 14 Gray, 52.
(7) Roberson v. Lambertville, 38 N. J. L. 69.

cient to constitute the offense, proof of any one will sustain a conviction. The remaining allegations are surplusage.¹

In order to properly advise the defendant of the charge made against him, not only must the act be particularly described, but the complaint must allege when, where, and how it was committed. A simple charge that he has committed a described offense is indefinite.² So, a charge that the defendant " knowingly associated with thieves previous to August 21, 1871," is bad for not stating when, where, and with whom he associated.³ This principle is most frequently invoked in complaints that charge offenses against the ordinances regulating the traffic in intoxicating liquors. If the offense consists in keeping a saloon open at unlawful hours, or in allowing persons to enter at unlawful hours, it is immaterial who entered, or who utilized the breach of the law; but if the offense lies in selling to persons in the habit of getting intoxicated, or in a state of intoxication, or to minors, the complaint must state either the names of those to whom the liquor was sold, or that their names are unknown to the informer.⁴

The allegations of the complaint must bring the offender clearly within the class of persons against whom an ordinance may be directed. If it is unlawful for any person in control of a saloon or house to do some act, the defendant prosecuted under that ordinance must be alleged to be *in control* of the saloon or house in question.⁵

§ 174. **Reference must be made to the ordinance violated.**—Under the common-law procedure, the only remedy for violation of municipal ordinances was an action

(1) Commonwealth *v.* Curtis, 9 Allen, 266; Stevens *v.* Commonwealth, 6 Met. 242.

(2) Memphis *v.* O'Connor, 53 Mo. 468.

(3) St. Louis *v.* Fitz, 53 Mo. 582.

(4) Hill *v.* Dalton, 72 Ga. 314; Sparks *v.* Stokes, 40 N. J. 487; Flanagan *v.* Plainfield, 44 N. J. L. 118; Greeley *v.* Passaic, 42 N. J. L. 87; Roberson *v.* Lambertville, 38 N. J. L. 69

(5) Napman *v.* People, 19 Mich. 352.

in debt or assumpsit, and it was deemed necessary to plead every fact that went to constitute the right to recover. The ordinance itself was considered a fact, and had to be pleaded. Following this rule many cases hold that the ordinance, or at least that portion which is directly violated, should be embodied in the complaint.[1]

Considered purely as a declaration in debt, the complaint would needs contain allegations as to the time of passage of the ordinance, by whom and by what authority enacted, the ordinance itself, and the acts constituting the breach.[2]

The strictness of the rule is sometimes modified by holding that only the substance of the ordinance need be pleaded.[3]

The existence of municipal ordinances must be noticed by all who come within the corporate jurisdiction in the same degree that state laws must be noticed by those within the limits of a state. State statutes are not specially pleaded in criminal prosecutions, and it is not plain why the same principle might not be as well extended to prosecutions under ordinances. The fact that it is not commonly extended to them, would seem to indicate very strongly that prosecutions under ordinances are still considered as civil rather than as criminal actions. Decisions have been rendered in a few states, which deny wholly or qualifiedly the necessity of pleading the existence of an ordinance. Thus it is held in Minnesota not to be necessary to refer to the ordinance.[4] In Wisconsin it has been

---

(1) Railroad v. Klauber, 9 Ill. App. 613; Railroad v. Godfrey, 71 Ill. 500; Van Dyke v. Cincinnati, 1 Dis. (Ohio), 533; Green v. Indianapolis, 25 Ind. 490; Pomeroy v. Lappens, 9 Oreg. 363; Harker v. New York, 17 Wend. 199; People v. New York, 7 How. Pr. 81; Greensborough v. Shields, 78 N. Car. 417; Hendersonville v. McMinn, 82 N. Car. 532; State v. Edens, 85 N. Car. 522.

(2) Coates v. New York, 7 Cow. 585.

(3) Clevenger v. Rushville, 90 Ind. 258; Keeler v. Milledge, 24 N. J. 142; Sanesville v. Railroad, 7 Wis. 484; People v. Justices, 12 Hun, 65; Case v. Mobile, 30 Ala. 538; Charleston v. Chur, 2 Bailey, 164; Council v. Seeba, 4 Strobh. 319; Kip v. Patterson, 26 N. J. L. 298.

(4) State v. Richards, 21 Minn. 47; Rochester v. Upman, 19 Minn. 108. But contra, Winona v. Burke, 23 Minn. 254. See Meyer v. Bridgetown, 37 N. J. 160.

held that a prayer that the defendant "may be arrested and held to answer," could be construed to refer to the ordinance as though imported in the complaint.¹ A conclusion against the peace of the city has been held to have the same effect.² But these decisions are surely not consonant with the current of authority. On the one hand municipal ordinances are looked upon by the American courts as quasi-public laws; as such, all who come within their operation are obliged to take notice of them, and it would therefore seem useless to plead them specially when sought to be directly enforced. On the other hand, actions to enforce ordinance penalties still have many features in common with the civil action in debt; they are generally considered as but semi-criminal, and some regard must still be had to the requirements of the civil rules of pleading. As these conflicting considerations can not be wholly reconciled, the best rule seems to be that the complaint should refer to the ordinance in some manner that will enable it to be easily identified; that it ought not to entirely ignore its existence, but also that it need not plead the ordinance or even its substance. Although the weight of authority is nearly evenly divided among these varying views, there is ample authority favorable to the doctrine that the ordinance need only be referred to, to justify its adoption by any court that is not yet committed to another view.³ If only one ordinance was passed on a certain day, it might be sufficient to refer to the ordinance as passed on that day. Where the ordinances are numbered, a reference to the number is sufficient. And in general a reference to the title of the ordinance, or some other feature by which it is commonly known, and which will enable the defendant to easily identify it and single it out from all

---

(1) Oshkosh *v.* Schwartz, 55 Wis. 483.
(2) Information *v.* Oliver, 21 S. Car. 318.
(3) West *v.* Columbus, 20 Kan. 633; State *v.* Merritt, 83 N. Car. 677; Watts *v.* Scott, 2 Dev. (N. Car.) 1; Goldthwaite *v.* Montgomery, 50 Ala. 486; Huntington *v.* Pease, 56 Ind. 305; Goshen *v.* Kern, 63 Ind. 468; Auburn *v.* Eldridge, 77 Ind. 126; Whitson *v.* Franklin, 34 Ind. 392; State *v.* Cainan, 94 N. Car. 880; Faribault *v.* Wilson, 34 Minn. 254.

other ordinances, will satisfy the requirements of good pleading.

If the ordinance has been properly referred to, or its substance pleaded, where that is deemed essential, it is not necessary to allege power in the corporation to enact the ordinance,[1] nor to plead or refer to the charter or general law by which that power was conferred.[2] It need not be alleged that all proper formalities were observed in its passage,[3] nor that the corporation has legal capacity to sue.[4]

§ 175. **Exceptions need not be negatived.**—Where certain acts or classes of acts are expressly excepted from the operation of an ordinance, it is unnecessary and unadvisable to negative the exception. If the act complained of comes within the exception, and is therefore lawful, it is a good defense to the action, and should be left to the defendant to prove.[5]

§ 176. **The conclusion.**—In those states where actions are properly brought in the name of the corporation, it is undoubtedly sufficient if the information or complaint concludes with such an expression as "contrary to the form of the ordinance in such case provided."[6]

In Massachusetts, where ordinances are considered as a part of the general scheme of state legislation, and where actions are brought in the name of the commonwealth, it is considered essential that the ordinance conclude either " contrary to the form of the statute in such case provided," or " contrary to the form of the ordinance in such case made and provided, and to the peace and dignity of

---

(1) Janesville v. Railroad, 7 Wis. 484.

(2) Winooski v. Gokey, 49 Vt. 282. *Contra*, Washington v. Frank, 1 Jones, 436.

(3) Hardenbrook v. Ligonier, 95 Ind. 70.

(4) Janesville v. Railroad, 7 Wis. 484.

(5) McGear v. Woodruff, 33 N. J. L. 213; Roberson v. Lambertville, 38 N. J. L. 69; Lynch v. People, 16 Mich. 472; Farwell v. Smith, 16 N. J. L. 133; Shaw v. Poynter, 2 Ad. & El. 312; Martinsville v. Frieze, 33 Ind. 507.

(6) Winooski v. Gokey, 49 Vt. 282.

the state."[1] A very convenient and ample form of conclusion includes a distinct reference to the ordinance violated, such as "contrary to the ordinance entitled 'an ordinance against the obstruction of the streets,' passed October 10, 1882, and to the peace and dignity of the state."

§ 177. **Signature to complaint.**—The person who makes the complaint or files the information upon which the complaint is based, must sign his declaration and make affidavit to its truth. Here, as in regard to other formalities, the making of the affidavit and the signature as a means of identifying the informer are the essence of the formality, and slight errors, not going to material features, are mere irregularities.[2]

§ 178. **Arrest of offender.**—In actions instituted against a person who has allowed his property to violate the local ordinances, the remedy is more directly against the property, and the notice to be given him of the pendency of the proceeding has already been considered.[3] But where the remedy is wholly against the person of the offender, the filing of a proper affidavit or complaint is followed by the issuing of a warrant to some police officer, commanding him to arrest the defendant, and to bring him before the court. At common law, local magistrates had no power to order the arrest of an offender and to take a bail bond for his due appearance, but, as the form of action has now been changed, and other punishments than fines imposed, the common-law rule has ceased to be applicable.[4] Some kind of process must issue, unless expressly declared unnecessary by statute.[5] Lack of process may be waived by the voluntary appearance of the defendant, but such

---

(1) Commonwealth v. Gay, 5 Pick. 44; Commonwealth v. Worcester, 3 Pick. 462.

(2) Cherokee v. Fox, 34 Kan. 16.

(3) *Ante*, § 162.

(4) Canthorn v. State, 43 Ark. 131.

(5) People v. Miller, 38 Hun, 82; Alexander v. Bethlehem, 27 N. J. L. 377.

appearance to be an effectual waiver must be made with a knowledge of the actual pendency of a charge or action. Thus, when a person came before a magistrate informally, and questions were put to him which induced the court to believe him guilty of the violations charged, and a fine was thereupon imposed, but the defendant did not know, when the questions were being asked him, that an actual complaint had been made before that magistrate, his appearance was held not to be an effectual waiver of process, and the judgment was held void.[1]

§ 179. **What the warrant should contain.**—The warrant issued should contain facts sufficient to inform the person arrested of what he stands charged. It generally gives the title of the action, the name of the court in which it is brought, and brief reference to the nature of the accusation, besides the formal command to the officer to take the person named therein into custody, and to bring him before the court. The prosecution actually conducted can not deviate materially from the facts contained in the summons or warrant, else a conviction would be voidable; that is, a person who is summoned to answer for the violation of one ordinance can not be punished in that proceeding for a breach of a different ordinance.[2] No man can be punished for that to which he has not been called to answer. The tribunal must likewise be accurately described. Thus, if a magistrate, who has jurisdiction over a whole township, the municipality included, in civil cases, but only over the municipality in cases arising under ordinances, should summon a defendant to appear in his court "in the township of B." instead of "in the city of B.," the summons is fatally defective.[3]

The person to be summoned or arrested should be as definitely named in the writ as is possible. If his Chris-

(1) Merkee v. Rochester, 13 Hun, 157.
(2) Mayor v. Arnold, 30 Ga. 517; Lesterjelle v. Mayor, 30 Ga. 936.
(3) Hershoff v. Beverly, 43 N. J. 139.

tian name is unknown, that fact should be stated; if omitted without any such explanation, the arrest will be void.[1]

§ 180. **Arrests made without a warrant.**—In order to secure the efficiency of the remedy against breaches of ordinances, the local police officers must be allowed to arrest for violations committed in their presence without having first secured a warrant.[2] For the purpose of legalizing arrests, municipal ordinances must be considered as equal to the criminal laws of the state. It has, however, been held that the act, though committed in the presence of the officer, must be one which amounts to a breach of the peace.[3] A warrant is certainly necessary if the offense was not committed in the presence of the officer.[4] Greater freedom in the making of arrests can not be conferred by ordinance that would be lawful at common law.[5] It has been held in Georgia that power to pass all ordinances necessary and proper for the good government of the town and for the subjection of all persons whatever authorizes an ordinance which permits arrests on view and without a warrant.[6] But it is apprehended that such power and ordinance confer no additional or novel powers on the local police. Still, under the charter of Newark, New Jersey, power to arrest on view alone must be expressly conferred upon the officer.[7]

An arrest for an offense committed in the officer's presence may be made on any day, but an arrest or warrant can not lawfully be made on Sunday.[8]

The simple service of a warrant to arrest without actually taking the person into custody is not an arrest, and

(1) Prell v. McDonald, 7 Kan. 426.
(2) White v. Kent, 11 O. S. 550; Bryan v. Bates, 15 Ill. 87; Main v McCarty, 15 Ill. 441; State v. Lufferty, 5 Harr. 491.
(3) Hennessy v. Connolly, 13 Hun 173.
(4) Knoxville v. Vickers, 3 Coldw. 205; State v. Cantieny, 34 Minn. 1.
(5) Quinn v. Heisel, 40 Mich. 576.
(6) Johnson v. Americus, 46 Ga. 80.
(7) Newark v. Murphy, 40 N. J. 145.
(8) Wood v. Brooklyn, 14 Barb. 425.

such a proceeding is considered to be such duress as would vitiate a confession of judgment or plea of guilty.[1]

An arrest, to be lawful, must be made as a preliminary step to an actual *bona fide* complaint and action. An arrest is for that reason unlawful, if made in pursuance of an ordinance that provides that any person who shall refuse to obey the orders of the officers present at a fire "may be arrested and *detained in custody until the fire is extinguished.*" The object of such an arrest is not to subject the offender to any legal action, and no *process of law* is contemplated. If such an arrest were to be followed by a prosecution under an existing ordinance prohibiting the obstruction of the fire department, or the like, it would be lawful.[2]

§ 181. **Trial by jury.**—In all prosecutions which may result in the imprisonment of the offender as a part of the penalty for his offense, the right of trial by jury must not be denied, but in prosecutions for petty offenses against ordinances passed in the exercise of police powers, and in which a pecuniary penalty alone can be inflicted, such a right can not be demanded.[3] And it does not matter that provision is made for enforcing the payment of the fine by imprisonment.[4] Nor can a jury trial be demanded in proceedings to determine and abate nuisances.[5]

In cases where a jury trial can be insisted upon, or in which it is allowed, either party may exercise the same right of challenge that is allowed by statute or the common law in other actions.[6] If the action is considered civil in its nature, or only quasi-criminal, the number of challenges would accord to the practice in civil causes, otherwise to the practice in criminal cases under the state laws

(1) Baldwin *v.* Murphy, 82 Ill. 487.
(2) Judson *v.* Reardon, 16 Minn. 431.
(3) Ex parte Kiburg, 10 Mo. App. 442; Hill *v.* Dalton, 72 Ga. 314; Inwood *v.* State, 42 O. S. 186.
(4) Inwood *v.* State, 42 O. S. 186.
(5) Hart *v.* Albany, 9 Wend. 571.
(6) Charleston *v.* Kleinback, 2 Spears, 418.

In West Virginia a jury trial can be had on appeal, but can not be insisted on in the magistrate's court.[1]

§ 182. **Arraignment and plea.**—It is certainly just to the offender and not injurious to the speediness of the remedy, that he should be formally arraigned and allowed to plead.[2] If he is not allowed to do so, costs of the action incurred after the point where he should have had this privilege, can not be charged against him, as they might have been saved by a plea of guilty. Whether the action be civil or criminal an opportunity to plead to the complaint should be given to the defendant. Under the liberal procedure followed in Missouri, it seems that these formalities are only considered essential in cases where indictments under the state law would be for the same act.[3]

§ 183. **Evidence.**—The methods adopted to prove the issues made in cases based on violations of municipal ordinances and the rules of evidence are subtantially the same as in cases in the state courts. The actual practice presents a strange mixture of civil and criminal rules. It is always safer to observe the established rules of evidence in criminal cases, though not always necessary to a valid judgment or conviction. The ordinary rules of evidence may be to some extent illustrated and even supplemented by minor rules dependent upon the peculiar nature of this class of actions, and upon the variation in the nature of the offense. It is, however, impracticable to formulate any well defined modification of the law of evidence, that can be considered as belonging peculiarly to practice in ordinance cases.

§ 184. **Judicial notice.**—In those states which adhere to the rule of common law that the complaint or petition must plead the ordinance on which the prosecution is based

---

(1) Beasley *v.* Beckley, 28 W. Va. 81; Moundsville *v.* Fountain, 27 W. Va. 183; Jelly *v.* Dills, 27 W. Va. 267.

(2) Mayor *v.* Nell, 3 Yeates, 475.

(3) Lexington *v.* Curtiss, 69 Mo. 626; St. Louis *v.* Knox, 74 Mo. 79.

as a fact, it is held consistently with that view that the local court will not take judical notice of the municipal ordinances. The same view is entertained in many states where there is no longer any reason for the rule. At common law ordinances, or by-laws, were not part of the public laws, having been originally enacted solely by the guilds, which were private corporations. The distinction seems, however, either to have been wholly overlooked, or other considerations have outweighed it in the minds of the courts. Cases are numerous which deny the right of the local courts to take judicial notice of the local ordinances.[1] In cases where the state statutes provide that ordinances may be proved in a specified manner, it would seem to be the legislative intent that they shall not be judicially noticed. Under the circumstances, it is certainly advisable to either plead or prove in evidence the ordinance relied on. In those states where no indication of legislative intent is conveyed by statute, and especially in those where prosecutions under ordinances are considered criminal actions, it is difficult to understand why ordinances need to be proved. Of course it would be necessary whenever their validity is attacked on the ground of an alleged informality in their passage. It is well established that the residents within a municipality must take notice of the ordinances, and it is frequently stated that ordinances have the force and effect of laws within the limits of the corporation. Why, then, are they not such public laws as to the locality which they govern, and matters of such public knowledge as to be brought within the judicial notice of the tribunals charged with their enforcement? The local court takes judicial notice of corporate existence, and the law by which it exists; in fact, corporate existence can not be questioned in the prosecution for the violation of an

---

(1) Winona v. Burke, 23 Minn. 254; Cox v. St. Louis, 11 Mo. 432; Mooney v. Kennett, 19 Mo. 551; Garvin v. Wells, 8 Ia. 286; Goodrich v. Brown, 30 Ia. 291; Case v. Mobile, 30 Ala. 538; Porter v. Waring, 69 N. Y. 250; Harker v. Mayor, 17 Wend. 199; People v. Mayor, 7 How. Pr. 81.

§ 185.] PROCEDURE—PLEADING—EVIDENCE. 159

ordinance.¹ And as to other matters of general public knowledge, local courts will take notice of materially the same things as the state courts. Surely if analogy is to be drawn from criminal prosecutions, it ought not to be necessary to prove the law violated. There can be no valid criminal proceeding, unless some public law has been violated, and the prosecution ought not to be obliged to prove a law of which all people are presumed to have notice. The municipality ought not to do more than produce such evidence of the ordinance, or appertaining to the steps taken in its enactment, as is necessary to rebut any claim of invalidity that has been *prima facie* proved. And such is the position favored by the recent text writers basing their opinions upon a number of well considered cases.²

§ 185. **How ordinances are proved.**—When it is deemed necessary to establish the existence of an ordinance by evidence, or when the validity of the ordinance is attacked for informal enactment, questions arise as to how it should be done. Provision is ordinarily made for a simple method of proving ordinances, either by introducing a certified copy or the printed volume in which they are all collected. When the printed volume is made evidence, ordinances are in one sense put upon the same footing with the state statutes,³ and all other proof is unnecessary.⁴ Very often special rules of evidence are provided by statute or by the municipality under express charter authority for the proof of ordinances, but if no special rule exists the common rules of evidence apply.⁵

Even in the absence of statutory provision, the printed

(1) Elk Point *v.* Vaughn, 1 Dak. 108; Winooski, *v.* Gokey, 49 Vt. 282; Smith *v.* Adrian, 1 Mich. 495; People *v.* Potter, 35 Cal. 110; Beasley *v.* Beckley, 28 W. Va. 81. Of its powers, Dwyer *v.* Brenham, 65 Tex. 526.

(2) Dill. Mun. Corp., § 413, and note; Wharton on Evidence, § 293; Dubuque *v.* Lieber, 11 Ia. 407; Conboy *v.* Iowa City, 2 Ia. 90; Information *v.* Oliver, 21 S. Car. 318; Wheeling *v.* Black, 25 W. Va. 266.

(3) Napman *v.* People, 19 Mich. 352.

(4) St. Charles *v.* O'Mailey, 18 Ill. 407.

(5) Railroad Co. *v.* Engle, 76 Ill. 317.

volume containing the city ordinances is *prima facie* evidence and will be considered sufficient proof of their existence until controverted.[1] A book purporting to contain all the ordinances, and shown to be in the custody of the corporation clerk, will be received without further attestation.[2] The testimony of a policeman who is familiar with the book and with the signature of the mayor affixed thereto will render the book admissible.[3]

Where there is no book in which ordinances are regularly published or recorded together, a *prima facie* case may be made by offering in evidence a copy of the ordinance sued upon attested by some corporate officer, usually the clerk. A copy duly, that is plainly, certified by the clerk, is proper evidence of the existence of the ordinance.[4] The ordinance must be certified to, if it is not in some form which is upon its face sufficient to establish its genuineness and accuracy.[5] A copy of the ordinance shown to have come from the clerk, and bearing the indorsement, "A true copy, A. B., Clerk," is authentic.[6] Where the witness testified that he was the clerk of the corporation when the ordinance in question was passed; that he had compared the copy offered in evidence with the corporate records, and that it was correct—that evidence was considered sufficient to admit the paper as a sworn copy.[7]

(1) Barr *v.* Auburn, 81 Ill. 361; Independence *v.* Trouvalle, 15 Kan. 70; Prell *v.* McDonald, 7 Kan. 446; State *v.* King, 37 Ia. 462; Lindsley *v.* Chicago, 115 Ill. 120.
(2) Tipton *v.* Norman, 72 Mo. 380.
(3) Ottumwa *v.* Schaub, 52 Ia. 515.
(4) Pendergast *v.* Peru, 20 Ill. 1; Commonwealth *v.* Chase, 6 Cush. 248; People *v.* Buchanan, 1 Idaho, 681; Lindsley *v.* Chicago, 115 Ill. 120.
(5) Pugh *v.* Little Rock, 35 Ark. 75.
(6) Kinghorn *v.* Kingston, 25 U. C. Q. B. 130.
(7) Railroad Co. *v.* Shires, 108 Ill. 617. If the municipal charter provides that, "an ordinance shall be sufficiently proved by producing a copy certified by the clerk, a printed copy taken from a newspaper," or a printed pamphlet, provided the same appears to have been issued by the authority of the corporation, a copy cut from a newspaper, and entitled, "published by authority," and bearing, in printing, the signature of the president and clerk, is sufficient proof. Block *v.* Jacksonville, 36 Ill. 301.

Proof of the existence and identity of the ordinance offered should by rights be all that is required of the prosecution in any case, until some showing has been made that there was irregularity in the enactment of the ordinance, in which case it becomes necessary to prove that it was properly enacted in order to sustain a conviction or judgment. If no such question is raised the presumption that the ordinance was properly passed becomes conclusive.[1]

If it is deemed necessary to prove compliance with all formalties, none must be omitted which are prescribed by the charter or statute authorizing the municipality to enact ordinances.[2] The steps taken before the council must be proven.[3] Where publication is necessary, that must be shown, as must also formal adoption by the body of the electors when their approval is required.[4] Although an early case holds that no evidence of promulgation need be given.[5]

§ 186. **The record of council proceedings as evidence.** Some provision is generally made for keeping a record of the acts and proceedings of every local legislative body. A record so kept and duly identified is the only proper method of proving those acts, unless express provision is made for some other method.[6] Where there is a record book, as a rule, parol or extrinsic evidence is inadmissible for the purpose of proving ordinances. It is the best evidence.[7] The record is conclusive as to all its recitals, and if it is silent as to the taking of some necessary step, compliance with the requirement can not be shown by supple-

(1) Flora v. Lee, 5 Ill. App. 629.
(2) As to what are deemed essential, see *ante*, §§ 56, 57, 58.
(3) Elizabethtown v. Lefler, 23 Ill. 90; Willard v. Killingworth, 8 Conn. 247.
(4) Schott v. People, 89 Ill. 195.
(5) Charleston v. Chur, 2 Bailey, 164.
(6) Parsons v. Trusteés, 44 Ga. 529; Baker v. Scofield, 58 Ga. 182.
(7) Stewart v. Clinton, 79 Mo. 604.

mentary extrinsic evidence.[1] Thus, the city clerk's attestation on the record of the date of the mayor's approval can not be contradicted by parol evidence.[2] The mayor's approval can not be proved extrinsically.[3] It has, however, been held in Missouri that if the signature of the mayor to the ordinance that was read and adopted is lacking through an omission to record accurately, it may be shown extrinsically that he did in fact sign it.[4] The local court of Pittsburgh once held, though certainly contrary to all authority, that the provision for a record is only directory, that the passage of an ordinance could be proved outside of the record and a prosecution thus sustained.[5]

§ 187 **Proof of publication.**—Publication of the ordinance is the only formality, compliance with which may be proved outside of the record. The rule against the admissibility of parol evidence is relaxed in this one particular. Ordinances must be promulgated before they can have effect and parol or documentary evidence of promulgation is admissible.[6] If the publication is made by posting copies in public places, testimony given by the clerk of the corporation that the ordinance in question was so posted is good proof.[7] When the statute provides that publication may be made in that manner, if no newspaper is published in the village, proof must be offered to show that no paper was so published when the ordinance was promulgated in order to show that posting was lawful.[8] It is sufficient to show that the statutory provision has been complied with. No other evidence of publication need be

(1) Solomon v. Hughes, 24 Kan. 211; Covington v. Ludlow, 1 Metc. (Ky.) 295; Lexington v. Headley, 5 Bush. 508; Ball v. Fagg, 67 Mo. 841; St. Louis v. Foster, 52 Mo. 513; People v. Murray, 57 Mich. 396.
(2) Ball v. Fagg, 67 Mo. 481.
(3) Lexington v. Headley, 5 Bush. 508.
(4) Knight v. Railroad Co., 70 Mo. 231.
(5) Barton v. Pittsburgh, 4 Brewst. 373. As to the method of proving ordinances in New York city, see Logue v. Gillick, 1 E. D. Smith, 398.
(6) Eldora v. Burlingame, 62 Ia. 32.
(7) Teft v. Size, 10 Ill. 433; Newton v. Aurora, 14 Ill. 364.
(8) Raker v. Maquon, 9 Ill. App. 155.

given than the printed ordinance book issued by the local authorities, if printing the ordinance in a book be recognized by statute as a lawful mode of publication.¹ If an issue is made as to proper publication in a newspaper, and the record does not show on its face that the statutory requirement was fulfilled, a sworn certificate of one of the publishers of the newspaper in which it was printed will be received.² The ordinance, as passed, need not be written in the record book. A copy cut from the newspaper and pasted in is sufficient.³ Similarly, publication may be shown by attaching the publisher's affidavit to the manuscript copy in the record book, instead of to a printed copy cut from the newspaper.⁴ Where the statutes declare that proof of publication shall be unnecessary unless the fact of proper publication be denied under written oath, an affidavit to that effect is defective which merely states that " affiant is informed and believes" that due publication was not made.⁵

It may be observed that Illinois furnishes most of the decisions cited in this section. This arises from the existence in that state of a statute permitting publication by posting notices in certain cases. The same principles should, however, be equally applicable in any other state, because publication is not strictly one of the proceedings in the council. The record book derives its unimpeachable authority from the fact that it is supposed to be a record of council proceedings made at the time and by the hand of an officer appointed for that purpose, and while it may be the most available and most natural place for preserving due evidence of what is done with ordinances after their passage by the council, as to such subsequent proceedings, the reason ceases for considering that evidence conclusive. It is possible to produce other evidence of

(1) Raker v. Maquon, 9 Ill. App. 155; Bethalto v. Conley, 9 Ill. App. 339; Faribault v. Wilson, 34 Minn. 254.
(2) Kettering v. Jacksonville, 50 Ill. 39.
(3) Ewbanks v. Ashley, 36 Ill. 177.
(4) Albia v. O'Harra, 64 Ia. 297.
(5) Green v. Indianapolis, 25 Ind. 490.

publication equally as good and worthy of credit as the record book, which is in that particular, at best, a piece of secondary evidence.

§ 188. **Presumption that ordinances are reasonable.**—
It is not necessary on the trial of a prosecution under a municipal ordinance to adduce proof of the power under which it was passed. If the ordinance is on its face absurd or unreasonable the court may and ought to dismiss the complaint,[1] and the court can, of course, take judicial notice of the power if conferred by statute, and determine whether the ordinance has any authorization.[2] Unless the invalidity of an ordinance is apparent on its face, there is a very strong presumption that it is valid. Whenever a question is raised the court will be governed by the following well established rules:

1. If the ordinance is passed in pursuance of a specific and definite power and includes nothing beyond the letter of that power, the presumption in favor of its validity becomes conclusive.

2. If the ordinance is based on a general power, and its provisions are more detailed and minute than any expression of power, the court may look into the question of its reasonableness. It may determine whether the power has been exercised in a reasonable manner, and if such determination depends on the existence or non-existence of certain facts, evidence may be introduced to prove or disprove them. The burden of proof is upon the party who denies the validity of the ordinance.[3]

The court will not investigate the reasonableness of an ordinance which has been enacted in pursuance with a definite power.[4] But if the power is expressed in such

(1) State Center v. Barenstein, 66 Ia. 249.
(2) Alton v. Hartford Ins. Co., 72 Ill. 328.
(3) Van Hook v. Selma, 70 Ala. 361; Bolton v. Cleveland, 35 O. S. 319; Reynolds v. Cincinnati, 27 O. S. 312; Douglasville v. Johns, 62 Ga. 423; State v. Gas Co., 37 Ohio, 45.
(4) Ex parte Chin Yan, 60 Cal. 83; Peoria v. Calhoun, 29 Ill. 317; St. Paul v. Colter, 12 Minn. 41; Grierson v. County, 9 U. C. Q. B. 623; Dist. of Columbia v. Waggaman, 4 Mackey, 328.

general terms that an ordinance which adopts its phraseology would be too indefinite to be enforceable, it becomes necessary for the local legislature to determine the precise regulation or control which is necessary to meet the needs of the public. The council will be protected by the courts in this exercise of its discretion to every reasonable extent. The main test is the ordinance itself. If it bears no apparent connection with any grant of power and is of a restrictive nature it might be just to oblige the corporation to show how its enactment could be justified.[1] "Within the power granted, the degree of necessity or propriety of its exercise rests exclusively with the proper corporate authorities; but in all cases the power exercised, or attempted to be exercised, must depend upon the nature and extent of the power granted, and whenever the question of the existence or limit of power is raised it becomes the plain duty of the courts to see that the corporate authorities do not transcend the power delegated to them."[2] As is said by Freeman, J.: "I have always thought the only test of general legislative action should be, was the law passed in pursuance of and in accordance with the constitution, and in the exercise of the constitutional powers of the legislative body. In the case of a municipal corporation, the question is, whether it is in accord with our constitution, state and federal, and, then, within the powers granted in the charter of the corporation, or necessary, as an implied power, to the exercise of the powers expressly granted. If so, the propriety and mode of its exercise is one solely for the legislative body exercising it. That is, in my judgment, a legislative, not a judicial, question, when the power to do the thing is conceded. . . . It seems to be sustained by the current of authority that an ordinance may be held void for oppression or irregularity."[3]

It is not quite clear just how far this right to review the exercise of discretion by the council extends. The

---

(1) Glenn *v.* Baltimore, 5 Gill & J. 424; Dunham *v.* Rochester, 5 Cow. 462.

(2) State *v.* Mott, 61 Md. 297; s. c., 48 Am. Rep. 105.

(3) In Knoxville *v.* Bird, 12 Lea, 121; s. c., 47 Am. Rep. 326.

court say in an early case in Pennsylvania that "where the municipal legislature has authority to act, it must be governed not by our discretion, but by its own, and we shall not be hasty in convicting them of being unreasonable in the exercise of it."[1] If the ordinance bears plain evidences of unreasonableness, or of unjust discrimination, or of fraud in its inception, it should undoubtedly be set aside.[2] Otherwise the results of its enforcement must be shown to cause great irregularities of burdens, or to effect a violation of some constitutional or statutory right. An ordinance is not defective because the mode of regulation adopted by the council does not accord with the views of the judicial power.[3] In the absence of evidence of pernicious results the ordinance will be presumed to be reasonable.[4] Courts should construe ordinances to be a valid exercise of the corporate powers except when the power has been grossly abused.[5] Especially is that so if the power vested in the corporation is exclusive in its nature. When limited to, or concurrent with, regulation also exercised by the state, more strict adherence to the power must be demanded.[6] Every presumption should be admitted to support an ordinance which reasonably intends to effect a lawful purpose.[7] In Illinois it has been held that, in the absence of express statutory authority, courts are not authorized to indulge in presumptions in favor of the validity of ordinances.[8] Whereas, the California courts go to the other extreme and hold that police ordinances as a class are valid, and that all questions, as to whether a certain ordinance is directed against an actual evil, or falls within the terms of the power contained in the statute or charter, are concluded by the discretion of the council.[9] In the last

(1) Fisher v. Harrisburgh, 2 Grant's Cas. 291.
(2) Alberger v. Mayor, 64 Md. 1; Rensselaer v. Leopold, 106 Ind. 29.
(3) Knoxville v. Bird, 12 Lea, 121.
(4) Commonwealth v. Patch, 97 Mass. 221.
(5) Elk Point v. Vaughn, 1 Dak. 108.
(6) Baltimore v. Clunet, 23 Md. 464.
(7) Gabel v. Houston, 29 Tex. 336.
(8) Schott v. People, 89 Ill. 195.
(9) Ex parte Smith, 38 Cal. 702; Ex parte Delaney, 43 Cal. 478.

§ 188.] PROCEDURE—PLEADING—EVIDENCE. 167

case cited, Ex parte Delaney, the power was to prohibit practices against good morals, and the decision of the council as to what is contrary to good morals was held final.[1]

But such holdings are certainly extreme. So long as the means adopted are not plainly and clearly unreasonable on their face, the ordinance provision will be upheld.[2] And the legal presumption is in favor of the validity of the ordinance.[3]

The reasonableness of an ordinance must at all events be judged solely from the wording of its provisions and from its results. The *motives* of the legislative body can under no circumstances be inquired into.[4]

Summary. Were the council to be bound down by severe rules it would be little more than a ministerial body, but the purpose and essence of its existence consist in the exercise of legislative functions. All legislation, to be effective, must be based upon the discretion of the law-making power, in view of all the circumstances of each case, as to the particular remedies that need to be provided. What is proper for one city is seldom exactly adapted to the necessities of other cities. The location of the community, the nature of its industries, the compactness of its population, and the character and sentiment of its citizens, among other things, are elements to be considered in determining just what measures are most appropriate to its needs and consonant with its policy. It follows that a wide discretion must be vested in the council. They are in the best possible position to understand all these varying elements, and to judge of the best course to pursue. The main object of local legislation, the very purpose of municipal organization, would be defeated, did not the courts recognize the full

---

(1) Likewise in Baker *v.* Boston, 12 Pick. 184; Grierson *v.* County, 9 U. C. Q. B. 623.

(2) McArthur *v.* Saginaw, 58 Mich. 357; Ex parte Gregory 20 Tex. App. 210; 15 Bull. 363; Dillon Mun. Corp., § 328.

(3) Railroad Co. *v.* Springfield, 85 Mo. 674.

(4) Freeport *v.* Marks, 59 Pa. St. 253; Knoxville *v.* Bird, 12 Lea, 121; s. c., 47 Am. Rep. 826.

extent of this discretion, and refuse to interfere with its exercise, except in cases of gross abuse. The unreasonableness of the ordinance must plainly appear upon its face, or it must as evidently appear to have been passed in a spirit of wantonness, or to be based on mistake or fraud, before the court will declare it void.[1] The council discretion is not reviewable unless private rights are wantonly invaded or the power exceeded.[2] When the power is not evidently abused and made a pretext for doing what is a violation of constitutional rights, the court ought not to interfere with the municipal discretion.[3] The general proposition is sustained by numerous authorities, and with the limitations just stated, the courts ought never to set up their judgment in place of the judgment of the council as to the manner and means of exercising delegated powers involving more or less discretion.[4]

Special illustrations. An ordinance is valid which authorizes the mayor to revoke the license issued for the sale of liquors, upon conviction of the licensee of keeping a disorderly house. Courts will not interfere with a municipal regulation, unless clearly shown that it is not authorized by the power, or that it is in conflict with the constitution or statutory law.[5] A fee of $200, charged for a license to keep a butcher's stall, is reasonable. The legislative discretion is not to be questioned, unless grossly and manifestly absurd.[6] If power is granted to fix wharfage charges, the courts will

---

(1) White v. Kent, 11 O. S. 550; Sargent v. Railroad Co., 1 Handy, 52; Neier v. Railway Co., 12 Mo. App. 25; Brust v. Carbondale, 78 Ill. 74; Brewster v. Davenport, 51 Ia. 427; Eric v. Reed's Executors, 113 Pa. St. 468.

(2) State v. Clarke, 54 Mo. 17; Gas Co. v. Des Moines, 44 Iowa 509; St. Louis v. Boffinger, 19 Mo. 15.

(3) Van Baalen v. People, 40 Mich. 258.

(4) Harrison v. Baltimore, 1 Gill, 264; Church v. Baltimore, 6 Gill, 391; State v. Mott, 61 Md. 297; Watson v. Turnbull, 34 La. Ann. 856; Los Angeles v. Waldron, 65 Cal. 283; Holland v. San Francisco, 7 Cal. 361; Morehouse v. Norwalk, 6 Ohio Law Bull. 267; St. Louis v. Knox, 6 Mo. App. 247.

(5) Towns v. Tallahassee, 11 Fla. 130.

(6) St. Paul v. Colter, 12 Minn. 41.

not undertake to determine the limit to the amount which the municipal authorities may exact, that being an administrative, not a judicial, function.[1] Nor can the court review the decision of the council that certain improvements are necessary.[2] Under power *to define* and punish misdemeanors, an ordinance is valid which enumerates the acts that shall be deemed misdemeanors, and its definition of those acts is final and binding on the courts.[3]

But, under power to establish markets at such places as the council may deem fit, it would be unlawful to authorize their establishment in a public highway.[4]

§ 189. **Reasonableness a question of law.**—It does not fall within the province of the jury to decide upon the validity of an ordinance; they are restricted to consider whether the evidence is sufficient to prove the commission of the act charged as an offense in the complaint.[5] The question as to whether a certain ordinance is a reasonable exercise of the discretion vested in the council, when proper to be considered at all, is one of law, and for the court to decide;[6] unless it depends, in the estimation of the court, on the existence of particular facts which are disputed.[7] What will amount to a prohibitory tax, so as to render an ordinance a virtual prohibition of a lawful trade, is a question of fact, and evidence may be admitted to show its effect.[8] It has, though, been held that witnesses may not be called to show that the restriction imposed by an ordinance is detrimental to certain businesses.[9] But, in an action brought to punish an alleged violation of an ordinance regulating the sale of fresh meats, it is error to in-

(1) Municipality *v.* Pease, 2 La. Ann. 538.
(2) Keasy *v.* Louisville, 4 Dana, 154.
(3) People *v.* Miller, 38 Hun, 82.
(4) St. John *v.* New York, 3 Bosw. 483.
(5) Washington *v.* Frank, 1 Jones (N. Car.), 436.
(6) Kirkham *v.* Russel, 76 Va. 956; St. Louis *v.* Weber, 44 Mo. 547; Elk Point *v.* Vaughn, 1 Dak. 108; Kip *v.* Paterson, 26 N. J. 298.
(7) Clason *v.* Milwaukee, 30 Wis. 316.
(8) Sweet *v.* Wabash, 41 Ind. 7.
(9) Launder *v.* Chicago, 111 Ill. 291.

struct the jury that the ordinance is valid, *unless* they find that it is in restraint of trade. That is for the court to find.[1] Evidence tending to show that the ordinance is in fact unreasonable is inadmissible.[2]

The unreasonableness of the ordinance must appear clearly.[3]

§ 190. **Proof of time and place of committing the offense.**—If an act is an offense only when committed on a certain day, such as a violation of the Sunday laws, it must be alleged and proven to have been committed on such a day.[4] Otherwise, any slight variance between the complaint and the proof is immaterial. So with regard to the place of commission. If necessary to be alleged, it must be proven to a reasonable certainty, and under all circumstances the act, must be proven to have been done within the territorial limits of the corporation.[5]

§ 191. **Proof that act does not fall within exceptions.**—Ordinances are frequently drawn so as to exclude certain persons or acts committed under certain circumstances from their operation. In such cases it is unnecessary for the prosecution to adduce evidence to show that the act complained of does not fall within the exception. The exception need not be negatived either by the evidence or by the allegations of the complaint.[6] The burden of proof is on the defendant to prove that the act complained of is such a one as falls within the exception.

§ 192. **Testimony of defendant.**—It seems that an action brought to punish a violation of an ordinance is so

(1) Peoria *v.* Calhoun, 29 Ill. 317.

(2) Corrigan *v.* Gage, 68 Mo. 541; Commonwealth *v.* Worcester, 3 Pick. 462. Held error to exclude all evidence of reasonableness in an action brought to test the validity of an ordinance. Railroad Co. *v.* Brooklyn, 37 Hun, 413.

(3) St. Louis *v.* Weber, 44 Mo. 547.

(4) Hershoff *v.* Beverly, 45 N. J. 288.

(5) Mayor *v.* Nell, 3 Yeates, 475; Taylor *v.* Americus, 39 Ga. 59.

(6) Flora *v.* Lee, 5 Ill. App. 629; Harbaugh *v.* Monmouth, 74 Ill. 367. *Contra*, Regina *v.* Pipe, 1 Ont. 43.

far criminal in its nature that the defendant can not be compelled to testify.[1]

§ 193. **Construction of ordinances.** — The general rules followed in construing statutes are as well applicable to the construction of ordinances.[2] A distinction must be drawn between the rules applied when considering whether an ordinance as enacted falls within the terms of the power or not, and those applied in determining whether a certain act complained of falls within the prohibition of an ordinance; the rules in the former case being much more lenient than in the latter. If doubt arises in the latter case the construction adopted is strict and in favor of the accused, although not quite so strict as in regard to penal laws of the state.[3] But in regard to their validity under the power expressed, ordinances are specially entitled to a reasonable construction, because they are less artificially expressed than other laws.[4] They are enacted by bodies less used to the exercise of legislative power, and less capable of observing niceties of distinction in the language employed. Very few ordinances would stand the test of rigid scrutiny.[5] An ordinance is frequently capable of two constructions, one which would bring its provisions within the limits of the power conferred upon the corporation, another which would invalidate it. That one should be adopted which gives effect to the ordinance.[6]

Questions of construction are for the court and not for the jury.[7]

(1) Day v Clinton, 6 Ill. App. 477; Mobile v. Jones, 42 Ala. 630.

(2) State v. Kirkley, 29 Md. 85; Zorger v. Greensburgh, 60 Ind. 1 Quinette v. St. Louis, 76 Mo. 402; In re Yick Woo, 68 Cal. 294.

(3) Pacific v. Seifert, 79 Mo. 210; Schultz v. Cambridge, 38 O. S. 659 Chicago v. Rumpff, 45 Ill. 90; New Orleans v. Anderson, 9 La. Ann. 323.

(4) Whitlock v. Wilton, 26 Conn. 406.

(5) First Municipality v. Cutting, 4 La. Ann. 335.

(6) Commonwealth v. Dow, 10 Metc. 382; Baltimore v. Hughes, Adm'r, 1 Gill & J. 480; Merriam v. New Orleans, 14 La. Ann. 318; Johnson v. Philadelphia, 60 Pa. St. 445.

(7) Pennsylvania Co. v. Frana, 13 Ill. App. 91; Wells Law and Fact, § 71.

An ordinance is not void for want of clearness of expression or on account of a difficulty in construing or applying its provisions.[1]

The act complained of does not constitute an offense unless it falls plainly within the meaning of the words used by the legislative body in framing the ordinance. Unless some peculiarity of the subject-matter indicates otherwise the words used must be taken in their ordinary accepted meaning. But the rule of strict interpretation is not violated by permitting the words of the ordinance to have their full meaning, or the more extended of two meanings, nor by giving a reasonable meaning to the words according to the intent of the law-making body, disregarding captious objections and even the demands of an exact grammatical propriety.[2]

Although that meaning must be determined from the face of the ordinance, it is permissible to refer to the statements made in the debate on the ordinance on its passage in order to determine the mischief which led to its enactment.[3] It is to be presumed that the council intended to enact an ordinance that would be within the terms of their power, and therefore the ordinance ought to be upheld whenever plainly capable of a validating construction, but extrinsic evidence of the actual legislative intent is never admissible.[4]

Ordinances which regulate the property rights of the citizen are subject to the rules of construing contracts, and should not be invalidated unless plainly necessary.[5]

§ 194. Where an enumeration is made in an ordinance all things not specially named are impliedly excluded, and general words can not widen the scope of special words preceding them.[6] So, when the first section of an ordi-

(1) Smith v. Toronto, 10 U. C. C. P. 225.
(2) Bishop's Statutory Crimes, chap. XIII.
(3) Ah Kow v. Nunan, 5 Saw. 552.
(4) State v. Railroad Co., 55 Tex. 76.
(5) Holland v. San Francisco 7 Cal. 363.
(6) Schultz v. Cambridge, 38 O. S. 659.

nance enumerates the kinds of vehicles which shall be subject to the payment of a license fee, the use of general terms in the following section which prescribes the amount of the fee can not be held to extend the operation of the prior section to other vehicles than those therein designated.[1] If an ordinance imposing the payment of wharfage dues on companies using the public wharves specifies the companies to be affected no other companies than those enumerated, not even their successors or new companies subsequently established, can be compelled to pay the prescribed fee.[2]

§ 195. **Examples of the application of rules of construction.**—A short review of a few decided cases will show how the rules of construction are often modified and governed by the circumstances of the case. In order to sustain a charge of *suffering* domestic animals to run at large there must be proof that the defendant either caused them to run at large, or that he had notice of their being at large and took no steps to restrain them.[3]

In a prosecution under an ordinance that prohibits fast driving the motive for the alleged violation may be considered, not to entirely free the defendant from the penalty imposed, but to lessen the amount of the fine when discretion in adjudging the amount rests in the magistrate.[4] An ordinance required that all fish packed for sale should be first inspected and the packages branded by the inspector before being offered for sale. The defendant, after the packages were properly inspected and branded, repacked his fish in smaller packages and offered them for sale. This was held to be a sufficient compliance with the ordinance.[5] An ordinance that imposed certain restrictions upon persons coming "from a place" infected with the small-pox applies to those only who leave such a place after the pas-

(1) Snyder *v.* North Lawrence, 8 Kan. 82.
(2) Keokuk, etc., Co. *v.* Quincy, 81 Ill. 422.
(3) Collinsville *v.* Scanland, 58 Ill. 222.
(4) Morton *v.* Princeton, 18 Ill. 383.
(5) Chicago *v.* Hobson, 52 Ill. 482.

sage of the ordinance and come directly to the town.[1] An ordinance that makes it unlawful to associate with a prostitute "in any public place, street, alley, common, *or within the city*," is construed to cover only public places, streets, alleys, and commons.[2] A provision that street cars going in the same direction "shall keep a certain distance apart" does not apply to two cars fastened together.[3] The provision that no person shall put, or cause to be put, in any street or other public place "any dirt, filth, shavings, or other rubbish or obstruction of any kind" has been held broad enough to cover the obstruction of a street by the cars of a railroad company.[4] An ordinance prohibiting the storing of fertilizers within the city limits without obtaining permission from the city council does not apply to the transient storage of fertilizers in the store-houses of a railroad company.[5]

Under an ordinance, power to license a house for dancing, music, games, etc., a license may be granted for either one of those things separately, and things not enumerated in the license would still be unlawful.[6] The word "*and*" may be read disjunctively, but only when it becomes necessary to carry out the intention of the legislators as expressed by the context.[7] Where an ordinance named the businesses and professions to be taxed and concludes "and all other business, trades, avocations, and professions whatever," a license may be demanded from an architect. The maxim *expressio unius exclusio alterius* would not apply.[8] An assault made by one person upon another with a dangerous weapon can not be punished as a *disturbance*.[9] The

(1) Commissioners v. Powe, 6 Jones (N. Car.), 134.
(2) Zorger v. Greenbush, 60 Ind. 1.
(3) Bishop v. Railroad Co., 14 R. Id. 314.
(4) Ill. Cent. R. R. Co. v. Galena, 40 Ill. 344.
(5) Athens v. Railroad Co., 72 Ga. 800.
(6) Brown v. Nugent, 6 Q. B. 693.
(7) Philadelphia v. Arrott, 8 Phila. 41; Smith v. Madison, 7 Ind. 86; Wright v. Railroad Co., 7 Ill. App. 438.
(8) St. Louis v. Herthel, 88 Mo. 128.
(9) Walsh v. Union, 11 Pac. Rep. 312.

word *street* used in an ordinance means a street within the city limits and used as a public highway.¹

Numerous illustrations of the construction applied to ordinances will be found in the sections treating the ordinances according to their subject-matter, *post*, Chapter XI.

A punishment imposed for "public drunkenness" is not restricted to those who are drunk in a public place, for a man may be publicly drunk in a private place, if while in that condition he is visible or accessible to any portion of the populace.² The license demanded of "second-hand dealers" does not extend to those who buy and sell second-hand articles as a mere incident of their general business. It can only be collected from those whose main business is in second-hand goods.³

Punitive ordinances should be enforced with some regard to the ability of persons affected to comply with their provisions; thus, an ordinance which declares that the owner of a house used or reputed to be used to his knowledge as a house of ill-fame shall be deemed guilty of maintaining a public nuisance, applies to those only who both know of such use or reputation and have power to prevent it, but which they do not exercise.⁴

But, duties imposed on the "owner or driver" of certain vehicles are binding on the owner, although he be absent and ignorant of the violation of the ordinance.⁵ The prohibition of "keeping open" a certain place of business does not render an actual user of the place for the purposes for which it is kept open necessary to constitute an offense. A readiness and present ability to carry on the usual business therein is a keeping open within the contemplation of the ordinance.⁶ A provision in an ordinance granting franchises to a railroad company, that it shall ever be subject

---

(1) Philadelphia *v.* Hughes, 4 Phila. 148· Chicago *v.* Gosselin, 4 Ill. App. 571.·
(2) State *v.* McNinch, 87 N. Car. 567.
(3) Eastman *v.* Chicago, 79 Ill. 178.
(4) McAllister *v.* Clark, 33 Conn. 91.
(5) Dane *v.* Mobile, 36 Ala. 304.
(6) Lynch *v.* People, 16 Mich. 472.

to *all* the ordinances of a city, refers to such ordinances only as are reasonable. The city could not by a subsequent ordinance absolutely prohibit the running of trains upon certain of its tracks.[1] And an ordinance permitting a railroad company to use certain streets on condition that it permit other companies, not to exceed two, to use the main track, will not be construed to prohibit the company from extending the use of its tracks to more than two others if it should so desire.[2] Permission to lay tracks and to run cars "on, over, and along" certain streets does not give permission to run cars above or under the street. The word *along* is synonymous with *on*.[3]

Where privileges are granted to semi-public concerns or corporations, on condition of their doing certain things if ordered, the grantee is not restricted to await the prior order of the corporate authorities, but may perform the acts whenever they seem advisable.[4] Whenever public ministerial agencies are created for defined purposes, such as the supervision of the highways, and the ordinance provides that they shall execute all the orders of the council or public boards, they need not await such order or direction, but they may perform such acts as are within the scope of their agency under the general implied powers conferred by the creating ordinance.[5]

To "permit" may mean "to allow by not prohibiting."[6] Under power to purchase coffee for the poor, an article called "Ottoman cahvey" can not be purchased.[7]

§ 196. **Defenses to prosecutions.**—Causes of action arising from the violation of municipal ordinances are subject to the operation of the statute of limitations.

(1) Railroad Company *v.* Joliet, 79 Ill. 26.
(2) Chicago *v.* Railroad Co., 95 Ill. 74.
(3) Heath *v.* Railroad Co., 61 Ia. 11.
(4) Quincy *v.* Bull, 106 Ill. 337.
(5) Noyes *v.* Ward, 19 Conn. 250.
(6) Commonwealth *v.* Curtis, 9 Allen, 266.
(7) Ottomon Cahvey Co. *v.* Philadelphia, 4 Atl. Rep. 745.

Ignorance of the law excuses no one.¹ Neither is ignorance of an ordinance a defense to a non-resident, whose property becomes amenable to the local ordinances by lying or coming within the corporate limits.² Non-residence is in general no defense to any one who enters a municipality, and thereby puts himself within the jurisdiction of its court.³

§ 197. **Effect of a repeal of an ordinance.**—If, during the progress of a prosecution, the ordinance on which it is based is repealed, the prosecution must fail, unless the repealing ordinance contains some express provision whereby all pending prosecutions are saved from its operation.⁴

The repeal of a resolution which itself repealed a prior ordinance has been held to revive the ordinance by implication.⁵ The usual and proper method, however, is to formally re-enact the old ordinance.

§ 198. **Former conviction.**—We have seen that where the same act is punishable under an ordinance and under some penal law of the state, the offense is often considered so far double in its nature that a conviction under one law will not act as a bar to a prosecution under the other.⁶ But the reason for such a holding fails where the same act can be considered as an offense under either of two ordinances. The corporation may elect to prosecute for either offense, but a conviction would be a complete bar to a prosecution for the other.⁷ An acquittal would not

(1) Burmeister *v.* Howard, 1 Wash. Terr. 207; Palmyra *v.* Morton, 25 Mo. 593.
(2) Knoxville *v.* King, 7 B. J. Lea, 441. See *ante,* §§ 142, 143.
(3) Buffalo *v.* Webster, 10 Wend. 99; Marietta *v.* Fearing; 4 Ohio, 43.
(4) Naylor *v.* Galesburg, 56 Ill. 285; Kansas City *v.* Clarke, 68 Mo. 588.
(5) Mayor *v.* New York. 97 N Y. 275
(6) *Ante,* §§ 91-120; State *v.* Welch, 36 Conn. 215; Mayor *v.* Allaire, 14 Ala. 400.
(7) Eddleston *v.* Barnes, 1 Ex. Div. L. R. 67.

bar a prosecution under some other ordinance, unless the evidence that would be necessary to convict under the second ordinance would also suffice to convict under the first ordinance.[1]

§ 199. **Other defenses.**—It can not be urged as a defense that the municipal corporation was improperly organized or the trustees improperly elected who enacted the ordinance.[2] Nor is it a good defense that other persons had previously violated the same ordinance, against whom no actions had been brought.[3]

It is no defense to a prosecution for running a railroad train at a greater rate of speed than is permitted by ordinance, that the train was carrying the United States mail. Governmental agencies, in the absence of express exception by general statute, are just as much subject to local police regulation as are private persons.[4]

In proceedings to enforce an ordinance against strays, it is a good defense that the escape of the animals was unavoidable, and that the owner used due diligence in attempting to reclaim the animals.[5]

A principal is ordinarily liable for the unlawful acts of his agents when performed in connection with the scope of their employment, and even though he has expressly prohibited their performance, but the owner of a saloon is not liable for an unlawful sale of liquor made by an employe who has no authority at all to sell under any circumstances.[6]

§ 200 **The doctrine of estoppel as applied to defenses.**—The principle of estoppel may be invoked under certain circumstances to protect the offender from prosecution, or to bar him from setting up an otherwise valid

(1) McRea v Americus, 59 Ga. 168.
(2) Decorah v Gillis, 10 Ia 234; Redden v. Covington, 29 Ind. 118.
(3) Charleston v. Reed, 37 W. Va. 681.
(4) Whitson v. Franklin, 34 Ind 392.
(5) Spitler v. Young, 63 Mo. 42.
(6) Minden v. Silverstein 36 La. Ann. 912.

defense. No man may derive any benefit from his own wrong; hence he who derives some advantage or benefit from an ordinance and accepts it, can not attack its validity.[1] So, if a person accepts a license for carrying on a business otherwise unlawful, he subjects himself to every condition imposed by the ordinance which makes the license necessary, and so far recognizes its validity as to be estopped from attacking it.[2] It is too late to object to an ordinance, which provides for certain improvements, on the ground of irregularity in its passage after due notice has been given and the work completed.[3] Or when one aids in procuring the improvement and stands by while it is being made.[4] Where an ordinance for the construction of sidewalks provides for personal notice, and notice by publication to be given to the adjoining owners, the latter mode is intended to bind those who are not personally served, and one who was actually served will not be heard to object that publication was omitted.[5]

§ 201. **Estoppel of the corporation.**—The corporation may also be estopped of its remedy by the acts or omissions of its agents. When a person complies with every requirement of an ordinance demanding a license, and the city refuses or neglects to issue him a license, he can not be punished for failing to procure it.[6] So, if a city, having power to grant or to withhold a license, grants one, it can not thereafter enforce an ordinance against the licenses, which requires all dealers to close their doors and stop selling their goods while any denomination of Christians are holding services within the city limits.[7]

Corporations may in various ways waive strict com-

(1) Argenti v. San Francisco, 16 Cal. 255.
(2) Launder v. Chicago, 111 Ill. 291.
(3) State v. Paterson, 40 N. J. 244.
(4) Covington v. Dressman, 6 Bush, 210.
(5) Chariton v. Holliday, 60 Ia. 391.
(6) Zanone v. Mound City, 11 Ill. App. 334.
(7) Gilman v. Wells, 64 Ga. 192; Genoa v. Van Alstine, 108 Ill. 555.

pliance with its police regulations.¹ But where a municipal corporation is directed by the charter or statute as to the mode of regulating some matter of local interest, and a person fails to comply with an ordinance passed in compliance with such direction, there is no presumption of a waiver of a right to punish a failure to observe the ordinance, from simple omission to proceed immediately after notice of such failure.²

Corporations may be barred of their rights by their own acts passed subsequently to the commission of an offense. Still, it has been held that the right to enforce a penalty for the violation of a fire limit ordinance becomes vested in the public, and that the passage of a resolution permitting the erection of buildings of the same nature would not bar a suit to enforce the penalty.³

§ 202. **Form of judgment.**—In order that judgment may be rendered it must be preceded by a finding of guilt by a competent tribunal. There can be no conviction without a trial.⁴ When the liability is admitted by a plea of guilty there must be a formal determination of guilt by the magistrate before proceedings are taken to enforce the penalty.⁵

The judgment rendered should be unconditional. If its severity is to be modified, it can be accomplished by remitting part of the penalty. The judgment can be for nothing else than the penalty prescribed by the ordinance under which suit is brought. That is the measure of the court's power. If an act is threatened which would constitute a flagrant violation of some ordinance, and the evil results of which would entail irreparable injury, the remedy of injunction would lie in a higher court. The local court could exercise no jurisdiction until a breach of the ordinance. The local court can neither enjoin a

(1) Railroad Co. v. People, 73 Ill. 542.
(2) Urquhart v. Ogdensburg, 97 N. Y. 238.
(3) Clark v. Elizabeth, 43 N. J. 173.
(4) Craig v. Bennett, 32 Ala. 735.
(5) Ewbanks v. Ashley, 36 Ill. 177; King v. Jacksonville, 3 Ill. 305.

threatened act, nor can it enforce a positive act of compliance with the ordinance. Action of the latter sort would be in the nature of mandamus and beyond its jurisdiction.[1]

The only rule to be observed in formulating the judgment of the court is that it must find the defendant guilty *as charged*. This may be done by referring to the charge or complaint, or by embodying its language in the judgment rendered. The former method is preferable, because in the latter some risk is run of inadvertently omitting from the words of the judgment some essential element of the charge, which would be fatal to its validity. To say that "the court finds the defendant guilty as charged and decrees and adjudges that he pay a fine of $——, etc.," adapting the punishment to that authorized by the ordinance, is unobjectionable. Even when the form of the action is *debt*, a verdict of guilty is responsive to the issue.[2] In a jury trial the finding of guilt is the duty of the jury, and the court merely adjudges the penalty. If the section of the ordinance provides for an alternative penalty, the judgment is not defective for assuming the same form. Either of the penalties could be enforced.[3] But a judgment that consists solely of a repetition of the section of the ordinance, without any averment as to the issue found, is bad.[4] It seems that a judgment is not fatally defective which contains some surplusage, provided the surplusage and the material elements are separable. Thus, in a prosecution for selling beer and wine without a license, under an ordinance which makes a license necessary to authorize the sale of beer and wine, a finding that the defendant is guilty of selling *ale*, beer, and wine without a license will be sustained, although the corporation has no power to license the sale of *ale*, and such a sale could not be a violation of the local

(1) People *v.* Railroad Co., 11 Hun, 297.
(2) Wiggins *v.* Chicago, 68 Ill. 372; Pendergast *v.* Peru, 20 Ill. 51; Deitz *v.* Central, 1 Col. 323.
(3) Flanagan *v.* Plainfield, 44 N. J. 118; Ex parte Chin Yan, 60 Cal. 78.
(4) Long *v.* Brookston, 79 Ind. 183.

law. Enough remains in the finding, after striking out the word *ale*, to establish a breach of the ordinance.¹

All matters included in the charge or complaint are concluded by the judgment of the court. If the charter authorizes the recovery of several fines in one action, and the proof is clear as to several distinct violations of the ordinance, the judgment should include all the fines, because it would otherwise have the effect of an acquittal of those violations which are not fined, and would be a complete bar to a subsequent prosecution on them.² If the offense consists in the *wanton* commission of some act, the court must find that the act complained of was *wanton*.³

§ 203. **The order of commitment to jail.**—As soon as judgment has been passed, immediate steps are taken for its enforcement. If a fine alone is the penalty, execution may issue whenever the action is in the nature of debt, but usually it can only be enforced by committing the defendant to jail until paid. When the direct punishment is imprisonment, the offender is at once committed. In either case a formal *mittitur* or order of imprisonment is necessary. A verbal order is not sufficient.⁴ The order is directed to the keeper of the jail, and commands him to keep the offender in custody. The terms of the order or writ vary with the nature of the penalty, but in every case it must show the cause of the commitment, the length of the imprisonment and its nature. The rules of procedure must be strictly observed.⁵ Thus, when the ordinances provide that when judgment is rendered, if the fine and costs are not paid, the magistrate may commit the defendant until they are paid, unless an appeal is taken, it would be error to commit after an appeal had been taken. Every element of the judgment that might have a bearing to determine the duration or nature of the imprisonment

(1) Keokuk *v.* Dressell, 47 Ia. 597.
(2) St. Charles *v.* O'Mailey, 18 Ill. 407.
(3) Mayor *v.* Wards, 1 Phila. 517.
(4) Trustees *v.* Schroeder, 58 Ill. 353.
(5) Carson *v.* Bloomington, 6 Ill. App. 481.

must be clearly set forth in the order. If the imprisonment be ordered as a means of enforcing payment of a fine, the writ must state the amount of the fine, and that the person named in the writ is to be confined for a certain definite time, the time that may be provided for by law, *or* until the fine and costs have been paid. If the law obliges the offender to work out the fine, the rate per day at which his labor shall be estimated must be also designated. If the law allows the imprisonment to be coupled with labor, it is error to adjudge that the offender shall be kept at *hard* labor.[1] Not only the termination of the term of imprisonment must be definitely fixed, but also its commencement. Thus, where an offender is in jail for another offense when judgment is passed, it would be error to sentence him to a certain imprisonment *to begin* after the previous sentence should expire or be otherwise disposed of.[2]

It is always proper to include the costs of the prosecution in the amount that must be paid before the imprisonment shall cease. The municipal corporation is never liable for costs in prosecutions under its ordinances.[3]

(1) Ex parte Reed, 1 Cranch, C. C. 582.
(2) Larney v. Cleveland, 34 O. S. 599.
(3) Regina v. Johnston, 38 U. Can. Q. B. 549; Selma v. Stewart, 67 Ala. 338; Camden v. Bloch, 65 Ala. 236; Montgomery v. Foster, 54 Ala. 61. *Contra*, State v. Cantieny, 34 Minn. 1; *ante*, § 156.

CHAPTER IX.

PROCEEDINGS IN REVIEW.

§ 204. Certiorari.
§ 205. Habeas corpus.
§ 206. Injunction.
§ 207. Appeal.
§ 208. Error.
§ 209. The record.

§ 204. **Certiorari.**—At common law the only method of reviewing the validity of proceedings for violation of ordinances was by a writ of *certiorari*, and this is still the proper remedy unless abrogated or superseded by statute. It is properly used to review the judicial acts only of a municipal corporation.[1] The writ lies unless some other remedy is provided by statute, in which case the statutory mode alone can be used.[2] The writ will not issue if the injured party has any other remedy, and if the time within which the defendant might have perfected an appeal has expired, he can only have resort to *certiorari* on a special showing of the entire absence of negligence on his part.[3] Where no other remedy is provided by statute, the writ of *certiorari* is the only method of review.[4]

The writ of *certiorari* is in general of limited application. When permissible it only lies to review judicial acts for errors of law alone.[5] It does not lie after the fine has been paid or the penalty exacted, for there must be some sub-

---

(1) In re Wilson, 32 Minn. 144.
(2) Montgomery v. Belser, 53 Ala. 379; Camden v. Bloch, 65 Ala. 236; Intendant v. Chandler, 6 Ala. 297; Taylor v. Americus, 39 Ga. 59; Jackson v. People, 9 Mich. 111; State v. Bill, 13 Ire. (N. Car.) 373.
(3) Beasley v. Beckley, 28 W. Va. 81; Poe v. Machine Works, 24 W. Va. 517.
(4) Loeb v. Duncan, 63 Miss. 89; Corbett v. Duncan, 63 Miss. 84.
(5) In re Wilson, 32 Minn. 144; Camden v. Bloch, 65 Ala. 236.

stantial injury to warrant such interposition of a higher court.[1] Acts which involve the exercise of discretion are considered ministerial rather than judicial when sought to be reviewed.[2]

Certiorari does not lie at the instance of the corporation; so that, unless special statutory provision is made therefor, a trial and acquittal is final.[3]

The scope of the writ of *certiorari* has been extended in the State of New Jersey even beyond that occupied by it at common law. In that state it lies to review errors and remedy grievances whether they arise from the exercise of judicial or ministerial powers.[4] And it even lies to declare an ordinance void at the suit of a party who is affected, although the ordinance may not yet have been sought to be enforced against him by an action.[5]

§ 205. **Habeas corpus.**—Questions as to the validity of proceedings pending for violation of municipal ordinances are sometimes attempted to be reviewed through the medium of the writ of *habeas corpus*. The right can not be denied, but such procedure is to be deprecated as unnecessary, inasmuch as the defendant always has his recognized legal remedy by error, appeal, or *certiorari*. It can only avail when the ordinance under which the petitioner has been placed in custody is *as a matter of law* void. No questions of fact or of procedure can be examined under the writ.[6] It will not lie after judgment has been passed to review alleged errors.[7]

§ 206. **Injunction.**—The court will not enjoin proceedings brought to punish a violation of a municipal ordinance for any reason that would receive proper recognition

(1) People *v.* Leavitt, 41 Mich. 470; State *v.* Blauvelt, 34 N. J. 261.
(2) State *v.* Bill, 13 Ire. (N. Car.) 373.
(3) Cranston *v.* Augusta, 61 Ga. 572.
(4) Camden *v.* Mulford, 26 N. J. 49; Dillon Mun. Corp., § 927.
(5) State *v.* Jersey City, 29 N. J. 170.
(6) In re Wright, 29 Hun, 357.
(7) Madden *v.* Smeltz, 2 Circ. Ct. Rep. (Ohio) 168.

by a court of law in the regular form of proceeding brought to review the action of the local courts. That the ordinance has not been properly promulgated, or that no offense is charged, or that the action has been begun before a court which has no jurisdiction, is no ground for injunction.[1] If a court of competent jurisdiction has on appeal or error already declared an ordinance void, a court of equity might enjoin subsequent actions begun under the same ordinance on the ground that they are vexatious and oppressive.[2] As a rule, injunctions can only be decreed to prevent municipal corporations from abusing their franchises and powers when it appears that the acts complained of are unauthorized, injurious, and of such a character that proceedings at law will furnish no adequate relief, or will not prevent irreparable injury of consequence.[3]

It is equally true that an injunction will not lie to *enforce* a municipal ordinance. The power vested in corporations to enforce their own ordinances can not be supplemented by recourse to the courts of the state for provisional remedies. If an injunction will be granted it will not be because the act complained of or threatened is or would be an offense against some ordinance of the municipality, but because it is a nuisance *per se*, an act in regard to which the remedy of injunction would lie in the absence of any ordinance prohibiting it.[4] In such case an injunction might be granted at the instance of the corporation, but the right would not be influenced by its ordinances. If a building has been erected in violation of an ordinance

---

(1) Dodge v. Council Bluffs, 57 Ia. 560; Safe Co. v. Mayor, 38 Hun, 146; Schwab v. Madison, 49 Ind. 329.

(2) Safe Co. v. Mayor, 38 Hun, 146; Taylor v. Pine Bluff, 34 Ark. 603. It will not lie to restrain a prosecution on an alleged illegal ordinance. Poyer v. Des Plaines, 20 Ill. App. 30.

(3) Gartside v. East St. Louis, 43 Ill. 47; West v. Mayor, 10 Paige, 539; Banking Co. v. Jersey City, 12 N. J. Eq. 258.

(4) Hudson v. Thorne, 7 Paige, 261; Waupun v. Moore, 34 Wis. 450; 2 High on Injunctions, § 1243–1244.

its owner can not enjoin the mayor from tearing it down, although the mayor does so without special authority.[1]

§ 207. **Appeal.**—The different states have adopted varying policies as to the mode of reviewing the proceedings of local courts. A writ or petition in error is more frequently authorized, but an appeal is often allowed. Strictly speaking, an appeal is not pursued as a method of reviewing the judgment of a lower court, although it can never be taken until such judgment has been rendered, but it is the privilege of a new trial before a higher tribunal. It is pursued without regard to the errors that may have been committed below. Its effect is to entirely vacate the prior judgment and to secure a new trial. All defects or irregularities are cured by appeal, except that the appellant may still object to the jurisdiction of the lower court.[2] A variance on the former trial between the complaint and the evidence can not be taken into account.[3] The form and nature of the action remain the same; the court alone is changed.[4] It seems that where the right of appeal is given, it is such a certain indication that the action is considered civil rather than criminal in its nature, that the right may be exercised by the corporation as well as by the offender against its ordinances. In that case, the application of the constitutional privilege of the accused, that he shall not be twice put in jeopardy for the same offense, does not extend to prosecutions under municipal ordinances.[5]

When the judgment of the lower court is appealed from by the defendant, he must give a bond conditioned upon the due prosecution of the appeal and submission to the judgment that shall be rendered. If the appellate court finds the bond to be defective, it should order a new one

(1) Aronheimer v Stokley, 11 Phila. 283.
(2) Alton v. Kirsch, 68 Ill. 261; Byars v. Mt. Vernon, 47 Mich. 192; Coulterville v. Gillen, 72 Ill. 599.
(3) Harbaugh v. Monmouth, 74 Ill. 367.
(4) Webster v. Lansing, 47 Mich. 192.
(5) Greenfield v. Mook, 12 Ill. App. 281; Camden v. Bloch, 65 Ala. 236.

to be given, and, in default of compliance, should dismiss the appeal.[1]

Appeals from prosecution under ordinances, like appeals from magistrates' courts in civil causes, should be accompanied by a transcript of the proceedings below in order that the issues shall be before the appellate court. Then they are prosecuted as though the appellate court were the court of original jurisdiction. The appellate court will follow the same rules of pleading and evidence, so far as possible, that are observed in the court below. Thus, it should take judicial notice of the ordinance, when the lower court might do so.[2] If, according to the practice below, the complaint need not do more than state the date of passage and the substance of the ordinance, with sufficient particularity to enable it to be identified, and to allege a violation, the same requisites, if complied with, will be sufficient in the appellate court.[3]

§ 208. **Error.**—A writ of error, or a petition in error, as it is called in some of the states, is the usual method provided for reviewing convictions under municipal ordinances. The entire proceedings of the lower court may thereby be brought before a higher court for review; and if it appears that any errors were committed on the trial below which in any material degree might affect the finding of the court or the verdict of the jury, or if it plainly appears that the finding of the lower court was contrary to the weight of the evidence, the judgment will be reversed and the defendant ordered free from custody. A bond must be given, conditioned upon the due prosecution of the error proceeding, else the corporation could proceed to enforce the penalty adjuged.

§ 209 **The record.**—As nothing can be taken into consideration by the higher court except what appears upon the

(1) Greenfield v. Mook, *supra*.
(2) Solomon v. Hughes, 24 Kan. 211; March v. Commonwealth, 12 B. Mon. 25.
(3) Goldthwaite v. Montgomery, 50 Ala. 486.

face of the record, it becomes important to consider just how the record should be prepared and what it must show. It is advisable that the record should be an accurate statement of every thing that was done in connection with the case. It should contain not only the evidence given, but also such things as the court below was obliged to notice judicially in order to reach its conclusions. The defendant is, however, charged with the duty of bringing into the record every thing that was judicially noticed, in order to base error upon its insufficiency. If the court could take judicial notice of the ordinance and it was not put in evidence, the court above will presume that the complaint alleges an act which would constitute an offense under the ordinance, unless the defendant brings the ordinance into the record in order that it may be compared with the words of the complaint, and in order that the court may pass upon its validity.[1] It is always better to formally put the ordinance in evidence and to let it appear in the record; for, if it is not, it may be urged that the court had no right to take judicial notice of it. It would, however, hardly be error for a reviewing court to also take judicial notice of the ordinance if justice necessitates so doing.[2]

With the one exception of the ordinance itself in states where the local court may take judicial notice of it, the record must show compliance on the part of the prosecution with every step that is necessary to a conviction or to the rendition of judgment. It must show, to particularize:

1. The complaint or charge in full.

2. The process issued in pursuance of the complaint by which the presence of the defendant was secured in court; or the notice given.

3. The action taken by the police officer in executing that process.

(1) New Orleans v. Boudro, 14 La. Ann. 303; Baton Rouge v. Crémonini, 35 La. Ann. 367; *Idem*, 36 La. Ann. 247; Morgan v. Nolte, 37 O. S. 23.

(2) March v. Commonwealth, 12 B. Mon. 28.

4. The ordinance upon which the right to recover is based.

5. The presence or absence of the defendant at the trial.

6. That the defendant was given an opportunity to plead to the complaint, and his plea, if he makes one.

7. Formal trial in open court.

8. That evidence was introduced or witnesses examined under oath or affirmation.

9. Either from the complaint or the evidence that the court had jurisdiction, viz., that the offense was committed within the corporate limits.

10. That the defendant was allowed to be heard in his own defense.

11. The finding of the court.

12. The sentence or due entry of judgment.

13. The proceedings taken to execute the sentence or judgment.

14. And if it is a case in which a jury trial was had, the record must show who were summoned, and who served, that they were duly sworn, that they were charged by the court, and the verdict which they returned.[1]

In regard to all things which need not appear on the record, the reviewing court will presume the proceedings to have been regular; but in regard to things or steps which must have been done in order to find the defendant guilty, the presumption is in favor of the defendant. All jurisdictional matters especially must appear on the record.[2] If the record shows the offense charged, that evidence was given and the defendant found guilty, the court will presume that the evidence proved an offense as charged. Objections to the sufficiency or admissibility of evidence are of no avail unless the petitioner brings into the court above, as a part of the record, all the evidence given at the trial. Otherwise the opinion of the magistrate will be considered

---

(1) City v. Duncan, 4 Phila. 145; Keeler v. Milledge, 24 N. J. 146; Taylor v. Americus, 39 Ga. 59; City v. Hughes, 4 Phila. 148; Northern Liberties v. O'Neill, 1 Phila. 427; Philadelphia v. Roney, 2 Phila. 43; Camden v. Bloch, 65 Ala. 236.

(2) Elizabeth v. Woodruff, 30 N. J. 176.

final.¹ It is the right of the defendant to insist that every question made upon the trial shall be incorporated into the record, for he can only take advantage in the reviewing court of such errors as appear on the record. But all questions of fact or law must be raised in the cout below. Technical questions as to the jurisdiction and form of procedure, or as to the sufficiency of the pleadings, evidence, or judgment may be raised either in detail or generally, by demurrer to the pleadings, motion to quash, motion to dismiss the complaint after the evidence has all been given, and motion to suspend sentence after the court has made its finding, or after the jury has returned its verdict.² In order to avail the defendant of any errors or objections which do not appear upon the face of the record, he must take a *bill of exceptions*. If no provision is made for the preparation of a bill of exceptions after the close of the trial, the defendant may insist upon time during the progress of the trial to prepare the same and procure it to be signed by the trial magistrate. The bill of exceptions becomes a part of the record of the trial, and should be certified up with it as such. Mandamus will lie to compel the magistrate to sign the bill and to certify it as a part of the record. The record must at least show that a bill was presented and allowed, and there must be evidence on its face to show that it is the one which was actually allowed.³

The petitioner must not only cause the record to be certified up to the reviewing court, but he must also make a formal claim in his petition of the errors from which he seeks advantage. The defect or error, even though it appears affirmatively on the face of the record, must be specifically assigned or covered by the petition in error. The measure of the petitioner's claim is his petition, and if no claim of

(1) Lynch v. People, 16 Mich. 472.
(2) Smith v. Elizabeth, 46 N. J. 312; Selma v. Stewart, 67 Ala. 338; Tisdale v. Minonk, 46 Ill. 9; Jacksonville v. Holland, 19 Ill. 271; Moss v. Oakland, 88 Ill. 109; Stokes v. New York, 14 Wend. 87; Flora v. Lee, 5 Ill. App. 629; Bethalto v. Conley, 9 *Id.* 339; Kanouse v. Lexington, 12 *Id.* 318.
(3) Wertheimer v. Boonville, 29 Mo. 254.

error is made, no relief can be granted. All errors which are not alleged are taken to be waived.

In order to entitle the defendant to have his conviction reviewed, he must not in any way have recognized its validity. Thus, the voluntary payment of the judgment would bar error proceedings.² Payment under protest to avoid imprisonment is an involuntary payment, and if the judgment should afterward be reversed, the defendant could recover the amount paid with interest in an action brought for that purpose.³

(1) Fuhrman *v.* Huntsville, 54 Ala. 263 (see page 265).
(2) Powell *v.* People, 47 Mich. 108.
(3) Harvey *v.* Boyd, 42 Ill. 336.

CHAPTER X.

RESOLUTIONS.

§ 210. Resolutions.
§ 210a. What may be done by resolution.

§ 210. **Resolutions.**—An ordinance of a municipal corporation may be in the form of a resolution and still be valid, provided that its enactment and promulgation is accompanied by all the solemnities and formalities prescribed by law for the passage of ordinances.[1] But in all cases where the charter or statute which gives powers of local regulation makes use of the word ordinance in directing the method in which those powers are to be exercised the word is construed to be used in its legal signification and the direction is imperative. The powers can only be exercised by ordinances in *form* as well as effect. Where ordinances are specified, resolutions are not considered as their equivalents.[2]

A resolution is a less formal act than an ordinance. All legislative acts of a municipal corporation which are to have continuing force and effect, and which are to constitute regulations of local matters until repealed or supplanted, are permanent in their nature and must be expressed in the form of ordinances. But municipal corporations have many other acts to perform of a quasi-legislative nature which are purely temporary in their effect. Such are its assent to acts of a private citizen which affect the property or rights of the public temporarily, the granting of licenses for special purposes, the execution of contracts, the accept-

---

(1) Manufacturing Co. v. Schell City, 21 Mo. App. 175; Drake v. Railroad Co., 7 Barb. 539; Tipton v. Norman, 72 Mo. 380; First Municipality v. Cutting, 4 La. Ann. 336.

(2) Paterson v. Barnet, 46 N. J. 62; Cross v. Morristown, 18 N. J. Eq. 305; Nashville v. Toney, 10 B. J. Lea, 643; Bryan v. Page 51 Tex. 532; Delphi v. Evans, 36 Ind. 90.

ance of proposals, the declaration of its intention to undertake some public improvement, and the purchase by it of property for the use of its fire or police department. All acts of that temporary character which neither command nor prohibit any thing that the public at large can do, may, in the absence of any specific direction, be performed by resolution as well as by ordinance. In fact resolutions are the more proper, although an ordinance would be as effective.[1] As a rule, all matters upon which the council wishes to *legislate* must be put in the form of an ordinance, and all acts that are done in its *ministerial* capacity may be in the form of resolutions.[2] Of course, if any other mode is prescribed it must be closely adhered to. Resolutions are not subject to the formalities prescribed for the enactment of ordinances, unless specifically directed. They do not need to be submitted to the mayor for his approval.[3] In Canada provision is made whereby the court may set aside ordinances, or *by-laws*, as they are there designated, on the petition of a citizen of the municipality, if they prove to be invalid. It is held that resolutions are not *by-laws* within the meaning of that statute, and that the court has no jurisdiction to set them aside. If they are illegal, they are simply void and the corporation renders itself liable to an action for damages at the hands of any one who is thereby injured.[4]

§ 210a. **What may be done by resolution.**—The following acts performed through the medium of resolutions have been upheld: The opening of a new street;[5] the purchase of apparatus for the fire department;[6] the determination that a sewer shall be built, and ordering it done;[7]

(1) Los Angeles v. Waldron, 65 Cal. 283.
(2) Burlington v. Dennison, 42 N. J. 165; Quincy v. Railroad Co., 92 Ill. 21; Green v. Cape May, 41 N. J. 46; Grimmell v. Des Moines, 57 Ia. 144; Butler v. Passaic, 44 N. J. 171.
(3) Burlington v. Dennison, 42 N. J. 165.
(4) Caesar v. Cartwright, 12 U. C. Q. B. 341.
(5) Sower v. Philadelphia, 35 Pa. St. 236.
(6) Green v. Cape May, 41 N. J. 45.
(7) State v. Jersey City, 27 N. J. 493.

fixing the amount of a license fee previously directed by an ordinance to be exacted;[1] ordering improvements on a certain street;[2] authorizing its agents to enter into specified contracts;[3] appointing architects to inspect the safety of buildings in process of construction;[4] confirming past acts performed by its agents.[5]

The following acts attempted to be performed by resolution have been declared void: Prescribing the payment of license fees;[6] fixing the compensation of officers.[7]

Resolutions are special and temporary, applicable only to a single matter of passing moment; ordinances are permanent regulations, applicable to all states of fact thereafter arising within the scope of its provisions.[8]

(1) Burlington v. Insurance Co., 31 Ia. 102.
(2) Indianapolis v. Imberry, 17 Ind. 175; Commissioners v. Silvers, 22 Ind. 491.
(3) Alton v. Mulledy, 21 Ill. 76.
(4) Egan v. Chicago, 5 Ill. App. 70.
(5) Gas Company v. San Francisco, 6 Cal. 190.
(6) People v. Crotty, 93 Ill. 181; s. c., 3 Ill. App. 465.
(7) Central v. Sears, 2 Col. 588; Walker v. Evansville, 33 Ind. 393.
(8) Blanchard v. Bissell, 11 O. S. 96; State v. Bayonne, 35 N. J. 335; Kempner v. Commonwealth, 40 Pa. St. 124.

CHAPTER XI.

ORDINANCES CLASSIFIED ACCORDING TO THEIR SUBJECT-MATTER.

§ 211. Nature of police powers.
§§ 212, 213. Their general purpose.
§ 214. Necessity and scope of health regulations.
§ 215. Boards of health.
§ 216. Regulation of articles of food.
§ 217. Markets.
§ 218. Other regulations of the food supply.
§ 219. Slaughter houses.
§ 220. Other health regulations: Cemeteries, offal, dead animals, diseases, miscellaneous.
§ 221. Fire.
§ 222. Fire limits.
§ 223. Extent of the power.
§ 224. Streets.
§ 225. Care of the streets.
§ 226. Grading.
§ 227. Paving.
§ 228. Sidewalks.
§ 229. Protection of streets.
§ 230. Obstructions.
§ 231. Examples of lawful obstruction.
§ 232. Inclosures.
§ 233. Public buildings.
§ 234. Other buildings.
§ 235. Snow.
§ 236. Moving buildings.
§ 237. Miscellaneous obstructions.
§ 238. Steam railroads.
§ 239. Police regulation of steam railroads.
§ 240. Street railways.
§ 241. Regulations.
§ 242. Sewerage system.
§ 243. Water supply.
§ 244. Gas pipes.
§ 244a. Telegraph poles.
§ 245. Restrictions on ordinary use of the streets.
§ 246. Vehicles.
§ 247. Routes and stands.

§ 248. Construction of vehicle regulations.
§ 249. Strays.
§ 250. Nuisances.
§ 251. Definition.
§ 252. Must be an actual nuisance.
§ 253. Judicial determination.
§ 254. What are nuisances.
§ 255. What are not nuisances *per se*.
§ 256. Nature of license power.
§ 257. Nature of licenses.
§ 258. Must not amount to a tax.
§ 259. What amount may be charged.
§ 260. Examples.
§ 261. The license.
§ 262. The ordinance.
§ 263. Discretion in officers.
§ 264. The penalty.
§ 265. Effect of a license.
§ 266. Conditions.
§ 267. Revocability.
§ 268. Grading and discrimination.
§ 269. Miscellany.
§ 270. Business privileges.
§ 271. Transient dealers.
§ 272. Peddling.
§ 273. Amusements.
§ 274. Dogs.
§ 275. Liquor licenses.
§ 276. Ordinance provisions.
§ 277. Other regulations.
§ 278. Definitions.
§ 279. Evidence in liquor cases.
§ 280. Uniformity in licenses.
§ 281. Taxation.
§ 282. Local assessments.
§ 283. Other taxes.
§ 284. Mode of exercise.
§ 285. Amount.
§ 286. Constitutional restrictions.
§ 287. Discrimination.
§ 288. Sunday ordinances.
§ 289. Appropriations for police purposes.
§ 290. To aid the administration of justice.
§ 291. To employ attorneys.
§ 292. Wharves.
§ 293. Conclusion.

§ 211. **Nature of police powers.**—The term "police" in its broad sense includes all the power that may be lawfully exercised by governmental agencies, but it is beyond the scope of this work to consider that class of local legislation which relates to the exercise of the property rights vested in municipalities, such as taxation, local assessments, and municipal assistance of private or quasi-public enterprises. The term as used here is restricted to those powers which relate solely to the proper police government of the municipality. The greater part of the powers delegated to municipal corporations are of that class, and their exercise constitutes an element in the general system of police regulation of the state. The precise nature and extent of police powers demand investigation, because the legislative expression of the powers to be exercised by a corporation is frequently restricted to the one phrase "police powers," and the ordinances enacted must then be reasonable regulations upon subjects which are recognized as falling within the scope of such powers. Often, too, an ordinance which can not be sustained under any of the special powers granted to a municipality, may be sustained by a general power elsewhere granted of regulating the police of the municipality. A grant of police power, however, can never be taken to authorize ordinances upon some subject which is partially or imperfectly given to the control of the corporation by an express grant, for the existence of the express grant shows that the legislative mind was specially directed to that subject, and the grant must be taken as the limit of its intention. And where nearly all the ordinary police powers are made the subjects of express grants, only such additional ones can be exercised under a general grant of police power as are absolutely essential to the welfare of the community.

§ 212. **Their general purpose.**—Police powers may be exercised in regard to any thing that will further and protect the comfort and welfare of the public at large. Their exercise is superior to all considerations of private interest or benefit. Ordinances passed in the exercise of these powers are not obnoxious to constitutional provisions merely because they do not provide compensation to the individual who is inconvenienced by them. He is presumed to be rewarded by the common benefits secured. Pronounced instances are found in all quarantine and health regulations and in all laws for the abatement of existing and prevention of threatened nuisances. If the public safety or the public morals require the discontinuance of any existing condition of property, manufacture, or traffic, the council may provide for its discontinuance, notwithstanding that individuals or corporations may thereby suffer inconvenience.[1]

Police power authorizes all regulations tending to promote the public health, morals, security, and comfort of the community. The main subjects of police regulation may be enumerated as nuisances, markets, strays, vehicles, the use of the streets, the condition of public and private property, the sale of dangerous commodities, the keeping of animals, the conduct of places of public resort, the prevention of fires, and the observance of Sunday.

§ 213. To illustrate by examples, the following powers have been held properly exercised under the general police power:

1. As promoting the health of the community; to regulate markets;[2] to regulate slaughter-houses;[3] to prohibit the keeping of swine in certain districts;[4] to prohibit the cultivation of rice within the corporate limits.[5]

2. As protecting the public morals; to regulate the

(1) Beer Company *v.* Massachusetts, 97 U. S. 25; Bancroft *v.* Cambridge, 126 Mass. 438; King *v* Davenport, 98 Ill. 305; McKibbin *v.* Fort Smith, 35 Ark. 352.

(2) State *v.* Bean, 91 N. C. 554.

(3) Worthington *v.* Scribner, 109 Mass. 487; Vogel *v.* Granz, 16 Chic. Leg News, 191.

(4) Commonwealth *v.* Patch, 97 Mass. 221.

(5) Green *v.* Savannah, 6 Ga. 1.

traffic in intoxicating liquors;[1] to regulate bawdy houses;[2] to prohibit lewd women from waiting upon customers of saloons and restaurants, even though the prohibition extends to the proprietress of the place;[3] to regulate the renting of rooms to lewd women;[4] to prohibit lewd women from loitering on the streets.[5]

3. As necessary to personal security and comfort; to prevent the storage of dangerous articles;[6] to regulate the keeping of dogs;[7] to repress and restrain assaults, riots, disorderly conduct, unlawful assemblies and breaches of the peace;[8] to punish public libelous or slanderous language as tending to cause breaches of the peace;[9] to punish attempts to aid prisoners in escaping from the custody of officers;[10] to require dogs to be muzzled and to authorize the police officers to kill those found at large and unmuzzled;[11] to require the erection of guards around elevator walls;[12] to regulate the speed of railroad trains while running within the corporate limits;[13] to regulate the hours of transacting any business that may by misuse become injurious to the people;[14] to restrain and take up stray animals;[15] to provide for the prevention of fires;[16] to suppress

(1) Schwuchow v. Chicago, 68 Ill. 444; Miller v. State, 3 O. S. 475.
(2) Childress v. Nashville, 3 Sneed, 347.
(3) State v. Canton, 43 Mo. 48.
(4) New Orleans v. Costello, 14 La. Ann. 37.
(5) Braddy v. Milledgeville, 74 Ga. 516.
(6) Little Rock v. Barton, 33 Ark. 436.
(7) Carter v. Dow, 16 Wis. 298; Faribault v. Wilson, 34 Minn. 254; Commonwealth v. Markham, 7 Bush, 486; Commonwealth v. Steffee, 7 Bush, 161.
(8) Commonwealth v. Turner, 1 Cush. 493; Mayer v. Allaire, 14 Ala. 400; Trimble v. Bucyrus, 5 Cin. L. Bull. (Ohio), 15; People v. Miller, 38 Hun, 82.
(9) Commonwealth v. Turner, 1 Cush. 493.
(10) Independence v. Moore, 32 Mo. 392.
(11) Haller v. Sheridan, 28 Ind. 494.
(12) Mayor v. Williams, 15 N. Y. 502.
(13) Merz v. Railroad Co., 88 Mo. 672.
(14) Chebanse v. McPherson, 15 Ill. App. 311.
(15) Centerville v. Lanham, 67 Ga. 753; Wilcox v. Hemming, 58 Wis. 144; New Orleans v. Blanc, 1 La. Ann. 385.
(16) Wadleigh v. Gilman, 12 Me. 403; Brady v. Insurance Co., 11 Mich. 425; Mayor v. Hudson, 7 Paige, 261.

vagrancy;[1] to prescribe regulations of a sanitary nature;[2] to regulate the observance of the Sabbath;[3] to provide hospitals;[4] to regulate the use of the streets and to keep them in passable condition;[5] to require common carriers to take out licenses;[6] to prohibit deposits of rubbish and broken wares except in designated places;[7] at the time of the evacuation of Richmond to require the destruction of all liquors found within the city limits and to provide for indemnifying the owners of goods destroyed;[8] to require pawnbrokers to deliver to the police authorities before midnight of each day a list of all articles received that day, together with descriptions of the pledgors;[9] to compel all brokers to obtain a license.[10]

But it has been held unlawful under general police powers to punish assault and battery;[11] to grant the privilege of erecting and maintaining toll bridges;[12] to require cotton merchants to keep a record of their sales;[13] to punish all persons who may be found on the streets after ten o'clock P. M.;[14] to order the removal of buildings on the ground that they have been adjudicated to be within the line of a street;[15] to levy any form of taxes.[16]

The remaining pages of this chapter will be devoted to

(1) St. Louis v. Benzt, 11 Mo. 61.
(2) Bliss v. Kraus, 16 O. S. 54.
(3) Piqua v. Zimmerlin, 35 O. S. 507; St. Louis v. Cafferata, 24 Mo. 94
(4) Vionet v. First Municipality, 4 La. Ann. 42.
(5) Palmyra v. Morton, 25 Mo. 593; Palmer v. Way, 6 Col. 106; Railway Co. v. Hoboken, 41 N. J. 71.
(6) Havana v. Vanlaningham, 17 Ill. App. 62; Railway Co. v. Philadelphia, 58 Pa. St. 119.
(7) Ex parte Casinello, 62 Cal 538.
(8) Jones v. Richmond, 18 Gratt. 517.
(9) Launder v. Chicago, 111 Ill. 291.
(10) Little Rock v. Barton, 33 Ark. 436.
(11) People v. Brown, 2 Utah, 462, certainly not in accord with the weight of authority.
(12) Williams v. Davidson, 43 Tex. 1.
(13) Long v. Taxing District, 7 B. J. Lea, 134.
(14) Memphis v. Winfield, 8 Humph. 707.
(15) Dawes v. Hightstown, 45 N. J. 501.
(16) Desty on Taxation, 1380.

a detailed consideration of the various classes of police ordinances, arranged according to their subject-matter.

§ 214. Necessity and scope of health regulations.—

Among the more important of the police powers is that of caring for the health of the community. It may always be exercised, whether expressly granted or not, because the preservation of the health of the people is indispensable to the existence of the corporation. The power is hardly susceptible of exact definition, for the exigencies of each case are varying and the occasions innumerable when the health of the inhabitants is in some degree endangered. It is the policy of the law to favor such legislation as being humane and essential to the preservation of life, and when the council considers that some occupation or thing is dangerous to health the exercise of its discretion in the passage of regulatory ordinances will not be questioned by the court except in extreme cases. A greater degree of liberty of legislative action is allowed to municipalities in this direction than in any other, for the necessity of speedy prevention is more urgent and the consequences of neglect more detrimental to the public good than in regard to any other form of local evil. "No power is more important than that for the preservation of the public health. It is not only the right but the imperative duty of the city government to watch over the health of the citizens and to remove every nuisance, so far as they may be able, which may endanger it. And they have, necessarily, the power of deciding in what manner this shall be done, and their decision is conclusive, unless they transcend the powers conferred by the city charter or violate the constitution."[1]

In a general way, the power of caring for the health of the community includes power to enact ordinances in regard to the removal of offal, the cleaning of the streets, the location and use of cemeteries, the care of infectious diseases, the erection and maintenance of hospitals and pest-houses, the quarantine of vessels and trains, the public

---

(1) Baker v. Boston, 12 Pick. 184.

water supply, the sewerage system of the municipality, the purity and wholesomeness of food and drink, and the conduct and continuance of all trades, employments, and businesses, whether mercantile or manufacturing, which tend to pollute the air or the earth.

§ 215. **Boards of health.**—The power to enact ordinances of this class is plain. But, some provision must be made for an effective ministerial agency to supervise and direct the details of the execution of such ordinances, and to act in cases of emergency without the specific direction of the corporate council.[1] For this purpose *boards of health* may be organized and full powers of detailed supervision delegated to them. So far as possible, general regulations should be prescribed by the council, but as to all matter of temporary or sudden necessity the foresight of the council can not be relied upon, and broad powers must necessarily be delegated to the board of health.

The rules and regulations which the board of health may see fit to make are not ordinances in the sense which would demand the same formalities in regard to their adoption, or the same strictness in construing their provisions, although for their violation the same remedies may be authorized to be pursued. The only definite restriction on the power to pass ordinances regulating things that affect health, and to provide detailed regulations through a board of health, is that the ordinances and regulations must not be used as a cloak for other kinds of regulation. Thus, it is proper to regulate the quality of breadstuffs, but the weight and price of bread are beyond the province of health regulation.[2] It is proper to require that buildings shall be so erected as to be free from sanitary defects, but the thickness of the walls could not be regulated as having any thing to do with health.[3] So, the board of health could bind the municipality to pay for necessary medicines furnished to paupers, but it could not for medi-

(1) Boehm v. Baltimore, 61 Md. 259.
(2) Guillotte v. New Orleans, 12 La. Ann. 432.
(3) Hubbard v. Paterson, 45 N. J. 310.

cines, however necessary, furnished to persons who are able to pay for them.[1]

§ 216. **Regulation of articles of food.**—It is necessary to regulate the sale of articles of food in order that no impure or unwholesome food shall reach the consumer, and in order that the air may not be polluted by the improper exercise of any business which is devoted to the production or preparation of food, the former object being the most important. If every one may sell produce and articles of food at any place he chooses, the municipal authorities can not exercise an effective supervision over them; and, hence, it is first of all proper that the sale of such articles as are most apt to become stale or unfit for use, should be restricted to known localities. This necessity is recognized in the market laws of every city.

§ 217. **Markets.**—Cities have full power to restrict the sale of edible commodities, provided that the restriction is accompanied by a designation of some locality where sales may be lawfully made.[2]

In order to make such regulations effectual, market-places and houses may be erected. They must be suitable to the purpose, but as in the case of other public buildings, the corporation may build a larger market-house than is necessary for that one purpose, and may rent the upper part or unoccupied part to private individuals.[3]

Power to establish and regulate markets includes power to purchase a site, to build a market-house, and to enforce reasonable and just rules for its regulation, with reference to peace, health, and good order. Such rules must be of a police or sanitary character, and must not operate so as to restrain trade. They are restricted to reasonable regulation.[4] Here, as in other cases, every thing may be

(1) McIntire v. Pembroke, 53 N. H. 462.
(2) Lamarque v. New Orleans, 1 McGloin, 28.
(3) Spaulding v. Lowell, 23 Pick. 71.
(4) Caldwell v. Alton, 33 Ill. 416; Ketchum v. Buffalo, 14 N. Y. 356; Smith v. Newburn, 70 N. C. 14.

done that is necessary to the complete execution of the power. For instance, architects may be employed to prepare plans.¹ Power to build market-houses includes power to lease a building for market purposes, if the council deem that preferable to building.²

The power to establish markets implies of necessity the power to restrict the sale of certain articles of food to the locality provided. Thus it is proper to prohibit the sale of fresh meat in less quantities than a quarter, except at the market-house;³ and to prohibit the sale of oysters outside the market;⁴ and to prohibit the sale of meat in any quantity, except at specified places.⁵

But it has been held that an ordinance is unreasonable which prohibits the sale of fresh meats at any time during the day within the city limits, except at a single designated place. The restriction could only extend to reasonable market limits and during certain hours.⁶

If a public market adequate to every need be established, the opening of any other markets, however well regulated, may be made unlawful.⁷ Under a power to regulate the sale of meat an ordinance prescribing fixed markets and market limits is valid.⁸ But the same restriction is placed upon the freedom of corporate action as upon that of private persons, in that no market may be established so as to obstruct the street.⁹

After markets and market limits have once been established, it becomes necessary to prescribe regulations for their proper conduct. As to matters of detail and of a purely police nature, the markets may be placed under the

(1) Peterson v. New York, 17 N. Y. 449.
(2) Wade v. Newburn, 77 N. C. 460.
(3) Davenport v. Kelly, 7 Ia. 102.
(4) Morano v. Mayor, 2 La. 217.
(5) Buffalo v. Webster, 10 Wend. 99.
(6) Bloomington v. Wahl, 46 Ill. 489.
(7) State v. Gisch, 31 La. Ann. 544.
(8) St. Louis v. Jackson, 25 Mo. 37; St. Louis v. Weber, 44 Mo. 547.
(9) Wartman v. Philadelphia, 33 Pa. St. 203; State v. Mobile, 5 Port. 279; St. John v. New York, 3 Bosw. 483; Columbus v. Jacques, 30 Ga. 506.

supervision of the general police or of some officer specially appointed for the purpose. But as to general matters, the regulation should be imposed by ordinance. In order to reimburse the corporation for the expense of maintaining the market and of proper supervision it is only just that those enjoying the market privileges should be compelled to pay a license fee of some nature. The imposition of a fee of twenty-five cents per day and a fine of five dollars for non-payment is reasonable.[1] So, the market may be divided into stalls, and a license demanded for their occupancy.[2] It is held that an ordinance is valid that provides that no one living within twenty miles of the market shall occupy a stand until he shows that his goods are the produce of his own farm, or of some farm within three miles of his.[3] A clause in an ordinance prohibiting the sale of meat without license, excluding *farmers*, does not extend to a butcher by trade who sells meat from his own farm.[4]

Market regulations must be uniform in their operation on all persons. They must not discriminate or create monopolies.[5] Thus, the grant of an exclusive market privilege to one or more specified persons for a definite period of time is unlawful.[6] It is lawful, however, to prohibit the sale of meat except in places *to be designated* by a market board and in the public markets.[7] It is proper, too, to separate the wholesale and retail trade in the markets, prescribing a penalty for retailing within the wholesale limits.[8] After markets are established their use may be regulated by any reasonable rules or ordinances. The method of selling goods, the arrangement of the stalls and

(1) Cincinnati *v.* Buckingham, 10 Ohio, 257.
(2) Nightingale *v.* Petitioner, 11 Pick. 167.
(3) Commonwealth *v.* Rice, 9 Metc. 253.
(4) Rochester *v.* Pettinger, 17 Wend. 265.
(5) State *v.* Gisch, 31 La. Ann. 544.
(6) Gale *v.* Kalamazoo, 1 Mich. N. P. 5.
(7) Kelly *v.* Toronto, 23 U. C. Q. B. 425.
(8) Strike *v.* Collins, 54 L. T. Rep. (N. S.) 152; s. c., 34 Alb. L. J. 343.

the wares in them, and the mode of weighing produce and meat may all be prescribed.[1]

There is some restriction on the power of the municipality to locate markets. That the establishment of a market in a certain place obstructs a street to a small extent is no objection, but a whole street could not be appropriated for market purposes; for the public right of way is a prior and superior easement. Nor could the market be established on the curbstone and edge of the street in front of business places.[2]

§ 218. **Other regulations of the food supply.**—Under a power "to regulate *the vending* of meats, vegetables, etc.," an ordinance imposing a fine for selling putrid meats has been held void, the power being construed to apply to *the mode of vending* and not to the character of the thing sold.[3] Under power to regulate the police and to maintain the good order of the community, an ordinance is unreasonable which provides that a fee of five cents shall be paid for every sale and delivery of hay and other produce.[4] But it is otherwise where provision is made for weighing hay by a public weigher, a reasonable fee for the service being proper. Thus, under power to regulate the place and manner of selling hay, an ordinance is valid that forbids the exposure of hay for sale without a prior weighing and the obtaining a certificate to be shown to the purchaser, a charge of twelve cents per load being made for the weighing.[5] Such weighing may be made compulsory under a heavy penalty for neglecting to comply with the ordinance.[6] So, as to coal.[7] In the exercise of health powers the corporation may prohibit the sale of the milk of cows that are fed

(1) Snell *v.* Belleville, 30 U. C. Q. B. 81.
(2) Hites *v.* Dayton, 6 Ohio Law Bull. 142; Wells on Law and Fact, § 253.
(3) Mayor *v.* Rood, Hill & Den. Supp. 146.
(4) Kip *v.* Paterson, 26 N. J. 298.
(5) Yates *v.* Milwaukee, 12 Wis. 673.
(6) Taylor *v.* Pine Bluff, 34 Ark. 603.
(7) Ex parte Heilbron, 65 Cal. 609.

on slops or other improper food.¹ The sale of milk that is in any degree adulterated may be prohibited; and, as a means of rendering such a regulation effectual, a license fee may be demanded from every peddler.² An adequate supply of wholesome water may be provided by the corporation for the use of the inhabitants, and regulations made to preserve its purity, under any general grant of police powers.³

§ 219. **Slaughter-houses.**—The business of slaughtering is inseparable from sanitary evils, and it may properly be excluded from the corporate limits, or at least under power granted to regulate and restrain slaughter-houses.⁴ A power " to direct the location and management of slaughter-houses " authorizes the restriction of slaughtering to a single building.⁵ But it has been held that the power to prohibit and prevent the location or construction of buildings used for slaughter-houses does not authorize a total prohibition, and that the regulations must be limited to the prohibition of future erections and to the regulation of those already in use.⁶ The slaughtering a single animal, or even several animals, if not a regular occurrence, does not make the place where it was done a slaughter-house within the meaning of that term as used in ordinances.⁷ An ordinance prohibiting slaughter-houses may be enforced by abating the business if carried on regardless of the ordinance.⁸

Such houses may be restricted to certain specified parts of the city.⁹ The limits must be defined by the ordinance and not left to the discretion of the board of health or of

(1) Johnson v. Simonton, 43 Cal. 242.
(2) People v. Mulholland, 82 N. Y. 324; Polinsky v. People, 73 N. Y. 65.
(3) Livingston v. Pippin, 31 Ala. 542; Rome v. Cabot, 28 Ga. 50.
(4) Pierce v. Bartrum, Cowp. 269; Ex parte Heilbron, 65 Cal. 609.
(5) Milwaukee v. Gross, 21 Wis. 241.
(6) Wreford v. People, 14 Mich. 41.
(7) St. Paul v. Smith, 25 Minn. 372.
(8) Wreford v. People, 14 Mich. 41 (only if it is an actual nuisance).
(9) Board v. Heister, 37 N. Y. 661.

some officer, or even to the subsequently expressed will of the council itself.[1]

§ 220. **Other health regulations—Cemeteries.**—Cemeteries are not *per se* nuisances or injurious to the public health, but they become so if closely surrounded by dwelling or business houses, or if not properly cared for.[2] The council must determine when they have become such, and when it is necessary to exercise control over them, and the exercise of its discretion can not be reviewed unless plainly unavoidable or unnecessarily destructive of private property. It would be unreasonable to prohibit any burials inside of the city limits in a sparsely populated municipality.[3] It is always lawful to prohibit burials within certain densely populated districts, even though the original right to use a cemetery lying within the proscribed limits came from the city and has been exercised for over a hundred years.[4] Whenever it is lawful to bury the dead inside of the corporate limits, all burials may be regulated, but not entirely controlled by the municipality. The right to bury the dead belongs to the family of the deceased or to his friends, and it can not be taken away from them so long as they are able and willing to conform to the regulations prescribed. The corporation is limited to defining the limits within which burials may be made, and to regulating the time of day, the depth of the burial, the distance between graves, the use of the vaults, and similar details.[5]

Offal.—The removal of offensive substances and offal from public or private premises is accompanied by a degree of danger, or at least inconvenience to the people, and may lawfully be regulated. It is customary to provide some public agency for the removal of offal and waste, and

---

(1) Barthet *v.* New Orleans, 24 Fed. Rep. 563; s. c., 9 Am. & Eng. C. C. 509.
(2) Lake View *v.* Letz, 44 Ill. 81.
(3) Austin *v.* Murray, 16 Pick. 121.
(4) Church *v.* New York, 5 Cow. 538; Coates *v.* New York, 7 Cow. 585.
(5) Bogert *v.* Indianapolis, 13 Ind. 134; Graves *v.* Bloomington, 17 Ill. App. 476.

to prohibit private persons from removing the same, either absolutely or except on condition that they first obtain a permit from the board of health.

Some effective agency must be provided to do the work, or else the prohibition of the ordinance could not be enforced against a person who, using due care, removes the offal from his premises himself.[1] Private individuals may be compelled to aid the officers in the performance of their duty by providing adequate means of enabling the officer to obtain access to and to transport offal from places where it has accumulated. But they can not be directed to leave an alley or roadway over which the officer can gain access to ash-pits and privies.[2]

Dead animals. Provision may be made by ordinance for the prompt removal of dead animals,[3] prescribing the mode and terms of using the streets in their removal, and, if desirable, confining the duty or privilege to a single agency subject to express contract.[4]

This right extends simply to the *removal* of the carcass. It is unlawful to give a single person the right to remove and *dispose* of the animal. Opportunity should, if practicable, be given to the owner to direct what he wishes done with the animal to be removed. If it is not given, or if he can not be notified, the limit of the corporate power is to remove the animal and dispose of it to the best advantage, holding the *proceeds*, less some reasonable charge for the removal, for the owner.[5]

Diseases. The care and prevention of contagious diseases belong within the province of health regulations. Whenever contagion is feared from vessels landing at a port or harbor the corporation may subject all vessels com-

(1) Vandine, Petitioner, 6 Pick. 187; Boehm v. Baltimore, 61 Md. 259.
(2) Waite v. Garston, 3 L. R. Q. B. 5.
(3) Underwood v. Green, 3 Robt. 86.
(4) Rendering Co. v. Behr, 7 Mo. App. 345; Morgan v. Cincinnati, 12 Ohio L. Bull. 41.
(5) Rendering Co. v. Behr, 77 Mo. 91; Alpers v. Brown, 60 Cal. 447.

ing into port to reasonable quarantine regulations.[1] It is immaterial what the disease is so long as it is contagious.[2] The officers can not take quarantined vessels into their own possession and control to the exclusion of the owner or captain; they can only exercise control as to those things that would tend to facilitate the spread of the disease.[3] The right to detain and disinfect any kind of property ceases as soon as reasonable disinfection has been exercised, or as soon as all appearance of disinfection is lost.[4] If a contagious disease is prevalent, hospitals and pest-houses may be erected and those suffering from the disease forced to remove to those places for treatment.[5] And competent nurses and physicians may be employed at public expense to care for those who are confined to pest-houses.[6] The municipal power extends only to public hospitals; it has nothing to do with private institutions.[7]

Miscellaneous health provisions. In a city of any size, it is lawful to prohibit the keeping of hogs, except as necessary for a short time for commercial purposes,[8] and provision may be made for abating such hog-pens as may be kept in violation of an ordinance.[9] So, it is lawful under general power to care for the public health, to prohibit the keeping of more than two cows in the populous districts of a city.[10] An ordinance may be enforced which provides that all wells under the streets, having more than six grains of chlorine to a gallon of water, shall be filled up, although the wells are private property and dug in pursuance of a license from the corporation.[11]

(1) DuBois v. Augusta, Dudley, 30; Harrison v. Baltimore, 1 Gill, 264.
(2) Mitchell v. Rockland, 41 Me. 363.
(3) *Idem.*
(4) Sumner v. Philadelphia, 9 Phila. 408; s. c., 6 Am. L. T. 476.
(5) Aull v. Lexington, 18 Mo. 284.
(6) Labrie v. Manchester, 59 N. H. 120.
(7) Bessoinies v. Indianapolis, 71 Ind. 189.
(8) Cedar Rapids v. Holcomb, 68 Ia. 107 (15,000 inhabitants).
(9) Boehm v. Baltimore, 61 Md. 259.
(10) In re Lineman (Cal. 1887), 13 Pac. Rep. 170.
(11) Ferrenbach v. Turner, 86 Mo. 416.

Penalties for breaches of the peace can not be imposed under power to regulate the public health and comfort.[1]

§ 221. Fire.—The power to take all measures necessary to prevent fires and their spread is of prime importance to the citizens of every community. It belongs to that class of powers exercised for self-preservation, which are inherent in every municipality, and which do not need the authorization of an express grant. Every precaution possible should be taken to prevent the destruction to property and the danger to life incident to conflagration, and for this purpose as great a degree of interference with personal rights is permitted as under any other power. Private interests are entirely subservient to the public safety.

§ 222. Fire limits.—The first preventive step taken is usually to prescribe fire limits; that is, territorial limits within which it shall be unlawful to erect certain classes of buildings. This is always permissible.[2] Owing to the extreme importance of such regulations, and their vital interest to the community, one would hardly think that the power of erecting fire limits in a thickly built up district would ever be denied; still it is surprising to note that two courts have insisted that express authority must exist for such regulations. It seems that their regard for personal rights has been carried to an unwarranted extent in view of the importance of preventing the destruction of property by fire, and great as our regard must be for their reasoning and conclusions, the rule above enunciated seems to be the true one, and the great majority of the well advised decisions tends to its support. Thus, it has been held in Texas that there must be express authority to create fire limits and to prohibit under penalties the erection of

(1) Raleigh v. Dougherty, 3 Humph. 11.
(2) King v. Davenport, 98 Ill. 305; Hine v. New Haven, 41 Conn. 478; Alexander v. Council, 54 Miss. 659; Baumgartner v. Hasty, 100 Ind. 575; Monroe v. Hoffman, 29 La. Ann. 651; Charleston v. Reed, 27 W. Va. 681; Wadleigh v. Gilman, 12 Me. 403.

wooden buildings therein.¹ A recent Pennsylvania case holds that such an ordinance must rest either upon an express grant or upon an urgent necessity.² One would think that the necessity would be urgent in every case. If the legislature has attempted to define the powers that may be exercised in regard to preventing fire, the corporation will be bound by the limits of the definition, although it may thereby be hindered from exercising as much power as it could have done had there been no grant at all. Under power to regulate the materials, construction, alteration, and use of dwellings, a permit can not be required to build any building except a dwelling.³

§ 223. **Extent of the power.**—The extent to which the power may be exercised is greatly in dispute. It is claimed that the removal of structures existing at the time of the passage of the ordinance would be giving a retroactive effect to the ordinance, and would be in excess of the power; and this position seems well taken, unless some existing building is in bad condition, and by reason of the use to which it is put becomes thereby extra-dangerous;⁴ or in case an old structure were partially destroyed by fire.⁵ It is proper to prohibit the erection of wooden buildings within fire limits, and to provide for the removal by police authorities of buildings thereafter built in defiance of the law.⁶ And the ordinance would be applicable even in cases where the foundation of a building of the prohibited class is already laid and the plans and contracts completed. The individual must suffer for the public good.⁷ As a total prohibition of such erection might sometimes work in-

(1) Pye v. Peterson, 45 Tex. 312.
(2) Kneedler v. Norristown, 100 Pa. St. 368.
(3) Newton v. Belger (Mass.) 10 East. Rep. 77. *Contra*, Ex parte Fiske (Cal. 1887), 13 Pac. Rep. 310.
(4) Green v. Lake, 60 Miss. 451.
(5) Brady v. Insurance Co., 11 Mich. 425.
(6) Wadleigh v. Gilman, 12 Me. 403; King v. Davenport, 98 Ill. 305; Monroe v. Hoffman, 29 La. Ann. 651.
(7) Salem v. Maynes, 123 Mass. 372; Knoxville v. Bird, 12 B. J. Lea, 121.

equalities of burdens, it is proper to allow their erection under license from the municipality, discretion as to granting the license being considered a sufficient safeguard,[1] and a reasonable fee may be charged for issuing the license.[2] So, it is proper to compel persons about to erect any kind of building to give the authorities notice of their intention and file plans of the proposed structure;[3] but such regulations would not apply to mere temporary structures.[4] Where the power of removal is defined by the charter, the power should be construed in favor of the owner of the building.[5] An ordinance passed prohibiting the erection of *any* building *other than* of brick, stone, iron, or other incombustible material, would not be sustained under a power to prevent the erection of *wooden* buildings.[6] An ordinance provision that the *lower story* of every bath room must be constructed of non-combustibles does not apply to bath houses which begin on the second story of the building which they occupy.[7] The making of ordinary repairs to existing buildings can not be prohibited. They must amount to additions or material alterations.[8] Reshingling a building, for example, is an ordinary repair.[9] The ordinance usually prohibits the *erection* of certain classes of buildings within defined limits. An enlargement and elevation of a building so as to change its character is an erection within the meaning of the term.[10] Changing, by repairs, a joiner's shop into a dwelling-house is not an erection;[11] nor is the

(1) Welch v. Hotchkiss, 39 Conn. 141; Hine v. New Haven, 40 Conn. 478.
(2) Welch v. Hotchkiss, *supra.*
(3) Hall v. Nixon, L. R. 10 Q. B. 152; s. c., 12 Moak Eng. R. 218.
(4) Fielding v. Commissioners, 3 C. P. Div. 272; s. c., 30 Moak Eng. R. 155.
(5) Louisville v. Webster, 108 Ill. 414.
(6) Attorney-General v. Campbell, 19 Grant's Ch. (U. C.) 299.
(7) Bowers v. Coultson, 11 Phila. 182.
(8) Brown v. Hunn, 27 Conn. 332; Stewart v. Commonwealth, 10 Watts, 307; Brady v. Insurance Co., 11 Mich. 425.
(9) Regina v. Howard, 4 Ont. 377.
(10) Douglass v. Commonwealth, 2 Rawle, 262.
(11) Booth v. State, 4 Conn. 65.

building of an addition of the same height and slope of roof onto the rear of a structure having only one story.[1] The corporation may prohibit the removal of wooden buildings from one site to another. Such a *removal* can not be prevented under a prohibition of *erecting* wooden buildings.[2] An ordinance prohibiting the erection of wooden buildings "having *in* them" a chimney, fire-place, or stove, is not violated by an outside chimney. This is, however, a very extreme stretch of the rules of construction.[3]

Reasonable time should be given to the owner of the unlawful structure to remove it or alter it so as to comply with the requirements, before a removal is made by the corporate authorities,[4] unless the necessity is urgent, in which case it may be removed without notice or any form of judicial proceeding.[5]

Regulations of this nature are not restricted to the erection of buildings. It would also be reasonable to prohibit the erection of wooden fences or sidewalks.[6] Of the same nature are ordinances prohiting the storage of dangerous and inflammable subtances in any considerable quantity; for instance, the keeping of more than five tons of straw, unless in a fire-proof inclosure.[7]

The proper cleaning of chimneys may be made compulsory, but an ordinance would be void which attempts to restrict the right of cleaning chimneys to an official inspector.[8]

It can not be expected that fires can be controlled unless adequate means are at hand to check their progress. Hence it is essential that every municipality be provided.

(1) Tuttle *v.* State, 4 Conn. 68 (contrary to rule).
(2) City *v.* Lenze, 27 O. S. 383. *Contra,* Wadleigh *v.* Gilman, 12 Me. 403.
(3) Daggett *v.* State, 4 Conn. 60.
(4) Louisville *v.* Webster, 108 Ill. 414; Hine *v.* New Haven, 40 Conn. 478.
(5) McKibben *v.* Fort Smith, 35 Ark. 352; King *v.* Davenport, 98 Ill. 305.
(6) Macon *v.* Patty, 57 Miss. 378.
(7) Clark *v.* South Bend, 85 Ind. 276.
(8) Regina *v.* Johnston, 38 U. C. Q. B. 549.

with fire engines, and no express power is needed to authorize their purchase.¹

Reservoirs for the storage of a sufficient supply of water are also necessary to an effective fire department, and may be constructed without express power.² Under power to *contract* with individuals for water, machinery and pipes, it is not lawful to purchase a *site* on which to locate and erect water-works.³

§ 224. **Streets.**—Highways are primarily under the control of the state, but as soon as a municipal corporation is organized, those highways or portions of highways which lie within its boundaries are subject to its powers of police regulation. These powers extend to the making of repairs and improvements, to the freeing them from obstruction and to preventing their improper use, and these ends may be accomplished by the passage and enforcement of suitable ordinances. The precise extent of this power depends on the terms of the charter or enabling statute. The authority of the municipality supplants that of the state, county, or township only as regards police supervision, unless the contrary is indicated by some express grant. It has been held in Alabama that the creation of an incorporated town *ipse facto* gives it exclusive jurisdiction over the public roads and highways within its limits, and even the right to abolish them entirely.⁴ But, as a rule, no power to vacate streets is thus conferred by implication. And when expressly granted, such a power must be strictly construed. Thus, under power to open and vacate streets, it is unlawful to grant the use of a street to private persons for a period of years, then to revert to the public.⁵ But under general police powers, portions of a street or park which are not

(1) Van Sicklen *v.* Burlington, 27 Vt. 70; Green *v.* Cape May, 41 N. J. L. 45; Allen *v.* Taunton, 19 Pick. 485; Mayor *v.* Rumsey, 63 Ala. 352; Desmond *v.* Jefferson, 19 Fed. Rep. 483.
(2) Hardy *v.* Waltham, 3 Metc. 163.
(3) People *v.* McClintock, 45 Cal. 11.
(4) McCain *v.* State, 62 Ala. 138.
(5) Glasgow *v.* St Louis, 87 Mo. 678.

needed or used for travel may be sodded and set apart to beautify the general appearance.¹ And, in general, the width of streets may be regulated under power to regulate them.² Under power "to alter streets," it is held to be unlawful to attempt to diminish their width by releasing a portion thereof to the adjoining owners.³ Free bridges to connect one street with another, or a street with a highway outside of the city limits, may be constructed under police powers. Such power as "to open" or "to extend" streets has been construed to mean "to construct, establish, and lay out."⁴ Power to construct streets must be reasonably exercised with due regard to private rights. Unnecessary harm should not be done. Thus, it would be improper to establish a new street longitudinally over the right of way of a railroad.⁵ But there is no objection to constructing a street *across* a railroad.⁶

For all purposes of police regulation it matters not whether the fee to the streets is in the public, in the adjacent owners, or in a company organized for the purpose of establishing the road.⁷ The question of ownership is only important, as will be seen later, in considering the right of the municipality to devote its streets to extraordinary uses. So long as the street is a public and not a private one full powers of police regulation may be exercised.⁸

An alley is not a street, the word *alley* meaning a passage-way on private property, or a public way too narrow to admit vehicles.⁹ A street, within the meaning of statutes and ordinances, includes every thing up to the fences or

(1) Murphy v. Pearce, Ill. Jan. 25, 1887.
(2) State v. Morristown, 33 N. J. 57. *Contra*, State v. Mobile, 5 Port. 279.
(3) Asylum v. Troy, 76 N. Y. 108.
(4) Hannibal v. Railroad Co., 49 Mo. 480; Sugar Co. v. Jersey City, 26 N. J. Eq 247.
(5) Railway Co. v. Faribault, 23 Minn. 167; Railroad Co. v. Long Branch, 39 N. J. 28.
(6) Hannibal v. Winchell, 57 Mo. 172.
(7) State v. New Brunswick, 30 N. J. 395.
(8) Quinn v. Paterson, 28 N. J. 35.
(9) Paul v. Detroit, 32 Mich. 108.

walls of the private premises adjoining it. It includes gutters, curbstones, and sidewalks, the air over the street and the earth beneath it.[1]

§ 225. **Care of the streets.**—The extent of municipal police power over streets can be summed up by saying that it includes everything necessary to render them easy of access and use to the public, and to preserve their usefulness unimpaired. Their surface may be made as convenient and safe as possible, they may be kept free from obstructions, and they may be artificially lighted at night.[2] For the purpose of better supervision, surveys may be made of the streets and squares and maps drawn of the city.[3] The extent of municipal control over the streets is usually defined by statute or the charter, and, in such case, the power is limited to that which is granted or necessary to effectuate that which is granted.

§ 226. **Grading.**—In populous places the streets " need to be graded and brought to a level; and, therefore, the public or municipal authorities may not only change the surface, but cut down trees, dig up the earth, and may use it in improving the street, or elsewhere, and may make culverts, drains, and sewers upon or under the surface. Whether the municipal corporation holds the fee of the street or not, the better doctrine is that the municipal authorities may, under the usual powers given them, do all acts appropriate or incidental to the beneficial use of the street by the public."[4]

Power to grade streets does not mean simply to level down the surface inequalities, but it extends to *establishing*

---

(1) Wallace *v.* New York, 2 Hilt. 440; In re Burmeister, 76 N. Y. 174.

(2) As to lighting, see Nelson *v.* La Porte, 33 Ind. 258; Gaslight Co. *v.* Middleton, 59 N. Y. 228; New Orleans *v.* Clark, 95 U. S. 644; Garrison *v.* Chicago, 7 Biss. 480; Horst *v.* Moses, 48 Ala. 129.

(3) People *v.* Flagg, 17 N. Y. 584; Randall *v.* Van Vechten, 19 Johns. 60.

(4) Cinciunati *v.* White, 6 Pet. 431; Dill. Mun. Corp., § 688.

the grade,¹ and implies power to materially raise or lower portions of a street in order to facilitate traffic.² Power to pave includes power to grade, because it would be impracticable to pave a street stably without prior grading.³ In grading, the municipality may use any surplus soil in grading any other street or the same street, and if not needed for such purpose, could dispose of it to the best advantage to third parties, unless the fee of the street is in the adjoining owner, who claims and removes such surplus.⁴ But soil can not be removed from one street to be used on another except in the execution of an ordinance or order for grading the street from which the soil is taken ⁵

The ordinance should specify, if possible, the general measures to be adopted when the cost is to be assessed on abutting owners.⁶ The power to grade streets is continuing, but any special damage suffered by an adjoining owner who has erected buildings in conformity to an established grade, by reason of a considerable change of grade, can be collected from the city.⁷

§ 227. **Paving.**—The word "pavement" is used in a conventional sense to express any thing that answers the purpose of a substantial covering for the surface of a street.

(1) Himmelmann v Hoadley, 44 Cal. 213.
(2) Karst v. Railway Co., 22 Minn. 118; Delphi v. Evans, 36 Ind. 90; State v. West Orange, 40 N. J. 122; Lewis v. Toronto, 39 U. C. Q. B. 343.
(3) State v. Elizabeth, 30 N. J. 365; Williams v. Detroit, 2 Mich. 560; In re Belmont, 12 Hun, 558.
(4) Smith v. Washington, 20 How. 135; Griswold v. Bay City, 35 Mich. 452; Denniston v. Clark, 125 Mass. 216; Hovey v. Mayo, 43 Me. 322. *Contra*, Smith v. Rome, 19 Ga. 89.
(5) Delphi v. Evans, 36 Ind. 90.
(6) Railway Co. v. Jacksonville, 114 Ill. 562.
(7) Karst v. Railway Co., 22 Minn. 118; Smith v. Washington, 20 How. 135; O'Connor v. Pittsburg, 18 Pa. St. 187; Macy v. Indianapolis, 17 Ind. 267; Hoffman v. St. Louis, 15 Mo. 651; Markham v. Mayor, 23 Ga. 402; New Haven v. Sargent, 38 Conn. 50; Delphi v. Evans, 36 Ind. 90; McCormick v. Patchen, 53 Mo. 33; Gall v. Cincinnati, 18 O. S. 563; Plum v. Canal Co., 2 Stockt. 256; Dunham v. Hyde Park, 75 Ill. 371.

It is not limited to any particular material. Neither is it "limited to uniformly arranged masses of solid material, or blocks of wood, brick or stone, but it may be as well formed of pebbles, or gravel, or other hard substances which will make a compact, even, hard way or floor."[1] Power to repair is held not to include macadamizing.[2]

Power to pave includes the power to furnish and do all that is necessary, usual or fit for paving. It includes power to grade, to provide gutters and curbstones, trimmings, and even sidewalks.[3]

Power to pave is not at all restricted because a railroad, however created, runs along or over the surface of the street.[4] Paving must extend uninterruptedly along the street within the limits determined upon by the council, and includes, of necessity, cross-walks, street intersections, and the like.[5]

Power to *repair* does not include power to pave originally.[6]

The power to pave, like that of grading, is continuing and is not exhausted by having been once exercised.[7] In Pennsylvania, alone, the opposite rule obtains.[8]

(1) Burnham *v*. Chicago, 24 Ill. 496; Warren *v*. Henly, 31 Ia. 31; In re Phillips, 60 N. Y. 16; Railroad Co. *v*. Mt. Pleasant, 12 Ia. 112.

(2) Watson *v*. Passaic, 46 N. J. 124.

(3) Dill. Mun. Corp., § 797; Schenley *v*. Commonwealth, 36 Pa. St. 29; Steckert *v*. East Saginaw, 22 Mich. 104; Dean *v*. Borchenius, 30 Wis. 236; McNamara *v*. Estes, 22 Ia. 246; Williams *v*. Detroit, 2 Mich. 560; People *v*. Brooklyn, 21 Barb. 484; O'Leary *v*. Sloo, 7 La. Ann. 25; Railroad Co. *v*. Mt. Pleasant, 12 Ia. 112; State *v*. Elizabeth, 30 N. J. 365; People *v*. Brooklyn, 21 Barb. 484.

(4) State *v*. Atlantic City, 34 N. J. 99.

(5) Powell *v*. St. Joseph, 31 Mo. 347; Creighton *v*. Scott, 14 O. S. 438; In re Burke, 62 N. Y. 224; In re Phillips, 60 N. Y. 16; Williams *v*. Detroit, 2 Mich. 560; Lawrence *v*. Killam, 11 Kan. 499; In re Eager, 46 N. Y. 100; Hines *v*. Lockport, 41 How. Pr. 435; State *v*. Elizabeth, 30 N. J. 365.

(6) State *v*. Jersey City, 28 N. J. 536.

(7) Morley *v*. Carpenter, 22 Mo. App. 640; Williams *v*. Detroit, 2 Mich. 560; McCormick *v*. Patchins, 53 Mo. 33, s. c., 14 Am. Rep. 440; Gurner *v*. Chicago, 40 Ill. 165; Municipality *v*. Dunn, 10 La. Ann. 57.

(8) Hammett *v*. Philadelphia, 65 Pa. St. 148; Wistar *v*. Philadelphia,

§ 228. **Sidewalks.**—Authority to pave includes authority to construct sidewalks.[1] It is held in California, though, that an ordinance or resolution of intention to macadamize and curb does not include work on sidewalks.[2] But sidewalks are part of the street and any measure applicable to the *street* should also be held to include the sidewalks. The mere fact that passage is facilitated by using one part of the street for vehicles and another for foot passengers should not lead to any material distinction in the character of the two parts.[3] This respective arrangement being purely conventional, it is not at all necessary that a sidewalk be constructed on each side of a street, and locating a walk on one side only, under power to improve the street, is permissible.[4]

Sidewalks may include gutters as a matter of necessity.[5] But it has been held not to include cross-walks,[6] though we can see no reason for the distinction, except the accidental form of the word. With reference to the use to which walks are put, they could just as lawfully be constructed along the center of the street as along the sides. As their obvious purpose is to accommodate foot passengers, and as people are obliged to cross the streets frequently in a thickly peopled community, it is difficult to see why cross-walks are not a very important accommodation, and why the term "walks" or "sidewalks" should not be construed to include them.

It is upon the same principle of so arranging the streets as best to accommodate the public, that councils, in the exercise of regulatory powers over streets, and aided by their superior knowledge of the relative needs of the various

---

80 Pa. St. 112. A petition from the property owners is a condition precedent to *repaving* in New York. In re Garvey, 77 N. Y. 523.

(1) Warren *v.* Henly, 31 Ia. 31; O'Leary *v.* Sloo, 7 La. Ann. 25; Railroad Co. *v.* Spearman, 12 Ia. 112.
(2) Dyer *v.* Chase, 52 Cal. 440; Himmelmann *v.* Satterlee, 50 Cal. 68.
(3) Woodruff *v.* Stewart, 63 Ala. 212.
(4) Christopher *v.* Portage, 12 Wis. 562.
(5) Robins *v.* New Brunswick, 44 N. J. 116.
(6) Péquignot *v.* Detroit, 16 Fed. Rep. 211.

modes of travel, are allowed to determine the relative *width* of the street and walk, namely, the space to be apportioned and occupied by each.[1]

The adjoining owner can not, however, be heard to complain if the council deems best to exclude the sidewalks from the operation of an ordinance ordering a pavement to be laid.[2]

Unless some statutory or charter provision permits the burden of constructing sidewalks, paving and like street improvements to be assessed upon the adjacent owners, or those benefited, the burden rests upon the corporation at large both to construct and to repair. When this burden is shifted by law upon the adjacent owners, it is permissible, because the benefits of street improvement are not only greater to that class, out more capable of equitable apportionment, than are the benefits arising from other classes of municipal regulation involving expense and outlay. It would be just as competent for the legislature to impose the entire expense incident to the exercise of any police power upon those benefited thereby, if it were possible to locate the benefit. A similar situation is the detail of a police officer to watch the property or premises of an individual, when his particular property is extraordinarily exposed to danger by his own act. The municipality would have a perfect right to collect of him a sufficient amount to meet the additional expense, in spite of the fact that he is entitled to general police protection. The burden of street improvements is not, however, to be entailed upon the adjoining owners, without express authority, for the general public as well as they derive a degree of benefit.[3]

§ 229. **Protection of streets.**—Whenever the control of the streets is thus delegated to the local government, they become, in one sense, the property of the corporation, and the duty would be incumbent upon the corporation to

---

(1) State *v.* Morristown, 33 N. J. 58.
(2) Moran *v.* Lindell, 52 Mo. 229.
(3) Chicago *v.* Crosby, 111 Ill. 538.

protect and guard them from injury. This duty does not rest upon express authority, but is to be exercised in pursuance of the general police power.[1] The pavements of a city are constructed with a view to ordinary and careful usage, and as the transportation of very heavy loads upon vehicles having tires of the ordinary width might easily displace, crush, or otherwise injure the materials used in paving, it is proper to prescribe the width of tires that must be used on vehicles heavily laden, or to prescribe certain streets over which heavy burdens, except in cases of necessity, must be conveyed. As mere regulations of the manner of using the streets, such ordinances are valid. The same object could be lawfully attained by demanding a license from those using the streets for the transportation of heavy loads.[2]

The trees that grow along the line of a public street are likewise within the regulatory powers of municipal corporations. If their roots tend to cause inequalities or breaches in the pavement under which they grow they may be removed. But unless injurious to the surface of the street, trees are to be protected. When the street has been unreservedly dedicated to the public, the trees become public property, but they can not for that reason be cut down by the supervisor of streets.[3] And when the adjacent owners retain the fee in the streets the corporation has no right to destroy the trees, unless they grow within the street, or so as to obstruct traffic.[4] It is even held, in that case, that an ordinance punishing injuries to, or the removal of, trees on the public streets, would have no application to the owner of the fee.[5] But the better rule seems to be that the municipality has a right to protect

(1) Dill. Mun. Corp., § 681; Korah v. Ottawa, 32 Ill. 121; Hooksett v. Amoskeag Co., 44 N. H. 105.
(2) Nagle v. Augusta, 5 Ga. 546; Brooklyn v. Breslin, 57 N. Y. 591; Gartside v. East St. Louis, 43 Ill. 47.
(3) McCarthy v. Boston, 135 Mass. 197.
(4) Bliss v. Ball, 99 Mass. 597; White v. Godfrey, 97 Mass. 472; Taintor v. Morristown, 19 N. J. Eq. 46; Cross v. Morristown, 18 N. J. Eq. 313; Bills v. Belknap, 36 Ia. 583; Everett v. Council Bluffs, 46 Ia. 66.
(5) Lancaster v. Richardson, 4 Lans, 136.

such trees from injury, even as against the owner. Thus the adjoining owner would not be exempt from the operation of an ordinance, which prohibits the hitching of horses to shade trees.[1]

§ 230. **Obstructions.**—Among other duties relative to the streets, that are imposed upon municipal corporations, is that of preventing any obstruction of the right of passage. As the power to remove obstructions extends only to clear cases,[2] and as the decision of the council or ministerial officers is subject to review by the courts, the question arises, what is an obstruction. It may be defined as any thing which, without reasonable necessity, impedes the use of the streets for lawful purposes. We proceed to consider the main adjudications as to what the council may prohibit as coming within the definition. In the first place, if a reasonable necessity for the obstruction exists it is lawful, unless *per se* a nuisance.

§ 231. **Example of lawful obstructions.**—In an early and often cited case,[3] the general principle is thus admirably stated: "Necessity justifies actions which would otherwise be nuisances; this necessity need not be absolute; it is enough if it be reasonable. No man has a right to throw wood or stones into the street at pleasure; but inasmuch as fuel is necessary, a man may throw wood into the street for the purpose of having it carried to his hours, and it may lie there a reasonable time. So, because building is necessary, stones, brick, lime, sand, and other materials may be placed in the street, provided it be done in the most convenient manner."[4]

Streets may be obstructed by building materials, if lack of room elsewhere renders it necessary, but the occupa-

(1) Baker *v.* Normal, 81 Ill. 108.
(2) State *v.* Jersey City, 34 N. J. 31.
(3) Commonwealth *v.* Passmore, 1 Sarg. & R. 217.
(4) Dill. Mun. Corp , § 730; Commonwealth *v.* Passmore, is cited with approval in Clark *v.* Fry, 8 O. S. 358; People *v.* Cunningham, 1 Denio, 524; St. John *v.* New York, 3 Bosw. 483.

tion must not be unreasonably prolonged. An ordinance is reasonable which allows one-third of the street to be thus occupied.¹ Moving buildings in proper streets and with expedition and care is not an unreasonable obstruction.²

As many residences and business houses in crowded parts of the city have no rear ingress, every thing taken into them must be unloaded and transferred in front and across the sidewalk. Mere temporary obstructions, necessary in the unloading of goods, are lawful, but all reasonable haste must be made, and the public inconvenienced as little as possible.³

As these lawful obstructions are easily allowed to become unlawful, by negligence, it is competent for municipalities to regulate them. They may pass ordinances defining the exact extent to which building materials may occupy the streets, regulating the length of time, the space used and even the height of the piles of materials. Or, a license may be required as a condition precedent to the right to so obstruct the streets.⁴ Such a license may be revoked at the will of the council.⁵ So, a certain location on the street adjoining the public wharves may be set aside for the unloading of spars and masts.⁶

§ 232. **Inclosures.**—Public premises of every kind, whether streets, parks, or squares, must be kept open to the free use of the public, and any inclosure of a part of their territory is *per se* an obstruction.⁷ In Michigan a technical distinction, based on the wording of the charter, is made between encroachments and incumbrances, incumbrances being restricted to impediments to travel

(1) Wood *v.* Mears, 12 Ind. 515; State *v.* Taylor, 59 Md. 338.
(2) Graves *v.* Shattuck, 35 N. H. 257.
(3) Mathews *v.* Kelsey, 58 Me. 56; Davis *v.* Winslow, 51 Me. 264; Wharf Co. *v.* Portland, 67 Me. 46.
(4) Lowell *v.* Simpson, 10 Allen, 88; State *v.* Taylor, 59 Md. 338.
(5) Indianapolis *v.* Miller, 27 Ind. 394.
(6) Municipality *v.* Kirk, 5 La. Ann. 34.
(7) State *v.* Woodward, 23 Vt. 92; State *v.* Atkinson, 24 Vt. 448; Rex *v.* Ward, 31 Eng. Com. Law, 180.

placed upon the open streets, while the former is the actual inclosure of a part of the street, or its occupation by a building.[1]

§ 233. **Public buildings.**—The erection of any kind of public building, as a market-house, in the center of a street, is an obstruction. The public nature of its use in nowise excuses the inconvenience to those who use the streets.[2]

§ 234. **Other buildings.**—As a general thing in cities a great many blocks and houses are built close up to the street line, and render the obstruction of the street easier in various ways. While the adjoining owner has, to be sure, the right to occupy every inch of his own ground, he has no right to trespass upon the public easement in the street, either by permanent structures or by temporary obstructions. Theoretically, no part of a building should project into the street, but the strictness of the rule is often relaxed, either by custom or by a desire to grant such slight privileges to adjacent owners as in reality do not inconvenience the public.

It is a public nuisance to erect a stall for the sale of goods or produce on the street or sidewalk, and the consent of the adjoining proprietor in nowise legalizes the obstruction.[3] Under power to regulate the streets, an ordinance providing that any building extending over the line of the street shall be torn down is valid.[4] It is apprehended that the owner should first be given an opportunity to remove the projecting part and that in case of his omission the municipal authorities would only be justified in abating that part of the building occupying the street. It is held in New Hampshire that a building so constructed that its roof projects over the line of the street is an unlawful

---

(1) Grand Rapids *v.* Hughes, 15 Mich. 54.
(2) State *v.* Mobile, 5 Port. 279; Columbus *v.* Jacques, 30 Ga. 506; Savannah *v.* Wilson, 49 Ga. 476; Ketchum *v.* Buffalo, 14 N. Y. 374.
(3) Commonwealth *v.* Wentworth, Bright. 318.
(4) Daublin *v.* New Orleans, 1 Martin (La.) 184.

obstruction,[1] but, though it might become a nuisance to other property owners by reason of obstructing their light, it is difficult to see how the mere projection of a roof on a structure of ordinary height could in any way interfere with the free use of the right of way by the general public, and it has been so held in England.[2] The erection and maintenance of awnings, posts, and the like, may be either regulated or prohibited as liable to impede and endanger passers-by, and the ordinance may provide a mode of removing them.[3] But it would not be reasonable to provide that no goods or articles should be suspended from or attached to buildings (doors, shutters, and the like not being excepted), so as to project over six inches into the street.[4] An ordinance that prohibits the hanging of goods or other things on the front of a building so that they project more than one foot does not apply to a temporary scaffolding.[5] But porches, or stairways leading to the upper stories of buildings constructed even with the street line, would be too material obstructions to be lawful.[6] An ordinance could not be enacted prohibiting the maintenance of door steps leading to the main entrance of a building on the ground floor.[7] And ornaments attached to buildings so as to project slightly over the street can not be restrained, and this is especially so where such ornaments are customary.[8]

Under power to regulate bay-windows, it is unlawful to authorize the erection of *any* bay-window. Some limit to their depth must be prescribed, such as one or two feet.[9] Nor may special licenses be granted to exempt particular

(1) Garland *v.* Towne, 55 N. H. 55.
(2) Goldstraw *v.* Duckworth, 5 Q. B. Div. (L. R.) 275.
(3) Fox *v.* Winona, 23 Minn. 10; Pedrick *v.* Bailey, 12 Gray, 161.
(4) Carlisle *v.* Baker, 1 Yeates, 471.
(5) Hexamer *v.* Webb, 101 N. Y. 377.
(6) People *v.* Carpenter, 2 Doug. (Mich.) 273; Pettis *v.* Johnson, 56 Ind 139
(7) Cushing *v.* Boston, 128 Mass. 330.
(8) Philadelphia *v.* Board, 29 Leg. Int. 53; Commonwealth *v.* Blaisdell, 107 Mass. 234.
(9) Commonwealth *v.* Harris, 15 Phila. 10.

bay-windows from the operation of a prohibitory ordinance.¹ It is held that prohibition of bay-windows does not apply to such structures built out from the second story of a building.²

Doors and window-shutters may be so hung that they swing out over the street line without being unlawful obstructions.³ So may iron gratings, trap-doors, and like arrangements for lighting and gaining access to underground rooms, be suffered in the sidewalk, and when necessary to open such passage-ways for the purpose of putting in goods and the like they may be left open a reasonable lenght of time.⁴ Although ingress to cellars may be had through gratings in the sidewalk, the grating must be securely fastened. Any unprotected or unguarded opening in a street or sidewalk is *per se* a nuisance and an obstruction to travel.⁵

As Judge Dillon says : " The owners of lots bordering upon streets or ways have, or may have, a right to make a reasonable and proper use of the street or way. What may be deemed such a use depends, in the absence of legislative or authorized municipal declaration, much upon the local situation and public usage—that is, the use which others similarly situated make of their land, this being evidence of a reasonable use." ⁶

§ 235. **Snow.**—While it is clear that municipal corporations can prevent private individuals from obstructing travel on the streets by their own acts, it is somewhat doubtful whether they have power to compel adjoining owners to keep the sidewalks clear from snow, so as to be passable. Such power is frequently exercised and seldom

(1) Commonwealth *v.* Reimer, 15 Phila. 72.
(2) Bowers *v.* Coultson, 11 Phila. 182.
(3) O'Linda *v.* Lothrop, 21 Pick. 292; Underwood *v.* Carney, 1 Cush. 285.
(4) Underwood *v.* Carney, 1 Cush. 285; Irvine *v.* Wood, 51 N. Y. 224.
(5) Dill. Mun. Corp., § 734.
(6) Beatty *v.* Gilmore, 16 Pa. St. 463; Runyon *v.* Bordine, 2 Green (N. J.) 472; Scammon *v.* Chicago, 25 Ill. 424; Dill. Mun. Corp., §§ 699, 670.

questioned, but the courts of Illinois have held that this is a duty belonging exclusively to the public, and that private persons, being in no way responsible for the obstruction, can not be compelled to remove it. The same would be true of regulations as to sprinkling sand or ashes on slippery walks.[1] Though this view is in one sense correct, still considerations of public benefit should overbalance any slight inconvenience to the individual. The inconvenience of a considerable depth of snow on the public walks is very great, and the most perfectly organized police system would be ineffectual to remove the obstruction expeditiously. Adjoining owners are so situated as to be able to clear the walks in a short time, and though a slight inequality of burden may fall upon the citizens thereby, such regulations ought to be sustained as proper and reasonable police measures. And such is the conclusion of the courts of Massachusetts and other states where the question has been thoroughly considered.[2]

§ 236. **Moving buildings.**—The moving of buildings over the public streets is a use which could not help but greatly impede travel unless conducted with great care and rapidity. General police powers are sufficient to authorize the passage of regulations governing their removal.[3] When the subject is not covered by ordinance, the moving of a building on suitable streets with expedition and care is not unlawful.[4]

§ 237. **Miscellaneous obstructions.**—Among other things that have been held to be obstructions, may be mentioned the following. These illustrations are not use-

(1) Gridley v. Bloomington, 88 Ill. 554; Chicago v. O'Brien, 111 Ill. 532.

(2) In re Goddard, 16 Pick. 504; Railway Co. v. Cambridge, 11 Allen, 287; Kirby v. Market, 14 Gray, 252; Taylor v. Railway Co., 45 Mich. 74. Rule approved in Dill. Mun. Corp., § 394; Bonsall v. Lebanon, 19 Ohio, 418; Paxton v. Sweet, 13 N. J. 196; Mayor v. Mayberry, 6 Humph. 368; Woodbridge v. Detroit, 8 Mich. 274.

(3) Day v. Green, 4 Cush. 433.

(4) Graves v. Shattuck, 35 N. H. 257.

ful simply to show what are considered obstructions, but principally to show what may be lawfully ordained against as obstructions, under general police powers, and power to regulate streets:

A truck backed up against the sidewalk and *across a street railroad track* for the purpose of unloading, is an unnecessary obstruction.[1]

If the nature of a person's business is such that its pursuit tends to partially block a street, the fact that the business is otherwise lawful does not excuse him. He must remove his stand to a location that is more convenient. For example, a congregation of carts to receive the refuse from a factory or manufacturing establishment is inexcusable.[2] A timber dealer can not use the highway as a depository for his timber.[3]

The highway may not be used as a stone-yard;[4] nor as a stable yard;[5] nor as a place in which to deposit the materials of any business.[6] It is unlawful to obstruct the streets by attracting crowds around a place where goods are being sold,[7] or by preaching,[8] or speeches.[9]

Though obstructions of any kind may generally be legislated *against* by the municipality, it is not lawful for it to authorize an obstruction, or any thing that amounts to a nuisance, unless express power is given.[10]

(1) State *v.* Foley, 31 Ia. 527.
(2) People *v.* Cunningham, 1 Denio, 524.
(3) Rex *v.* Jones, 6 East, 230; Rex *v.* Moore, 3 B. & Ald. 184; Thorpe *v.* Brumfitt, L. R. Ct. App. 650.
(4) Cushing *v.* Adams, 18 Pick. 110; Commonwealth *v.* King, 13 Metc. 115.
(5) The King *v.* Cross, 3 Campb. 224.
(6) Queen *v.* Davis, 24 U. C. C. P. 575; Vars *v.* Railway Co., 23 U. C. C. P. 114; The King *v.* Russell, 6 East, 427.
(7) The King *v.* Carlisle, 6 C. & P. 636; White *v.* Kent, 11 O. S. 550.
(8) Commonwealth *v.* Davis, S. C. Mass., Jan., 1886.
(9) Barker *v.* Commonwealth, 19 Pa. St. 412.
(10) State *v.* Mobile, 5 Port. 279; Columbus *v.* Jacques, 30 Ga. 506; State *v.* Woodward, 23 Vt. 92; Commonwealth *v.* Rush, 14 Pa. St. 186; Att'y. Gen'l. *v.* Heisohn, 18 N. J. Eq. 410; Stetson *v.* Faxon, 19 Pick. 147; State *v.* Railroad, 23 N. J. 360; State *v.* Laverack, 34 N. J. 20; Dill. Mun. Corp., §§ 645, 660, 383.

§ 238. **Steam railroads.**—The occupation of the streets by the tracks and rolling stock of steam railroads, results in more interference with other modes of travel and with the free use of the streets than any other lawful obstruction, and for that reason needs to be more closely guarded. The primary right to authorize railroad companies to select and appropriate rights of way lies with the state, and when exercised, the right of way may be laid out through a municipal corporation as well as anywhere else. Express power must be given to a municipality in order to authorize it to grant a right of way to a railroad company over the streets.[1] It is even held that power to grant the use of the streets to railroads is limited to street railroads, and does not apply to steam railroads.[2] Power to regulate the streets, together with a statutory provision that no railroad shall be constructed through a municipal corporation, without the consent of the council, imply powers in the council to consent to such construction.[3] In Kansas municipalities may provide for and regulate the passage of steam railroads along the streets.[4] And in Kentucky municipal consent may be given to such use.[5] Whenever municipalities may consent to the occupation of the streets by steam railroads, they have a right to couple with their consent any condition that they may see fit, and compliance with such condition becomes a condition precedent to the right to exercise the franchise. The railroad can not use the streets, even by consent of the council, so as to affect the public easement to a greater extent than is necessary to enable it to pass through or get into the corporate territory. The power to construct a railroad can never be construed to allow the occupation of a street longitudinally.

(1) Railway Co. v. Covington, 9 Bush, 127; Perry v. Railroad Co., 55 Ala. 425.

(2) State v. Railroad Co., 85 Mo. 263; Railroad Co. v. Railroad Co., 20 N. J. Eq. 69.

(3) Brown v. Duplessis, 14 La. Ann. 842.

(4) Railroad Co. v. Garside, 10 Kan. 552.

(5) Railroad Co. v. Brown, 17 B. Mon. 763; Wolfe v. Railroad Co., 15 B. Mon. 404; Cosby v. Railroad Co., 10 Bush, 288.

That could not be done without express legislative authority.[1] Under all circumstances, the municipality may prescribe the grade and such conditions as to paving as it may deem necessary to preserve the usefulness of the street.[2] A grant of *exclusive* control over the street authorizes an ordinance permitting the location of a railroad.[3] But not when the construction of the railroad would materially interfere with the established street grade.[4]

New York and New Jersey seem to be exceptions to the general rule that steam railroads are subject to municipal police regulation under their general police powers. In New York the whole subject of railroad management is covered by statute, and it is held that it is not the policy of the state to give to municipalities any power to regulate it.[5] Although this adverse policy is less pronounced in New Jersey, it has been held there that the power of police regulation of railroads must either be expressly granted to the municipality, or must be found as a condition in the grant of the franchise to the railroad company.[6]

§ 239. Police regulation of steam railroads.—Authority to occupy and use the streets of a corporation, however conferred, never acts to exempt the railroad from reasonable police regulation. Under general police powers any restriction may be made upon the mode of using the streets by railroads that look to the security and comfort of the citizens. Unless restricted by the legislature the use of steam motors may be prohibited.[7] If once permission is given to use steam motors, no subsequent prohibi-

---

(1) Ingham v. Railroad Co., 34 Ia. 249; Railroad Co. v. Newark, 2 Stockt. 352.

(2) Railway Co. v. Louisville, 8 Bush, 415; Slatten v. Railroad Co., 29 Ia. 148.

(3) Moses v. Railroad Co., 21 Ill. 516.

(4) Railroad Co. v. Shields, 33 Ga. 601.

(5) City v. Railroad Co., 79 N. Y. 561.

(6) Hoboken v. State, 30 N. J. 225.

(7) Railroad Co. v. Buffalo, 5 Hill, 209; Donnaher v. State, 16 Miss. 649.

tion destructive of the privilege would be lawful. It falls within the province of police regulation to limit railroad trains to a certain comparatively slow rate of speed while in motion within the limits of the corporation.[1] A restriction to six miles an hour is neither unreasonable nor in restraint of trade.[2] Or even to four miles.[3] And such a provision operates over the whole city whether platted or not.[4] It would also operate over such portions of the right of way as lie within the private yards of the railroad, unless it is so drawn as to exclude such a construction.[5] The municipality may regulate the mode of laying tracks, and may compel reasonable precautions to be taken to guard the public from danger at street crossings and other exposed places.[6] It would, for instance, be reasonable to compel the stationing of a flagman at any crossing which in the judgment of a prudent man would be considered dangerous, but not if so isolated and open to view that there would be hardly any danger.[7]

An ordinance directed against "any kind of obstruction" to the streets applies to the case of a railroad company.[8] Under general police powers an ordinance may provide that boys and other persons not connected with a railway, except passengers and others in the act of taking passage, are prohibited from getting on trains or cars within the city limits.[9] The ringing of bells, whistling,

(1) Railroad Co. v. Chenoa, 43 Ill. 209; Robertson v. Railroad Co., 84 Mo. 119; Gahagan v. Railroad Co., 1 Allen, 187; Railroad Co. v. Galena, 40 Ill. 344; Myers v. Railroad Co., 57 Ia. 555.

(2) Knobloch v. Railway Co., 31 Minn. 402; Railroad Co. v. Haggerty, 67 Ill. 113.

(3) Whitson v. Franklin, 34 Ind. 392.

(4) Whitson v. Franklin, 34 Ind. 392.

(5) Crowley v. Railroad Co., 65 Ia. 658; Green v. Canal Co., 38 Hun, 51. *Contra*, State v. Jersey City, 29 N. J. 170. See *ante*, sec. 145.

(6) Textor v. Railroad Co., 59 Md. 63; Railroad Co. v. People, 92 Ill. 179; Railroad v. Chenoa, 43 Ill. 209.

(7) Railway Co. v. Jacksonville, 67 Ill. 37; s. c., 16 Am. Rep. 611. *Contra*, Ravenna v. Penna Co., O. S. 1887, 44 or 45 O. S. Rep.

(8) Railroad Co. v. Decatur, 33 Ill. 381; Railroad Co. v. Galena, 40 Ill. 344.

(9) Bearden v. Madison, 73 Ga. 184.

letting off steam and general conduct of the train and engine may likewise be regulated.[1]

The leaving of cars, trains, or engines standing upon street crossings for more than three minutes at a time may be prohibited,[2] or for ten minutes, except in case of accident.[3] If a street is extended or opened across an existing railroad, but at a different grade, the railroad company can not be compelled to grade the street approaches.[4]

§ 240. **Street railways.**—Street railways must, of necessity, use the streets, and still, being an additional burden, such use must be authorized by legislative enactment. As a matter of fact, the right to charter street railways is generally left to the discretion of the local government.[5] And it is generally held that the usual powers over streets and their use will authorize municipalities to allow them to be occupied by street railways.[6] This power is subject to three limitations: First, that the road to exercise the francise must be for the public use, and not merely to accommodate some one business or individual;[7] second, that the franchise can not be granted to one railway to the exclusion of all others. If attempted the ordinance, in so far, is void.[8] Third. The grant must not exclude or restrict the use of the street as a public highway.[9]

§ 241. **Regulations.**—Under general power to control the use of the streets, the use of steam motive power on street railways may, by ordinance, be declared a nuisance.[10]

(1) Merz v. Railway Co., 14 Mo. App. 459.
(2) Railroad Co. v. Jersey City, 47 N. J. 286
(3) McCoy v. Railroad Co., 5 Houston, 599.
(4) Railroad Co. v. Bloomington, 76 Ill. 447.
(5) Boston v. Richardson, 13 Allen, 146; Railway Co. v. Railway Co., 2 Col. 673.
(6) Dill. Mun. Corp., § 719; Brown v. Duplessis, 14 La. Ann. 842.
(7) State v. Trenton, 36 N. J. 79.
(8) Railroad Co. v. Transit Ry., 24 Fed. Rep. 306; Railroad Co. v. Smith, 29 O. S. 292; State v. Coke Co., 18 O. S. 292.
(9) Railroad Co. v. Belleville, 20 Ill. App. 584.
(10) Railroad v. Lake View, 95 Ill. 207; Railroad Co. v. Richmond, 96 U. S. 521 (over certain streets).

After a railroad company has received authority to use the streets it is, as we have seen, subject not only to the charter conditions but also to such further police regulations as the public safety and convenience may require. So, under general police power, street railway companies may be compelled, in pursuance of an ordinance, to construct their tracks of a certain width, so as to enable other vehicles than the cars to use them.[1] A license may be exacted for each car in use under power to license hackmen, draymen, omnibus drivers, cabmen, and all others pursuing like occupations.[2] But power to regulate common carriers and carriers of passengers does not authorize an ordinance requiring a conductor on every car.[3] The ordinances may provide for a reasonable and safe rate of speed; that the cars shall not be stopped upon the space formed by the intersection of two streets; that lights and signals of warning shall be carried; that sufficient brakes are provided, and similar regulations tending to public security.

Power to "open, alter, abolish," etc., streets does not warrant a grant to a railroad company of the right to obstruct a street by permanent structures so as to wholly destroy its usefulness.[4]

As with steam railroads, any reasonable conditions may be attached to the grant of a franchise to a street railroad company, with which it must comply. But after the franchise has been accepted and acted upon no further conditions can be imposed, unless they are such as fairly come within the designation of police regulation. For example, unless it is so provided in the original grant a street railroad company can not be compelled to pave the street between its tracks.[5]

(1) Railroad Co. v. Lake View, 95 Ill. 183.
(2) Allerton v. Chicago, 9 Biss, 552; s. c., 6 Fed. Rep. 555.
(3) Railroad Co. v. Brooklyn, 37 Hun, 413. See further as to general principle, Railway Co. v. Philadelphia, 58 Pa. St. 119; State v. Herod, 29 Ia. 123; Railway Co. v. Louisville, 4 Bush, 478.
(4) Lackland v. Railroad Co., 31 Mo. 180.
(5) Kansas City v. Corrigan, 86 Mo. 67. *Contra*, Columbus v. Street Railway Co., 44 or 45 O. S. (1887.)

A railroad company is neither a "*person*" nor an "*employment*" within the meaning of those words as used in an ordinance requiring the payment of a license tax.[1]

Though the railroad company has agreed to keep the street in repair, it can not be compelled to lay a *new* pavement.[2]

It has been held reasonable to compel a street railway company to report quarterly the number of passengers it has carried.[3] And to prescribe the manner of constructing the road, and, in general, the mode of its operation.[4] If a street railway was built under an ordinance that reserves no taxing power to the city, the city can not afterward tax it beyond the rate at which all property is taxed.[5] And when the company is chartered subject to such tax as the city may impose, the city is restricted to its ordinary powers of taxation unless the city charter allows special taxation of railroads.[6] Except under special power, an exclusive right to use a street can not be granted for any length of time.[7]

§ 242. **Sewerage system.**—Under power to control the use of the streets a corporation may authorize almost any use which is for the manifest good of the public, and without regard to whether the fee to the streets is vested in the public or only the right to use. Among such cases are sewerage, a system of pipes for the transportation of water, gas, steam, and other conveniences, and, under exceptional circumstances, underground railways. The right to devote the street to such purposes must be exercised so as to inter-

---

(1) Lynchburg *v.* Railway Co., 80 Va. 237.

(2) State *v.* Railroad Co., 85 Mo. 263; *contra*, City *v.* Erie Railroad Co., 7 Phila. 321.

(3) St. Louis Ry. Co. *v.* St. Louis, 89 Mo. 44.

(4) Wyandotte *v.* Corrigan, 35 Kan. 21.

(5) Mayor *v.* Second Ave. Railroad Co., 32 N. Y. 261.

(6) Mayor *v.* Railroad Co., 97 N. Y. 275; Mayor *v.* Railroad Co., 33 N. Y. 42.

(7) Railway Co. *v.* Jonesville, 8 Bush, 415; Davis *v.* Mayor, 14 N. Y. 506; Milhau *v.* Sharp, 27 N. Y. 611; Coleman *v.* Railroad Co., 38 N. Y. 201.

fere as little as possible with the rights of adjoining owners. The construction of a system of sewerage is a lawful use of the streets.¹ And power to open streets and construct sidewalks implies power to construct a sewer under the sidewalk as well as under the street.² It is manifest that sewerage can not safely be conducted in open ditches or gutters over the surface, but must be carried away beneath the surface. The necessity of disposing of sewerage does not, however, imply any power in the corporation to condemn private property for that purpose. Unless specially authorized, the entire system must be constructed under the public streets.³ When a sewerage system is once established, reasonable regulations may be imposed upon those individuals who desire to participate in its benefits. They may be compelled to make certain specified kinds of connections and to bear the entire expense of laying the connecting pipes. In this expense could be included a fair charge for supervision and inspection.⁴

This right to repair and construct sewers can not be divested by contract or otherwise.⁵

§ 243. **Water supply.**—A municipality may, in pursuance of its ordinary power of street control, and with a view to the public health and convenience, construct cisterns under the streets for the storage of water with which to extinguish fires or to sprinkle the streets.⁶ Although this is undoubtedly the correct view, still the courts of Iowa have held that the cities of Keokuk and Dubuque,

(1) Traphagen *v.* Jersey City, 29 N. J. Eq. 206; Stondinger *v.* Newark, 28 N. J. Eq. 187, 446; In re Fowler, 53, N. Y. 60; Quincy *v.* Bull, 106 Ill. 337; Cincinnati *v.* Penny, 21 O. S. 499. But see Glasby *v.* Morris, 18 N. J. Eq. 72.
(2) Americus *v.* Eldridge, 64 Ga. 524.
(3) Allen *v.* Jones, 47 Ind. 438.
(4) Borough *v.* Shortz, 61 Pa. St. 399; Commonwealth *v.* Hartford, 28 Conn. 363; State *v.* Jersey City, 30 N. J. 148; Stroud *v.* Philadelphia, 61 Pa. St. 255; Boston *v.* Shaw, 1 Met. 130; In re Workman, 7 Ont. 425.
(5) Railway Co. *v.* Louisville, 8 Bush, 415.
(6) West *v.* Bancroft, 32 Vt. 367; Louisville *v.* Osborne, 10 Bush, 226.

on account of the nature of the right vested in the public to their streets, are exceptions.¹ But still the use must be reasonable, and a cistern occupying half the width of a street, having a steam engine in connection therewith, is an unlawful erection, although its purpose is lawful.²

The use of the streets for the laying of water pipes to supply the citizens and to provide for fires is proper and necessary,³ and the adjoining proprietor is not entitled to compensation.⁴

It has been held in Connecticut that power to regulate or prohibit the opening of streets for public or private purposes, and to regulate the laying of gas and water pipes, does not authorize any assessment in the form of a license, and that a charge of $1 for a license, and an additional $10 for each nine hundred feet of pipe laid in an unpaved street and $50 for the same length in a paved street, was unlawful.⁵ It is proper to assess the cost of such improvements upon adjoining owners, only under statutory or charter authority. Otherwise being a public use, the burden of providing for it would rest upon the municipality at large.

§ 244. **Gas pipes.**—As water is necessary to protect the city from disastrous fires, so is gas necessary to light the streets, and proper provision for its distribution becomes of public moment, as well as beneficial to the individual consumer. Although a municipality under power to light the streets, or even under power to control the streets, and to provide for the security and convenience of its citizens, might engage in the construction of a system of gas pipes as a public work, still it is customary, on account of the large capital necessary and the profit to be derived from

(1) Dubuque v. Maloney, 9 Ia. 450; Dubuque v. Benson, 23 Ia. 248; Davis v. Clinton, 50 Ia. 585; Cook v. Burlington, 30 Ia. 94; Des Moines v. Hall, 24 Ia. 234.

(2) Morrison v. Hinkson, 87 Ill. 587.

(3) Dill. Mun. Corp., § 697; Milhau v. Sharp, 15 Barb. 210; Kelsey v. King, 32 Barb. 410; Quincy v. Bull, 106 Ill. 337.

(4) Commissioners v. Hudson, 2 Beasley (N. J.) 420.

(5) New Haven v. Water Co., 40 Conn. 106.

the sale of gas to private consumers, to vest the privilege of laying pipes in private persons.¹ In order, however, to grant such privileges the municipality must have express power at least to light the streets.² The municipality can never grant an *exclusive* right to use the streets for such purpose, except as it has express power to grant such privileges for a limited time. Such power may be necessary to encourage the investment of capital in such useful enterprises, but care must be exercised not to create a monopoly,³ and power to regulate gas pipes after they are laid can not be delegated.⁴

§ 244a. **Telegraph poles.**—Telegraph companies, although of great service to the public, must, like railroads, have express authority to use the streets of a city for the support of their wires.⁵ And the city may impose any reasonable restrictions upon the mode of conveying the wires through the city. It may prescribe the streets over which they may be strung, the size, height, and frequency of the poles; and if compelled to lay the wire underground, the manner of so doing.⁶

A telegraph company is subject to all reasonable ordinances, and the actual erection of poles may be lawfully put entirely under the control of the police or fire department.⁷

(1) Garrison *v.* Chicago, 7 Biss. 480.
(2) Nelson *v.* La Porte, 33 Ind. 258; State *v.* Gas Co., 18 O. S. 262; Milhan *v.* Sharp, 15 Barb. 210; Gas Light Co. *v.* Gas Co., 25 Conn. 19; Smith *v.* Gas Co., 12 How. Pr. 187; People *v.* Benson, 30 Barb. 24; New Orleans *v.* Clark, 95 U. S. 644; Gas Light Co. *v.* Middleton, 59 N. Y. 228; East St. Louis *v.* Gas Light Co., 98 Ill. 415.
(3) Dill. Mun. Corp., § 692–696; State *v.* Gas Co., 18 O. S. 262; Indianapolis *v.* Gas Co., 66 Ind. 396; Gas Light Co. *v.* Gas Co., 25 Conn. 19, and other cases cited above; Gas Co. *v.* Des Moines, 44 Ia. 508.
(4) Anderson *v.* Gas Co., 12 Daly, 462.
(5) Commonwealth *v.* Boston, 97 Mass. 555; Domestic Telegraph Co. *v.* Newark, 10 East. Rep. 122. (N. J. 1887).
(6) Telegraph Co. *v.* Chicago; 16 Fed. Rep. 309; s. c., 11 Biss. 539.
(7) City *v.* Telegraph Co., 11 Phila. 327.

§ 245. **Restrictions on ordinary use of the streets.**—
It is lawful for a municipal corporation to restrain by ordinance any immoderate or incommodious use of the streets, to insure freedom of passage and the absence of any thing that might be dangerous. The streets may be kept free from all things which are *per se* nuisances and from many other things which become nuisances from improper use. Hawkers and peddlers, stands for the sale of fruits and nuts, and any thing that tends to attract a crowd of persons and thereby impede progress of wayfarers, may be prohibited from being on the streets, whenever the council deems it necessary.[1] Any method of selling goods by outcry in the streets or public places, or by attracting persons to purchase goods exposed at such place, by signals or placards, or by going from house to house selling or offering goods for sale at retail to persons who are not dealers in such commodities, whether for future or immediate delivery, constitutes hawking or pedding within a statute or ordinance prohibiting those things.[2]

The streets are open to the public for all ordinary uses, and it is considered that marching in procession through the streets with torches, flags, or musical instruments is a lawful use, and that associations or organizations of persons can not be prohibited from so doing without the consent of the local authorities.[3]

Hours of the day may be fixed during which it shall be unlawful to drive cattle either singly or in droves through the streets.[4] Such an ordinance would not be violated by transporting cattle over the streets in vans drawn by horses.[5]

§ 246. **Vehicles.**—In order that traffic may not be impeded upon the streets of a corporation, and to prevent the use of the streets by vehicles and loads of a nature to injure the pavement or damage the road-bed, corporations are

(1) Caldwell *v.* Alton, 33 Ill. 416; St. Paul *v.* Traeger, 25 Minn. 248.
(2) Graffty *v.* Rushville, 107 Ind. 502.
(3) Frazee's Case, 35 Alb. L. Jour. 6 (Mich. 1886).
(4) Board *v.* Heister, 37 N. Y. 661.
(5) Triggs *v.* Lester, 1 L. R. Q. B. 259.

generally empowered to regulate the use of vehicles. This power is reasonably exercised by requiring the owners of such vehicles as tend from the nature of their use to obstruct the streets, or such as may endanger the security of foot passengers, to procure a license, or by regulating the use of vehicles kept for hire. It does not authorize restrictive regulations upon all classes of vehicles indiscriminately, nor even upon all classes of vehicles used in the conduct of any business. A license imposed upon vehicles used in any business without exempting those whose use can in no way be dangerous to public security, or annoying to the citizens, would be nothing less than a tax measure. It would cease to be regulatory in its nature, and would therefore be void.[1]

§ 247. **Routes and stands.**—It is proper to ordain certain routes to be followed by such vehicles as tend from the nature of their use either to hinder traffic, or to be offensive to passers-by.[2] In this category would fall all vehicles whose loads render rapid motion impossible, or whose loads are unusually bulky, as hay-wagons or wagons loaded with lengthy building material; wagons used for transporting offal, garbage, or fertilizers of offensive odor; and vehicles of such gaudy appearance or peculiar appearance as to tend to frighten horses.

That people may be protected from imposition, it is lawful to ordain that fixed tariffs must be charged for the use of vehicles kept for hire for the transportation of passengers or merchandise, and prescribing the rates for different distances.[3] In such case the ordinance provision becomes imperative and the drivers of such vehicles are precluded from asking higher rates, and even from making a special contract varying the lawful charges to the disadvantage of the passenger.[4]

(1) Brooklyn *v.* Nodine, 26 Hun, 512; Ex parte Gregory, 20 Tex. App. 210.
(2) Commonwealth *v.* Stodder, 2 Cush. 562.
(3) Commonwealth *v* Gage, 114 Mass. 328.
(4) Commonwealth *z.* Duane, 98 Mass. 1.

Inasmuch as the general public would inevitably suffer annoyance from the promiscuous and unrestrained solicitation of passengers or trade by those in charge of vehicles used for hire, it is lawful to prescribe defined stands for hacks and drays, and to prohibit them from standing elsewhere when not employed.[1] But the location of such stands must be selected so as to avoid annoyance to those whose premises are adjacent. No ordinance of this nature could legalize any hinderance to the free use of the streets. So, if the hacks standing in their prescribed places tend to interfere with access to the adjacent premises of private individuals, the ordinance virtually works an appropriation of private property without making compensation, and is void to that extent.[2]

Bicycles come within the reason of such regulation and their use may be regulated.[3]

§ 248. **Construction of vehicle regulations.**—The general propriety and scope of such ordinances is evident, but many contests arise as to the lawful extent of an ordinance with reference to the wording of a power. When the power enumerates the classes of vehicles that may be regulated, all others are excluded, and construction is often invoked to determine whether a class ordained against is reasonably within the meaning of the terms of the power. Thus, it is held that an ordinance requiring a license for drays, carts, wagons, or other vehicles used for hire, does not include the delivery wagons of wholesale merchants.[4] Such wagons are used for private persons, but they come within the reason and letter of the ordinance whenever the merchant makes a charge for delivery.[5] An ordinance regulating wagons, drays, carts, and other vehicles of burden used to convey loads, includes wagons used by retail grocers

(1) Commonwealth v. Matthews, 122 Mass. 60.
(2) Branahan v. Hotel Co., 30 O. S. 333; McCaffrey v. Smith, 41 Hun, 117.
(3) Recent unreported case in New Jersey; In re Wright, 29 Hun. 357.
(4) Farwell v. Chicago, 71 Ill. 269.
(5) Knoxville v. Sanford, 13 B. J. Lea, 545

for delivering goods sold.¹ But when the same provision in the ordinance is followed by a provision relative to fixing the rates to be charged, this evidence of the legislative intention as to the scope of the ordinance would exclude retail delivery wagons:² Where one section of an ordinance requires a license for keeping a livery-stable, to let out horses, carriages, etc., and other vehicles, providing that it should not extend to drays used for hire, and a separate provision is made for the regulation of drays, it is held that under a livery license a wagon might be let by the day for hauling lumber, without securing the license required for drays by the second section of the ordinance.³ *Street cars* are properly vehicles. They may be regulated under a power to regulate omnibuses and vehicles in the nature thereof,⁴ or under a power to license hackmen, omnibus drivers, and others pursuing like occupations.⁵

Under the designation "public vehicles" are included sprinkling carts,⁶ but not a hotel free bus.⁷

"Cars" include steam cars.⁸ A ferry-boat is not a "vehicle."⁹ A livery-stable man, who hires out vehicles by the day to draw ice, is not a common-carrier.¹⁰

§ 249. **Strays.**—Perhaps, upon no subject connected with municipal powers does there seem to be less uniformity in adjudicated cases than in regard to strays, or animals found running at large. If animals are at large upon the public streets or commons of a populous city, they are certainly apt to impede traffic, to render the streets filthy, and

(1) Gartside *v.* East St. Louis, 43 Ill. 47.
(2) Joyce *v.* East St. Louis, 77 Ill. 156.
(3) Griffin *v.* Powell, 64 Ga. 625.
(4) Railway Co. *v.* Philadelphia, 58 Pa. 119.
(5) Allerton *v.* Chicago, 6 Fed. Rep. 555; s. c., 9 Biss. 552; Johnson *v.* Philadelphia, 60 Pa. St. 445; Provision Co. *v.* Chicago, 88 Ill. 221; Munn *v.* Illinois, 94 U. S. 113. *Contra*, Mayor *v.* Second Ave. R. R. Co., 32 N. Y. 261; Railroad Co. *v.* Philadelphia, 6 Phila. 238.
(6) St. Louis *v.* Woodruff, 71 Mo. 92.
(7) Oswego *v.* Collins, 38 Hun, 171.
(8) Cumming *v.* Railroad Co., 38 Hun, 362.
(9) Duckwall *v.* New Albany, 25 Ind. 283.
(10) Havana *v.* Vallaningham, 17 Ill., App. 62.

to greatly annoy many who have occasion to use the public ways. It would seem most reasonable that strays should be considered *per se* nuisances, and that every municipal corporation should have an incidental power to restrain them, and to pass ordinances providing for reasonable prevention of the evil.[1]

But it has been held that pounds can only be established under express power,[2] and that ordinances against strays can not be sustained under power "to abate nuisances," nor under power to pass ordinances for the "well regulation, interest, health, convenience, etc.," of the corporation.[3] These decisions are based upon the idea that an ordinance of this nature must, to be in any way effective, authorize a summary proceeding against property, and that express authority must be given in order to warrant such proceedings. But the evident impracticability of making the remedy other than summary, and the evident inconvenience of having animals running on the public streets, ought to establish a case where the public good is to be preferred to the rights of the individual. The regulation of strays ought to be considered as fairly within the police powers vested in every corporation.[4] Of course, like all other police powers, the prescribed mode of exercise must be strictly observed.[5]

However summary the seizure of strays may be, there must be some notice given to the owner, actual or constructive, and some form of judicial determination before the animal taken up can be forfeited and sold to pay the expenses incurred in its seizure and keeping.[6] The remedy

(1) Roberts v. Ogle, 30 Ill. 459; Hellen v. Noe, 3 Ired. 493; Whitfield v. Longest, 6 Ind. 268; Waco v. Powell, 32 Tex. 258; Gilchrist v. Schneidling, 12 Kan. 263.
(2) White v. Tallman, 26 N. J. 67.
(3) Collins v. Hatch, 18 Ohio, 523.
(4) Cartersville v. Lanham, 67 Ga. 753.
(5) Greencastle v. Martin, 74 Ind. 449.
(6) Cotter v. Doty, 5 Ohio, 395; Cincinnati v. Buckingham, 10 Ohio, 257; Rosebaugh v. Saffin, 10 Ohio, 32; Jarman v. Patterson, 7 Monroe, 647; Varden v. Mount, 78 Ky. 86; Donovan v. Vicksburg, 29 Miss. 247; and cases cited *ante*, §§ 159–161.

is, however, not confined to seizing and selling the stray itself. The owner may be fined for violating the ordinance in allowing his animal to run at large, and on default of payment the fine may be added to the amount to satisfy which the animal is sold.[1]

The main difficulty that arises in enforcing this class of ordinances is in determining whether an animal is "running at large" within the meaning of the ordinance. In the first place, the animal must be found on the public streets or places. An animal that has escaped from one private inclosure to another is not at large.[2] An animal that is accompanying some person upon the street is at large as soon as the circumstances show that it is beyond that person's control. The test is simply whether the person has immediate control of the animal. A dog running close to his master, or a trained horse following him, would not be at large.[3]

§ 250. **Nuisances.**—The power to prevent and remove nuisances is one of the most important to be noticed under the general head of police powers. It is difficult to draw any distinct class line between the various police powers, for the same act may have several bearings. Thus, a building which violates the fire limit ordinance may also be in such condition of dilapidation as to be *per se* a nuisance, or dangerous to health.

§ 251. **Definition.**—All things are nuisances which are detrimental to the health, dangerous to life, or productive of serious inconvenience.[4] Municipal corporations have inherent power as absolutely essential to the corporate purposes to take measures to remove nuisances.[5] Nor is the power restricted to simple abatement. It extends to all

---

(1) Roberts *v.* Ogle, 30 Ill. 359; Kinder *v.* Gillespie, 63 Ill. 88; Waco *v.* Powell, 32 Tex. 258.

(2) Shepherd *v.* Hees, 12 Johns. 433.

(3) Commonwealth *v.* Dow, 10 Metc. 382; Welsh *v.* Railway Co., 53 Ia. 632.

(4) State *v.* Jersey City, 29 N. J. 170.

(5) Kennedy *v.* Phelps, 10 La. Ann. 227.

steps necessary to prevent nuisances from arising. An ordinance may be passed in advance looking toward prevention.¹ Though, as has been held in Illinois, the power to abate nuisances does not warrant an ordinance prohibiting the establishment of a cemetery.² This power, like all others, is not self-executing, and an actual abatement can not be made unless an ordinance has first been passed defining the mode of procedure, and establishing the law.³ When such ordinance once exists, the corporation may intrust the execution to the police officers, or it may direct the abatement of certain nuisances as they may arise. And the resolution expressing the corporate determination that a specified thing is a nuisance is legal. It must not be confused with an ordinance directed against an individual, which would be bad.⁴

Unless general power is given to punish for violations of all ordinances, the single power to abate nuisances does not carry with it the power to punish the person at whose instance, or by whose neglect, a certain nuisance exists.⁵

§ 252. **Must be an actual nuisance.**—Nuisances can not be declared in contravention of the general law; for instance, a railroad expressly authorized by state law can never be of itself a nuisance, though it might be so conducted as to create nuisances.⁶

Neither may the power be exercised unrestrictedly. When the corporation is authorized to abate nuisances in any manner deemed expedient, only such means as are for the public good are lawful. No wanton or unnecessary injury may result from the means adopted.⁷ Due provision may be taken to prevent any business or structure from be-

(1) Gregory v. City of N. Y., 40 N. Y. 273.
(2) Lake View v. Letz, 44 Ill. 82.
(3) Lake v. Aberdeen, 57 Miss. 260.
(4) Kennedy v. Phelps, 10 La. Ann. 227.
(5) Nevada v. Hutchins, 59 Ga. 506.
(6) State v. Jersey City, 29 N. J. 170; Ward v. Little Rock, 41 Ark. 526.
(7) Babcock v. Buffalo, 56 N. Y. 268; affirming Babcock v. Buffalo, 1 Sheldon, 317.

coming a nuisance, but must not go so far as to practically prohibit. Businesses that are lawful *per se*, and which may be so conducted as to be free from nuisance, can only be so regulated as to prevent their improper conduct.[1] Power to compel the cleansing and abating of slaughter houses whenever necessary to the health of the city can only be exercised when an actual nuisance exists.[2] The nuisance may be abated when it arises, but care must be taken that no unnecessary damage results. The nuisance alone may be proceeded against, and the cause is to be separated if possible from its surroundings. So, if a certain trade or business becomes a nuisance, the trade or business may be stopped, but the remedy would not extend to the place or building in which the nuisance is maintained. Buildings can never be removed simply because they have been put to an unlawful use.[3]

A corporation has no right to declare that to be a nuisance which is not so in fact. This power is exercised in derogation of property rights, and must be strictly followed. Nuisances are declared at the risk of the corporation, and its determination, however formal, is never conclusive.[4] Its judgment is always subject to revision.[5] And if in fact erroneous, the corporation owes restitution to all who have suffered injury to their property rights. But "in doubtful cases, where the thing may or may not be a nuisance, depending upon a variety of circumstances requiring judgment and discretion on the part of the town authorities in exercising their legislative functions, their action would be conclusive of the question."[6]

§ 253. **Judicial determination.**—There should, then,

(1) Weil v. Ricord, 24 N. J. Eq. 169.
(2) Wreford v. People, 14 Mich. 41.
(3) Miller v. Burch, 32 Tex. 208.
(4) Howard v. Robbins, 1 Lans. 63.
(5) Everett v. Council Bluffs, 46 Ia. 66; Pye v. Peterson, 45 Tex. 312; State v. Mott, 61 Md. 297; Davis v. Clifton, 8 U. C. C. P. 236.
(6) Railway Co. v. Lake View, 105 Ill. 207; s. c., 44 Am. Rep. 788; Denver v. Mullen, 7 Col. 345.

always be some judicial determination of the existence of a nuisance.¹ A board of health vested with power to proceed against nuisances must give notice to the owner or party in control, and must allow him an opportunity to be heard.² An ordinance that authorizes the closing of a saloon by force, without a prior judicial determination that it is a nuisance, is void.³ It is even held that a resolution for the removal of a person sick with an infectious disease is void unless he consent to the removal.⁴ But this is surely not the accepted rule, especially not during the prevalence of such disease, when public health and safety make such removal an imperative necessity. But if a thing is in fact a nuisance, and its abatement is effected without doing unnecessary damage, the fact that the owner was not notified would only be so far material as to throw the cost of removal on the corporation. In order to impose the cost on the owner, he must be first given a reasonable opportunity to remove the nuisance himself.⁵

Under the Georgia statute, a municipal corporation may punish for continuing a nuisance, *before* notice is given to abate it, but not after, when such continuance becomes a penal offense.⁶

§ 254. **What are nuisances.**—The following things have been held to be nuisances and properly prohibited by ordinance: Exposing articles for sale that are in a condition unfit for use;⁷ public exhibition of stud horses;⁸ depositing rubbish except in places designated by some board or

(1) Gates *v.* Milwaukee, 10 Wall. 497; Monroe *v.* Gerspach, 33 La. Ann. 1011.
(2) People *v.* Board of Health, 33 Barb. 344; Weil *v.* Ricord, 24 N. J. Eq. 169.
(3) Baldwin *v.* Smith, 82 Ill. 163.
(4) Boom *v.* Utica, 2 Barb. 104.
(5) Baumgartner *v.* Hasty, 100 Ind. 575.
(6) Vason *v.* Augusta, 38 Ga, 542.
(7) Shillito *v.* Thompson, L. R., 1 Q. B. Div. 12.
(8) Nolin *v.* Franklin, 4 Yerg. 163; Ex parte Shrader, 33 Cal. 279.

officer;[1] smoke from chimneys;[2] houses of ill-fame;[3] swine running at large in the streets;[4] growing rice within city limits; keeping swine.[5]

§ 255. **What are not nuisances per se.**—Many things that are not nuisances *per se* may become nuisances under special circumstances. Such are a blacksmith's shop;[6] a cornice projecting over the street;[7] keeping pigs or cows in stables in close proximity to dwelling-houses;[8] burning lime;[9] cemeteries.[10]

In order to make this class of things nuisances it must appear that they cause some actual inconvenience or discomfort, or some actual damage to life or health.[11]

The consideration of what acts amount to nuisances is one involving too much space to be treated at length. Reference must be made to the text-books on that subject.

§ 256. **Nature of license power.**—Among other means in common use to effect the purposes of police regulation is the prohibition, except under license from the corporation, of such occupations and pursuits as need to be conducted with more than ordinary care. The power to license must be granted in express terms, although it is merely a police power. It is one mode of regulation, but one that can not be exercised under general police author-

(1) Ex parte Casinello, 62 Cal. 538.
(2) Harmon *v.* Chicago, 110 Ill. 400.
(3) McAlister *v.* Clark, 33 Conn. 91.
(4) Roberts *v.* Ogle, 30 Ill. 459; Hellen *v.* Noe, 3 Ired. 493; Whitfield *v.* Longest, 6 Ired. 268; Waco *v.* Powell, 32 Tex. 258. *Contra,* Collins *v.* Hatch, 18 Ohio, 523.
(5) Green *v.* Savannah, 6 Ga. 1; St. Louis *v.* Stern, 3 Mo. App. 48.
(6) Terre Haute *v.* Turner, 36 Ind. 522.
(7) Grove *v.* Ft. Wayne, 45 Ind. 429.
(8) McKnight *v.* Toronto, 3 Ont. 284.
(9) State *v.* Mott, 61 Md. 297.
(10) Musgrave *v.* Church, 10 La. Ann. 244.
(11) Ewbanks *v.* Ashley, 36 Ill. 177; Poyer *v.* Des Plaines, 18 Ill. App. 225; Everett *v.* Council Bluffs, 46 Ia. 66.

ity.[1] And like all other express powers it must be strictly followed.[2] So, power to enact ordinances "*relative to*" certain occupations does not warrant the passage of an ordinance imposing a license.[3] Even a power "to make such assessments for the safety, convenience, benefit, and advantage of said city" as may be deemed expedient, would not suffice.[4] But it must not be supposed that the word "license" must itself appear in the grant of power, for the right to subject occupations to licenses may be, and is, conferred by a grant of power superior in grade to that of licensing. For example, a grant of *entire control*, or of power to *suppress* and restrain, would enable the corporation to adopt any mode of regulation within the limit of those powers, license included.[5] So, a license would be lawful under power to declare the selling of certain commodities a nusiance.[6] In Illinois the courts have gone to the extreme limit, and have even held that power to license is implied by power to *regulate*,[7] or power to *restrain*.[8] The claim is often made that a distinction should be drawn in this respect between such occupations as afford special opportunities to defraud and impose upon the public and those of a more harmless nature, but there is no reason for maintaining such a distinction. The same degree of regulation can be attained by other means than licenses, even

(1) Railway Co. *v.* Hoboken, 41 N. J. L. 71; Fowle *v.* Alexandria, 3 Pet. 399; Sanders *v.* Butler, 30 Ga. 679; Ordinary *v.* Retailers, 42 Ga. 325.
(2) Jackson *v.* Bowman, 39 Miss. 671; House *v.* State, 41 Miss. 737; Dill. Mun. Corp. 361.
(3) Dill. Mun. Corp. 361.
(4) Charleston *v.* Oliver, 16 S. C. 47.
(5) Martin *v.* People, 88 Ill. 390; Burlington *v.* Lawrence, 42 Ia. 681; Smith *v.* Madison, 7 Ind. 86; Ex parte Mount, 66 Cal. 448.
(6) Martin *v.* People, 88 Ill. 390.
(7) Chicago Packing Co. *v.* Chicago, 88 Ill. 221.
(8) Mt. Carmel *v.* Wabash Co., 50 Ill. 69. Wherever the right to license is sustained under a general power of regulation, the provisions of the license ordinance must be strictly adapted to the maintenance of good order, and only reasonable means to that end employed. State *v.* Hoboken, 33 N. J. 280. "To tax" does not mean "to license." Leonard *v.* Canton, 35 Miss. 189.

though perhaps more arduous; and, without express authority so to do, no lawful business should be prohibited.

§ 257. **Nature of licenses.**—The power to license depends upon a concurrent power to prohibit. The business or occupation is declared unlawful, except upon compliance with certain condition. A license, then, " is a privilege granted to carry on some occupation or exercise some right which could not be legally exercised without the grant of such license. The pursuit of the prohibited occupation becomes a franchise in the power of the municipality to grant, and the license fee is the price exacted for the right to exercise the franchise."[1]

A license is in no sense a tax.[2] The distinction between the two is of the utmost importance, and is the turning point upon which the validity of a large class of license ordinances depends. The basis of all license ordinances is police regulation, and all are valid which do not exceed the proper limits of such regulation. The questions to be propounded in order to test such ordinances are:

1. Is the ordinance provision within the express authority of the power? If so, it is valid, however high the fee imposed, or however severe the conditions.

2. If the amount of the fee demanded or the conditions imposed are not expressly authorized by the power to enact the ordinance, do they exceed the limits of reasonable regulation?

§ 258. **Must not amount to a tax.**—When rightfully imposed the license fee will never be construed to be a tax within the meaning of constitutional provisions, although the term "license tax" is frequently used to designate it.[3]

(1) Desty Tax, § 193; Chilvers v. People, 11 Mich. 43.
(2) Desty Tax, § 193; Coe v. Hall, 103 Ill. 30; State v. Herod, 29 Ia. 123; Livingston v. Trustees, 99 Ill. 564; Ferry Co. v. East St. Louis, 102 Ill. 560; East St. Louis v. Trustees, 102 Ill. 489; Walker v. Springfield, 94 Ill. 364; Ducat v. Chicago, 48 Ill. 172; Johnson v. City Leg. Int. 1869, p. 269.
(3) Distilling Co. v. Chicago, 112 Ill. 19; Leavenworth v. Booth, 15 Kan. 627; Fort Smith v. Ayers, 43 Ark. 82; Ash v. People, 11 Mich 347.

And courts will not interfere with the discretion of the council unless the amount imposed is plainly unreasonable.[1] A tax is levied for the purposes of revenue, and the power to levy taxes must be granted in the plainest language, the policy of some states even forbidding by constitutional inhibition any delegation of the power. Power to license gives no right to enact ordinances for the purpose of increasing the municipal revenues.[2] It is within the province of the court to decide in each case whether the amount of the fee is upon its face so high as to make it in effect a revenue measure. But a fee may be entirely reasonable as a police regulation, and at the same time in fact swell the municipal revenues. The precise extent to which the ordinance may go is the point upon which the courts of the different states vary, and in regard to which it is impossible to lay down exact rules. The standard is reasonableness, in itself a very indefinite and unsatisfactory basis, varying, as it must, with the individual opinions of those called upon to judge and with the character of the thing to be regulated.[3]

§ 259. **What amount may be charged.**—The strictest rule limits the amount of the fee to the actual expense of issuing the license. This is upon the theory that the sole object of regulation by licensing is to prevent improper persons from obtaining permission to carry on the prohibited trade, and that this may be accomplished by the exercise of discretion in the selection of the licensees by the officer who issues the licenses. This rule restricts the lawful amount to a very small sum and is adopted by very few states,[4] and is only recognized in some of the earlier decisions.

(1) Burlington v. Insurance Co., 31 Ia. 102; Mankato v. Fowler, 32 Minn. 364.

(2) Mankato v. Fowler, 32 Minn. 364; Van Hook v. Selma, 70 Ala. 361; Railway v. Hoboken, 41 N. J. 71; Burlington v. Insurance Co., 31 Ia. 102. But see Ferry Co. v. East St. Louis, 102 Ill. 560; Lynchburg v. Railway Co., 80 Va. 237.

(3) Kitson v. Ann Arbor, 26 Mich. 325; Railway v. Hoboken, 41 N. J. 71.

(4) Commonwealth v. Stodder, 2 Cush. 562; Mobile v. Yuille, 3 Ala. 137.

The wider and almost universally adopted rule recognizes the fact that different occupations need different restrictions, varying with the character of the people and the size of the city, and reposes a very broad, generous confidence in the judgment of the law-makers as to the needs of each particular case. Thus the amount charged often swells the local treasury without exceeding the bounds of proper regulation. As was said by Gholson, J., in Baker v. Cincinnati, 11 O. S. 534: "Things licensed may be such as should only be permitted under the regulation or supervision of public functionaries. A tax or charge may have reference to such regulation and supervision. Such is the case of exhibitors of shows and performances. An inquiry has to be made into the character of those who propose to exhibit, and as to the nature of the thing exhibited. Then the exhibition may require additional attention from those intrusted with the care of public peace to prevent disorder and disturbance. The burden thus devolved on public officials, requiring, perhaps, an increase in their number or compensation, for the benefit of exhibitors of shows or performances may justly authorize a charge beyond the mere expense of filling up a blank license. The same principle that would authorize a charge for one extends to the other. To say that it is a tax and goes into the public treasury does not disprove this object. There is no magic in names."

The holding in this case is that generally recognized as the true rule. The amount of the fee should depend on the nature of the business, and should not be scrutinized too narrowly. A reasonable addition to cover the cost of police supervision may always be made.[1] The whole expense attending the additional supervision should be met.[2]

The law is stated very clearly in Van Hook v. Selma, 70 Ala. 361; s. c., 45 Am. Rep. 81, as follows: "We declare the true rule to be, in the case of useful trades and em-

(1) Van Hook v. Selma, 70 Ala. 361; Ash v. People, 11 Mich. 347; In re Wan Yin, 22 Fed. Rep. 701; Cincinnati v. Bryson, 15 Ohio, 625; Johnson v. Philadelphia, 60 Pa. St. 445; comparatively strict holding in Mays v. Cincinnati, 1 O. S. 268; Fort Smith v. Ayers, 43 Ark. 82.

(2) Ash v. People, 11 Mich. 347.

ployments, and *a fortiori* in other cases, that as an exercise of police power merely, the amount exacted for a license, though designed for regulation and not for revenue, is not to be confined to the expense of issuing it; but that a reasonable compensation may be charged for the additional expense of municipal supervision over the particular business or vocation at the place where it is licensed. For this purpose, the services of officers may be required and incidental expenses may be otherwise incurred in the faithful enforcement of such police inspection or superintendence."

The amount thus reached may be *much greater* than the mere cost of issuing, and a considerable surplus fund may go into the treasury to swell the general revenue fund.[1]

The Kansas courts have even gone so far as to hold that the amount of the fee should include not only the value of the labor and material involved in allowing and issuing the license, and the value of the inconvenience and cost of additional supervision, but also the value of the franchise granted to the licensee, and that the fee could even be still increased so as to prevent improper persons from engaging in the business.[2]

These additional elements are, however, justly excluded from the general rule. It certainly adds nothing to the burden of regulation, that the privilege granted is of special benefit to the licensee, and in proper persons can be excluded from the licensed business by the exercise of discretion on the part of the ministerial officer charged with the duty of allowing the licenses, although they could lawfully refuse only those who were notoriously and evidently unfit to be vested with the privilege. The Kansas doctrine is expressly based on the theory that a license is "a *sale* of a benefit or privilege to a person who would otherwise not be entitled to the same."

§ 260. **Examples.**—To illustrate the extent to which the courts allow license fees to exceed the bare cost, and to

---

(1) Leavenworth *v.* Booth, 15 Kan. 627; Johnson *v.* Philadelphia, 60 Pa. St. 445.

(2) Leavenworth *v.* Booth, 15 Kan. 627.

which they trust to the judgment of the council, the following fees have been sustained: $5 on every meat market;[1] $200 on pawnbrokers;[2] $63.50 for a six months' license for a theater;[3] $5 to $10 on milk peddlers;[4] $500 a year for retail liquors;[5] $500 per year for a theater;[6] $500 per year for brewer's license;[7] $300 for the privilege of keeping billiard tables;[8] $25 for sale of liquors;[9] $15 for each peddler;[10] $50 a year on each street car used by street railway companies;[11] $1,000 annually on a theater under power to license "on such terms and conditions as may seem just and reasonable."[12]

§ 261. **The license.**—The grant of a license is usually evidenced by a written certificate, stating the amount paid, the name of the licensee, the duration of the license and the particular franchise or privilege granted. Still, it is not essential that the license should be in writing.[13] And when so evidenced, its form and manner of execution are immaterial.[14]

§ 262. **The ordinance.**—Whenever power to license certain occupations is given to a municipal corporation, it becomes discretionary with the council to exercise the power.

(1) Ash *v* People, 11 Mich. 353.
(2) Van Baalen *v.* People, 40 Mich. 258.
(3) Baker *v.* Cincinnati, 11 O. S. 534.
(4) People *v.* Mulholland, 82 N. Y. 324.
(5) Wiley *v.* Owens, 39 Ind. 429; Perdue *v.* Ellis, 18 Ga. 586.
(6) Hospital *v.* Stickney, 2 La. Ann. 550.
(7) Distilling Co. *v.* Chicago, 112 Ill. 19.
(8) In re Neilly, 37 U C. Q. B. 289.
(9) Ex parte Benninger, 64 Cal. 291.
(10) People *v.* Russell, 49 Mich. 617.
(11) Allerton *v.* Chicago, 9 Biss. 552; s. c., 6 Fed. Rep. 555; Railway Co. *v.* Philadelphia, 58 Pa. St. 119; Johnson *v.* Philadelphia, 60 Pa. St. 445. In New York the contrary is held as to street cars under an ordinance imposing the same amount. Mayor *v.* Railway Co., 32 N. Y. 261.
(12) Boston *v.* Schaffer, 9 Pick. 415.
(13) Boston *v.* Schaffer, 9 Pick. 415.
(14) Swarth *v.* People, 109 Ill. 621.

The necessary degree of police regulation could often be attained by other local means. And when the license power extends to businesses which are unlawful under the state laws, a simple local option is thereby conferred, which is in nowise mandatory.[1]

Power to license includes, as incident thereto, power to determine the exact sum to be enacted and extent and duration of the privilege.[2] This power must be conclusively exercised by the council, and the main features of the regulation incorporated in the ordinance. The ordinance, too, must be general in its terms, and its benefits capable of enjoyment by any one who is willing to comply with its requirements.[3] The licensees can not be nominated by the ordinance.[4] Where the power is silent as to the manner in which it should be executed, the amount of the license may be fixed by resolution as well as ordinance.[5]

§ 263. **Discretion in officers.**—As has been already stated no discretionary powers should be vested in the officers whose duty it is to execute the provisions of ordinances, and the rule is entirely applicable to this class of ordinances. The ordinance itself should specify every condition of the license and the officer should be merely intrusted with the duty of issuing licenses to all who comply with the prescribed conditions. If it is feared that irresponsible and unprincipled persons may thus receive rights whose exercise in their hands might be injurious to the public, the remedy can not be provided by placing a discretion in the hands of the ministerial officer, but lies with the council itself. A bond may be required of the applicant conditioned upon the proper conduct of the business

(1) Louisville v. McKean, 18 B. Mon. 10.
(2) Boston v. Schaffer, 9 Pick. 415; Darling v. St. Paul, 19 Minn. 389.
(3) The ordinance should be general and uniform, and not discriminating, but it need not be so general that all persons complying with its terms may receive the license, without regard to their moral fitness. Crotty v. People, 3 Ill. App. 465.
(4) In re Coyne, 9 U. C. Q. B. 448.
(5) Burlington v. Insurance Co., 31 Ia. 102.

licensed, or the ordinance may provide for a forfeiture of the license *ipse facto* in case the business privilege is misused. The expression in the ordinance, "which license shall be granted by the mayor," makes the issuing of a license to every comer mandatory upon the mayor.[1] But, if discretion is rightfully vested in the mayor, he violates no rights by refusing an applicant.[2] And it has been held in Alabama that a note may be taken for the amount of the license fee, to be collected, if necessary, by suit in assumpsit.[3] An early case in Iowa holds that the mayor may lawfully be vested with a discretion, within specified limits, as to the amount to be paid for auction licenses,[4] but a similar discretion in regard to peddlers' licenses was defeated in a later case,[5] and the rule may be considered universal that no judicial discretion may be conferred upon the officer issuing the license.[6]

Even the council itself can not lawfully limit the number of licenses to be granted. Its power extends only to the prescription of conditions.[7] And when they have power "to limit the number of licenses," under express grant, the language will be strictly construed, and at least *two* licenses, to comply with the use of the word in the plural, must be authorized.[8] But if authorized to grant or refuse a license, power is thereby conferred to grant an

(1) Commonwealth *v.* Stokley, 12 Phila. 316.
(2) People *v.* New York, 7 How. Pr. 81.
(3) Powers *v.* Decatur, 54 Ala. 214.
(4) Decorah *v.* Dunstan, 38 Ia. 96.
(5) State Center *v.* Barenstein, 66 Ia. 249.
(6) It may delegate its authority to issue licenses, by requiring five citizens to sign a petition therefor, and allowing the officers to investigate the character of the applicant. Such provisions only relate to the mode of applying for the license. In re Bickerstaff, 11 Pac. Rep. 393, Cal. 1886. But an ordinance is void which provides that the mayor shall license entertainments, but only at fair times, and then not, if three citizens should so petition. This places the discretion entirely in the hands of the citizens. Elwood *v.* Bullock, 6 Q. B. 383.
(7) In re Barclay, 12 U. C. Q. B. 86; In re Greystock, 12 U. C. Q. B. 458; In re Brodie, 38 U. C. Q. B. 580.
(8) Terry *v.* Haldimand, 15 U. C. Q. B. 380. For further consideration of the discretion that may be vested in ministerial officers, see § 13.

exclusive license.[1] Mere power "to license" does not include power to enact a monopoly.[2]

§ 264. **The penalty.**—Like all other classes of ordinances that aim at police regulation, ordinances which demand a license fee as a condition to engaging in some prohibited business, may be enforced by proper penalties. And the same modes of punishment for an omission to take out a license may be adopted as would be lawful for other offenses against local laws.[3] This is based upon the theory that the business authorized to be regulated by license, becomes unlawful without the license, immediately upon the exercise of the power vested in the corporation.[4]

Where imprisonment may be prescribed for other offenses, it may also for any violation of a license ordinance.[5]

In prosecutions for failure to secure a license no question of evil intent arises. The essence of the offense consists in pursuing the avocation without a license, when one is required by law.[6]

It is held in England that the offense of pursuing a prohibited business without the necessary license can only be punished once during the period for which the license should have been secured.[7] But this can not be taken as the American rule; for, under the policy of our laws, the punishment is a penalty, and in nowise acts as a license. The payment of a fine ought not to be considered as a substitute for the payment of the required license fee.

(1) Ferry Co. v. Davis, 48 Ia. 133.
(2) Logan v. Pyne, 43 Ia. 524; Chicago v. Rumpff, 45 Ill. 90.
(3) St. Louis v. Bank, 49 Mo. 574; St. Louis v. Life Association, 53 Mo. 466; St. Louis v. Sternberg, 69 Mo. 289; St. Louis v. Laughlin, 49 Mo. 559; St. Louis v. Green, 70 Mo. 562; s. c., 6 Mo. App. 591; Cincinnati v. Buckingham, 10 Ohio, 257; Vandine, Petitioner, 6 Pick. 187; Shelton v. Mobile, 30 Ala. 540; Chilvers v. People, 11 Mich. 43; Brooklyn v. Cleves, Hill & Den. L. S. 231; Desty Taxation, 770; Distilling Co. v. Chicago, 112 Ill. 19.
(4) Hershoff v. Beverly, 45 N. J. 288.
(5) Appleton v. Hopkins, 5 Gray, 530; Commonwealth v. Byrne, 20 Gratt. 165; Desty Tax. 770.
(6) St. Louis v. Sternberg, 69 Mo. 302, and other Missouri cases there cited.
(7) Garrett v. Messenger, 10 Cox C. C. 498; s. c., 36 L. J. C. P. 337.

§ 265. **Effect of a license.**—It follows from the nature of license exactions as mere police regulations, that the payment of a license fee in nowise exempts the licensee from any of the burdens imposed by other laws and ordinances.[1]

The grant of a license does not waive the right of the corporation to subject the business licensed to all further reasonable police regulations.[2] But even if the business, by the express language of the license, were still to be subject to *all* ordinances, no ordinance would be included which the council has no power to pass. Such language is construed to mean all *lawful* ordinances.[3] The license is a grant of a privilege, and exempts from no duty or burden, either of regulation or taxation.[4] The licensee by accepting the license thereby assents to the terms imposed by the license and ordinance, and by the general law.[5] Thus it would be no bar to the exercise, as against his property, of the right of eminent domain.[6] Nor could the license be set up in defense of a prosecution under the general law.[7]

§ 266. **Conditions.**—Under power to license, the council may impose such reasonable conditions precedent or subsequent as they may see fit. Only in such manner can the license be made efficacious as a mode of police regulation.[8] The ordinance may require proof of fitness of the applicant, and may impose conditions for the breach of which

(1) If the bond requires obedience " to *all* other ordinances," only such would be included as relate to the subject-matter of the thing licensed. In re Schneider, 11 Oreg. 288.

(2) Maxwell v. Jonesboro, 11 Heisk. 257; Bowling Green v. Carson, 10 Bush, 64; Baldwin v. Smith, 82 Ill. 162.

(3) Gilham v. Wells, 64 Ga. 192.

(4) State v. Herod, 29 Ia. 123; Railway Co. v. Louisville, 4 Bush, 478; Walker v. Springfield, 94 Ill. 364; Cole v. Hall, 103 Ill. 30; East St. Louis v. Trustees, 102 Ill. 489. Does not exempt from the payment of ordinary taxes. State v. Bennett, 19 Neb. 191; Wendover v. Lexington, 15 B. Mon. 358.

(5) Schwuchow v. Chicago, 68 Ill. 444.

(6) Branson v. Philadelphia, 47 Pa. St. 329.

(7) Paton v. People, 1 Col. 79.

(8) Launder v. Chicago, 111 Ill. 291.

the license may be declared forfeited.[1] Any reasonable conditions will be sustained.

§ 267. Revocability.—Licenses, being mere grants of privileges issued in the exercise of police power, do not create contractual obligations, and are revocable at the discretion of the municipal authorities.[2] The power of revocation should, however, be exercised by a formal act of the law-making body, unless it is made an express condition in the grant that the license shall become forfeited by any breach. So, when a person accepts a license, under an ordinance which gives the mayor authority to revoke it for cause, and the license recites this provision, he can not be heard to say that the mayor has no power and that the license can only be revoked by judicial sentence.[3] Licenses may be revoked for a violation of the ordinance under which they were granted.[4] But there should be some cause for revocation. And it has been held that the council can not reconsider a grant of a license at a subsequent meeting.[5] The revocation of a licnse granted upon the condition of its due observance is not a forfeiture beyond the power of the corporation. Such revocation is not depriving the licensee of his property without compensation.[6] It has been held in Canada that a forfeiture for a breach of the ordinance is lawful.[7]

Revocation must be express even when authorized. It may not be indirectly effected, as by the prohibition of the vocation licensed, or by the enactment of such unreason-

(1) In re Bickerstaff, 11 Pac. Rep. 393 (Cal. June, 1886).
(2) Board of Excise v. Barrie, 34 N. Y. 657; Commonwealth v. Brennan, 103 Mass. 70; Commonwealth v. Kurby, 5 Gray, 597; Columbus v. Cutcamp, 61 Ia. 672.
(3) Wiggins v. Chicago, 68 Ill. 373; Schwuchow v. Chicago, 68 Ill. 444.
(4) Ottumwa v. Schaub, 52 Ia. 515.
(5) Laurtz v. Hightstown, 17 Vroom, 102, p. 107. An ordinance providing that the license should be *ipso facto* revoked as a part of the penalty for breach of the ordinance under which it was granted. held void. Towns v. Tallahassee, 11 Flor. 130.
(6) Baldwin v. Smith, 82 Ill. 162.
(7) Bright v. Toronto, 12 U. C. C. P. 433.

able regulations as will amount to a prohibition.[1] Neither the repeal of the ordinance authorizing the license,[2] nor a decree of a court that the ordinance is void,[3] will render the licensee liable to conviction until the expiration of the time for which the license was granted. Likewise, a license granted by a *de facto* officer protects the licensee until the license is formally revoked and the money paid, or a proportional part thereof returned.[4]

§ 268. **Grading and discrimination.**—Where power is given to a municipal corporation to license certain enumerated occupations, the power may be exercised as to any or all of them, in the discretion of the council, and it can not be objected that a certain business is thereby discriminated against. The restriction might lawfully be placed upon a single kind of business.[5] And where several occupations are licensed, they need not all be treated alike. It is within the council discretion to say that one occupation needs further restriction than another. For this purpose all trades and occupations may be classified and each class required to pay different amounts. Ordinances which distinguish thus between classes are valid, so long as they treat all the members of the same class alike.[6] The difficulty naturally consists in determining the proper basis of classification. It is certain that the nature of the occupation may be used as a basis. For instance, peddlers, auctioneers, vendors of meat, and brokers, exercise clearly distinguishable callings. But there is a strong tendency to the classification of members of the same apparent class, based upon minor differences in the locality, extent, and other peculiarities. Where the classification is distinct it can never be objected that the burden of a uniform license

(1) Wiggins *v* Chicago, 68 Ill. 373.
(2) Boyd *v.* State, 46 Ala. 329.
(3) Regina *v.* Stafford, 22 U. C. C. P. 177.
(4) Martel *v.* East St. Louis, 94 Ill. 67.
(5) Ex parte Hurl, 49 Cal. 557; Athens *v.* Long, 54 Ga. 330.
(6) New Orleans *v.* Kaufman, 29 La. Ann. 283; New Orleans *v.* Dubarry 33 La. Ann. 481; Davis *v.* Macon, 64 Ga. 128; Cutliff *v.* Albany, 60 Ga. 597; Grand *v.* Guelph, 29 U. C. Q. B. 46; Kelly *v.* Dwyer. 7 Lea, 180.

fee falls heavier upon some licensees than upon others. Every person in the eye of the law has equal facilities to do business, and if one is more prosperous than another the difference need not be noticed by the law-making power. Thus, an ordinance exacting a fee for a license to erect or alter a building within established fire limits is not inequitable because it does not discriminate between classes and sizes of buildings sought to be erected.[1]

But a serious question arises so soon as the corporation sees fit to recognize these inequalities among members of the same class and to make them the foundation for discrimination in the amount of the fee demanded. The discrimination must not be arbitrary, but must, in all cases, be based upon some reasonable advantage possessed by one class over another.[2] Thus, it has been held that a license ordinance, which demands $10 from a dray drawn by over three horses, and $75 from an omnibus, discriminates unjustly against the latter.[3] It would seem natural that the opportunities to do harm and infringe upon the public rights would be directly proportionate to the amount of business done, and the ability or facility to conduct an occupation; and, in fact, the true rule seems to be, although not by any means generally recognized, that the amount of the fee must be uniform as to all having the same or equal facilities for profit.[4] Under power to license, dealers may be classified according to the nature and amount of business and the fee graded accordingly.[5] So, under powers to fix and collect a license tax on all trades, professions, and businesses, an ordinance is valid which grades the amount according to the gross sales. It is not void for lack of uniformity. The tax is on the *trade* and not on the

---

(1) Welch *v.* Hotchkiss. 39 Conn. 140.
(2) Zanone *v.* Mound City, 11 Ill. App. 334.
(3) Van Sant *v.* Stage Co., 59 Md. 330
(4) East St. Louis *v.* Wehrung, 46 Ill. 392; Kaliski *v.* Grady, 25 La. Ann. 576; Vosse *v.* Memphis, 9 B. J. Lee, 294.
(5) Vosse *v.* Memphis, 9 B. J Lee, 294; Cincinnati *v.* Bryson, 15 Ohio, 643. Grading license for laundries, according to number of persons employed, has been held valid. Ex parte Sisto Li Protti, 68 Cal. 635 Theaters, according to seating capacity Marmet *v.* State, Ohio, 1887.

goods or person exercising the trade.[1] The amount of the license may be graded according to the income.[2] Location of the business may be justly considered as a facility within the meaning of the rule and the fees graded according to locality.[3] Thus, a fee of $50 for persons selling liquor on boats plying to and from a city, and of $85 for persons selling on land, is a proper discrimination. The same amount is imposed on persons pursuing the traffic in the same way.[4] But there are authorities to the contrary.[5] An ordinance dividing occupation into classes, and imposing a certain sum on each class, and directing the finance committee to classify the occupations is not a delegation of the power to tax.[6] An ordinance imposing a license tax on businesses and vocations, and discriminating as to the amounts to be paid by different classes of persons, is not within the inhibition of the state constitution against unequal taxation.[7]

There is no law governing the amount of the license fee that the city of New Orleans may demand of any particular occupation. The council is the sole judge.[8]

§ 269. **Miscellany.**—Until a power to license is exercised it lies dormant, and none can be required until an appropriate ordinance is passed.[9] Nor can the license power be put in operation by resolution.[10]

§ 270. **Business privileges.**—Under this and subsequent sections are grouped together numerous decisions

(1) Sacramento v. Crocker, 16 Cal. 120.
(2) Burlington v. Insurance Co., 31 Ia. 102.
(3) East St. Louis v. Wehrung, 46 Ill. 392.
(4) Kaliski v. Grady, 25 La. Ann. 576.
(5) St. Louis v. Spiegel, 75 Mo. 145; Donelly v. Clarke Township, 38 U. C. Q. B. 599.
(6) Ould v. Richmond, 23 Gratt. 464; Telegraph Co. v. Richmond, 26 Gratt. 1.
(7) State v. Columbia, 6 Rich. 1.
(8) Goldsmith v. New Orleans, 31 La. Ann. 646.
(9) Bull v. Quincy, 9 Ill. App. 127.
(10) People v. Crotty, 93 Ill. 181.

based upon the construction of various license powers and ordinances.

A statute authorizing the licensing of specified vocations and "all other places of business conducted for profit," applies to merchants, bankers, and brewers, in addition to those enumerated, or similar to those enumerated.[1] Attorneys at law do not exercise an avocation or business within the meaning of a licensing power.[2] Nor are insurance companies included by the term "works of all kinds."[3] But if rightfully included, a foreign insurance company may be compelled to pay a percentage on their business, and the same is not a tax. The agent is amenable.[4] Unless specifically imposed upon the individual by the power, it is the business which is licensed, and a partner subsequently taken in by the licensee is protected.[5] To be a live stock dealer, one must not only buy live stock, but buy with the intent to sell.[6] A license imposed on persons or corporations whose business extends beyond the limits of the city or even into other states, such as express companies, is not void as being a regulation of commerce.[7] Where the charter fixes a minimum and maximum limit the fee exacted must neither fall below the minimum nor exceed the maximum.[8] When a person is engaged in two occupations, each may be licensed, unless a clear custom can be shown to consider them as one business.[9]

§ 271. **Transient dealers.**—The class of dealers who come into a locality temporarily, in order to represent some business located elsewhere and to solicit orders or sell on

(1) Butler's Appeal, 73 Pa. St. 448.
(2) St. Louis v. Laughlin, 49 Mo. 559.
(3) State v. Smith, 31 Ia. 493.
(4) Trustees v. Roome, 93 N. Y. 313; Ex parte Schmidt, 2 Tex. App. 196.
(5) Carter v. State, 60 Miss. 456; Sacramento v. Crocker, 16 Cal. 119.
(6) Saunders v. Russell, 10 Lea, 293.
(7) Osborne v. Mobile, 16 Wall. 479; Sacramento v. Stage Co., 12 Cal, 135; Harrison v. Vicksburg, 3 S. & M. 581; Ferry Co. v. East St. Louis, 108 U. S. 18; Los Angeles v. Railroad Co., 61 Cal. 59.
(8) Kniper v. Louisville, 7 Bush, 599.
(9) Savannah v. Feeley, 66 Ga. 31; Wilder v. Savannah, 70 Ga. 760.

commission, are, in distinction from peddlers, known as transient dealers. Ordinances imposing a license tax upon them must be clearly authorized.[1] The fact that they do not carry with them the goods sold has been considered as an additional feature distinguishing them from peddlers. Regulations demanding license fees from transient dealers are not regulations of commerce.[2]

A non-resident who sends goods to a local dealer to be sold on commission is not a transient dealer.[3] Where the sole power of the kind is to license peddlers, an ordinance is void which requires a license from persons sent out by local business houses to solicit orders and supervise delivery of the goods. Such are not peddlers.[4] So, a drummer or commercial traveler, who sells by sample for future delivery, is neither a merchant nor a peddler.[5] The term *merchant* has, however, been held to include an itinerant trader who ships produce to an agent who goes about the city soliciting orders and delivering goods from the freight depot.[6]

§ 272. **Peddling.**—A peddler is one who sells from place to place, or offers for sale commodities, which he carries with him.[7] Selling goods by sample is not peddling, although an occasional order is filled by delivering the sample.[8] It makes no difference that the peddler has regular customers.[9] The usual method is to grant licenses for a year or fraction thereof.[10]

The term peddler includes milkmen.[11] The license imposed is a personal privilege to the one actually selling

(1) Ex parte Taylor, 58 Miss. 478.
(2) Colson *v.* State, 7 Blackf. 590; Sears *v.* Commissioners, 36 Ind. 267; In re Rudolph, 2 Fed. Rep. 65.
(3) Regina *v.* Cuthbert, 45 U. C. Q. B. 19.
(4) Regina *v.* Coulter, 5 Ont. 644.
(5) City of Kansas *v.* Collins, 34 Kan. 434.
(6) Burr *v.* Atlanta, 64 Ga. 225.
(7) Cook *v.* Pennsylvania, 97 U. S. 556.
(8) Commonwealth *v.* Farnum, 114 Mass. 267; Commonwealth *v.* Jones, 7 Bush, 502. *Contra,* Morrill *v.* State, 38 Wis. 428.
(9) Chicago *v.* Bartee, 100 Ill. 61.
(10) Wilmington *v.* Roby, 8 Ired. Law, 250.
(11) Chicago *v.* Bartee, 100 Ill. 57.

the goods. He can not even employ another to drive his wagon and transact business under his license. The privilege can be exercised only by the person named in the license.[1] Under power to license peddlers, a fee of $15 per year, or, at the option of the applicant, $3 per day is not excessive.[2] An ordinance providing that "hawkers and peddlers of any article kept for sale by merchants of the city to pay a license of $2.50 per day for selling the same is not void for discrimination, partiality, or on grounds of public policy.[3] The fact that a person is peddling an article covered by a patent right, owned by him, in nowise releases him from the duty of securing the regular peddler's license.[4]

§ 273. **Amusements.**—Exhibitions may be regulated or restrained by means of a license system.[5] Theatrical entertainments are not confined to pure drama, but include negro minstrelsy.[6] A license to keep a theater will, however, not entitle the licensee to produce feats of legerdemain.[7] Amateur performances, if produced on successive nights, come within the provision of amusement license ordinances.[8]

Owners of billiard halls may be licensed in accordance with the number of tables kept.[9] A license tax may be imposed upon billiard saloons as a reasonable police regulation,[10] and power to restrain and suppress them includes power to license.[11]

(1) Temple v. Sumner, 51 Miss. 13; Gibson v. Kaufield, 63 Pa. St. 168; Stokes v. Prescott, 4 B. Mon. 37; Mabry v. Bullock, 7 Dana, 337.
(2) People v. Russell, 49 Mich. 617.
(3) Cherokee v. Cox, 34 Kan. 16.
(4) People v. Russell, 49 Mich. 617.
(5) Boston v. Schaffer, 9 Pick. 415; Baker v. Cincinnati, 11 O. S. 534.
(6) Taxing District v. Emerson, 4 Lea, 512.
(7) Jacko v. State. 22 Ala. 73.
(8) Society v. Diers, 10 Abb. Pr. 216.
(9) Merriam v. New Orleans, 14 La. Ann. 318.
(10) Peay v. Little Rock, 32 Ark. 35; Washington v. State, 13 Ark. 752.
(11) Burlington v. Lawrence, 42 Ia. 681.

§ 274. **Dogs.**—The keeping of dogs is an act that may be regulated by requiring a license fee.[1] Such fee is not in the nature of a tax on property, but is essentially a police regulation.[2]

In the District of Columbia an ordinance requiring a license for the privilege of keeping a dog, and prescribing fine and imprisonment for omission to secure the same, is void.[3]

§ 275. **Liquor licenses.**—The power to regulate the sale of intoxicating liquors is one that has always been exercised by the general government, and one that may be lawfully, and generally is, delegated to municipal corporations. But the grant must be express, and the right can not be exercised by municipalities under general language of any kind.[4]

An ordinance declaring a penalty for selling liquors without having first obtained a license is valid, under power to license retailers of liquor and general police power.[5] Under power "to license and regulate groceries, ale-houses, and confectioners" an ordinance regulating "grocery shops or the vending by retail bread, cakes, ale, wine, porter, beer," etc., is valid.[6]

In Goddard v. Jacksonville, 15 Ill. 589, it was held that towns being empowered to pass such by-laws as should not

(1) Cranston v. Augusta, 61 Ga. 573; Shelby v. Randles, 57 Ind. 390.
(2) Mowery v. Salisbury, 82 N. C. 175; Van Horn v. People, 46 Mich. 183; Carter v. Dow, 16 Wis. 317; Morey v. Brown, 42 N. H. 373.
(3) Washington v. Meigs, 1 McArthur, 53.
(4) Commonwealth v. Turner, 1 Cush. 493; e. g. in Indiana, Lawrenceburg v. Wuest, 16 Ind. 337; Commonwealth v. Dow, 10 Met. 382; Ex parte Burnett, 30 Ala. 461. In the entire absence of state laws the subject may be regulated under general power. Heisembrittle v. City 2 McMull. 233; City v. Ahrens, 4 Strob. 241; City v. Church, 4 Strob. 306. And in Illinois the sale of liquors is regulated under power to prevent *nuisance.* Block v. Jacksonville, 36 Ill. 361; Pekin v. Smelzel, 21 Ill. 464; Byers v. Trustees, 16 Ill. 35; Goddard v. Jacksonville, 15 Ill. 588.
(5) Meyer v. Bridgeton, 37 N. J. 160.
(6) Thomas v. Mt. Vernon, 9 O. S. 290.

be inconsistent with the laws of the state, and as they should deem necessary to prevent and remove nuisances, an ordinance might be passed declaring the selling of spirituous liquors a *nuisance* and imposing a fine under the general power to provide penalties.

Power "to tax or entirely suppress all petty groceries" gives no right to license the retailing of liquors.[1] Nor does power "to regulate, tax, and prohibit tippling-houses, ale, and porter shops" authorize a total prohibition of the sale of liquors.[2]

Power to prohibit tippling-houses and dram shops does not authorize the passage of an ordinance forbidding the sale of spirits and beer, in any quantity or for any purpose, except by persons authorized to sell for mechanical, medicinal, and manufacturing purposes.[3] Partial prohibition may be exercised under power to prohibit. The greater includes the less.[4]

§ 276. **Ordinance provisions.**—An ordinance closing the bar-rooms of inns during a certain time, when "no liquor is to be sold or furnished to any one," is void for not excepting guests of the inns from its provisions.[5]

Under a charter provision that the council might suppress disorderly houses, and that the mayor might order saloons closed at such hour as the council should designate, it is held that the council may ordain that saloons shall close from 10:30 P. M. to 5 A. M., under a penalty of $25 for failure.[6] Among other provisions relative to the hours of closing saloons, the following have been sustained: Compelling saloons to close at 10 P. M.;[7] at 9 P. M. under gen-

---

(1) Leonard v. Canton, 35 Miss. 189.
(2) Tuck v. Waldron, 31 Ark. 462; Pekin v. Smelzel, 21 Ill. 465.
(3) Strauss v. Pontiac, 40 Ill. 301.
(4) Gunnarssohn v. Sterling, 92 Ill. 569; Schwuchow v. Chicago, 68 Ill. 444; Harbaugh v. Monmouth, 74 Ill. 371; Martin v. People, 88 Ill. 390, and other cases cited there.
(5) Baker v. Paris, 10 U. C. Q. B. 621.
(6) State v. Welch, 36 Conn. 215.
(7) Staates v. Washington, 44 N. J. 605; Bauer v. Avondale, 4 Cin. Law Bull. 12; s. c., 8 L. Rec. 478; Platville v. Bell, 43 Wis. 488.

eral powers;[1] at dark;[2] from 10 P. M. to 5 A. M.;[3] from 10 P. M. to 4 A. M.[4] Such provisions need not be based upon power over saloons or the liquor traffic, but can be sustained under general police powers of regulation. The reasonable sale of liquors is in no way hindered. A regulation that requires saloons to be closed twelve hours out of the twenty-four would be unreasonable under any power.[5]

§ 277. **Other regulations.**—Under power to regulate ale, beer, and porter-houses it is proper to ordain that girls shall not be employed in such places, the regulation being reasonable as tending to preserve the public morals.[6] Under general power to regulate, the council may, by the terms of the license, confine the sale of liquors to a particular room in a house, as to the front room on the ground floor, for instance.[7] If the power is to license, regulate, restrain, or suppress, the sale may be prohibited; and if permitted under license, the license may provide for its forfeiture as a penalty for any breach of the provisions of the ordinance authorizing the license. Other restrictions may be imposed, such as requiring the place licensed to be closed at certain hours, on Sundays, holidays, and election days.[8] Saloons may be closed on Sundays under power to enact police regulations and to control the sale of liquors.[9] An ordinance inflicting a penalty on any one selling domestic liquors which have not been gauged according to fixed regulations, and charging a small fee for such gauging, has been held constitutional.[10] In Alabama, under power to prohibit drunkenness, to license retailers of spirits, and to

(1) Smith v. Knoxville, 3 Head, 245.
(2) Maxwell v. Jonesboro, 11 Heisk. 257.
(3) Ex parte Wolf, 14 Neb. 24.
(4) Staats v. Washington, 45 N. J. 318.
(5) Ward v. Greenville, 8 J. Bax 228.
(6) Bergman v. Cleveland, 39 O. S. 651.
(7) Sanders v. Elberton, 50 Ga. 178.
(8) Schwuchow v. Chicago, 68 Ill. 444.
(9) Minden v. Silverstein, 36 La. Ann. 912.
(10) Green v. Savannah, R. M. Charlt. 368.

regulate and restrain them whenever deemed a nuisance, an ordinance was sustained which exacted an annual fee of $1,000, and inflicted a penalty of $10 for each day when sales were made without any license.[1] An ordinance prohibiting physicians from giving prescriptions to persons in good health to enable them to obtain liquor and thereby evade the law is neither unreasonable nor oppressive.[2]

Power "to prohibit tippling houses" does not authorize the prohibition of sales of beer by brewers.[3] An ordinance prohibition of the sale of liquors, without any further definition of the persons arrived at, will not be construed to apply to sales by manufacturers, but simply by retailers.[4]

Power "to regulate, restrain, and suppress shops and places for the sale of ardent spirits by retail," authorizes a total prohibition on the theory that the suppression of the place where sold is equivalent to the suppression of the sale itself.[5]

A transaction may be a *retail* sale, even though no consideration passes.[6] *Taverns* are not necessarily places where liquor is sold, so long as they accommodate and entertain guests.[7] A *sale* includes an *exchange* of commodities.[8]

§ 278. **Definitions.**—An ordinance that provides that "*no person* shall sell liquor without a license applies to druggists."[9] So, power to license retailers of spirituous liquors would authorize the extension of the restriction to druggists who sell liquors only on prescription.[10]

Considerable flexibility is given to the meaning of the words "*wholesale*" and "*retail*," which are necessarily of frequent use in this class of ordinances. To illustrate their

(1) Marion v. Chandler 6 Ala. 889.
(2) Carthage v. Buchner 4 Ill. App. 317.
(3) Strauss v. Pontiac, 40 Ill. 301.
(4) St. Paul v. Troyer, 3 Minn. 291.
(5) Clintonville v. Keeting, 4 Denio, 341.
(6) Markle v. Akron, 14 Ohio, 586.
(7) St. Louis v. Siegrist, 46 Mo. 593.
(8) Buffalo v. Webster, 10 Wend, 99.
(9) Rochester v. Upman, 19 Minn. 108.
(10) Sparks v. Stokes, 40 N. J. 487.

respective limits, "wholesale" has been held to mean selling liquor by the *quart*.¹

If the power authorizes the prohibition of minors except on the consent of a parent, the ordinance may require that consent to be in writing.²

§ 279. **Evidence in liquor cases.**—In actions to recover the penalty imposed by ordinances upon engaging in the liquor traffic without first obtaining a license, it is not incumbent upon the prosecution to prove the failure to secure a license. The defendant must prove compliance with the law, because the fact lies peculiarly within his knowledge.³ No proof negativing the having a license is necessary.⁴ In a suit for violating such an ordinance, the defendant testified that he could not afford to pay for a license and plead guilty to violating the ordinance. The ordinance contained other prohibitory provisions. It was held that these facts proved that he had no license, that he sold liquors, and that his plea of guilty had reference to the failure to procure a license.⁵

The proof used only sustains the essential elements of the violation. Under an ordinance prohibiting the sale of beer within the corporate limits it is not necessary to prove that the beer sold was intoxicating. The offense consists in selling beer to any character.⁶ So, where the ordinance forbids the keeping open of *licensed* saloons on Sunday, it becomes necessary to convict to prove that the saloon in question is a *licensed* one.⁷

In a prosecution for selling intoxicating liquors to a minor, it is sufficient to show that the liquor sold was intoxicating, without showing that the vendor knew it to be

(1) Roberson *v.* Lambertville, 38 N. J. 69.
(2) Arkell *v.* St. Thomas, 38 U. C. Q. B. 594.
(3) Information *v.* Oliver, 21 S. C. 318; State *v.* Geuing, 1 McCord, 574.
(4) Smith *v.* Adrian, 1 Mich. 495. *Contra*, Bull *v.* Quincy, 9 Ill. App. 127.
(5) Pendergast *v.* Peru, 20 Ill. 51.
(6) Kettering *v.* Jacksonville, 50 Ill. 39.
(7) Bloomington *v.* Strehle, 47 Ill. 72.

so. Knowledge or intent is immaterial to the offense.[1] So it is not necessary to prove that the liquor was actually sold. The burden of the offense consists in allowing the person to procure the liquor, and it matters not whether it was sold' or given away.[2] Under an ordinance against selling liquors in less quantities than a quart, the sale of a single glass is enough to constitute the offense.[3]

It is also unnecessary to prove that the sale was made by the defendant in person. The owner of a saloon is responsible for the unlawful act of his agents and employes, even though he may have given his agent express instructions not to make such sales as the one complained of.[4] The act of one partner, too, can be proven to convict the other.[5]

§ 280. **Uniformity in licenses.**—Ordinances have frequently been attacked, but invariably without success, on the ground that the amount of the license fee demanded is greater than that imposed by similar ordinances in other towns, more or less universally in the same state. But in this respect license fees do not differ from other charges authorized to be imposed by ordinances. They are, as we have seen, in no sense taxes, but merely incidents of effective police regulation, and the constitutional requirement of uniformity of taxation has no sort of application. The amount is to be defined by the council of each municipality, within certain express statutory limits as to the maximum, or within the limits of reasonableness, when not expressly limited, and that a higher or lower rate should, in the opinion of the council, be necessary or advisable in one community than in another is natural, and no objection to the validity of the ordinance.[6]

(1) Byars v. Mount Vernon, 77 Ill. 467; St. Louis v. Sternberg, 69 Mo. 303.
(2) Council v. Van Roven, 2 McCord, 465.
(3) Kansas City v. Muhlbach, 68 Mo. 638.
(4) Council v. Van Roven, *supra*.
(5) Smith v. Adrian, 1 Mich. 495.
(6) Louisiana v. Lathrop, 10 La. Ann. 398; Morrill v. State, 38 Wis. 428; Fire Dept. v. Helfenstein, 16 Wis. 136; Baker v. Cincinnati, 11 O. S. 534; People v. Moore, 1 Idaho (N. S.) 504; Leavenworth v. Booth,

§ 281. **Taxation.**—Inasmuch as the aim of this volume is to deal specially with police regulations proper, it will be inconvenient to consider at any length subjects connected with property rights of corporations. Municipal taxation has received thorough treatment by several authors,[1] and except as municipal taxes have an indirect connection with police regulations, it answers every purpose to state general rules alone. One of the most important topics connected with local taxation is that of assessments for local improvements. In this connection, the summary given by Judge Dillon in his treatise on municipal corporations expresses the law in an admirable manner.

§ 282. **Local assessments.**—He says:

"1. A local assessment upon property immediately and specially benefited by a local improvement of a street, although resting for its taxation upon the taxing power, is distinguishable in many respects from a tax levied for the general purposes of the state or the general purposes of the municipality. The soundness of this proposition is recognized by the legislation of perhaps every state in the Union. Hence, a statutable exemption of designated property from 'taxation' does not include an exemption from local assessments. Hence, also, provisions in state constitutions concerning equality of 'taxation' are generally, though not invariably, held not to apply by their intrinsic force to local assessments.

"2. A local assessment or tax upon the property benefited by a local improvement may be authorized by the legislature.

"3. Special benefits to the property assessed—that is, benefits received by it in addition to those received by the community at large—is the true and only solid foundation upon which local assessments can rest; and, to the extent of special benefits, it is every-where admitted that the

---

15 Kan. 527; Washington v. State, 13 Ark. 752; Livingston v. Trustees, 99 Ill. 564; Slaughter v. Commonwealth, 13 Gratt. 767.

(1) Dill. Mun. Corp., §§ 735 to § 822; Desty on Taxation; Cooley on Taxation.

legislature may authorize local taxes or assessments to be made.

"5. The assessments may be made upon all the property *specially* benefited by the particular improvement according to the exceptional benefit each lot or parcel of property *actually and separately* receives. This is the method . . . which, in our judgment, is right in principle and the most just in its practical workings.

"6. When the property is urban, and has been platted into blocks, with lots of equal depth which abut the local improvement for which the assessment is made, and there are no special constitutional restrictions in the way, and nothing in the nature and circumstances of the particular case to make assessments in proportion to the *frontage* of the lots upon the improvement work manifest injustice, it is generally, but not always, regarded as within the competency of the legislature to provide that it may be so made.

"7. Under the same conditions and restrictions, the legislature may authorize the assessment upon the lots benefited, in proportion to their *superficial area.*"

This power of levying taxes to meet the cost of local improvements is necessarily delegated to municipal corporations, and when the grant does not specify the mode of distributing the burden, the rules just stated must be followed. When, however, the grant indicates the mode, then the assessment must be made in strict conformity thereto.

§ 283. **Other taxes.**—Local assessments are necessary from the nature of things and are generally directed with so much certainty that only questions of construction of special language arise. But in many states the legislative policy permits a delegation to municipal corporations of the power of general or limited taxation for the purpose of swelling the general revenue fund of the corporation. Under such delegation many important questions arise in the construction of the power and in the extent of its application.

The power to tax for revenue need not be granted in *specific terms*, but it must, nevertheless, be plainly and unmistakably conferred. It can never be deduced by implication or inference. The only apparent exception is where its exercise is *absolutely essential* to the complete exercise of some express power.[1] It can not be inferred from the general welfare clause, because taxation is an attribute of sovereignty, only to be exercised by express delegation.[2] Nor can the power to tax for one purpose be implied from power to tax for other specified purposes.[3] And when permitted, taxes can only be levied for corporate purposes.[4] Under power "to license and regulate," taxes for revenue can not be imposed.[5]

§ 284. **Mode of exercises.**—Power to impose a tax upon sales may be exercised by a direct tax, or by requiring a license to sell.[6] So, it is held in Louisiana, that ordinances making certain things unlawful without a license, and prescribing a penalty, are measures for revenue and can not be enforced under the power to punish transgressions of police regulations.[7]

A penalty imposed for selling liquors without a license is not a tax.[8] Under power to tax business an assessment

(1) State v. Smith, 31 Ia. 493. Must be plainly conferred. In re Church, 66 N. Y. 395; Sewall v. St. Paul, 20 Minn. 511; Vance v. Little Rock, 30 Ark. 439; Heine v. Commissioners, 19 Wall. 660; Dill. Mun. Corp., § 763.

(2) Mays v. Cincinnati, 1 O. S. 268.

(3) Asheville v. Means, 7 Ire. Law, 406; Dill. Mun. Corp., § 765.

(4) Foster v. Kenosha, 12 Wis. 616.

(5) Van Sant v. Stage Co., 59 Md. 330; St. Louis v. Trust Co., 47 Mo. 150; Clark v. New Brunswick, 43 N. J. 175; State v. Bean, 91 N. C. 554; Mühlenbrinck v. Commissioners, 42 N. J. 364. *Contra*, Hodges v. Nashville, 2 Humph. 61; Ex parte Frank, 52 Cal. 606. Under power "to regulate and prohibit and to fix the amount." Flanagan v. Plainfield, 44 N. J. 118. But not under power "to prevent," Fennell v. Guelph, 24 U. C. Q. B. 238.

(6) Carroll v. Tuscaloosa, 12 Ala. 173; Wright v. Atlanta, 54 Ga. 646.

(7) State v. Patamia, 34 La. Ann. 750; Municipality v. Pance, 6 La. Ann. 515

(8) King v. Jacksonville. 3 Ill. 305.

of one-tenth per cent on gross sales is invalid, it being the occupation and not the receipts therefrom that may be taxed.[1]

§ 285. **Amount.**—A charge will be construed a tax which exceeds plainly the reasonable limits laid down in the foregoing chapter.[2]

Failure to pay taxes in the nature of regulations is as much a violation of an ordinance as any other, and is equally punishable.[3]

§ 286. **Constitutional restrictions.**—Although taxes for revenue are taxes in name and nature, they are excluded by implication from the operation of constitutional prohibitions against inequality of taxation, and directions as to the mode of levying. So, when the constitution demands that all taxes shall be levied *ad valorem*, taxes imposed by municipal corporations for purposes of regulation as well as revenue are exempted.[4] But powers of this kind should never be exercised so as to virtually effect a total prohibition of the occupation taxed.[5]

§ 287. **Discrimination.**—The same general rules that apply to the graduation and classification of the objects of a license system are applicable to taxation. "Certain occupations may be taxed for a greater amount and others for less, and to that end the city may divide occupations and callings into several classes and impose a different tax on each class, but upon all objects of taxation in the same class there must be equality."[6] No regard need be paid to

(1) Columbus *v.* Flournoy, 65 Ga. 231; Hatcher *v.* Columbus, 69 Ga. 581; Insurance Co. *v.* Augusta, 50 Ga. 530; Alton *v.* Insurance Co., 82 Ill. 45.

(2) Mayor *v.* Railroad Co., 32 N. Y. 261; Collins *v.* Louisville, 2 B. Mon. 134.

(3) St. Louis *v.* Green, 70 Mo. 562.

(4) St. Louis *v.* Green, 70 Mo. 562; Glasgow *v.* Rowse, 43 Mo. 490.

(5) Sweet *v.* Wabash, 41 Ind. 7.

(6) New Orleans *v.* Dubarry, 33 La. Ann. 481. To the same effect are: Athens *v.* Long, 54 Ga. 330; Cutliff *v.* Albana, 60 Ga. 597; New

the amount of income; it is the business and not the extent that is taxed.[1] Nor need each class be taxed. The fact that the tax actually imposed virtually exempts all of one or more classes does not invalidate the ordinance.[2]

The classification must rest upon some plain and reasonable distinction. Such is held to be the amount of the income, when power is conferred to tax incomes as such. Therein lies the chief difference between general, state, and municipal taxation.

An ordinance is valid, although it exempts from dealers in meat those farmers who sell their own produce. In such case butchers residing outside, but delivering within the city, do not come within the exemption.[3] Residence is not essential. Thus, a tax levied on all vehicles *using* the streets of a city is equally applicable to vehicles owned by non-residents.[4] Discrimination may be made between domestic and foreign insurance companies.[5] An ordinance taxing the sale of goods need not distinguish between goods of domestic and foreign manufacture, and is not, therefore, a regulation of commerce.[6] Chartered banks may be taxed as a business to the same extent as private banks.[7] Under power to tax all peddlers bringing commodities into the city, a tax may be imposed on all strangers and non-residents. The amount was $10 per capita. The court held that this was not unjust discrimination, because discrimination in taxation is only an ob-

Orleans v. Kaufman, 29 La. Ann. 283; Express Co. v. St. Joseph, 66 Mo. 675; St. Louis v. Transportation Co., 84 Mo. 156; Nashville v. Althrop, 5 Coldw. 554.

(1) St. Louis v Sternberg, 69 Mo. 289.

(2) Bright v. McCullough, 27 Ind. 223; Insurance Co. v. Augusta, 50 Ga. 530; Burch v. Savannah, 42 Ga. 596; Holberg v. Macon, 55 Miss. 112; Glasgow v. Rowse, 43 Mo. 479; New Orleans v. Bank, 10 La. Ann. 735.

(3) Davis v. Macon, 64 Ga. 128; Burr v. Atlanta, 64 Ga. 225.

(4) St. Louis v. Green, 70 Mo. 562; s. c., 7 Mo. App. 468; Chess v. Birmingham, 1 Grant Cas. 438; Bennett v. Birmingham, 31 Pa. St. 16; Gartside v. East St. Louis, 43 Ill. 47.

(5) State v. Lathrop, 10 La. Ann. 398.

(6) Ex parte Hanson, 28 Fed. Rep. 127.

(7) Macon v. Bank, 60 Ga. 133.

jection when plainly oppressive, whereas the amount imposed was a reasonable protection to local merchants.[1] Where a classification has been made the same individual may be obliged to pay two taxes when he is engaged, although in the same locality, in the sale of two classes of goods.[2] Under authority to tax all *persons* engaged in a certain business, each member of a firm may be made amenable to a tax.[3] But when the power is to tax the *business*, the tax is levied on the partnership as a unit.[4]

It is apparent that very little distinction exists between taxes and license fees as regards the standard of their validity. Every thing that exceeds the limit of reasonability is a tax, and, when taxation is not permitted, is illegal; but, if taxation is allowed, the taxes imposed are not looked upon as falling within the constitutional and statutory meaning of the word, but merely as a more pronounced mode of regulation, inuring to the benefit of the corporate revenues.

§ 288. **Sunday ordinances.**—It is the policy of every state in the Union to enforce a proper observance of the first day of the week as a day of rest and quiet, and although no express power is granted to a municipality to further that policy by ordinances directed at the observance of Sunday, such ordinances may be passed under implied police powers. Under power to regulate any subject of municipal control, special regulations applicable to Sunday alone may be passed. Additional regulation is necessary on that day in order to preserve the comfort of the inhabitants. It is universally held, therefore, that trades, occupations, and businesses, which are not works of necessity, may be restrained or totally prohibited on Sunday. This may be done under a general welfare clause in the statute or charter,[5] or under any grant of general

(1) Three Rivers *v.* Major, 8 Quebec, 181.
(2) Keeley *v.* Atlanta, 69 Ga. 583.
(3) Wilder *v.* Savannah, 70 Ga. 760; Lanier *v.* Mayor, 59 Ga. 187.
(4) Savannah *v.* Hines, 53 Ga. 616.
(5) State *v.* Welsh, 36 Conn. 215; Megowan *v.* Commonwealth, 2 Metc. (Ky.) 3.

police power.¹ So, when power is granted to regulate the police of a city, to pass and enforce all necessary police regulations, and to impose penalties for violations of the ordinances, places of business may be required to be closed on Sunday.² Especially is this true of such businesses as from their nature are generally looked upon as liable to interfere with the public security and to promote disorders. The sale of intoxicants and noisy and public occupation may be prohibited on Sunday. This will not be so far extended as to cause great financial loss or great loss of time in businesses which depend largely on uninterrupted prosecution for success. It is, for example, improper to close large mills and manufacturing establishments.

Even if the state law only goes to the extent of forbidding all labor on Sunday, which disturbs "the peace and good order" of the community, places of ordinary commercial business may be closed on that day.³

Ordinary regulations against carrying on mercantile pursuits on Sunday are not in derogation of the rights of religious liberty.⁴ But an ordinance would be void which orders the closing of *all* places of business on Sunday, without making some provision for works of charity and necessity and for the transaction of business by those who from religious motives observe some other day as a day of rest.⁵ The offense in such cases depends on the publicity of the business, on its conduct as a *public* business, to which every one who wishes may have access. Thus, it is not at all impossible or inconsistent to have a business place closed for one purpose and open for another.⁶ Hotels and

---

(1) Specht v. Commonwealth, 8 Pa. St. 312; St. Louis v. Cafferata, 24 Mo. 94; Hudson v. Geary, 4 R. I. 485; Cincinnati v. Rice, 15 Ohio, 225; State v. Ames, 20 Mo. 214; Karwisch v. Atlanta, 44 Ga. 204; Gabel v Houston, 29 Tex. 336.

(2) McPherson v. Chebanse, 114 Ill. 46.

(3) McPherson v. Chebanse, 114 Ill. 46.

(4) Charleston v. Benjamin, 2 Strobh. 508.

(5) Canton v. Nist, 9 O. S. 439. *Contra,* Shreveport v. Levy, 26 La. Ann. 671. Ordinances can not distinguish between Jews and Gentiles.

(6) Lynch v. People, 16 Mich. 477.

inns are such places of business. Though the general public is prohibited from access to a hotel bar on Sunday, the hotel-keeper owes other duties to his guests, and he can not be punished for furnishing liquors to them. If the ordinance disregards their duty, and attempts to absolutely prohibit the sale of liquors on Sunday, it is voidable.[1] Travelers and boarders must be excepted.[2]

The municipality ought as a rule to follow the policy established by the state, and ought never to attempt to exceed its limits.

§ 289. **Appropriations for police purposes.**—Municipalities are generally provided by the laws of the state with a system of municipal courts and officers. It becomes a question of some importance as to how far the municipality may make appropriations to supplement the efficacy of the state laws. In the first place, suitable buildings or rooms must be provided for the use of the local officers and courts, and the incidental expenses of their operation and action must be defrayed. These are legitimate corporate purposes, and may be attended to without an express grant of power. A suitable municipal hall may be erected without express power.[3] And it may be built large enough to meet and supply the prospective as well as the present wants of the administration of the local government; and, until needed, the extra rooms may be rented to private persons, or their use permitted gratuitously.[4]

§ 290. **To aid the administration of justice.**—Occasions frequently arise when it seems eminently proper that the municipality should, by means of judicious appropriations, render additional aid and encouragement to the local authorities in the administration of the laws. But it is generally considered unlawful to offer special inducements

(1) Wood v. Brooklyn, 14 Barb. 425.
(2) Ross v. York, 14 U. C. C. P. 171.
(3) Torrent v. Muskegon, 47 Mich. 115.
(4) Worden v. New Bedford, 131 Mass. 23; French v. Quincy, 3 Allen, 9.

to the local officers to do their duty. It is the duty of every citizen to aid in making arrests when an opportunity offers itself; but private persons will undoubtedly be moved to greater activity to assist the local police if they have a prospect of reward for so doing, and it has been held lawful to offer rewards to citizens for the apprehension of criminals.[1] It is the duty of a police officer to do all he can to make lawful arrests, and in theory he needs no additional stimulus to urge him to properly perform that duty. The extra exertion made by a private citizen may constitute a consideration for the payment of a reward offered; but an officer who makes an arrest has done no more than his duty for which his salary is paid to him, and there is no consideration for such a payment or offer. It is accordingly generally held, and usually without drawing any distinction between officers and private persons, that it is unlawful for a municipal corporation to offer rewards for arrests.[2] The police power of the municipality is limited in this respect to allowing extra pay to officers who are obliged to do extra duty in time of great peril from riots, and to providing adequate means of defense against riots. Thus, it would be lawful to authorize the mayor, in anticipation of a riot, to borrow arms and to give a bond for their safe return.[3] As against dangers threatened *from without* the municipality, such as hostile invasions, or an attack of rebels, it is the duty of the state and nation to provide protection, and the municipality has no power by implication to expend public money for defense.[4]

§ 291. **To employ attorneys.**—As a rule, a municipal corporation may, without express authority, employ attor-

(1) York v. Forscht, 23 Pa. St. 391; Crashaw v. Roxbury, 7 Gray, 374.
(2) Cornwall v. West Nissouri, 25 U. C. C. P. 9; Hawk v. Marion County, 48 Ia. 472; Pool v. Boston, 5 Cush. 219; Gilmore v. Lewis, 12 Ohio, 281; Gale v. South Berwick, 51 Me. 174; Patton v. Stephens, 14 Bush, 324; Hanger v. Des Moines, 52 Ia. 193.
(3) New York v. Buffalo, 2 Hill, 434.
(4) Burrill v Boston, 2 Cliff. 590; Crowell v. Hopkinton, 45 N. J. 9; Stetson v. Kempton, 13 Mass. 272.

neys to look after the public interests and to aid in the execution of its laws.¹ A different question arises when suit is brought against some municipal officer for alleged injuries suffered at his hands in the performance of his official duties. The law presumes that every officer restricts his official acts to those which are lawful, and when the legality of his acts are questioned he must either defend himself or be defended by the public whom he serves. An attorney employed by a city to defend an action brought against a municipal officer for an alleged unlawful exercise of his powers can collect reasonable fees from the corporation. As was justly said by Zollars, J., in Cullen v. Carthage, 103 Ind. 196; s. c., 53 Am. Rep. 504: "In every community there is a greater or less number of people who yield obedience to the law, and respect the rights of others, simply because they fear the consequences of an opposite course. It is necessary that such shall be made to understand that the laws will be executed, and that the executive officers will be sustained in their efforts to execute them. If it should be understood that the marshal of the town is left without support of the governing body to defend himself against all manner of suits that might be instituted against him, the vicious and violent might, by a succession of annoying suits against him, greatly cripple the enforcement of the ordinances. Such an understanding would at least have a tendency to embolden the vicious and intimidate the marshal."

§ 292. **Wharves.**—In those municipalities which border on navigable waters, it is often important to determine the extent of their power to regulate the public wharves. The full power of police control extends only over those wharves that have been dedicated to or constructed by the corporation. Only such control can be exercised over private wharves as may be necessary by reason of the public nature of their use.² Public wharves can not be erected

(1) Memphis v. Adams, 9 Heisk. 518; Smith v. Sacramento, 13 Cal. 531.
(2) Horn v. People, 26 Mich. 222. See last note under § 144, *ante.*

except under special powers; but if their erection is in any way authorized, such powers of police control and regulation may be exercised over them as are necessary to preserve their usefulness. Neither power to regulate the streets nor to preserve good order and government authorize the imposition of wharfage fees as a method of police regulation.[1] Power " to erect" wharves includes power to establish new wharves and also to extend existing ones.[2] Power " to erect, repair and regulate " does not give any power to alienate the wharves or their franchises.[3]

The power of control does not exist in Louisiana except by express grant.[4] The better and general view is, however, that public wharves may be regulated to the same extent as any other public property, such as city parks and streets.[5] The wharves entail expense upon the corporation for their construction and care, and it is no more than just that the burden of the expense should fall upon those who are benefited by them and not upon the body of the taxpayers. Reasonable fees for the use of the public wharves may be exacted. This right is not a franchise to depend upon a grant of power, but it results from the proprietary interest of the corporation.[6] Such a charge is neither a tax in the constitutional sense, nor as a tonnage tax, obnoxious to the constitutional prohibition of any regulation of inter-state commerce. This is true, even though the tonnage of vessels is made the basis by which the amount charged is determined.[7] But the fee must only be a *reason-*

In California, no proprietary interest in wharves is vested in corporations. People *v.* Wharf Co., 31 Cal. 33; Miles *v.* McDermott, 31 Cal. 271.

(1) The Geneva, 16 Fed. Rep. 874; s. c., 28 Alb. L. J. 376.
(2) Hannibal *v.* Winchell, 54 Mo. 172.
(3) Railroad Co. *v.* St. Louis, 2 Dill. C. C. 70.
(4) St. Martinsville *v.* "Mary Lewis," 32 La. Ann. 1293.
(5) Muscatine *v.* Packet Co., 45 Ia. 185; Keokuk *v.* Packet Co., 45 Ia. 196.
(6) Murphy *v.* Montgomery, 11 Ala. 586; Mobile *v.* Moog, 53 Ala. 561; Campbell *v.* Kingston, 14 U. C. C. P. 285.
(7) Keokuk *v.* Packet Co., 45 Ia. 196; Packet Co. *v.* Catlettsburg, 105 U. S. 559; Packet Co. *v.* Keokuk, 95 U. S. 80. See *ante,* § 85.

able compensation for the actual use of the public wharves.[1] The owners of adjoining property may be prohibited from using the wharves without paying a fee and obtaining a formal permit from some corporate officer.[2]

Where a corporation is expressly authorized to charge wharfage, it becomes its duty to do so, in order not to throw the cost of supervising them on the general taxpayer, and it could not establish *free* wharves.[3] The payment of the fee could not be avoided on the ground that the wharf is not well built and that it needs further improvements.[4] The fee may be collected from all kinds of vessels, even such as are licensed by the state or federal government.[5]

Wharves are only those portions of the shore that have been improved in order to facilitate the landing of boats. The use of an unimproved part of a shore would not subject a vessel to the regular wharfage charge.[6]

Elevators, as beneficial to the public, may not be erected by the corporation, but it may allow others to erect them on the public wharves. They would not be considered public obstructions.[7]

Power to regulate the wharves does not imply power to improve the harbor, even though an improvement would greatly facilitate access to the wharves.[8] Nor could the corporation define high-water mark, and declare all erections of buildings below it to be nuisances.[9] It would be equally unlawful to create an artificial dock line further toward the shore than the navigable portion of the water,

(1) Cannon *v.* New Orleans, 20 Wall. 577; Railroad Co. *v.* Ellerman, 105 U. S. 166; Leathers *v.* Aiken, 9 Fed. Rep. 679; In re Hagaman, 20 U. C. Q. B. 583.
(2) Dubuque *v.* Stout, 32 Ia. 80.
(3) Mobile *v.* Moog, 53 Ala. 561.
(4) Prescott *v.* Duquesne, 48 Pa. St. 118.
(5) Packet Co. Keokuk, 95 U. S. 80.
(6) *Idem.*
(7) Canal Co. *v.* St. Louis, 2 Dill. C. C. 70.
(8) Spengler *v.* Trowbridge, 62 Miss. 45.
(9) Evansville *v.* Martin, 41 Ind. 145.

and by prohibiting the erection of wharves over or beyond that line, in fact prevent access to the navigable water.[1] After wharf lines are established, all the water beyond is considered as navigable.[2]

After wharves have been established their use may be regulated directly by ordinance, or through some public wharf or harbor-master, appointed for that purpose. Any reasonable rules may be adopted. The manner of landing at wharves, the place, the length of their occupation, the mode of their use, are all proper subjects of regulation.[3] The transportation of goods *along* the wharves may be regulated under general police power.[4]

§ 293. Conclusion.—After reviewing the decisions covered by this work, it is clear that the drafting of *valid* ordinances ought not to be a matter of great difficulty to any council. As a general rule any ordinance will stand the test of enforcement which has been enacted in good faith, after careful deliberation, and to remedy a real mischief or provide for a real want. Nearly every feature of local laws which has been held void or unlawful had its origin in local prejudice or in precipitate action. Ordinances should be enacted with the legislative mind directed to rights of offenders, as well as to those of the public; penalties should be made as light as possible and still preserve their effectiveness; burdens of every kind should be distributed as equably as possibly; plain words should be used and in their ordinary sense; and the remedy should be carefully limited to accomplish the cure of the evil or mischief against which the ordinance is directed, and not extended so that it affects or restrains harmless acts or occupations.

(1) Yates *v.* Milwaukee, 10 Wall. 497.
(2) Winpenny *v.* Philadelphia, 65 Pa. St. 136.
(3) Horn *v.* People, 26 Mich. 222; Keokuk *v.* Packet Co., 45 Ia. 196.
(4) Ex parte Cass, 13 Pac. Rep. 169 (Cal. 1887).

The ordinance book of a municipal corporation should neither be incumbered with useless laws nor should the community be obliged to suffer inconveniences or to endure evils which the corporation has ample power to prevent and correct.

APPENDIX.

FOUR SAMPLE ORDINANCES.

I. An ordinance. To regulate strays.

Be it ordained by the [council of the village of B.], that:

SECTION 1. The [mayor] shall select and establish a place within the corporate limits for impounding stray animals.

SEC. 2. The marshal [*or*, any police officer] shall take up any animal found running at large on the public streets or places, and impound it; he shall at once give notice by one week's publication in some newspaper of general circulation in the [village], [describing the animal, and giving the date and place of sale]; that it will be sold to defray costs, if it is not reclaimed and costs paid within a week from the publication of the notice; if not then reclaimed, he shall sell said animal at public auction, apply the proceeds to the payment of the poundage and expenses, and retain the balance in trust for the owner of the animal. If the balance is not claimed within a year from the sale, it shall be paid into the general fund of the [village].

SEC. 3 The following shall be the fees charged as poundage, one-half of which shall be paid to the marshal [*or*, pound-keeper], who shall have charge of the pound, and the other half to the treasurer of the village on account of the general revenue fund: For each seizure, fifty cents; for each day's retention of each animal, of the horse, cattle, ass, goat, sheep, or swine kind, fifty cents; for each day's retention of any other animal, twenty-five cents; for preparing any advertisement and for each auction, regardless of animals sold, one dollar.

SEC. 4. Any person who permits an animal belonging to him to run at large upon a street or public place within the corporate limits shall, on conviction thereof, be fined in any sum not more than five dollars and not less than one dollar.

SEC. 5. This ordinance shall take afect five days after its publication, as provided by statute.

II. **An ordinance.** To regulate peddlers.

Be it ordained by the [council of the village of B.], that:

SECTION 1. A peddler is a person who carries goods with him, either on his person or in some vehicle, and sells them or offers them for sale, barter or exchange, on the streets or public places, or at stores or residences.

SEC. 2. The mayor shall issue a license to peddle to each applicant, on the payment of fifty cents,[1] unless the applicant is known to him to have a bad reputation, which license shall be good for three months.

SEC. 3. Any person who peddles without such license shall, on conviction thereof, be fined not less than five nor more than twenty-five dollars.

SEC. 4. This ordinance shall be in effect on and after its due publication.

III. **An ordinance.** To regulate the erection of buildings, so as to insure safety from fire.

Be it ordained by the [council of the village of B.], that:

SECTION 1. It shall be unlawful for any person to erect, within the limits hereinafter defined, any building, more than ten feet square, or eight feet high, unless the outer walls thereof are constructed of iron, stone, brick and mortar, or some of those materials, eight inches thick, in a building less than twenty feet in height to the eaves, twelve inches thick in a building less than forty and more than twenty feet in height, and four inches additional thickness for each additional twenty feet in height, and unless the roof is covered with some non-combustible material.

SEC. 2. Erections include removals from one lot to another.

SEC. 3. Any person who violates section one of this ordinance shall, on conviction thereof, be fined in a sum not less than twenty and not more than one hundred dollars. [*The limit must be confined to the amount of fine lawful for the corporation to impose.*]

SEC. 4. [*Describe the limits.*]

SEC. 5. Whenever any building shall be erected, or in progress of erection, in violation of section one of this ordinance, the mayor [or, chief of the fire department] shall notify its owner in writing to either remove it or alter it so as to comply with the requirements

---

(1) The fee may be made higher for a peddler who carries his goods in a vehicle than for one who carries them on his person.

of this ordinance, and if such notice is not complied with within [twenty] days, the mayor [or, chief] shall cause such building to be removed at its owner's expense, the material removed to remain in charge of the corporation until the expense of its removal is paid; if not paid within five days from its removal, such material shall be sold at public auction, and the proceeds, after satisfying the expense of removal and sale, paid over to the owner of the building. Such auction to be held at a time and place designated in a notice to be published in a newspaper of general circulation in the [village].

SEC. 6. [Provision may be made, if desirable, for the erection of a prohibited building under license or permit to be granted by the council or the chief of the fire department.]

IV. An ordinance. To protect public property from injury.

Be it ordained by the [council of the village of B.], that:

SECTION 1. No person shall cut, mark, burn, tear down, deface, or destroy any building, or portion of a building, any walk, bridge, fence, tree, plant, ornamental structure or object, post, pipe, stone, wire, or any other property not included in the foregoing enumeration, belonging to or used by the village or located on, above, or under its streets, or public places, or buildings, without lawful authority.

SEC. 2. Any person violating the provisions of this ordinance shall, on conviction thereof, be fined in a sum not less than two dollars nor more than fifty dollars.

SEC. 3. [As to date of going into effect.]

INDEX.

[REFERENCES TO SECTIONS.]

Abatement of unlawful business, 219.
Acquittal, effect of on subsequent prosecution, 198.
Action, when brought in state court, 166.
    restricted to special tribunal, 166.
    form of, 168.
    nature of, 169.
    civil or criminal, 169, 174.
    quasi-criminal, 169.
    joinder of causes of, 171.
    when enjoined, 206.
Adjournment of council, 38.
    See MEETINGS.
Alabama, law of double offenses in, 92.
    nature of action in, 170.
Alleys. See STREETS.
Amendments to ordinances, 64.
Amusements, license of, 273.
"And" used disjunctively, 195.
Animals, what are reasonable regulations of, 130.
    what are not, 131.
    belonging to non-resident, 137.
    remedies against strays, 161.
    See STRAYS.
    use of streets for driving, 245.
Appeal, remedy of, 207.
    how effected, 207.
    what considered on, 207.
    rules of practice on, 209.
    record of lower court, 209.
Appropriations, for police purposes, 289.
    to aid the administration of justice, 290.
    for defense, 290.
    to pay attorneys, 291.
Arraignment, of the defendant, 182.

Architects, when may be employed, 217.
Arrests, of the offender, 178.
    with or without warrant, 178, 180.
    form of warrant, 179.
    what constitutes, 180.
    must be as preliminary to action, 180.
    what are not reasonable regulations of, 131.
    rewards for, 290.
Assaults, when may be regulated, 213, 220.
Assessments, charged against realty, 164.
    for building sidewalks, 228.
    local, for police purposes, 282.
Assumpsit, action in at common law, 168.
Attorneys, not in a "business," 270.
    employment of corporation, 291.
Auctions, what is reasonable regulation of, 131.
    when regulation is in restraint of trade, 133.
Authority to pass ordinance need not be recited in ordinance, 73.
Bay-windows, 234.
    right of action for unlawfully constructing, 7
Bill of exceptions, what should contain, 209.
    when taken, 209.
Billiard tables, amount of license fee, 260, 273.
Board of health, when may pass rules, 195.
    erection and powers of, 209.
Bond on appeal, 207.
Breaches of the peace, under what power may be punished, 213, 220.
Bread, extent of regulation of, 215.
    reasonable regulations of, 130.
    when may be forfeited, 160.
Bridges, what is reasonable regulation of, 130.
Buildings, power to provide public, 15, 289.
    reasonable regulation of, 130.
    removal under police powers, 213.
    extent of health regulations of, 215.
    used for slaughter houses, 219.
    within fire limits, 222, 223.
    obstructing the streets, 233, 234.
    moving, 236.
Building materials, when allowed on street, 231.
Burials, regulation of, 220.
Businesses, what regulation of conduct reasonable, 130, 213.
    what not reasonable, 131.

Businesses—*Continued.*
    classified for police purposes, 135.
    licensing of business privileges, 270.
    closing on Sunday, 288.

Butchers, reasonable regulation of, 130.
    See SLAUGHTER-HOUSES.

Bicycles, 247.

By-law, definition of, 1.

California, nature of action in, 170.

Canada, mode of declaring ordinance void, 210.

Cemeteries, reasonable regulation of, 130.
    unreasonable regulation of, 131.
    when may be regulated, 220.
    not nuisances *per se*, 255.

Certiorari, remedy of, 204.
    what reviewed thereby, 204.
    municipal corporation can not have, 204.
    record from the lower court, 209.

Charter, must be observed, 125.
    nature of, 2.
    prohibition in, needs no ordinance, 4.

Chinamen, unlawful regulation of, 84.

Clerk of council, signature to ordinance, 48.
    deputy, 48

Closing hours of saloons, 277.

Coal, weighing of, 218.

Colorado, law of double offenses in, 93.

Commerce, must not be regulated, 85.
    regulation of by license, 270.

Commitment, order of, 203.
    form, contents, when made, 203.

Common carrier, regulation under police power, 213.

Compensation, benefits derived are sufficient, 212.

Complaint, must be in writing, 172.
    little formality in, 172
    what must state, 172.
        See TITLE.
    full allegation of offense, 173.
    how offenses described in, 173.
    must follow definition of ordinances, 173.
    surplusage in, 173.
    must refer to ordinance and how, 174.
    how ordinance pleaded, 174.

Complaint—*Continued.*
  need not negative exceptions, 175.
  form of conclusion, 176.
  signature to complaint, 177.
Conclusion. See complaint.
Concurrent powers construed, 21.
Condition precedent to exercise of power, 24, 35.
  compliance need not be pleaded, 73.
Connecticut, law of double offenses, 94.
Constitutional provisions, as to scope of law, 74.
  effect on tax ordinance, 286.
Construction of ordinance, like that of statute, 2.
  of power, against corporation, 17.
  of enumeration, 18, 194.
  rule of *ejusdem generis*, 20.
  intention of legislature governs, 17.
  of statutory directions, 35.
  general rules as to powers, 33.
  of common phrases in grants of power, 25–32.
  of concurrent powers, 21.
  general rules as to ordinances. 193.
  leniency toward, 193.
  words have full meaning, 193
  examples of application of rules of construction, 195.
  of regulations of vehicles, 248.
Corporate powers, scope of, 8.
Corporate purposes, scope and construction, 26.
Costs, when collected of defendant, 154.
Council, alone can pass ordinances, 5.
  can not bind successors, 9, 82.
  de facto can not act, 36.
  members properly elected, 36.
  meetings of, 37.
  joint action of bi-cameral, 39.
  what constitutes, 39.
  quorum, 40–45.
  members disqualified by interest, 42.
  vote of mayor, 44.
  suspension of the rules, 45.
  when may reconsider, 46.
  readings of the ordinance, 47.
  unfinished business, 47.
  clerk's signature, 48.
  record of its action, 56–58.
  informalities subsequently cured, 59.
  power to repeal, 60, 60a.

Court, only such as authorized can be erected, 166.
    limited in jurisdiction, 166.
Dakota, law of double offenses, 95.
Dead animals, removal of, 220.
Debt, when action in will lie, 168.
Defendant, testimony of, 192.
Defenses, prior conviction under state law, 91, 92, 120.
    non-residence, 143, 196.
    ignorance of the law, 143, 196.
    former conviction under ordinance, 198.
    irregularities in formation of corporation, 199.
    other persons not punished, 199.
    offense unavoidable, 199.
    statute of limitations, 196.
    repeal of ordinance, 197.
Defense, appropriation for public, 290.
Defininiteness, in ordinance terms, 78–81.
Definitions, "corporate powers," 8.
    "corporate purposes," 26.
    "general welfare," 27.
    "peace and good government," 28.
    "to regulate," 30.
    "to suppress and restrain," 31.
    "to establish," 32.
    "newspaper," 54.
    "drove," 78.
  of state statute followed, 122.
    "penalty," 147.
    "crime, criminal prosecution," **169.**
    "within the city," 195.
    "street," 195, 224.
    "second-hand dealers," 195.
    "keeping open," 195.
    "along," 195.
    "alley," 224.
    "paving," 227.
    "sidewalk," 228.
    "obstruction," 230, 232.
    "encroachment," 232.
    "running at large," 249.
    "nuisance," 251.
    "license," 257.
    "peddler," 272
    "retail," 277, 278.
    "sale," 277.
    "wholesale," 278.

Discretion, in council, 8a.
    in officer granting license, 13, 263.
    when its exercise conclusive, 128, 129.
    as to penalty, 148.
    presumed to be reasonable, 188.
    how and when questioned, 188.
    of board of health, 219.
    in declaring nuisances, 253.
    in fixing amount of license, 258, 280.

Discrimination, as test of validity, 135, 136.
    as to non-residents, 137.
    in granting licenses, 268, 280.
    in taxing, 287.

Diseases, prevention of, 220.

Distress, can not be resorted to, 84, 159.

Dogs, regulated to preserve security, 213.
    license of, 274.
    reasonable regulations, 130.
    regulated, not prohibited, 84.

Doorsteps, how restricted, 234.

Drummers, license of, 271.
    regulation of, 85.
    non-residents, 137.

Ejusdem generis, rule of in construction of powers, 20.

Elevators, regulation of, 213.

England, action in nature of debt, 166.

English language, ordinance must be in, 68.

English decisions, when applicable, 123.

Enumeration, how construed, 18, 19, 194.
    part void, 139.

Establish, scope of power to, 32.

Error, writ of, 208.
    petition in, 208.
    what reviewed under, 208.
    record from lower court, 209.
    petition on writ must assign errors, 209.

Estoppel, 200.
    of the corporation, 201.
    to claim error by payment of fine, 209.

Evidence, of legislative intent, 17.
    rules to be adopted, 183.
    judicial notice, 184.
    proof of ordinance, 185.

Evidence— *Continued.*
    how proved, 185, 186.
    what not necessary to prove, 185.
    record of council proceedings as evidence, 186.
    proof of publication of ordinance, 187.
    how publication proved, 187.
    presumption that ordinance is reasonable, 188.
    when and how rebutted, 188.
    reasonableness a question of law, 189.
    proof of time and place of offense, 190.
    proof that act not within exceptions, 191.
    testimony of the defendant, 192.
        See CONSTRUCTION OF ORDINANCES.
    in liquor cases, 279.

Ex post facto ordinances, 23.

Exceptions, proof that act not within, 191.

Execution, when issued to collect fine, 155.

Express companies, reasonable regulation of, 130.

Expressio unius est exclusio alterius, 18, 195.

Ferry, regulation of, not regulation of commerce, 85.

Fine, for owning stray, 249.
    when recovered back after payment, 209.
        See REMEDIES.

Fire, what may be delegated to fire department, 12.
    power to purchase engine, 15.
    unreasonable regulations, 131.
    regulations to prevent, 221, 222.
    limits, 222.
    erection of buildings, 222, 223.
    water supply for, 243.
    license to erect buildings, graded, 268.

Fisheries, denial of use to non-residents, 137.

Florida, law of double offenses, 96.

Foreign goods, regulation of sale, 85.

Foreign sovereigns, powers derived from, 124.

Food supply, regulation of, 217, 218.

Forfeiture of property, 159–161.
    notice to owner, 162.
        See REMEDIES.
    of stray animals, 249.

Form of ordinance, 68.
        See ORDINANCE.

Gambling, reasonable regulations of, 130.

Gas company, regulation of, 131.

Gas supply, use of streets for, 244.
General welfare clause, construction and scope of, 2 7.
Georgia, nature of action in, 170.
    law of double offenses in, 97.
Grading, of streets, 226.
    of licenses, 268.
    of taxes, 287.
Gravamen criminis, proof of, 190.
Gunpowder, reasonable regulation of, 130.
Habeas corpus, writ of, 205.
    what examined under, 205.
Hay, regulation of sale of, 218.
Health, power to protect, implied, 15.
    reasonable regulations, 130.
    unreasonable regulations, 131.
    regulations to promote under police power, 213.
    necessity and scope of regulation, 214.
    boards of health, 215.
        See BOARDS OF HEALTH.
    regulations of articles of food, 216, 218.
    market regulations, 217.
    slaughter-houses, 219.
    cemeteries, 220.
    offal, 220.
    dead animals, 220.
    diseases, 220.
    hospitals, 220.
    hog-pens, 220.
    odors, 220.
Hogs, regulation of keeping, 220.
Hospitals, erection of, 220.
    regulation of, 213.
Hotels, regulation of on Sunday, 288.
Ignorance of ordinance, no excuse, 196.
Ill-fame, houses of regulated, 213, 254.
Illinois, nature of action in, 170.
    law of double offenses in, 98.
Imprisonment, in default of payment, 155, 156.
    does not satisfy judgment, 157.
    does not entitle to jury trial, 84.
    form of judgment to imprison for, 156.
    must be a lawful judgment, 158, 163.
    as a penalty, 158.

Imprisonment—*Continued.*
  in default of payment, 155, 156.
Inclosures, on streets, 232.
Income, licenses graded according to, 268.
Indiana, nature of action in, 170.
  law of double offenses in, 99.
Information. See COMPLAINT.
Injunction, of passage of ordinance, 6.
  in higher court, 202.
  not in local court, 202.
  when will lie, 206.
  not to enforce ordinance, 206.
Insurance companies, license of foreign, 270.
Intent, of violation can not be considered, 264, 279.
Interest of magistrate, by reason of citizenship, 167.
Intoxicating liquors, what regulation reasonable, 130.
  what not reasonable, 131.
  what in restraint of trade, 134.
  what discriminating, 136.
  allegations of the person to whom sold, 173.
  regulated to preserve morals, 213.
  regulation of by license, 275.
  as nuisances, 275-278.
  other regulations than by license, 277.
  definitions of ordinary terms, 278.
  evidence in liquor cases, 279.
  how regulated on Sunday, 288.
Introduction to ordinance, 72.
Iowa, law of double offenses in, 100.
  nature of action in, 170.
  joinder of causes of action in, 171.
Jews, regulation of on Sunday, 288.
Joinder of causes of action, 171.
  option with plaintiff, 171.
Joint sessions, of council, 39.
Judgment, form to imprison for non-payment of fine, 156.
  must be a lawful judgment, 158, 163.
  form of ordinary, 202.
  in action of debt, 202.
  when may be passed, 202.
  unconditional, 202.
  what may include, 202.
  surplusage in, 202.
  conclusiveness of, 202, 209.

Judicial notice, of ordinance by state court, 209.
Jurisdiction, restricted to statutory limits, 166.
    objections must be made in lower court, 166.
    does not depend on validity of ordinance, 166.
    over private property of railroad, 239.
        See REMEDIES; TERRITORY.
Jury, can not consider reasonableness, 189.
    nor questions of construction, 193.
Jury trial, must be provided for, 169.
    when, if compulsory in other cases, 170a.
    only applies to offenses covered by the state law, 169.
    when must be granted, 181.
    rights of challenge, 181.
Kansas, nature of the action in, 170.
Kentucky, law of double offenses in, 102.
Laundry, reasonable regulation of, 130.
Law of the land, what is, 123.
Libel, regulations of as against security, 213.
License, no action for unlicensed competition, 7.
    what power over may be delegated to officers, 12.
    power to decide fitness of applicant, 12, 13.
    contents of the ordinance, 80.
    state and municipal licenses, 121.
    when revoked as a penalty, 150, 160.
    exempts from unreasonable ordinance, 195.
    effect of refusal on proper application, 201.
    amount fixed by resolution, 210a.
    for market privileges, 217.
    regulation by, 256–280.
    power to, how granted, 256.
    .nature of license, 257, 265.
    limit of license regulation, 257.
    must not amount to a tax, 258.
    what amount may be charged, 259, 270.
    examples of amount, 260.
    form of the license, 261.
    contents of the license ordinance, 262.
    amount fixed by resolution, 262.
    imposing discretion in officers, 263.
    number can not be limited, 263.
    the penalty for refusal to take out, 264.
    offenses under license ordinance continuing, **264.**
    effect of a license, 265.
    does not exempt from other regulations, 265.
    conditions to the grant, 266.

License—*Continued.*
  revocability, 267.
  when and how revoked, 267.
  grading and discrimination, 268.
  classification of things licensed, 268.
  power dormant until exercised, 269.
  not provided by resolution, 269.
  of business privileges, 270.
  same person in separate business, 270.
  of transient dealers, 271.
  of peddlers, 272.
  of amusements, 273.
  of dogs, 274.
  of sale of liquors, 275–279.
  a personal privilege, 272.
  uniformity in, 280.
  distinct from taxation, 284.
  not in Louisiana, 284.

Lotteries, may be regulated, 87.

Louisiana, law of double offenses in, 103.

Magistrate, not disqualified by citizenship, 167.

Markets, amount of meat license fee, 260.
  power to establish not to be delegated, 11.
  what regulations are reasonable, 130.
  what are not, 131.
  what in restraint of trade, 133, 134.
  regulations under health power, 213.
  houses, when and how erected and extent of regulation, 217.
    See HEALTH.

Maryland, law of double offenses in, 104.

Massachusetts, law of double offenses in, 105.
  nature of action in, 170.

Mayor, when may vote, 44.
  signature of ordinance by, 49.
  approval of ordinance, 50, 49.
  what needs approval, 50.
  how approval signified, 51.
  veto, 51.

Meat. See MARKETS.

Medicines, to whom may be furnished, 215.

Meetings of council, 37.
  adjourned and special, 38.
  quorum, 40.

Merchant, who is a, 271.

Michigan, nature of the action in, 170.
  law of double offenses in, 106.
Minnesota, nature of action in, 170.
  law of double offenses in, 107.
Missouri, nature of action in, 170.
  law of double offenses in, 108.
Mittimus, form of, 203.
Monopolies, unlawful, 132.
    See DISCRIMINATION and RESTRAINT OF TRADE.
Morals, regulations to protect, 213.
Motion, what made on trial, 209.
Motives, for violation, when considered, 195.
Municipal corporations, considered as an agent, 8.
  three classes of power, 8.
  source of power, 14, 15.
Navigable waters, extent of jurisdiction over, 142.
Nebraska, nature of action in, 170.
  law of double offenses, 109.
North Carolina, law of double offenses, 110.
New Hampshire, nature of action in, 170.
New Jersey, nature of action in, 170.
  certiorari in, 204.
  law of double offenses, 111.
New Orleans, not limited as to the amount of license, 268.
New York, nature of action in, 170.
  law of double offenses, 112.
New York City, jurisdiction over adjoining waters, 142.
Notice, judicial, 184.
  to owner of nuisance, 253.
  when estoppel to object to form, 200.
Non-residents, taxation of, 287.
  how affected by penal ordinances, 143.
  discrimination as to, 137.
    See REMEDIES.
Nuisances, can not be abated without ordinance, 3.
  can not be legalized by ordinance, 7.
  what the ordinance should provide, 81.
  when abated, 160.
  regulation of under police power, 250.
  definition, 251.
  how regulated, 251.
  must be an actual nuisance, 252.
  must be a judicial determination, 253.

Nuisances—*Continued.*
    examples of nuisances, 254.
    of things that are not *per se*, 255.

Obstructions, to streets, 230, 231–237.
    by unloading goods, 231, 237.
    by building material, 231.
    by inclosures, 232.
    by public buildings, 233.
    by other buildings, 234.
    projections into the street, 234.
    stalls and booths, 234.
    snow, 235.
    moving buildings, 236.
    by attracting crowds, 237.

Offal, regulation of, 130, 220.

Offense, may be double, 89 *et seq.*

Officers, rewards to for arrests, 290.
    their right to their salaries, 67.

Ohio, nature of action in, 170.
    law of double offenses in, 113.

Opium smoking, when punishable, 144.

Ordinances, definition of, 1.
    are laws, 2.
    power to pass. See POWER.
    necessity of formal passage, 3, 34.
    not self-executing, 3.
    not necessary to enforce charter prohibition, 4.
    passed by governing body, 5.
    must regulate corporate affairs, 6.
    uniformity within municipality, 6.
    must not regulate civil liabilities, 7.
    retroactive, 23.
    statutory direction mandatory, 35.
    passed by *de facto* council, 36.
        See PASSAGE and COUNCIL.
    changes during passage, 47.
    veto of, 51.
    publication of, 52–55.
    record of, 56–58.
    repeal of, 60–65.
    must be by council, 60a.
    effect on vested rights, 67.
    form of, 61.
    by implication, 62, 63.

Ordinances—*Continued.*
    saving clause, 66.
    amendments to, 64.
    form of ordinance, 68.
    constituent parts of, 69.
    like resolutions in form when, 70, 210.
    title of, 71.
    introduction to, 72.
    need not refer to power, 73.
    scope of, 74.
    reference to existing ordinances, 75.
    time of going into effect, 76.
    must fix penalty, 77.
    definiteness of its terms, 78.
    as to penalty, 79.
    in license ordinances, 80.
    in nuisance ordinances, 81.
    can not bar further legislation, 82.
        See RULES OF VALIDITY.
    against offense under state law, 89–90.
    may be retroactive, 138.
    once void, always void, 138.
    partial invalidity, 139.
    must be reasonable, 127–131.
    must not restrain trade, 132–134.
    must not discriminate, 135–136.
    must accord to charter and state law, 88–125.
        See REMEDIES.
    operate over whom. See REMEDIES.

Oregon, law of double offenses, 113.

Partial invalidity of ordinances, 139.

Parties, corporation proper plaintiff, 168.

Partners, liability for unlawful acts, 279.
    each liable to tax, 287.

Passage, statutory directions are mandatory, 35.
    by council *de facto*, 36.
    meetings of council, 37.
        See MEETINGS.
    in joint session, 39.
    quorum, 40, 41.
    majority of, sufficient, 43.
    in joint session, 40.
    special holdings as to, 42.
    vote of mayor, 44.
    suspension of the rules, 45.
    reconsideration of vote, 46.

Passage—*Continued.*
 readings of the ordinance, 47.
 change in ordinance during passage, 47.
 signature of clerk, 48.
 signature of mayor, 49.
 approval by mayor, 49–51.
 veto, 51.
 publication, 52–55.
 record of ordinance, 56.
 what it must show, 57.
 record of vote, 58.
 informalities subsequently cured, 59.

Patented articles, sale of restricted, 272.

Paving, of the streets, 227.
 by railroad company, 241.

Pawnbrokers, regulation of, 213.
 amount of license fee, 260.

Payment of fine acts as estoppel, 209.

Peace and good government, scope of, 28.

Peddlers, not transient dealers, 271.

Peddling, reasonable regulation of, 130.
 license of, 272.

Penalty, must be fixed by ordinance, 77.
 definitely fixed, 79.
 when part void, 129, 159.
  See REMEDIES.
 may be double, state, and local, 169.
 effect of conviction of either, 198.
 in license ordinances, 264.

Pennsylvania, nature of the action in, 170.
 rule as to power being continuing, 227.

Plea, to complaint, 182.

Pleading. See COMPLAINT.

Police regulations, examples of scope of, 28.
 nature of, 211.
 scope and purpose, 212.
 regualting Sunday, 288.
 regulating liquors, 275–279.
 appropriations for, 289.

Pounds, when established, 249.
 for animals, 161.

Power to pass ordinances, statutory directions mandatory, 227.
 need not be referred to in ordinance, 73.
 continuing, 82.

Power to pass ordinances—Continued.
    derived from foreign sovereignties, 124.
    may be delegated to municipal corporation, 2.
    may not be delegated by municipal corporation, 5, 10.
    not a vested right, 8.
    discretionary, 8a.
    continuing, 9.
    what may be delegated to officers, 10-12.
    source of power, 14, 15.
    can not be enlarged by council, 15.
    what are implied, 15.
    limitations of inherent power, 16.
    construed strictly against the corporation, 17.
    construction of enumeration in, 18, 19.
    construction of special grants of power, 19.
    rule of *ejusdem generis*, 20.
    rule when two powers concur, 21.
    general grant limited by special, 21.
    greater includes less, 22, 23.
    conditions to their exercise, 24, 35.
    construction of common phrases in grants, 25-32.
    "corporate purposes," 26.
    "general welfare," 27.
    "peace and good government," 28.
    other expressions, 29.
    "to regulate," 30.
    "to suppress and restrain," 31.
    miscellaneous particular expressions, 32.
    "to establish," 32.
    general rules of construction, 33.
Presumption, of regularity of proceedings, 209.
Principal and agent, liability of principal, 199.
    in sale of liquors, 279.
Private property, how far regulated, 144.
Procedure, on appeal and error, 207-209.
    must conform to state court, 169, 170a.
    arraignment and plea, 182.
Processions, unreasonable regulations of, 131.
Prostitutes, unlawful regulation of, 84, 131.
Publication, proof of, 187.
    of ordinance, 52.
    construction of statutory provisions for, 53.
    time of, 53
    in what paper, 54.
    form of the notice, 55.

Punishment. See REMEDIES.
Quarantine regulations, 220.
Quorum, 39-43.
Railroads, may not delegate power to grant franchises to, 11.
    what regulations are reasonable, 130.
    what are not reasonable, 131.
    what restrain trade, 134
    its premises quasi-public, 145.
    authority to run over private streets, 146.
    regulation of speed of trains, 213.
    regulation of steam railroads, 238, 239.
    use of streets for, 238.
    rule in New York and New Jersey, 238.
    rate of speed, other conditions, 239.
    street, right to permit, 240.
    regulations of, 241.
Ratification to validate void acts, 138.
Readings of ordinance, 47.
Realty, remedy against, 155, 164.
Reasonableness, presumption in favor of, 188.
    evidence to rebut, 188.
    question of law, 189.
    as test of validity, 127-131.
Reconsideration of vote, 46.
Record of passage of ordinance, 56.
    what must contain, 57.
    of votes, 58.
    use as evidence, 186.
Record of court proceedidgs, what must contain, 209.
    on error, 209.
    on appeal, 207-209.
    mention of bill of exceptions, 209.
Reference in ordinance to other ordinance, 75.
Regulation, scope of, 30.
Religious liberty, and Sunday regulations, 288.
Remedies, nature and necessity of, 140.
    over what teritory effectual, 141.
    extraterritorial effect, 142.
    affects what persons, 143.
    when part of corporate territory exempt, 144.
        railroad premises, 145.
        streets, regardless of title, 146.
    penalties, definition, 147.
        power to inflict, when implied, 147.

Remedies—*Continued.*
>what kind lawful, 148.
>are not licenses, 149.
>fines, 150.
>amount, 151.
>cumulative, 152.
>for second offense, 153.
>costs, 154.
>imprisonment in default of payment, 155, 156.
>does not satisfy judgment, 157.
>labor during, 157.
>imprisonment as a penalty, 158.
>forfeiture, 159, 160.
>destruction of property, 160.
>against strays, 161.
>>disposition of proceeds of sale, 161,
>>notice to owner, 162.
>>judicial determination, 163.
>forfeiture of realty, 164.
>distress not lawful, 84.

Repeal of ordinance, effect on license, 266.
>effect on prosecution, 197.
>of repealing ordinance, 197.
>general treatment, 60–65.
>must be by council, 60a.
>form of repealing act, 61.
>by legislature by implication, 62.
>by council by implication, 63.
>saving clause, 66.
>effect on vested rights, 67.
>of state law, does not invalidate ordinance when, 138.

Residence, when a defense, 196.

Resolution, when ordinance may be in form of, 70.
>nature of and effect, 210.
>when sufficient, 210, 210a.
>how passed, 210.
>to fix license fee, 262, 264.
>to ordain license, 269.

Restaurant, reasonable regulation of, 130.

Restraint of trade, 132–134.

"Restrain," meaning of "to restrain," 31.

Retroactive ordinances, 23.

Revenue, power to tax for, 283.

Reward for arrests, 290.

Rhode Island, law of double offenses in, 115.
Riots, regulation of to insure security, 213.
Rubbish, regulation of, 213.
Rules of validity, 83–139.
    fidei, legii et rationalii, 83.
    must accord to U. S. constitution and laws, 84.
    law of the land, 84, 123, 124.
    regulation of commerce, 85.
        of U. S. mails, 86.
    interference with U. S. license laws, 87.
    consistence with state law, 88.
        as to minor offenses, 89.
        punishment may be greater, 90.
        one conviction to bar, 91.
        holdings in the various states, 92–120.
    consistency with state license laws, 121.
    policy of state legislation, 122.
    corporate charter, 125.
    reasonableness, 127–131.
    restraint of trade, 132–134.
    discrimination, 135–136.
        against non-residents, 137.
    once void, always void, 138.
    partial invalidity, 139, 159.

Sale of commodities, what reasonable regulation of, 130.
    what is not, 131.

Saloons, regulations of, 276–279.
Saving clause in ordinance, 66.
School, unlawful regulation of, 131.
Security and comfort, regulations to preserve, 213.
Selling goods on the streets, 245.
Sewerage system, 242.
    beyond corporate limits, 142.
    reasonable regulation of, 130.
    power to fix size may not be delegated, 11.

Shore, reasonable regulation of, 130.
Sidewalks, power to regulate may not be delegated, 11.
    reasonable regulation of 130
    unreasonable regulation of, 131.
    extent of control over, 228.
    snow on, 235.

Signature to ordinance, of clerk, 48.
    of mayor, 49.
    when proved extrinsically, 186.

Signature to complaint, 177.
Slaughter-houses, regulation of under health powers, 213.
 what reasonable regulation of, 130, 219.
 what is not, 131.
Smoke, may be regulated, 85.
Snow, on the sidewalks, 130, 235.
South Carolina, law of double offenses, 116.
State law, must be conformed to, 88, 121, 122.
Statute of limitations, 196.
Strays, remedy against, 161.
 notice to owner, 162, 249.
 reasonable regulation of, 130.
 unreasonable regulation of, 131.
 of non-residents, 137.
  See REMEDIES.
 may be regulated, 249.
 pounds, 249.
 proof of owner's knowledge, 195.
 regulation under police powers, 213.
Streets, power to improve may not be delegated, 11.
 nor to determine boundaries 11.
 lights for, who may erect, 136.
 regulations under police power, 213.
 may not be obstructed by markets, 217.
 power to regulate implied, 15.
 use of by non-residents, 143.
 jurisdiction over, 146.
 under police control, 224.
 no power to vacate, 224.
 extent and scope of power, 224.
 care of the streets, 225.
 lighting, 225.
 grading, 226.
 paving, 227.
 sidewalks, 228.
 protection of, 229.
  See VEHICLES.
 obstructions to, 230–237.
  inclosures, 232.
  public buildings, 233.
  other buildings, 234.
  snow, 235.
  moving buildings, 236.
  other obstructions, 231.
  railroads, 238–241.

Streets—*Continued.*
    openings in, 234.
    sewerage, 242.
    water-pipes, 243.
    gas, 244, 225.
    telegraphs, 244a.
    restrictions on the ordinary use, 245.
    sale of goods on, 245.
    processions, 245.
    use by vehicles, 246.
        See VEHICLES.
Street railways, 240, 241.
Subject, covered by a single ordinance, 74.
Sunday ordinances, when against religious freedom, 122.
    when discriminating, 136.
    to insure peace and comfort, 213.
    closing saloons, 277.
    regulating trades, 288.
Suppress and restrain, scope of power to, 31.
Suspension, of council rules, 45.
Swine, when nuisances, 254.
    regulation under health powers, 213.
Taxes, not levied under police power, 213.
    limit of for police purposes, 281.
    local assessments, 282.
    other taxes, 283.
    mode of exercising the power, 284.
    amount of the the tax, 285.
    limited by the constitution, 286.
    discrimination in, 287.
Telegraph poles, 244a.
Tennessee, law of double offenses in, 117.
Territory, over which ordinance takes effect. See REMEDIES.
Texas, law of double offenses in, 118.
Theater, amount of license fee, 260.
    definition of the word, 273.
    unreasonable regulation of, 131.
Title to property, not affected by ordinance, 166.
Title, of ordinance form and contents, 71.
Title of complaint, object of, 172a.
    form of, 172a.
    total lack of, 172a.
    slight inaccuracy not fatal, 168, 172a.
    ordinary name of corporation, 168.
    exception to, taken in the court below, 172a.

312 INDEX.

Time of going into effect, 76.
Toll-bridges, not to be erected under police power, 213.
Transcript. See RECORD.
Transient dealers, license of, 271.
Trees, regulation of on streets, 229.
    owner's remedy in case of injury, 7.
Trial by jury, inviolable, 84.
Uniformity in licenses, 280.
United States mail, transport of subject to regulation, 86, 199.
United States law, to be observed, 84.
    license laws, 87.
    law of double offenses, 120.
Utah, law of double offenses in, 199.
Vagrants, what regulation of reasonable, 130.
Validity. See RULES OF VALIDITY.
Vehicles, what regulation reasonable, 130.
    what is not, 131.
    what is in restraint of trade, 133, 134.
    of non-residents, 143.
    on railroad grounds, 145.
    use of street by, 229, 246.
    what regulation lawful, 246.
    routes and stands, 247.
    kept for hire, 247.
    construction of special regulations, 248.
Waiver of right to object to offense, 201.
Warrant of arrest, form of, 179.
    what it must contain, 179.
    of imprisonment, 203.
        See COMPLAINT; COMMITMENT.
Water, provision for supply of, 218.
    for use of fires, 222.
    use of streets to convey, 243.
Weighing of produce, 218.
Wells, regulations of when obnoxious, 220.
Wharves, what power over delegated to harbor-master, 12.
    regulation of not a regulation of commerce, 85.
    discrimination against non-residents, 137.
    may not regulate private wharves, 144.
    what regulation valid, 292.
Wisconsin, nature of the action in, 170.
Women, unlawful discrimination against, 84.
Wyoming, nature of the action in, 170.

LAW TREATISES AND REPORTS

PUBLISHED BY

ROBERT CLARKE & CO.,

61, 63, and 65 West Fourth Street, Cincinnati, Ohio.

ATKINSON. Township and Town Officers' Guide for the State of Indiana. By F. Atkinson. 12mo. Net. Cloth, $2.00; sheep, 2 50

BARTON. History of a Suit in Equity, from its Commencement to its Final Termination. By Charles Barton. New edition, revised and enlarged, by Hon. H. H. Ingersoll. Net. 2 50

BATES. Ohio Pleadings, Parties, and Forms under the Code. By Clement Bates. 2 vols. 8vo. Net. 12 00

BEEBE and LINCOLN. Ohio Citations, Corrections of Errors in Citations, and Table of Cases. By F. N. Beebe and A. W. Lincoln. 8vo. Net. 6 00

BENT. Digest of the Decisions of the Court of Appeals of West Virginia. (29 vols), 1863–1887. By J. A. Bent. Royal 8vo. Net. 8 00

BEST. An Exposition of the Practice relative to the Right to begin and Reply in trials by Jury, and other Proceedings, Discussions of Law, etc. By William M. Best, LL.D. With Annotations by J. J. Crandall. 8vo. Net. 2 00

BIBLE in the Public Schools. Arguments in Favor and Against, with Decision of the Cincinnati Superior Court. 8vo. Cloth. 2 00

—— The Arguments in Favor of and Against. Separate. Paper. Each. 50

BOND. Reports of Cases Decided in the Circuit and District Courts of the United States for the Southern District of Ohio. By L. H. Bond. 2 vols. 8vo. 14 00

BREWER and LAUBSCHER. Ohio Corporations other than Municipal, as Authorized by the Former and Present Constitutions of the State, and Regulated by Statute; with Notes of Decisions, and a Complete Manual of Forms for Organizing and Managing all kinds of Companies and Associations. By A. T. Brewer and G. A. Laubscher. Second edition. 8vo. Net. 3 00

CARLTON. The Law of Homicide; together with the Celebrated Trial of Judge E. C. Wilkinson, Dr. B. R. Wilkinson, and J. Murdaugh, for the Murder of John Rothwell and A. H. Meeks, including the Indictments, the Evidence and Speeches of Hon. S. S. Prentiss, Hon. Ben Harding, E. J. Bullock, Judge John Rowan, Col. Geo. Robertson, and John B. Thompson, of Counsel, in full. By Hon. A. B. Carlton. 8vo. Net. 2 50

CARUTHERS. History of a Lawsuit. By Abraham Caruthers. Third edition. Enlarged, Annotated, and Revised by Andrew B. Martin, LL.D. 8vo. Net. 6 00

CINCINNATI ORDINANCES. The General Ordinances and Resolutions of the City of Cincinnati, in force April, 1887. Compiled under Authority and Direction of the City Council. By Frank M. Coppock, City Solicitor, and Fred. Hertenstein, of the Cincinnati Bar. 8vo. 924 pages. Net. 6 50

CINCINNATI Superior Court Reporter. 2 vols. 8vo. Net. 10 00
See also Handy, Disney.

COCHRAN. The Student's Law Lexicon. A Dictionary of Legal Words and Phrases, with Appendices explaining Abbreviations and References to Reports, and giving the meaning of Latin and French Maxims commonly found in law books. By William C. Cochran. 12mo. Net. 2 50

CONSTITUTIONS of the United States and State of Ohio, with Amendments, Annotations, and Indexes; also the Articles of Confederation, 1777, and Ordinances of 1787. Royal 8vo. Net. Paper, 50c.; half sheep, 1 00

COX. American Trade Mark Cases. A Compilation of all Reported Trade Mark Cases decided in the United States Courts prior to 1871. By R. Cox. 8vo. 3 00

CURWEN. Manual of Astracts of Title to Real Property. By Hon. M. E. Curwen. New edition by W. H. Whittaker. 12mo. Net. 2 00

DISNEY'S REPORTS. Cincinnati Superior Court. 2 vols. 8vo. Net. 10 00

·FISHER. Reports of Patent Cases decided in the Circuit Courts of the United States, 1843–1873. By Hon. S. S. Fisher, late Commissioner of Patents. 6 vols. 8vo. Vols. 3 to 6, each. Net. 25 00

FISHER. Reports of Patent Cases decided in the Courts of the United States, 1827–1851. By W. H. Fisher. 8vo. 6 00

FISHER. Digest of English Patent, Trade Mark, and Copyright Cases. By R. A. Fisher. Edited by Henry Hooper. 8vo. 4 00

FORTESQUE. De Laudibus Legum Angliæ. A Treatise in Commendation of the Laws of England. By Sir John Fortesque. 8vo. Cloth. 2 00

GIAUQUE. The Election Laws of the United States. Being a Compilation of all the Constitutional Provisions and Laws of the United States relating to Elections, the Elective Franchise, to Citizenship, and to the Naturalization of Aliens. With notes of Decisions affecting the same. By F. Giauque. 8vo. Paper, 75c.; cloth, 1 00

GIAUQUE. Election Laws of the State of Ohio and the United States. 8vo. Paper, $1.00; cloth, 1 50

GIAUQUE. A Manual for Notaries Public, General Conveyancers, Commissioners, Justices, Mayors, Consuls, etc., as to Acknowledgments, Affidavits, Depositions, Oaths, Proofs, Protests, etc., for each State and Territory, with Forms and Instructions. By F. Giauque. 8vo. Net. Cloth, $2.00; sheep, 2 50

GIAUQUE. The Revised Statutes of the State of Ohio. Revised and Annotated to embrace the Laws and Notes of Decisions to January, 1890. 2 vols. Royal 8vo. Net. $12.00. Or, 3 vols. Net. 13 00

GIAUQUE. Manual for Road Supervisors in Ohio. By F. Giauque. 16mo. Boards. 25

GIAUQUE. Manual for Assignees and Insolvent Debtors in Ohio. By F. Giauque. Net. Cloth, $2.00; sheep, 2 50

GIAUQUE. Manual for Guardians in Ohio. By F. Giauque. Second edition, revised, 1886. Net. Cloth, $2.00; sheep, 2 50

GIAUQUE. The Law Relating to Roads and Ditches, Bridges and Watercourses, in the State of Ohio. By F. Giauque. 8vo. Net. 5 00

GIAUQUE and McCLURE. Dower and Curtesy Tables, for ascertaining, on the Basis of the Carlisle Tables of Mortality, the Present Value of Vested and Contingent Rights of Dower and Curtesy, and other Life Estates. By F. Giauque and H. B. McClure. 8vo. Net. 5 00

GILMORE. Practice and Precedents in the Probate Courts of Ohio in Civil and Criminal Proceedings; with Forms, Notes of Decisions, and Practical Suggestions. By Hon. J. A. Gilmore. 8vo. Net. 5 00

HANDY'S REPORTS. Cincinnati Superior Court. 2 vols. in 1. 8vo. Net. 5 00

HANOVER. A Practical Treatise on the Law relating to Horses. By M. D. Hanover. Second edition. 8vo. 4 00

HARRIS. Principles of the Criminal Law. A Concise Exposition of the Nature of Crime, and the Law of Criminal Procedure. By Seymour F. Harris, B.C.L., A.M. Edited by Hon. M. F. Force. 8vo. Second edition. Net. 4 00

HARPER. Inter-State Commerce Act. The Provisions of the Constitution as to the Regulation of Commerce. With Notes of Decisions and the Act of Congress to Regulate Commerce, approved February 4, 1887. With References to Decisions under analogous Statutes. By J. C. Harper. 8vo. Half sheep, net, $2.00; full sheep, net. 2 50

HORR and BEMIS. A Treatise on the Power to Enact, Passage, Validity, and Enforcement of Municipal Police Ordinances, with Appendix of Forms and References to all the Decided Cases on the Subject in the United States, England, and Canada. By N. T. Horr and A. A. Bemis. 8vo. Net. 4 00

HUTCHINSON. Land Titles in Virginia and West Virginia, including Tax Sales, Deeds, Forfeitures, Ejectment, Adverse Possession, Boundaries and Surveys, Unlawful Detainer, Claims for Improvement, Authentication of Deeds, etc. By Hon. John A. Hutchinson. 8vo. Net. 5 00

HUTCHINSON. A Treatise on the Laws of West Virginia pertaining to the Powers and Duties of Justices of the Peace, Clerks of Courts, Prosecuting Attorneys, Sheriffs, Constables, and Notaries. By Hon. John A. Hutchinson. 8vo. Net. 6 00

INTERROGATORY LAW. Over One Thousand Law Questions, being a Complete Compilation of the Questions submitted to the Graduating Class of the Cincinnati Law School, from 1879 to the Present Time. 8vo. Paper. Net. 50

JOHNSTON. Arguments to Courts and Juries. By William Johnston, late Judge of the Superior Court of Cincinnati. 8vo. Cloth. Net. 3 00

KENTUCKY REPORTS. Reports of Cases decided in the Court of Appeals of Kentucky. 1785–1885. 82 vols in 67.

KING. A Commentary on the Law and True Construction of the Federal Constitution. By J. King. 8vo. Cloth. 2 50

McDONALD. Treatise on the Law relating to the Powers and Duties of Justices and Constables in Indiana. By D. McDonald. Edited by L .O. Schroeder. 8vo. Net. 6 00

McLEAN. Reports of Cases decided in the Circuit Court of the United States for the Seventh District. 1829–1855. By Hon. John McLean. 6 vols. 8vo. Vols. 2, 4, 5. Each. 6 50

MATTHEWS. A Summary of the Law of Partnership. For use of Business Men. By Hon. Stanley Matthews. 12mo. Cloth, $1.25; sheep, 1 50

MILLER. A Treatise on the Law of Conditional Sales of Personal Property. By Charles B. Miller. 8vo. Net. 3 50

MONTESQUIEU. The Spirit of Laws. By Baron D. Montesquieu. Translated from the French by Thomas Nugent. New edition, with Memoir. 2 vols. 8vo. Cloth. 4 00

MORGAN. An English Version of Maxims, with the Original Forms, alphabetically arranged, and an Index of Subjects. By J. Appleton Morgan. Second edition. 12mo. Cloth. 2 00

NASH. Pleading and Practice under the Codes of Ohio, New York, Kansas, and Nebraska. By Hon. J. Nash. Fourth edition. 2 vols. 8vo. 10 00

OHIO DIGEST. Digest of the Decisions in all Ohio Courts to 1882. By J. B. Walker and C. Bates. 3 vols. Royal 8vo. Net. 17 00
Vol. 3, 1874–82. By C. Bates. Royal 8vo Separately. Net. 5 00

OHIO and Ohio State Report. Reports of Cases decided in the Supreme Court of Ohio. 1821–1890. 66 vols. Net. 132 00

OHIO REVISED STATUTES. New edition, thoroughly revised to embrace all Laws in force January, 1890. By Florien Giauque. 2 vols. Royal 8vo. Net. $12.00. Or, 3 vols. Net. 13 00

OHIO STATUTES at Large. Embracing:
Curwen's Statutes at Large, 1833–1860. 4 vols. 8vo. Net. 20 00
Sayler's Statutes at Large, 1860–1875. 4 vols. 8vo. 20 00

PECK. The Law of Municipal Corporations in the State of Ohio. By Hon. H. D. Peck, late City Solicitor and Judge of the Superior Court of Cincinnati. Second edition. 8vo. Net. 5 00

PECK. The Township Officer's Guide of Ohio. By Hon. H. D. Peck. Sixth edition, 1889. Net. Cloth, $2.00; sheep, 2 00

POLLOCK. Principles of Contract at Law and in Equity. Being a Treatise on the General Principles Concerning the Validity of Agreements, with a Special View to the Comparison of Law and Equity. By Frederick Pollock, LL.D. Edited by G. H. Wald. Second edition. 8vo. Net. 6 00

RAFF. Guide to Executors and Administrators in the State of Ohio. Sixth edition. By Hon. G. W. Raff. Edited and Enlarged by F. Giauque. 12mo. Cloth, $2.00; sheep, 2 50

REINHARD. The Criminal Laws of the State of Indiana, with Precedents, Forms for Writs, Docket Entries, etc. By G. L. Reinhard. 8vo. 2 50

RITCHIE. Manual for Municipal Officers. Having Special Reference to the Duties and Powers of Mayors, Marshals, Councilmen, Clerks, and Treasurers in Ohio, and containing Forms for all the usual business incident to these Offices. By Edwards Ritchie. 12mo. Leatherette. Net. 1 50

ROSENTHAL. Manual for Building and Loan Associations. Embracing the Origin and History of Co-operative Societies; Objects and Benefits of Building Associations; Plans and Methods of Organizing and Conducting them; Legislation; Constitution and By-laws; Forms and Descriptions of Books, Blanks, and Papers; Interest and Dividend Tables; and a Comprehensive Variety of Practical and Useful Information and Suggestions. By Henry T. Rosenthal. 12mo. Cloth. 1 50

SAINT GERMAIN. The Doctor and Student; or, Dialogues between a Doctor of Divinity and a Student in the Laws of England, containing the grounds of those Laws. By Christopher St. Germain. Revised and corrected by Wm. Muchall. 8vo. Cloth. 2 00

SAUNDERS. A Treatise upon the Law of Negligence. By T. W. Saunders. With Notes of American Cases. 8vo. 2 50

SAYLER. American Form Book. A Collection of Legal and Business Forms for Professional and Business Men. By John R. Sayler. Second edition. Revised, 1886. 8vo. Cloth. Net. 2 .00

STANTON. A New Digest of the Kentucky Decisions; embracing all Cases decided by the Appellate Courts from 1875 to 1877. By Hon. R. H. Stanton. Second edition. 2 vols. 8vo. Net. 6 00

STANTON. A Practical Treatise of the Law relating to Justices of the Peace, etc., in Kentucky. By Hon. R. H. Stanton. Third edition. 8vo. 7 50

STANTON. Manual for the use of Executors, Administrators, Guardians, etc., in Kentucky. By Hon. R. H. Stanton. Second edition. 12mo. 1 75

SWAN. Treatise on the Law relating to the Powers and Duties of Justices of the Peace, etc., in the State of Ohio. By Hon. Joseph R. Swan. Thirteenth edition. 8vo. Net. 6 .00

SWAN. Pleadings and Precedents under the Code of Ohio. By Hon. Joseph R. Swan. 8vo. 6 00

SWAN and PLUMB. Treatise on the Law relating to the Powers and Duties of Justices, etc., in Kansas. By Hon. Joseph R. Swan and Hon. Preston B. Plumb. 8vo. 4 00

WARREN. Criminal Law and Forms. By M. Warren. Third edition. 8vo. 5 00

WELCH. Ohio Index-Digest of all the Cases decided in the Courts of Ohio. (Contained in 105 vols.) By Hon. John Welch, late Judge Supreme Court of Ohio. 8vo. 1887. Net. 6 00

WELLS. Treatise on the Separate Property of Married Women, under the recent Enabling Acts. By J. C. Wells. Second edition. 8vo. 6 00

WELLS. A Manual of the Laws relating to County Commissioners in the State of Ohio, with carefully prepared Forms and References to the Decisions of the Supreme Court. By J. C. Wells. Net. 3 50

WILD. Journal Entries under the Code of Civil and Criminal Procedure. With Notes of Decisions. By E. N. Wild. Third edition. 8vo. 4 00

WILCOX. The General Railroad Laws of the State of Ohio, in force January, 1874. By J. C. Wilcox. 8vo. 5 00

WILSON. The New Criminal Code of Ohio. With Forms and Precedents, Digest of Decisions, etc. By Hon. M. F. Wilson. Third edition. 8vo. Net. 5 00

WORKS. Indiana Practice, Pleadings, and Forms. By Hon. J. D. Works. Second edition. 3 vols. 8vo. 1887. Net. 18 00

WORKS. Removal of Causes from State Courts to Federal Courts, embracing the Act of Congress passed March 3, 1887, with Forms and References to Decisions. By Hon. J. D. Works. 8vo. 1 00

WRIGHT. Reports of Cases at Law and in Chancery, decided in the Courts of Ohio during the years 1831-1834. New edition, with Notes. By Hon. J. C. Wright, late Judge Supreme Court of Ohio. 8vo. Net. 5 00

YAPLE. Code Practice and Precedents. Embracing all Actions and Special Proceedings under the Civil Code of Ohio, and applicable to the Practice in all the Code States having a Similar Code System. By Hon. Alfred Yaple, late Judge Superior Court of Cincinnati. 2 vols. 8vo. 1887. Net. 12 00

www.ingramcontent.com/pod-product-compliance
Lightning Source LLC
Chambersburg PA
CBHW030306240426
43673CB00040B/1078